Vol 1

METTERNICH'S GERMAN POLICY

VOLUME I:

THE CONTEST WITH NAPOLEON, 1799–1814

METTERNICH'S
GERMAN POLICY

VOLUME I: THE CONTEST WITH

NAPOLEON, 1799–1814

BY ENNO E. KRAEHE

PRINCETON, NEW JERSEY

PRINCETON UNIVERSITY PRESS

1963

Publication of this book has been aided by
the Ford Foundation Program to support publication,
through university presses, of works in
the humanities and social sciences.

Printed in the United States of America
by Vail-Ballou Press, Inc., Binghamton, N.Y.

to M. A.

PREFACE

This volume is not an effort to explain the origins of Nazism or to solve today's diplomatic problems through the lessons of "Professor" Metternich. Those lessons may have some value for us; but they were not the reason for writing this book. Actually the study grew out of an investigation of the German Confederation. That an enterprise which started out to describe the historical development of an institution became instead an account of the German policy of Austria's great foreign minister is due to two considerations. One was the discovery that much detailed research on many special topics needs to be done before a balanced history of the Confederation can be written. The other was the realization that the description of an institution tends to impute ontological reality to super-personal entities and to make the values of the historian more important than the values of the human components of the institution. Examining the German Confederation within the categories of state *versus* nation, disunity *versus* unity, and reaction *versus* liberal reform, I discovered that I was pursuing issues that were somewhat remote from those that occupied Metternich, Stein, Hardenberg, and the other practicing statesmen of the time. An understanding of their ambitions and motives is a precondition for an objective history of the German Confederation, and since Metternich's role in the Confederation was paramount, the investigation led to him.

At first it appeared sufficient to begin with the Congress of Vienna, where the Confederation was founded. Further investigation, however, disclosed in Metternich's German policy such a continuity with the period of the French Revolution and Napoleon that an earlier start was indicated. The present volume, which centers on Metternich's contest with Napoleon, is the result. A second volume will follow, dealing with the years from 1814 to 1820 and stressing the contest with Alexander of Russia.

The need for a study of Metternich's German policy *after* the Congress of Vienna has long been felt. (See A. O. Meyer, "Der Streit um Metternich," *Historische Zeitschrift*, CLVII [1937], 75–84; and Paul W. Schroeder, "Metternich Studies

Since 1925," *Journal of Modern History*, XXXIII [1961], 259.) By contrast, much of the ground covered in the present volume has been treated before. Yet the literature of the Napoleonic era has dealt only haphazardly with Metternich's German policy, allowing the subject to fall between general diplomatic histories and specialized monographs on minute points. For all Metternich's renown as a diplomat, neither his diplomacy as a whole nor broad regional aspects of it have been so carefully treated as is true, for example, of Napoleon or Castlereagh. An excellent beginning was made toward the end of the last century when the European archives for this period were opened, enabling such dispassionate pioneers as Adolf Beer, Eduard Wertheimer, August Fournier, Wilhelm Oncken, and Fedor von Demelitsch to produce monographs and publish documents which even today remain the basis of investigation. But death carried off the older men and the first world war interrupted the work of the others.

The war did more: it plunged the history of the nineteenth century into the political and ideological disputes of the twentieth. Thus Viltor Bibl, in his *Metternich, der Dämon Österreichs* (Vienna, 1936), instead of reflecting the objectivity ordinarily to be expected with the passage of time, returned to the older practice of blaming Metternich for every mishap of Austria, including the catastrophe of 1918—just as many German writers began to blame Bismarck for the collapse of Germany. Heinrich Ritter von Srbik, the successor to Fournier at the University of Vienna, constructively revised our notions of Metternich's political and social values but diverted attention from his diplomacy to his philosophy. Later, Srbik played a leading role in entangling Metternich studies in the revival of the *grossdeutsch-kleindeutsch* controversy from which they had earlier been on the verge of rescue. As far as historical scholarship is concerned, the *grossdeutsch* doctrines popular in Nazi Germany provided a desirable antidote to the Prussia-centered emphasis of an earlier day and, in moderate hands, inspired a good many useful monographs and source collections we would not otherwise have had. Nevertheless, the polemical tone of this literature and its tendency to read twentieth-century interests into the world of Metternich have left unfulfilled the promise of Fournier's generation.

Taken as a whole, the literature bearing directly and indirectly on Metternich's German policy in the Napoleonic era is enormous and on some topics exhaustive. In this volume therefore it has been neither necessary nor physically possible to utilize unpublished sources throughout. The several chapters relating to Metternich's role in the war of 1809 are based primarily on records in the *Haus- Hof- und Staatsarchiv* in Vienna, but otherwise I have found the published documents and literature adequate—in contrast to volume two, where the situation will be reversed.

This is not to say that the problem was simply one of putting the pieces together as in a jigsaw puzzle. On the contrary, as the larger picture emerged, it often revealed shapes and colors not apparent in the specialized studies. As a result, although I have gratefully made use of the facts unearthed by others, I have frequently been compelled to correct the arrangement of them. My method—insofar as I have stressed anything beyond the usual canons of historical scholarship—has been to maintain, within the bounds of intelligibility, a conscious and scrupulous attention to chronology, and this in turn has led to a predominantly narrative presentation. That this procedure is any the less analytical, however, I would deny. The truth is that an abstract analysis which cannot be expressed in narrative form— which is never retested against the sequence of events it purports to explain—is more apt to satisfy the intellect of the historian than the facts of history. The important thing is that the narrative take into account not merely external deeds but also internal events, the mental states of the principals.

This note is offered as a long-overdue explanation to the many friends, colleagues, employers, and benefactors who in recent years have discreetly ceased to inquire about my progress. To them collectively I extend thanks for patience and interest. In particular, however, I am happy to register at last my gratitude for a Fulbright research grant to Austria for the year 1952–1953 and for a John Simon Guggenheim fellowship in 1960–1961, which enabled me to complete my research in

Vienna. Without these I should never have known the gracious hospitality and renowned service of the *Österreichische Staatsarchiv,* for which I wish to thank the General Director, Hofrat Dr. Gebhart Rath and his expert staff. Similar thanks I owe to the *Nationalbibliothek* in Vienna, the *Historisches Institut* of the University of Vienna, the Library of Congress, and the libraries of the University of Kentucky, the University of Minnesota, the University of Texas, and the University of Virginia. All have shown unfailing sympathy and rendered invaluable assistance. I am also indebted to the Research Fund Committee of the University of Kentucky for financial assistance at many crucial points in the course of my research, and to Professor H. Clay Reed of the University of Delaware for an unusual act of generosity some years ago which has ever since been an incentive to me.

The manuscript at various stages has been read by Professor Emeritus Lawrence D. Steefel of the University of Minnesota, Professor Carl B. Cone of the University of Kentucky, and Professor Robert A. Kann of Rutgers University. Without their discerning suggestions as to style and content the book would have been far worse, nor is it their fault that it is no better. To Professor Kann in particular I am indebted both for encouragement and for timely advice that altered the direction of the investigation. I have also profited from the leads and suggestions of Dr. Walter Leitsch and Dozent Dr. Fritz Fellner of the University of Vienna, Professor Karl Bosl of the University of Munich, and Professor Guillaume de Bertier de Sauvigny, of the Institut Catholique of Paris.

Finally and most important, I want publicly to acknowledge the gratitude I owe my wife and children for their aid and forbearance in the preparation of this work. I can only hope that they regard two years' exposure to the charms of Vienna as adequate compensation.

Lexington, Kentucky
July, 1963

CONTENTS

Preface   vii

    I. Clemens Metternich, Count of the
       Holy Roman Empire   3

   II. The Decline and Fall of the Reich   25

  III. The War to Restore
      the Reich   58

  IV. War and Peace: The Maturing of a
      Foreign Minister   82

    V. 1809–1812: The Contest Suspended   119

  VI. The Grand Mediation Attempt   147

 VII. Rival Plans for Germany   187

VIII. Saving the German Sovereigns   219

  IX. Germany and Europe   250

    X. Rapprochement with Hardenberg
      and Castlereagh   281

  XI. Conclusion: The Contest Ended
      and Begun   313

Bibliography   327

Index   339

METTERNICH'S GERMAN POLICY

VOLUME I:

THE CONTEST WITH NAPOLEON, 1799–1814

CHAPTER I

CLEMENS METTERNICH, COUNT OF

THE HOLY ROMAN EMPIRE

The first thing to remember about Clemens Lothar Wenzel von Metternich-Winneburg-Beilstein is that he was not an Austrian but a Rhinelander. It was not until he was twenty-one years old that he traversed the *Wiener Wald* and first beheld the baroque splendor of the *Ballhaus,* where he was to spend some forty years as foreign minister. The only tangible connection the Metternich family had with the sprawling territories bound together by the Pragmatic Sanction of 1723 and known as "Austria" was an estate at Königswart in Bohemia, and Königswart was of minor significance in comparison to the family seat on the Mosel River midway between Trier and Coblenz. This consisted of the seigniory called Winneburg on the left bank and a smaller fief, Beilstein, on the right bank. Together they constituted a fertile property of about 75 square miles, 6200 inhabitants, and an annual revenue of 50,000 guilders, which enabled the family to live in muted elegance at nearby Coblenz.[1] It was here, at the confluence of the Rhine and Mosel, in sight of moldering castles and terraced vineyards, that Clemens Metternich was born in 1773.

The Rhineland in the twilight of the old regime was a mélange of French and German cultures, at least among the bilingual aristocratic families to which the Metternichs belonged. Politically the region was a part of the *Kreis* Lower Rhine-Westphalia in the Holy Roman Empire. Clemens' father, Franz Georg, was a *Reichsgraf* or imperial count, one of about 400 princes who formed the highest German nobility, the *Standesherren.* These princes were the immediate vassals of the emperor and were represented at Regensburg in that august assembly known as the Reichstag. The Metternichs, it must be

[1] Heinrich Ritter von Srbik, *Metternich der Staatsmann und der Mensch,* 1 (Munich, 1925), 79.

said, were just barely of this group. Above them in the social hierarchy stood princes, margraves, dukes, and electors; counts were the lowest of those represented in the Reichstag, and not all of them were in it. The Metternichs had but a small fraction of a vote at Regensburg, since the counts-of-the-empire were grouped into four councils which voted as units when the Reichstag met. In the Council of the Counts of Westphalia the name of Metternich was twenty-first on a list of thirty-two.[2]

Without this seat the family would have been considered part of the *lower* imperial nobility, a designation reserved for those who held their fiefs directly from the emperor but had no representation in the Reichstag. Most of this group, which included a handful of counts, about 350 families with the title of *Freiherr* (baron), and some 1500 imperial knights, belonged to a corporate order called the *Reichsritterschaft,* which had many of the privileges of the higher nobility, such as exemption from imperial taxes. Thus they enjoyed a higher status and more material benefits than many German nobles who had larger domains but were vassals of some other prince and subject to his legislation. Nevertheless, on the imperial level the punctilious protocol of a decadent feudal order drew a sharp line between the higher and lower nobility, and it was just at this line that the Metternichs, like many another *gräfliche* house, maintained their ambivalent position. They could, by straining, enjoy every luxury; they could hire the best tutors; and they could, as *Standesherren,* mingle socially with any of the great in Germany. Young Clemens, for example, was the childhood friend of young princesses who became the queens of Hanover and Prussia; and later, while a student at Strasbourg, he was on intimate terms with a future king of Bavaria, Prince Maximilian of Zweibrücken. All the same, it not not usual to marry above one's rank; when Clemens did so in 1795, it was regarded as an extraordinary coup, a tribute to Franz Georg's salesmanship as well as to his son's good looks and intelligence.[3]

Yet the real divergence within the ranks of the *Standesherren*

---

[2] Prince Jean-Engelbert d'Arenberg, *Les princes du St-Empire a l'époque Napoléonienne* (Louvain, 1951), 43–44.

[3] Srbik, *Metternich,* I, 66; Egon Cäsar Conte Corti, *Metternich und die Frauen,* I (Zürich and Vienna, 1948), 26.

was political. Since the Peace of Westphalia in 1648 some forty of the leading imperial estates had enjoyed the exercise of *Landeshoheit,* a constitutional status which removed them from the jurisdiction of the *Reichskammergericht* (imperial supreme court), made them masters within their territories, and allowed them to conclude alliances with one another and even with foreign powers. Many maintained their own military establishments and, despite the nominal homage they owed the emperor, conducted their affairs as if they were sovereigns. Some of the princes were in fact sovereign in other capacities—the elector of Hanover, for example, as king of England, the elector of Brandenburg as king of Prussia, or the duke of Holstein as king of Denmark, not to mention the various titles and functions of the Habsburgs. Thus the "armed estates," as those with private armies were called, tended to pursue an egocentric *Staatsraison,* striving to create centralized despotism within their territories, reaching out to seize smaller holdings on their borders, and forming alliances, even with France or Russia if need be, to advance their interests. For such rulers the Reich was an unwelcome encumbrance, an anachronism that dimmed their glory. As for the houses of Habsburg and Hohenzollern, their status as great powers was so well established that one often disregarded their provinces in referring to the empire; in popular usage the term "Reich" connoted simply that part of Germany west of the Elbe River and the Bohemian Forest.[4]

To the lower orders of the *Standesherren,* on the other hand, the Reich was not merely a living tradition; it was a necessity. It was the guarantee of their possessions; it was the source of their equality with the great houses; it was their protection against predatory neighbors; and, by the very mildness of the imperial restraints, it was a safeguard against outside interference in the management of their manors. A *Reichsgraf,* as opposed to a territorial count, was not importuned by zealous bureaucrats seeking to carry out the centralistic designs of an ambitious despot, and only rarely was he summoned before the *Reichskammergericht* on complaint of a neighbor or of one of

[4] Fritz Hartung, *Deutsche Verfassungsgeschichte vom 15. Jahrhundert bis zur Gegenwart,* 6th ed. (Stuttgart, 1950), 162ff. for this and the following.

his vassals. At the same time, the Reich provided opportunity for service and employment on a grander scale than was attainable within the confines of one's own patrimony. The emperor had many posts to offer, both in the imperial service as such and in the administrative hierarchy of the Habsburg crown lands, which, being educationally backward, were always in need of talent from the western part of the empire. There were also in the Reich a large number of ecclesiastical estates, some of which were nearly as large as the armed estates. These not only had offices to staff; they were sees to which any noble family might aspire that customarily sent sons into the service of the church. By the time Clemens was born, the Metternichs had already produced four electoral archbishops, who lifted the family to heights far above its purely secular standing. One of these prelates, in fact, was the source of the Lothar in the future diplomat's name, and the names Clemens and Wenzel were in honor of a godfather who was archbishop of Trier.[5]

And so the house of Metternich belonged with those who were of necessity champions of the Reich. The freedom that the largest estates sought through their own armed strength and their own foreign policies was found by the lesser houses in a benevolent imperial regime. However much they might boast of their equal birth with the mighty, their interests coincided more with those of the *Reichsritterschaft,* the ecclesiastical estates, and the imperial free cities, all of which hailed the emperor as the defender of "German liberties."

The future of German liberties in the second half of the eighteenth century was anything but bright. The ecclesiastical estates faced the Enlightenment's incessant demand for secularization and often suffered the rule of clerical princes who desired to become temporal rulers in their own right. The free cities and petty estates in their turn were exposed to absorption by powerful neighbors who desired to round out their frontiers, pocket additional tax revenue, and gain access to new military recruiting grounds. Inside the Reich, then, conditions bordered on anarchy, and after the demoralizing War of the Austrian Succession and the Seven Years' War, which ended just ten years

[5] Srbik, *Metternich,* I, 54–55.

6

before Clemens Lothar Metternich was born, it was clear that German liberties depended less on the protection of a benevolent emperor than on the checks and balances among the armed estates, and especially on the stalemate between Austria and Prussia.

Internal chaos inevitably brought foreign intervention. In 1778, when civil war again broke out, with Austria and Bavaria aligned against Prussia, Saxony, and Mecklenburg, it was the flanking powers, France and Russia, which were called in to mediate. For France, a voice in imperial affairs was hardly a novelty; for Russia, however, it marked a new pinnacle of European influence. Scarcely six years before, she had moved her boundary westward in the first partition of Poland; now, by the treaty of Teschen, which settled the German war, she became a guarantor of the *status quo* in the Reich.[6] Henceforward she too had to be counted among the powers with an interest in Germany.

The following year (1780), Joseph II launched his long-cherished program to transform the loose and variegated collection of provinces that was Austria into a modern centralized state. As a social reform the effort was a failure. For the Reich, however, it had a peculiar importance, drawing Austria more than ever into herself and promoting an exclusively "Austrian" outlook which valued territorial consolidation and neat frontiers above organic association with the Reich. It was in this spirit, for example, that Joseph hoped some day to exchange the distant Austrian Netherlands for Bavaria—almost as if the remains of the empire were something to be parceled out among the powers. Those remains—the "Reich" of eighteenth-century parlance, the "third Germany" in the idiom of a later age—had become a power vacuum, the counterpart in Western Europe of decrepit Poland in the East.

But life in Swabia, Westphalia, Franconia, and the Rhineland, where the petty estates tended to be clustered, still went on in ways blessed by time. Among the servants of the empire

---

[6] Text of treaty of Teschen in Georges Frédéric de Martens, *Recueil de traités . . . des puissances et états de l'Europe*, II (Göttingen, 1817), 661–667. Note in particular Arts. XII and XVI.

there were many abler than Franz Georg Metternich, but none more devoted to its traditions. In 1768 he entered the service of the elector of Trier, representing him in Vienna until 1771, at which time he was recalled to Coblenz, the capital of the arch-bishopric, to serve as councillor and foreign minister. Needless to say, the "foreign affairs" of the archbishop seldom rose above matters of protocol, and Franz Georg discharged his duties well. Impeccably groomed, always amiable and polite, delighting in the company of attractive women, among them his wife Beatrice, a charming and talented woman née Kageneck from the Breis-gau, the *Reichsgraf* Metternich was ideally suited to rococo life in a petty eighteenth-century German court. Nor did that life change markedly when in 1773 he accepted service with the emperor. As imperial minister to the courts of Trier and Cologne, and later to the electoral court at Mainz and the *Kreis* Lower Rhine-Westphalia, he continued to reside in the *Met-ternicher Hof*, the large family residence at Coblenz, and there brought up his family: a daughter, Pauline, born in 1772, Clemens born the following year, and another son, Joseph, born in 1774.[7]

With an easygoing father and a mother who scarcely con-cealed her partiality toward the first-born son, Clemens Metter-nich could easily have grown up indolent and spoiled. Perhaps to some extent he did. At least there was nothing of the Prussian or the Puritan in his make-up. He inherited his full share of the Rhineland's celebrated flair for good living, to which he added a love of ease and comfort that was peculiarly his own. Over the years, his dalliance and habits of procrastination were the despair of his associates, and he sometimes displayed a diffidence and superciliousness that would have marked a man of lesser charm as a fop; in Metternich, however, they simply com-pleted the picture of a *grand seigneur*, fully at ease in the civilized aristocratic surroundings of the old regime. Still, the age was one that understood the art of combining pleasure with achievement, and Metternich was no exception. His activities were usually marked by great economy of effort, the result of a quick mind, intellectual discipline, and a *sangfroid* which

[7] Srbik, *Metternich*, I, 54–59.

looked like languor but actually disguised concentrated labor.

His intelligence, as well as an intellectual curiosity which made him a lifelong amateur of the sciences, was probably inherited from his mother. Yet, to give Franz Georg his due, he seems to have had the kind of good sense that mediocre men often display in the handling of their children. From the outset, he envisaged a diplomatic career for Clemens and, though it is impossible to say how much design informed his efforts, he provided, even for that cosmopolitan time, an unusually rich and varied background. No snob about languages, he admonished the son not to neglect German in his zeal for French, which the lad preferred to speak with his mother.[8] He also saw to it that the boy gained first-hand experience with public affairs, obtaining minor assignments for him at the coronation of Leopold as Holy Roman Emperor at Frankfurt in 1790 and again at the coronation of Francis II two years later—experiences which, on the surface at least, made it appear that the young Metternich would have the same affection for the Reich that his father had.[9]

Nowhere, however, was the influence of Franz Georg more important than in the youth's formal education. Two Catholic tutors were followed in the *Metternicher Hof* by a deist, Johann Friedrich Simon, who brought into the family circle not only the latest educational methods but the spirit of the Enlightenment as well. Simon was no mere pedagogue; when the Revolution came, he went to Paris, where he served a series of revolutionary governments and participated in the Reign of Terror. A Jacobin in the bosom of the family was an anomaly, to say the least, and it is interesting that it was the Countess Metternich, the intellectual in the family, who objected most strenuously to his ideas, while Franz Georg was unperturbed. As for young Clemens, he respected his teacher and, in six years of almost daily association, no doubt acquired through him those habits of rational analysis which later characterized his work. If there

[8] Franz Georg to Clemens, 9 April 1785, in Clemens Lothar Wenzel Metternich-Winnebrug, *Memoirs of Prince Metternich*, ed. by Prince Richard Metternich, I, English ed. (New York, 1880), 382.

[9] See Metternich's own account in his "Autobiographical Memoir," in *ibid.*, I, 7 and 12.

was paradox in the fact that the master traveled the road of revolution while the pupil became the defender of enlightened despotism, the fault was with the Enlightenment itself, which bequeathed an ambiguous legacy to the world.[10]

In 1788 Franz Georg enrolled his sons at the University of Strasbourg, sending them there in the company of a private tutor. Although the student body was predominantly French and German, the university in those days attracted students from most parts of Europe and from many social classes. The university was then in the midst of a mild renaissance, partly the result of the Seven Years' War, which had made the German universities temporarily inaccessible to many foreigners.[11] As a result, Metternich met an unusual assortment of nationalities, including such future associates as Prince Paul Stroganov and Count Andreas Razumovsky of Russia and the Corsican, Count Carl Pozzo di Borgo. The odd circumstance that the Metternich entourage lived in quarters usually reserved for scholarship students also brought Clemens into contact with a variety of commoners—though the experience apparently had little effect on his political views or even on his personal life, what with his expensive tastes, his riding and fencing lessons, and his well-filled social calendar.[12]

One of the specialties of Strasbourg at the time was law, particularly German law, which even French students studied in hopes of finding administrative careers in the many small courts to the east. The men under whom Metternich studied, notably Christopher William Koch, reflected the training of the renowned Göttingen school. The spirit was essentially secular and rationalistic. The study of positive law and its historical development was encouraged in order to gain practical knowledge of existing institutions, but one did not expect to find wisdom in it or traces of divine will. Justice was a matter of natural law, discoverable by human reason and best attained through enlightened human volition, in a word, through the despotic powers of the territorial princes. In this spirit one did not

[10] ibid., I, 4–6; Srbik, Metternich, I, 62ff.

[11] Franklin L. Ford, Strasbourg in Transition 1648–1789 (Cambridge, Mass., 1958), 167f.

[12] Cf. Michel Missoffe, Metternich 1773–1859 (Paris, 1959), 13–14.

mourn the decline of the Reich as an organic institution or as the expression of a universal Christendom. The Reich, in this conception, had become a league of states, a primarily secular corpus in the center of the continent, a constituent part of a European republic; and if it had any transcendent value, it was as a mainstay of the balance of power. For it stood to reason—and reason was the measure of all things in those days—that in a Europe culturally more or less homogeneous, but politically divided into egocentric sovereign states, the only alternative to balance was chaos. Since balance was also the first principle of the physical universe and since practical diplomats for a century had found in equilibrium a pragmatic solution of their problems, the balance of power as the regulator of international relations seemed a fact of nature, logically demonstrable. At Strasbourg, therefore, Metternich was almost daily immersed in speculation about the European equilibrium.[13]

The same was true when, in 1790, the young student of statecraft transferred to the University of Mainz. There he heard the lectures of Nicholas Vogt on the history of the German empire and made of this eminent scholar a lifelong friend. Vogt's philosophy was not so mechanistic as that of Koch; it stressed rather the historical development of institutions and their organic arrangement in a hierarchy of entities starting with the family, rising through provinces, estates and kingdoms, and culminating in the European republic. Nevertheless, balance was all-important. Indeed, for Vogt balance was not merely, as with Koch, a matter of relations among monolithic sovereign states—it was the informing principle of all human relations, all society, indeed of the universe itself; it was God's *modus operandi*. Whereas Koch's doctrine, when applied to the Holy Roman Empire, tended to justify absolutism and the ambitions of the greater territorial princes, Vogt's philosophy stressed the organic harmony of the whole and the importance of all estates, great and small, secular and ecclesiastical.

Thus Metternich found at Mainz a philosophy that not only met the current standards of intellectual respectability but also accorded well with the traditions and vital interests of his family.

[13] Srbik, *Metternich*, I, 88ff. for this and following.

No wonder he venerated Vogt and, many years later, when the scholar died, had his remains interred on the Metternich estate at Johannisberg.[14] Yet even if he claimed Vogt more than Koch as his mentor, the latter cannot be altogether dismissed. For—could the student have but known it at the time—between them the two professors had anticipated in academic form the central issue of Metternich's future German policy: whether post-Napoleonic Germany was to be reconstituted as a hierarchy of imperial estates or as a league of sovereign states.

In the meantime, the French Revolution was providing a school for statecraft which no classroom lectures could match in melodrama and raging emotion. For young Clemens, the Revolution was a sobering, intimate experience. Just a week after the Bastille fell he saw a frenzied mob storm the city hall of Strasbourg, plunder the city's renowned wine cellar, and launch an orgy of drunken looting that only Prince Max's regiment of guards was able to subdue. Later, to the young man's sorrow, he saw his old teacher, Simon, become the editor of a revolutionary weekly in the city and the local translator of the Declaration of the Rights of Man. From the beginning, then, as the horrified but fascinated student saw it, the Revolution was bathed in blood and whatever was good in it was negated by destructiveness.[15]

Despite the revulsion Metternich may have felt for the July violence, he continued his studies and spent another school year at Strasbourg. The summer of 1790 found him in Frankfurt, at the coronation of Leopold II, and under the circumstances the ritual was more than the crowning of an emperor; it was like the consecration of the old regime itself. Then followed the two years at Mainz and in July, 1792, Metternich was back in Frankfurt for the coronation of Francis II. If the previous crowning had commemorated the tenaciousness of the old regime, this one seemed designed to celebrate its triumph. At that very moment a Prussian army was assembling near Coblenz under the duke of Brunswick, and was preparing the attack

---

[14] Metternich, *Memoirs*, I, 11.
[15] Ford, *Strasbourg in Transition*, 245ff. and 252; Missoffe, *Metternich*, 24; and Metternich, *Memoirs*, I, 8.

which carried such high hopes of destroying the Revolution—the hopes not of the German princes alone but especially of the many French émigrés who had come for the coronation. The ceremony over, it was in a spirit of light-hearted gaiety that Metternich joined the throng of noblemen who trooped back to Coblenz to await the news of victory.[16]

It was news that never came. On September 20 the attack stumbled to a halt at Valmy, and the retreat began, the long retreat that in the next four months yielded Mainz and Frankfurt to the armies of the Revolution and cleared the way for the greater horrors yet to come. What now remained of society's "natural balances"? The French estates had been abolished, the royal family executed, and a terroristic dictatorship imposed. Vogt had spoken of a God-given balance between love and hate; where was the love that would stem the flood of hate that poured from Paris, edged across the Rhine, and threatened to engulf peaceful Winneburg and Beilstein, a scant fifty miles to the north?

A return to Mainz was out of the question, and besides, who could concentrate on the harmonies of the universe when each day the Revolution cast doubt on their existence? Metternich now continued his education in the world of practical affairs, assisting his father and acting as a courier between the armies and the political authorities of the Netherlands. In 1791 Franz Georg had been promoted to the post of resident minister to the Austrian Netherlands; he was a kind of prime minister, as Clemens later boastfully claimed, except that he was subject to the orders of the state chancellery in Vienna, which directed the affairs of the Habsburg crown lands. He was now technically in the service of Austria, not of the Holy Roman Emperor as he had been at Mainz, and the difference soon became evident.

With all the preconceptions of an imperial count, Franz Georg tended to treat the Netherlands more as a *Kreis* of the empire than as an Austrian crown land. His sympathies were entirely with the aristocratic estates, their desires for home rule, and their reluctance to raise taxes for the purposes of the far-off Austrian court. There was actually something to be said for

[16] *ibid.*, I, 12ff.

Franz Georg's policy, inasmuch as the estates had rebelled in 1789 against Joseph II's attempt to abolish their ancient constitution, and ever since had found it hard to choose between the evils of revolutionary France and the centralistic reform policies of Josephinism. Nevertheless, as Metternich's superiors in Vienna were for the most part Josephinists by conviction and distrustful of Belgium by experience, they opposed his conciliatory methods and constantly interfered in his administration. In the fall of 1793 Franz Georg, without consulting Vienna, collaborated with the estates in an attempt to raise a local militia by arming the peasants and organizing volunteer free corps to fight the invading French. The Vienna chancellery was aghast, not so much because it feared the arming of the masses—Austria had earlier appealed to the Reichstag for a *levée en masse* throughout the Reich [17]—but because it doubted the reliability of the Belgian estates. When the Netherlands were overrun in 1794 and the country did in fact desert Austria with disconcerting haste, it was all too easy to make Franz Georg the scapegoat. Early in July, Brussels was evacuated and an angry Kaiser abolished Metternich's post.[18]

These were trying days for the family, and Clemens felt the humiliation keenly. Through what remained of his father's influence he now received an assignment in England. Removed from the scene of violence, he had time to take stock of his tottering world and defend his father's policies. In a pamphlet which he wrote in August of that year, 1794,[19] he railed against the "boneheads," the old-school diplomats, "who consider the present war like any other and the Revolution in its commencement mere child's play, and who regard the general conflagration with the true coldbloodedness of a physician. . . ." Such men, he explained, referring to the chancellery, recoiled from putting arms in the hands of the mobs. "A bugbear was held up before the eyes of the monarchs, and this decisive measure of the Government of the Netherlands was prohibited."

[17] Ernst Rudolf Huber, *Deutsche Verfassungsgeschichte seit 1789*, I (Stuttgart, 1957), 29.
[18] Srbik, *Metternich*, I, 73–77.
[19] "On the Necessity of a general Arming of the People on the Frontier of France by a Friend of Universal Peace," in Metternich, *Memoirs*, I, 340–347.

But the truth was that a fundamental difference existed between the "mob" and the "people." The latter were men of property and would fight for it, "be it ever so small. . . . In a general arming of the people, I do not, therefore, understand the class of unoccupied, so dangerous to the state, men who possess nothing and are constantly ready for revolt. . . ." The important thing was to find masses of "citizens" and "yeomen" to pit against the armed hordes unleashed by the Revolution— the Revolution which threatened "the dissolution of all social ties, the destruction of all principles, and the spoliation of all property."

There is much of interest in this, Metternich's first essay on politics. With all the profundity of youth, he was sounding the first note in his lifelong polemic against revolution. *The* Revolution, as he called it, was not politics in the ordinary sense, a contest carried out within a mutually agreed upon set of rules; it was rather a demonic force which threatened civilization itself. Materially the issue was simple: it was a struggle between those with property and those without it. Monarchical governments and beleaguered propertied classes had better awake to the fact that they were engaged in a class struggle; they must suspend their petty, limited rivalries for the sake of collective action against the unlimited aims of the Revolution.

It was an eloquent denunciation; yet what Metternich affirmed was also important. This was the spirited defense of his father's policy in the Netherlands, his enthusiastic championing of a popular militia that would be neither an unfeeling band of mercenaries nor an undisciplined horde of fanatics. The tract preached the philosophy of a third force, that of the ancient estates pitted against absolutism on one side and revolution on the other. Beneath the polemic against revolution was an imperial count's affirmation of the Reich as an organic institution, a cry of concern lest the left bank of the Rhine be abandoned to France. The denunciation of the "boneheads" in Vienna was at bottom an outburst of dismay—"incomprehensible" was the word he used over and again—dismay that the court on which the aristocratic estates depended most should be so blind to its own vital interests. It was the eternal complaint of the front-line

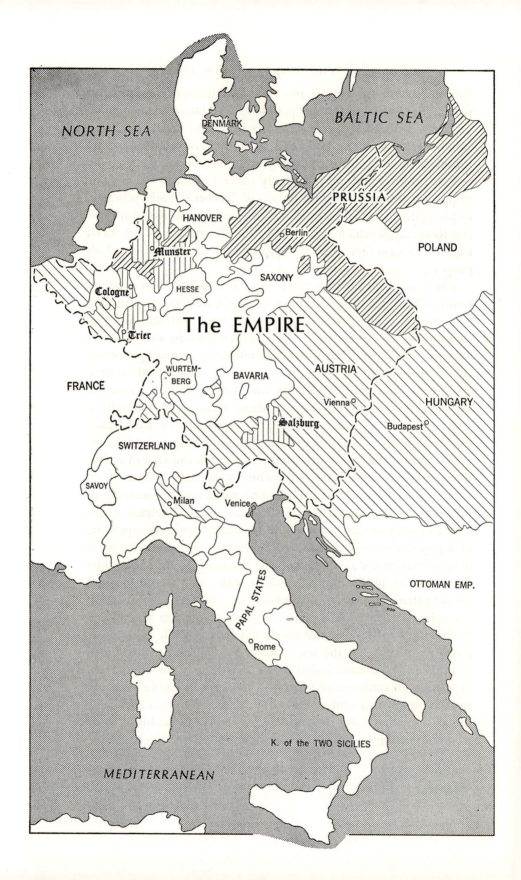

men against headquarters; and far from exhibiting a grasp of universal principles, as Heinrich Ritter von Srbik contends in his celebrated biography of Metternich,[20] the point of view was essentially parochial. Metternich's campaign against Revolution, whatever philosophical insights it acquired along the way, actually began as an effort to interest the Habsburgs in an all-out defense of the Reich.

If the chief concern of Metternich's German policy at that time was indeed the fate of Winneburg and Beilstein, his fears were justified. In October Coblenz fell, and by January, 1795, the entire Rhineland, with the exception of Mainz, was in French hands. The Metternichs were no longer merely "front-liners" in the fight against the Revolution; they were refugees— émigrés—and such a condition could only intensify their feelings. Without employment, thrown back on the puny resources of Königswart, Franz Georg took the family to Vienna; in November, 1794, Clemens Lothar saw the capital for the first time. The purpose of the sojourn on the Danube was threefold: to find a job for Franz Georg, a bride for Clemens and, insofar as it was in their power, to influence policy against a permanent cession of the Rhineland.

Circumstances were about as bad as they could be. It was hard enough for any outsider to break into the tightly drawn ranks of the higher Austrian nobility, but for the impecunious Franz Georg Metternich the barriers were almost insurmountable. He had antagonized the most important people, including the foreign minister, Baron Franz von Thugut; he was widely, though perhaps unfairly, blamed for the debacle in the Netherlands; and he was the conscience of the Reich in a capital that had many other interests besides Germany. He found no post. Clemens, however, had more success. Less than a year after his arrival he astounded the gossips of the capital by marrying the Princess Eleanor, only child of Prince Ernst von Kaunitz and granddaughter of the great chancellor himself. The opportunity was made by the connections and intrigues of Countess Metternich, but the victory was that of young Clemens alone. With courtly manners, keen wit, and handsome appearance he won the lady's

[20] Srbik, *Metternich*, I, 78.

heart, besting rival suitors from the great houses of Liechtenstein and Palffy. It was an important conquest, not merely because it routed the resistance of Viennese society but because it
liberated the young cavalier from his own family. After the
wedding in September, 1795, he took up residence in his father-
in-law's house at Austerlitz and, despite a personal aversion to
many of his newly acquired relatives, he was not above trading
on the name of Kaunitz. Henceforward the fortunes of the house
of Metternich depended more on him than on his father; they
were, in fact, now linked with Austria as much as with the
Rhineland.[21]

Under these circumstances, with Franz Georg discredited and
Clemens living in semi-seclusion at Austerlitz, Austrian policy
went its lumbering way without benefit of prompting from the
Rhenish émigrés. Thugut's policy was, as Clemens charged,
based on Austrian *Staatsraison* rather than on the principle of
an ideological struggle against the Revolution. This did not
mean, however, that Thugut lightheartedly accepted the loss of
the Netherlands or deliberately sabotaged the Reich. On the
contrary, the Belgian lands must be regained even if only to be
traded for nearby Bavaria. The Reich, moreover, still had much
value for Austria, notably advantageous commercial relations
with the imperial free cities and the exclusive right of military
recruitment in all the smaller fiefs which did not maintain
armies of their own. About half of every so-called German
regiment (as distinct from the Hungarian and Croatian units)
in the Austrian army was recruited in this way, and the per-
centage of non-commissioned officers was even higher because
of the greater literacy in western Germany.[22] Finally, there was
still a moral force in the Reich which, though feeble and intangible, could not be wholly discounted. Thugut, in one final
appeal to the spirit of imperial patriotism in March, 1793, induced the Reichstag to declare the struggle against France an

[21] Corti, *Metternich und die Frauen*, I, 30–44.
[22] Edmumund Glaise von Horstenau, "Altösterreichs Heer in der deutschen
Geschichte," in Karl Linnebach (ed.), *Deutsche Heeresgeschichte* (Hamburg,
1935), 127f.; Hermann Meynert, *Geschichte der k.k. österreichischen Armee*
(Vienna, 1852–1854), III, 47–49 and 147f.; and IV, 15ff. Also Harold C. Deutsch,
The Genesis of Napoleonic Imperialism (Cambridge, Mass., 1938), 218, note 18.

imperial war and to enjoin the armed estates to mobilize military contingents of triple the normal strength. Even the elector of Palatinate-Bavaria delivered the required troops, though in all other respects he continued to honor the neutrality pact which he had signed with France.[23]

Thus the Reich was still of use to the Habsburgs, and if Germany had been their only concern, even the Metternichs would probably have had little reason to complain. The main obstacle to a consistent imperial policy was the Polish question, which Catherine of Russia opened anew in the summer of 1792. "I am breaking my head to find a way to drive the courts of Vienna and Berlin to meddle in the affairs of France," she confided. "I want to have them involved in those affairs so as to have my elbows free." [24] By marching an army to Warsaw, she overturned the delicate three-way balance in the East and directly challenged the Austrian policy of preserving Poland as a buffer against Prussia and Russia. Nevertheless, Thugut and the Emperor Francis, both of them new to their jobs, continued to emphasize the western battlefront, foregoing a share in the second partition of Poland, which the other two eastern powers perpetrated in January, 1793. In return, Prussia and Russia pledged themselves to continue the war against France, to aid in the reconquest of the Netherlands, and to support the Austrian scheme to trade the Netherlands for Bavaria.[25]

The bargain from the Austrian standpoint was a poor one. Russia's aid in the West was negligible, and Prussia, her appetite for Polish territory whetted, could afford to risk the loss of her own Rhenish provinces (Cleves and Gelderland) in the hope of greater gains in the East. This hope was well founded, for the remnant of Poland was in a state of near-anarchy, and Prussia soon found a pretext for occupying still more territory. Unfortunately, the lands so entered included the region of Cracow, which commanded the "Moravian Gateway," the great pass leading directly to Vienna. In the face of this threat, which

[23] Huber, *Deutsche Verfassungsgeschichte*, I, 28–29.
[24] Quoted in Andrei A. Lobanov-Rostovsky, *Russia and Europe, 1789–1825* (Durham, N.C., 1947), 7. Cf. Peter Richard Rohden, *Die klassische Diplomatie von Kaunitz bis Metternich* (Leipzig, 1939), 50.
[25] Huber, *Deutsche Verfassungsgeschichte*, I, 37.

was concrete and immediate and not, like the French Revolution, vague and problematical, Thugut dropped his laissez faire policy and joined with Russia to expel the Prussians from the sensitive zones and partition Poland according to Austro-Russian convenience. In March, 1795, the court at Berlin responded by signing a separate peace with France at Basel. By the treaty of Basel, Prussia recognized the French claim to Belgium and the left bank of the Rhine and, in a secret clause, was assured that her own modest losses would be compensated on the right bank by the secularization of ecclesiastical territory. Thus extricated in the west, she pressed her claims in Poland and six months later took her share in the final partition of that unhappy land.

Such were the harsh realities which forced cruel choices on Austrian strategists. Metternich was no doubt right in an academic sense when he warned against the ultimate dangers of the Revolution and called for a halt to conventional political rivalries. But the message had no meaning unless heeded by all the continental courts, inside and outside the Reich. As long as Russia forced the issue in Poland, Thugut had no choice but to keep a large portion of Austrian military strength in the east, where Vienna itself was exposed. It was not his fault that Prussia abandoned the western front or that Saxony, Hanover, and Hesse-Cassel also made peace, leaving as the only belligerents the princes with lands at stake on the left bank of the Rhine. That a young man of twenty-one should overlook these facts is not surprising; what is remarkable is that years later at the height of his powers Metternich, with unbecoming conceit, continued to reproach Thugut's ministry for its "unbroken series of mistakes and miscalculations," and even then spoke only of the advance of France and not of the Polish question.[26] But that is often the way we treat those from whom we learn.

Austria fought on in Germany, with a fair degree of success; and it was only when France spread the war to Italy, with Napoleon Bonaparte commanding her armies, that Thugut finally sued for peace. The treaty was signed in October, 1797, at Campo Formio, and by its terms Austria ceded the Belgian

[26] Metternich, *Memoirs*, I, 33.

provinces to France, taking as compensation the Italian territories of Venice, Istria, and Dalmatia. Surrendering a crown land within the Reich for possessions entirely outside the imperial boundary was a clear case of *Österreich über Alles,* but that was not all. In secret clauses Austria agreed to the cession of much of the left bank of the Rhine, and in return was assured of French help in acquiring parts of Upper Bavaria as well as the sizeable archbishopric of Salzburg. The latter implied endorsement of the principle of secularization, so long resisted for fear of abolishing some of the most important props of the Empire.

Somewhat ironically, the treaty of Campo Formio, which had such ominous implications for the family Metternich, was the cause of both father and son being recalled at last to public life. As France was technically still at war with the Empire, the treaty had provided that a conference be held at Rastatt to discuss peace with the emissaries of the Reich. Count Ludwig von Lehrbach was appointed to represent the imperial *Kreis* known as "Austria," and Count Ludwig von Cobenzl, the negotiator of Campo Formio, was named the ambassador of the Emperor Francis in his capacity as king of Bohemia and Hungary. There remained the post of plenipotentiary for the Holy Roman Emperor, and this Franz Georg Metternich received through the influence of his friend, Cobenzl, who had suddenly attained new standing through the conclusion of the peace. Young Clemens was again named to represent the counts of Westphalia, as at the coronation of 1792.[27]

If Franz Georg had been a keener politician he might, even in his straitened circumstances, have hesitated to accept an assignment in which he would have to do his best for the Reich without impeding the endeavors of Cobenzl and Lehrbach to implement the secret clauses of Campo Formio. Indeed, the suspicion is strong that Thugut viewed the appointment as a fitting reward for Franz Georg's bungling in the Netherlands. He systematically excluded the emperor's plenipotentiary from the state secrets that he freely shared with Cobenzl and Lehrbach,

---

[27] For this and following see Corti, *Metternich und die Frauen,* I, 49ff.; and Srbik, *Metternich,* I, 82ff.

and there is considerable doubt that either of the Metternichs even knew of the commitments made at Campo Formio. Clemens, unfortunately, was more accurate than he knew when he said of his father, "no post could have suited him better, and no man could have better filled the post." [28]

At any rate, when the Congress opened in January, 1798, Franz Georg was virtually helpless, caught between the imperial deputation, which had instructions from the Reichstag to negotiate on the basis of the *status quo ante,* and the French envoys, who went beyond the terms of Campo Formio and demanded the entire left bank with no exceptions. In the end, of course, he had to follow the lead of Coblenzl and Lehrbach, who not only acquiesced in the new French demands but also influenced the other imperial estates to do the same, assuring them of compensation on the right bank. The imperial protection, Franz Georg finally confessed to a deputation of the *Reichsritterschaft,* was nothing but a "loud-sounding word." [29]

Metternich the younger did not share his father's sentimentality and stoic pride. Even before the treaty of Campo Formio he had abandoned hope for the left bank; [30] and now, at Rastatt, where his official duties were only nominal, he immediately took steps to assure adequate compensation for his own house. "I do not wish to be quoted," he wrote his wife, "but according to my way of seeing things, everything is gone to the devil and the time is come when everyone must save from the wreck what he can." [31] Four months later, when the congress adopted the principle of compensation, he already had his eye on a suitable estate and had staked his claim to it.[32] On the higher level of policy, too, he looked forward rather than back. Weighing the French program of complete secularization against what he understood to be the Austrian court's opposition to it, he favored a middle course; and when this was in fact adopted, he

---

[28] Metternich to wife, 6 Jan. 1798, in Metternich, *Memoirs,* I, 361.

[29] Srbik, *Metternich,* I, 85; Theodor Bitterauf, *Die Gründung des Rheinbundes und der Untergang des alten Reiches* (Munich, 1905), 77.

[30] Corti, *Metternich und die Frauen,* I, 47.

[31] Metternich to wife, 7 Dec. 1797, in Metternich, *Memoirs,* I, 350.

[32] Metternich to wife, 11 April 1798, in *ibid.,* I, 370.

was impatient with his father's continued and, as he believed, futile defiance.

While Franz Georg stubbornly defended the territorial integrity of the Reich and Clemens realistically bargained for compensations, the real issue at Rastatt was how the great powers would partition "the third Germany." Considered hypothetically, the situation presented a chance to dispose of the area much as Poland had been disposed of—by a three-way partition, France taking the left bank, Prussia assuming the hegemony of North Germany, and Austria, strengthened by Bavarian lands, commanding the South. Indeed, some such arrangement was the solution toward which old-regime diplomacy had been groping since the Peace of Westphalia—the "Polonization of Germany" some called it—and, had the precepts of classical diplomacy continued to prevail, it might in time have taken place.

It was not to be. Thugut would not allow Prussia her coveted territorial consolidation, and the French would not limit their influence to the Rhine. It was bad enough that they made secularization a universal principle. Even worse was their program of redistribution, which designated not the two German powers but the intermediate estates as the beneficiaries, in the hope that Prussia and Austria would be satisfied with mere ceremonial primacy in the Reich.[33] In addition, the French envoys planned to replace the three ecclesiastical electors by the secular houses of Hesse-Cassel, Würtemberg, and Orange-Nassau. Not since the Reformation had the scramble for land been so great, as the princes, led by the landgrave of Hesse-Cassel and the margrave of Baden, flocked to Paris and Rastatt seeking favors from victorious France. "The French lay down the law," was Clemens Metternich's comment, "and that with an arrogance and certainty of success incredible to those who do not know the secret supporters and authors of our evils."[34]

By this time one of the leading French imperialists was Bonaparte himself, and he appeared in person at Rastatt. His soldier's eye was dazzled by the rich manpower potential of the

[33] Bitterauf, Gründung des Rheinbundes, 66–81.
[34] Metternich to wife, 27 March 1798 in Metternich, Memoirs, I, 365–366.

Empire, and his keen political intelligence titillated by the opportunities of *divide et impera*. He envisioned a future of compensation for friends and punishment for enemies, with France the while exploiting the intimidating effects of her unique and terrifying capacity to raise mass armies.[35] Napoleon did not stay long at Rastatt, leaving several days before Clemens Metternich arrived, but his fame was great and his influence on French policy already considerable. Metternich, bitterly disappointed at missing him, carefully noted every rumor of his impending return to the congress, but the famous general never came. Thus the contest for Germany began without a personal encounter between the two antagonists.

Perhaps it is just as well. A meeting between the military hero and the obscure delegate of the counts of Westphalia would not have been a meeting between equals. Indeed, there was little outward sign that a future foreign minister was maturing; Metternich's stay at Rastatt was a lively round of balls and plays, casinos and concerts, spiced by scandalous behavior with the actresses and an occasional fling at conducting the orchestras. Inwardly he was beginning to evince some of the "physician's coldbloodedness," which he had once so heartily despised. He was getting a glimpse of Vienna's viewpoint; and if he had regrets at the loss of the left bank, it was less because he shared his father's affection for the Reich than because he could not "bear the idea of seeing my home in the hands of those rogues. . . ." [36] Nevertheless, the difference with his father was a matter of tactics rather than of principle. Stubborn resistance to all change, he feared, could well result in losing the left bank *without* compensation, and none of the Metternichs could afford that. The Reich as an institution was still to their interest regardless of its territorial extent and regardless of where the family seat might be. Clemens Metternich was still a *Reichsgraf* at heart, very much his father's son.

[35] Deutsch, *Genesis*, 39–40; Bitterauf, *Gründung des Rheinbundes*, 66–76.
[36] Metternich to wife, 7 Dec. 1797, in Metternich, *Memoirs*, I, 350.

CHAPTER II

THE DECLINE AND FALL OF THE REICH

In the summer of 1798 Metternich's wife and small daughter joined him in Rastatt. Otherwise there was little change. The principles of secularization and compensation were adopted but the efforts to implement them protracted negotiations interminably. By the beginning of the next year it was clear that the war would continue. In March, fearing unpleasantness and even danger in a border town like Rastatt, Clemens Metternich returned with his family to Austria. Still out of favor with Thugut, he resumed private life, alternating his scientific hobbies at Austerlitz with the observation of politics in the salons of the capital. Not until the fall of Thugut, after the disastrous peace of Lunéville in February, 1801, did he have another chance to pursue a diplomatic career.[1]

The events which he observed in those two years were associated with the War of the Second Coalition. Contrary to his own belief while at Rastatt, the congress did prove to be a sideshow, a "prearranged game," the outcome of which was determined not so much by the negotiations as by the actions of the two absent powers. One of these was Great Britain, which continued the war and thereby caused Bonaparte to turn his attention from Germany to Egypt. The other power was Russia, which was alarmed at French ambition in Central Europe, concerned for the fate of Bavaria, Würtemberg and Baden, her special wards in the empire, and outraged that her rights as a guarantor of the *status quo* in Germany had been totally ignored. Tsar Paul now attempted to reconstitute the coalition which had been broken by the separate peace treaties, and warned the Directory that he would not tolerate hostile acts against "our ally, the Emperor of the Romans or [leading to] the overthrow [of] the German Empire." [2]

If the First Coalition had been ruined by defeat, the Second

[1] Corti, *Metternich und die Frauen*, I, 63ff.
[2] Quoted in Lobanov-Rostovsky, *Russia and Europe*, 17.

foundered on victory. By routing the French army on the Nile, Britain found herself in a contest with her Russian ally over spoils in the Eastern Mediterranean. Austro-Russian relations took a similar turn. After several welcome victories in Italy the government in Vienna became uneasy about the presence of Russian troops in Central Europe and raised innumerable barriers to further collaboration. And Tsar Paul, convinced that the Austrians were bent on maneuvering his forces and the French into mutual destruction, withdrew his armies altogether and guided Russian policy toward a rapprochement with France. In this way Russia was soon able to obtain by negotiation what she had not achieved by war: a voice in the questions of Germany, Italy, and the Levant.[3]

Russia's change of course demonstrated the variety of choices open to the "flanking power" on the continent. However, Austria's choice was a simple one: either obstructing the common enterprise just when it approached success, or seeing the alliance through to victory only to find herself the captive of her stronger ally. Having chosen the first course, she now met defeat at Marengo (June 14, 1800) and at Hohenlinden (December 3) and sued for peace. And this time the French emissaries insisted that Francis of Habsburg sign in the name of the Reich as well; they had no desire to duplicate the Rastatt experience of Franz Georg's refusing for the emperor what Cobenzl had conceded for the king of Hungary.

By the treaty of Lunéville, February 9, 1801, Austria accepted all the losses discussed at Campo Formio and more. In Germany the principle of secularization was confirmed and the clause of Campo Formio relative to Cleves and Gelderland rescinded, so that Prussia, as a reward for her neutrality, would be compensated in Central Germany after all. The entire left bank of the Rhine, including the great fortress of Mainz, was now French in law as well as fact; while on the right bank the razing of all fortifications left South Germany at the mercy of the French, and access to the Danube valley, highway to Vienna, unimpeded. Another legacy of Campo Formio had been a plan

---

[3] *ibid.*, 59. Cf. Oskar Regele, *Der österreichische Hofkriegsrat 1556–1848* (Vienna, 1949), 62ff.

to remove Francis' uncle, the duke of Modena, to a territory in Germany; this was now confirmed, and a similar arrangement made for Francis' brother Ferdinand, the grand duke of Tuscany. The device not only terminated Austrian influence in Italy; it also compelled her to cooperate in the redistribution of territory in the Reich, else the relatives would not have anything at all.

Yet of Austria's compensations in Upper Bavaria and Salzburg, which had been the silver lining of Campo Formio, there was now no mention. The reason for the change was Bonaparte's desire to appease Russia, the self-appointed protector of the South German courts. For Napoleon had in the meantime become First Consul in France while Alexander had succeeded Paul as Tsar of Russia. Even more forcefully than his predecessor, Alexander demanded a voice in the reorganization of Germany. On October 10, 1801, Count Arcadi Markov for Russia and Prince Charles Talleyrand for France signed a peace convention which stipulated that France and Russia would jointly dictate terms in Germany and Italy, it being understood in advance that they would treat Bavaria, Würtemberg, and Baden with special benevolence. A wild scramble ensued as once more the estates of the empire vied for favored treatment, but this time they consulted Markov as well as Talleyrand, and some also dispatched lobbyists to St. Petersburg. The three-way contest for the "third Germany" had become a four-way contest.[4]

Once again Austria's misfortune was Clemens Metternich's personal gain. Baron Thugut, increasingly referred to in Vienna as Baron "Thunichtgut," had to pay the price for Austria's failures—this despite the fact that he had learned more than anyone, perhaps, about the dilemmas of the centrally located power, the options of Russia, and the insatiable ambition of Napoleon. His successor was Count Cobenzl, the old friend to whom Franz Georg owed his post at Rastatt. He was just as helpful now, and through his influence Clemens was offered, not only a ministerial post, but a choice of Dresden, Copenhagen, or Regens-

[4] Bitterauf, *Gründung des Rheinbundes*, 88–90; Deutsch, *Genesis*, 41–52; Lobanov-Rostovsky, *Russia and Europe*, 7off.; and André Fugier, *La révolution française et l'empire Napoléonnien* (Paris, 1954), 130–165.

burg. It was a big jump for so young a man without real experience in diplomacy; ordinarily a secretaryship would have been expected. But Cobenzl was close to the Kaunitzes and Liechtensteins; and his sister, the Countess Rombeck, was especially fond of the Rhinelander, who apparently had impressed everyone at her soirées. All in all, Metternich's entry into the state service of Austria was due not only to personal influence but also to a genuine recognition of his talent.[5]

Although the appointment was made in February, 1801, bureaucratic delays prevented Metternich's departure for Dresden until November. In the meantime, he used his position to gain access to official documents in Vienna and, under the tutelage of the seasoned expert, Carl Daiser von Sylbach, spent months studying the background of Austrian policy, making up, as it were, for the lack of conventional advancement through the ranks.[6] Metternich summarized the results of his labors in an elaborate state paper which he hoped to carry to Dresden as his instructions. The fact that the document was never used for the purpose does not detract from its value as a guide to the aspiring diplomat's thinking in the dark months following Lunéville.

Analyzing "the present state of European politics" in this paper,[7] Metternich still saw the French Revolution as the cause of all the changes that had occurred, changes greater than "the three great wars of the past century" had brought about. Nevertheless, his attention was drawn not so much to the social upheaval as to the shattered European state system. With an obvious effort to prove his "Austrian" point of view, he saw many "indirect advantages" both in the loss of the Netherlands, "the remotest and as regarded defense, the most expensive of all our states," and in the new arrangements in Italy, which amounted to trading primacy on the peninsula for control of the Adriatic. Thugut himself could not have rationalized the *Hausmacht* point of view better. There was one thing, however, which set Metternich apart from both Thugut and Cobenzl: the convic-

[5] Corti, *Metternich und die Frauen*, I, 66–67.
[6] Srbik, *Metternich*, III, 44.
[7] Text of instructions, dated 2 Nov. 1801 in Metternich, *Memoirs*, II, 3–19.

tion that Austria's welfare was linked far more closely to the European equilibrium than to any local advantages she might salvage in the form of territorial aggrandizement. And that is why he could not be satisfied with the *status quo* but could only regard it as an opportunity to recuperate, to put the Austrian house in order, and to seek new alliances for war.

One need hardly reiterate that, with Winneburg-Beilstein lost and still no compensation forthcoming, every private interest of the Metternichs cried out for the eventual resumption of hostilities. It is equally clear, however, that the advice was sound and on the whole objective; it remained, in fact, the essence of Metternich's policy long after he had abandoned his dreams of returning to the Rhineland and had become the very incarnation of the Austrian statesman. It is symptomatic of his increasingly dispassionate judgment that he did not dwell exclusively on the French part in destroying the balance of power. French acquisitions must of course be disgorged, but England too had "made so many conquests that peace can only be secured with this state by a great retrocession on her part." The partition of Poland he described as "contrary to all principles of sound policy," necessitated only by "the blind desire of aggrandizement" in Berlin and St. Petersburg. In like manner he had come to appreciate at last the westward thrust of Russia. "By internal resources not possessed by any other civilized state," he said almost enviously, "able to terminate every alliance and every war at her own pleasure, merely by the retreat of her army, unassailable within her frontiers, Russia is, by virtue of her geographical and political situation, always dangerous but especially so under a government which, without principles, acts from the convenience of the moment."[8]

Prussia he blamed most of all for the overthrow of the balance, and although he doubted that her gains really offset the risks she assumed in acquiring so long a common frontier with Russia, he denounced her schemes for hegemony in North Germany and warned the Saxon court against the danger of allying with her. Saxony's only hope, he concluded, surrounded as she was on three sides by Prussia, was Austria. Only in this con-

[8] *ibid.*, II, 8–9.

nection did he dwell with some sentimentality on the imperial constitution; there was after all little else he could say to a court which, no less than Prussia, hoped to devour the petty princes in the Reich when France and Russia gave the word.

There was in all this a dim awareness that the ideological struggle launched by the French Revolution was being assimilated into the familiar contests of the great powers even as the "boneheads" in Vienna had always believed. Whatever the Revolution might mean for the ancient social institutions of Europe, Metternich's earlier thinking, with its tendency to reduce everything to the two categories of Revolution and Old Regime, seemed superficial now. It was rather as if egalitarian France, liberal England, autocratic Russia, bureaucratic Prussia, and dynastic Austria, all of which differed widely with respect to their domestic institutions, were engaged in a relentless struggle over the weaker components of old Europe and her colonial appendages. Each contestant had some inherent advantage: France the unprecedented energies of her aroused masses, Britain her sea power, Russia her remoteness, and Prussia, though hardly in the same class, her frugality and perseverance. Only Austria, it seemed, lacked any peculiar asset save possibly her central position, and that could only be effectively exploited in a Europe to which equilibrium had been restored.

This new stress on the rivalry of states rather than the rivalry of doctrines did not mean that Metternich had repudiated the conservatism of his student days. On the contrary, it was during his stay at the Saxon court that he entered upon his long and intellectually stimulating association with Friedrich von Gentz, a leading continental disciple of Edmund Burke, whom Metternich had met during his stay in England.[9] Gentz tended to make a dogma of conservatism, opposing it to all revolutionary doctrines as if the dichotomy reflected a kind of worldwide contest between good and evil; Metternich, on the other hand, was groping his way toward a larger view, in which he did not, so to speak, ostracize revolution but included it among the facts of political life which the statesman must dispassionately take cognizance of and manipulate to his advantage. When Metter-

[9] Srbik, *Metternich*, I, 105ff.

nich boasted of his principles, he had reference not to political dogmas or propositions about the good society but simply to the maxims which described his technique, a technique which consisted mainly of handling each case on its merits. "My point of departure is the quiet contemplation of the affairs of this world," was the way he put it many years later.[10] By that time, it must be said, his methods had degenerated into the unadorned cynicism which lies in wait for one obsessed with technique alone.

In choosing the post at Dresden rather than that at Regensburg, seat of the Reichstag, Metternich was attracted by the opportunity of observing the affairs of Eastern Europe. The decision removed him from the center of German affairs, since it was at Regensburg that the momentous negotiation concerning the reconstruction of the Reich was about to begin. But in view of his father's experience with the thankless assignment at Rastatt, it is understandable that he had no desire "to witness the obsequies of the noble German Empire" [11] and (one may safely surmise) the possible burial of his budding career in diplomacy. After the peace of Lunéville there was no fame to be won at the capital of the Holy Roman Empire. Thus Metternich had no direct connection with the deliberations of the imperial deputation chosen by the Reichstag to negotiate with the French and Russian mediators. Nor was he present when on February 25, 1803, the deputies finally adopted the famous *Reichsdeputationhauptschluss,* or Imperial Recess, so basic to an understanding of German politics in the Age of Metternich.

The Imperial Recess laid the foundations of modern Germany, not by advancing unity, but by sweeping away the ecclesiastical and municipal fragments of the Middle Ages and by extending the sway of modern territorial government. The ecclesiastical estates were expropriated outright, and most of the fifty-one imperial cities were "mediatized," that is to say subordinated to the political authority of the larger secular princes, who henceforth stood between them and the emperor. There

<hr>

[10] Quoted in Henry A. Kissinger, *A World Restored. Metternich, Castlereagh, and the Problems of Peace 1812–1822* (London, 1957), 10.
[11] Metternich, *Memoirs,* I, 34.

were some exceptions, gestures to the habits of the past and concessions to the practical needs of the present. Carl Theodore von Dalberg, archbishop of Electoral Mainz and archchancellor of the empire, preserved his status and was given territory at Regensburg as a reward for cooperating with Napoleon. He and the Grand Master of the Teutonic Knights were the only ecclesiastical survivors. Six cities kept their freedom: Augsburg, Nuremberg, Frankfurt, and the Hanseatic towns of Lübeck, Bremen, and Hamburg. Similarly, the imperial knights, barons, and counts weathered the storm for a time, because Bonaparte prudently desired to hold back some patronage for future dispensation, and also probably because he had not yet decided how *la troisième Allemagne* was to be definitively reorganized.

For Austria, the Recess was a severe shock, acceptable only because her exhausted army and empty treasury did not permit physical resistance. In order to obtain compensation for the grand duke of Tuscany she had to give up her own claims to Salzburg, Berchtesgaden, and Passau, territories which would have given her a really strong frontier. The grand duke was Francis' brother Ferdinand, but that did not, as we shall see, guarantee a permanent association of his provinces with Austria. Worse still, the only way to indemnify the duke of Modena was to surrender Ortenau and the Breisgau, Austria's last remaining foothold on the Rhine and, incidentally, the home of Metternich's mother. As compensation Austria received Trent and Brixen in the South Tyrol; this had a face-saving value in connection with her extrusion from Italy, but hardly outweighed her withdrawal from the Rhine. The constitutional changes in the empire hurt even more. The margrave of Baden and the duke of Würtemberg replaced the archbishops of Trier and Cologne in the electoral college, and an additional electorate was created for Hesse-Cassel. In this body as well as in the Reichstag itself Protestants were now in the majority. In a new election the Habsburgs could not expect to win.[12]

In some ways this last circumstance was the most important of all in the determination of Austria's subsequent policy. For what would the Habsburgs be without the imperial title? In

[12] d'Arenberg, *Princes du St-Empire*, 63–72. Cf. Fugier, *La révolution*, 166–168.

European affairs they would merely be the kings of Hungary. Inside the Reich they would be nothing but the archdukes of Austria and kings of Bohemia, vassals of whoever succeeded them as emperors. There could be no "kingdom of Austria" because the Pragmatic Sanction had not created an Austrian monarchy; it had only assured a personal union of territories, no one of which enjoyed the status of a great power. Juridically the Pragmatic Sanction itself rested, as its name testified, on the precarious foundation of political convenience; it had once been challenged by Frederick the Great, and could easily be questioned again by those whom it inconvenienced. Fallen from imperial heights, the dynasty might find it difficult to keep even the crown lands together. Thus the Imperial Recess, although it formally pertained only to imperial affairs, cast a shadow over the Austrian *Hausmacht* as well, confronting Francis with a problem comparable to that which had plagued Charles VI.

To these adversities of the house of Habsburg were linked, as usual, the fortunes of the house of Metternich. The ecclesiastical estates had generally been Austrian pocket boroughs so far as their votes in the Reichstag were concerned; now that they were eliminated the court at Vienna tried desperately to find other ways of maintaining its influence. Count Franz von Colloredo, the vice-chancellor for imperial affairs (thus the counterpart of Cobenzl, who was court and state vice-chancellor), was extremely solicitous of the refugees from the Rhineland. Wherever possible he interceded to give their new fiefs the status of principalities rather than counties, hoping that they could then occupy the Reichstag seats formerly assigned to the ecclesiastical bench. As a result, Franz Georg Metternich not only received the former Abbey of Ochsenhausen, just south of Ulm in Swabia, a property considerably larger than Winneburg-Beilstein, but he was also granted the rank of prince, and potentially his own seat in the Reichstag. Financially the family fortunes were again on a solid footing. As the title, however, was attached to the territory and not to the family, only Franz Georg could use it; Clemens remained a count.[13]

[13] *Metternich, Memoirs*, I, 45–46.

Count Metternich's assignment, in the meantime, was to try to win the court at Dresden over to the new Austrian interpretation of the Reich. There was no longer any reason for Protestant Saxony to oppose Austria, especially as the elector of Saxony was the only member of the imperial deputation not involved in the territorial upheaval. On the contrary, so Metternich argued, Austria was Saxony's only support against the ambitions of Prussia, and the Reich was a bulwark which must be maintained for the good of all. His success, however, was minimal. The elector appeased Prussia and fawned on France, and in the matter of new votes in the Reichstag made it clear that, although he shared the Austrian view, he would not use his influence in her behalf. To this Metternich replied "that the Constitution of the Empire would necessarily fall if the chief courts adopted a purely passive system in such important discussions." [14] All that remained of Austrian prestige in Dresden, it seemed, was Metternich's knack for gaining precedence in matters of protocol, and even that was thwarted whenever the French minister chose to make an issue of it.[15]

The decline of Austrian influence in Germany was no doubt preordained by the shift of the continental balance. Still, most of the German princes, even those most benefited by the Recess, would have preferred a position of neutrality between France and Austria had not material conflicts of interest decreed otherwise. The main issue was the status of the imperial knights and counts, a majority of whom were left in the new order partly or wholly surrounded by the expanded holdings of the greater princes. The latter, led by Max Joseph of Bavaria (Metternich's friend of Strasbourg days) and Frederick of Würtemberg, soon proclaimed suzerainty over hundreds of *Reichsritterschaft* estates in Swabia, Franconia, and along the Rhine. Swabia was particularly important, for there Austria herself had expectations of annexing property by offering in return rich offices in the Austrian service. With prestige, vital recruiting rights, and future aggrandizement at stake, Cobenzl had to act. First he sent an army to the Bavarian frontier. Then, in January, 1804,

---

[14] Metternich to Cobenzl, 20. Nov. 1803, Metternich, *Memoirs,* II, 20.
[15] Missoffe, *Metternich,* 68.

he had the Aulic Council, the emperor's personal advisory board in Vienna, issue a *conclusum* which annulled all the acts of mediatization. That he was able to make the edict prevail was due largely to Bonaparte, who at the time desired tranquility in Germany and advised the predators to desist.[16]

The Aulic Council directed only the mildest strictures toward Frederick, who had been pro-Austrian even at the time of the Recess and whose marauding did not touch Austria directly. Nevertheless, he too eventually turned against the *Hofburg* in Vienna. Würtemberg had long been renowned for the vigor of its estates, which had managed to preserve "the good old law," as it was fondly called, against the trend of the age toward absolutism. Frederick was therefore often at odds with his estates, and in the summer of 1804 he challenged them by refusing to seat one of their officials. It was a challenge to Austria, too, since what was left of imperial law was violated, and the estates lost no time in appealing to the Aulic Council, where they had often before found succor. The issue thus forced, the Council on August 16 ordered the official in question to be installed. Frederick refused, turned to France for assistance, and became, despite his close kinship with the tsar, one of Bonaparte's most reliable allies.

Austria stood out once again as the protector of the estates, her cause more than ever identified with the fate of the lesser nobility, both the mediate estates of the duchies and the immediate estates of the Reich. Given the determination to shore up the truncated Reich as best one could, the decision of the Aulic Council was no doubt the proper one. In the long run, however, association with the weakest elements in Germany at the cost of alienating the strong was a heavy liability—one that Metternich, when at last he occupied Cobenzl's place, was careful to avoid.[17]

Cobenzl's eagerness to stand by the petty estates was partly a matter of traditional policy, but it also had an air of seeking to give reassurance about Austria's own relations with the

[16] Deutsch, *Genesis*, 214–218; d'Arenberg, *Princes du St-Empire*, 74–77.

[17] Deutsch, *Genesis*, 238–239. Also Hans Rall, *Kurbayern in der letzten Epoche der alten Reichsverfassung, 1745–1801* (Munich, 1952), 171–172.

Reich. Only a few months before, in May, 1804, the French senate had proclaimed Napoleon emperor and had sought Austria's recognition of the act. As a *quid pro quo* Cobenzl's first demand was the right to convert the Reich into an hereditary monarchy under the Habsburgs, thus dispelling once and for all the grave uncertainty about future elections. Only when that was refused did he fall back on a more radical plan: the creation of a new, a genuine Austrian empire, comprising the lands hitherto joined only by the Pragmatic Sanction. This arrangement Napoleon at length accepted, probably fully realizing how much the new crown would prejudice the one that Francis already wore. For under the Austrian crown sovereignty was claimed for lands which were fiefs of the other—an ominous example to set for all the intermediate houses, which likewise yearned for sovereignty.[18]

Cobenzl, of course, realized this too, but he was acting on the premise that under existing circumstances Francis was going to be the last Habsburg to wear the Roman crown regardless of what happened to the Reich itself. If the Reich should continue under another family (which would be worse: the Bonapartes or the Hohenzollerns?) there was all the more reason to establish between the German and non-German lands of Austria a bond equal, if not superior, to the ancient ties with Germany. The vice-chancellor thus arranged in advance for a graceful withdrawal. Sentimental pamphleteers to the contrary, Cobenzl was only doing his duty, and it must be said that of the two empires founded in 1804, his empire outlived Napoleon's by a hundred years.[19]

The time was to come when Metternich, even more emphatically than Cobenzl, would make the new empire of Austria the cornerstone of his policy. At the time of its creation, however, his heart was all with the other Reich, at least to the extent that he strongly opposed the recognition of Napoleon's crown. Indeed, it may truthfully be said that he disagreed with most of Cobenzl's policies. Where the vice-chancellor viewed the

[18] Heinrich von Srbik, *Die Schicksalsstunde des alten Reiches* (Jena, 1937), 13–23.

[19] Cf. *ibid.*, 16, who charges that for Cobenzl it was merely "a question of rank and etiquette."

German princes as "a regrettable following" for France,[20] Metternich regarded their defection from the Reich as "inconceivable." [21] Where Cobenzl considered Napoleon the tamer of the Revolution, a man with whom one could reason, Metternich followed Gentz's doctrine that the Corsican was the instrument of the Revolution.[22] Where Cobenzl cautiously desired a rapprochment with Russia for the sake of greater leverage with France, Metternich favored a total commitment that would make possible a united front against France. Cobenzl, in short, desired reconciliation and peace; Metternich wanted war. It is possible that Cobenzl sensed their differences, for in an instruction of November, 1803, he stressed the importance of the envoy's being "in complete agreement with our aims and actions." [23]

The instruction in question was the general directive for a new assignment: the embassy in Berlin. Compared to the attitude of the South German courts, the neutrality of Saxony had put Clemens Lothar's performance in Dresden in a favorable light. "The Count Metternich is young but he is not maladroit," Colloredo said of him,[24] and as early as February, 1803, the appointment had been made. The occasion was the adoption of the Imperial Recess, which put Austro-Russian relations on a normal footing once more and brought about the transfer of the ambassador in Berlin, Count Philip Stadion, to St. Petersburg. But again the wheels turned slowly in the well-known *Schlamperei* of Vienna: Metternich remained three months longer in Dresden, spent several more on leave in Ochsenhausen, and not until November did he actually set out for the Prussian capital.

In Berlin his assignment was not primarily to cultivate Prussia, whose neutrality on the whole suited Cobenzl's policy of reconciliation, but to reinforce Stadion's efforts toward an entente with Russia. The task was almost embarrassingly easy, for before long it was Russia that was pressing the matter, mainly

---

[20] "Instruktion für den Grafen Metternich," 5 Nov. 1803, in August Fournier, *Gentz und Cobenzl, Geschichte der österreichischen Diplomatie in den Jahren 1801–1805* (Vienna, 1880), 208.

[21] Metternich to Colloredo, 29 Oct. 1805, in Metternich, *Memoirs*, II, 82.

[22] Srbik, *Metternich*, I, 105–107.

[23] "Instruktion für Metternich," *op.cit.*, 211.

[24] Corti, *Metternich und die Frauen*, I, 79.

because Napoleon's German policy completely ignored Russia's desire to neutralize the country. The affronts were legion. When Alexander proposed a joint mediation in Vienna of Austria's quarrels with Bavaria, Napoleon steered the issue into the diet at Regensburg, where Russia's wishes were ignored.[25] A few weeks later, when Alexander denounced the armed seizure of the Bourbon duke of Enghien on the soil of Baden, Napoleon declared the Franco-Russian mediation in Germany terminated. When Russia lodged a protest with the Reichstag, the only members who favored its discussion were the two with great-power affiliations (Hanover-England and Pomerania-Sweden), and the best they could do was to see that it was tabled rather than flatly rejected.[26] When war broke out again between France and England, Napoleon occupied Hanover and the Hanseatic free cities in order to control the commerce of the Elbe and Weser—this too in defiance of Russia. An intermediate zone is really neutral only if it separates equal forces, and that had only momentarily been the case between France and Russia. Like Napoleon's other creations, the Batavian, Helvetian, and Cisalpine republics, Germany was neutral in name only. Now Russia was only too anxious to win both Austria and Prussia to her side, that is to say to the Third Coalition, which was then forming.

Metternich was almost jubilant at the turn of events. Under Gentz's influence he had long favored an alliance between Austria and Prussia and, convinced that "it will only be the power which inspires terror here which can direct the movements of the Prussian cabinet . . . ,"[27] he believed that Russia alone could supply the necessary pressure. His procedure therefore was unstinting collaboration with the representatives of St. Petersburg, whether the resident minister Baron Maximilian von Alopeus, or the special emissary, General Ferdinand Winzingerode, or the tsar himself, who came to Berlin in October, 1805, to plead personally with Frederick William.

The trouble was that the Cobenzl-Colloredo ministry viewed an alliance for war quite differently from a rapprochement for

[25] Deutsch, *Genesis*, 218–228.
[26] Lobanov-Rostovsky, *Russia and Europe*, 76–77.
[27] Metternich to Colloredo, 29 Oct. 1805, in Metternich, *Memoirs*, II, 82.

peace. Cobenzl, moreover, was troubled by practical considerations that his Berlin envoy seemed to ignore. One was the imminent military threat posed by Bavaria if Max Joseph, as was likely, joined Napoleon. Sitting astride the Danube, the Bavarian army of 50,000 could either block Napoleon's way or become the spearhead of a drive to Vienna. The Austrian command could not wait to see which it would be; and therefore, when war finally came, Cobenzl resorted to crude intimidation, dispatching an ultimatum which did in fact drive Bavaria into Napoleon's arms.[28] Another problem was uncertainty about the Russian armies, which were distant and could easily be withdrawn in time of stress—this had happened in 1799. Indeed, it was Cobenzl's belief that their principal use would be to restrain Prussia. This pessimistic assessment of Prussian intentions and Russian capabilities was reason enough for peace, especially as the *Hofkriegsrat* in Vienna, headed by Archduke Carl, doubted Austria's own readiness.[29] At length, however, Napoleon's determination to dominate Germany was too obvious to be ignored. And so, after concluding a preliminary alliance with Russia in November, 1804, Cobenzl gave his ambassador in Berlin the signal to proceed.

The situation brimmed with opportunities for intrigue, and Metternich rapidly developed his native talent for it. Behind the back of the neutralist first minister, Count Christian August Haugwitz, he worked with the disgruntled Baron Carl August von Hardenberg, who, despite his role in negotiating the peace of Basel, was a man of broad European outlook.[30] Together with Alopeus he plotted to bring about the dismissal of the pro-French cabinet councillor John William Lombard. When Alexander peremptorily demanded permission to march his troops through Prussian territory, Metternich was among the first to applaud the gambit, seeing in it the application of his own conviction that one would have to "inspire terror" in Berlin.

He could not have been more mistaken. Frederick William,

[28] Cf. Hans Karl von Zwehl, *Der Kampf um Bayern 1805. I: Abschluss der bayerisch-französischen Allianz* (Munich, 1937), 140–141.
[29] Cobenzl to Colloredo, 9 March 1804, in Fournier, *Gentz und Cobenzl*, 215ff.
[30] Hans Hausherr, "Hardenberg und der Friede von Basel," *Historische Zeitschrift*, Bd. 184 (August–December, 1957), 292ff.

whose primary concern was his country's freedom of action, mobilized against *all* powers, and only later, after the French army had duplicated the tsar's mistake by violating Prussian soil in Ansbach, did he resume discussions with the Russians and Austrians. It was a blunder that could easily have been irreparable, and Metternich knew it, as he indicated in later years by denying that he had had anything to do with it. What he learned, both from this episode and from Cobenzl's ill-fated brusqueness toward Bavaria, was that a weak state, not being really free, is all the more apt to value the *appearance* of freedom, and to favor those who accord it dignity however much they may in reality control it. Later, as foreign minister, Metternich did not rule out intimidation as a technique, but he realized the importance of timing and came to see that threats and taunts, by adding insult to injury, usually leave more grievous wounds than the presentation of accomplished facts.

Except for this mistake, Metternich proved adept at following the twists and turns of the diplomatic labyrinth in Berlin, and his performance was almost universally commended. He was decorated with the order of St. Stephen, and Gentz, who undoubtedly had much to do with his friend's belief in the Prussian alliance—not merely as a temporary expedient but as the cornerstone of all future Austrian policy—considered him the only man fit to be foreign minister. This was rich praise, especially as the Berlin envoy did not actually accomplish his purpose. The best that he and Alexander could obtain from Prussia was a promise of armed mediation, inscribed in the treaty of Potsdam in November, 1805: if by December 15 Napoleon had not accepted the allied peace terms, Prussia would join the coalition with an army of 180,000. In return Alexander promised to obtain Hanover for Prussia *if he could*—a most improbable eventuality in view of England's attitude. This was vividly dramatized by the British envoy in Berlin, who fainted when Metternich told him of the plan.[31] To these terms Metternich, apparently on his own initiative, attempted to add an article pledging Prussia to intervene even if the Austrian

[31] The envoy was Lord Harrowby. Deutsch, *Genesis*, 395.

army was in the meantime defeated; [32] and although the proposal was rejected, it at least proved Metternich a good prophet
since the contingency it provided for was precisely what occurred. At Austerlitz on December 2 a combined Austro-
Russian army was routed in one of Napoleon's finest battles.

What followed was a tragedy of errors, errors traceable in the
final analysis to the indecision of Alexander, who could not
make up his mind between an all-out defense of the central
powers and a bargain with France at their expense. When the
Emperor Francis offered to continue the fight if Russia would,
Alexander temporized, refusing to sign peace but on the other
hand insisting on the withdrawal of his armies. Frederick William, whose guileless calculations seldom depended on legal
technicalities, took the generous view that the lost battle had
no bearing on his obligations under the Potsdam treaty, and
sent Colonel Phull as emissary to the allied sovereigns to announce that Prussia would abide by their wishes. [33] In the meantime, however, the Austrians, shaken by the Russian retreat,
tentatively undertook peace negotiations. Thereupon Count
Haugwitz, now the Prussian envoy to French headquarters, concluding that his government was about to be deserted, initialed
a separate pact of his own with Napoleon. By its terms Prussia
was to obtain Hanover after all, surrendering Ansbach, Neuchâtel, and the remainder of Cleves in exchange. This was in
Vienna, at the palace of Schönbrunn. In Berlin, on the other
hand, Metternich was working feverishly to bring Prussia into
the war, and on December 15 his efforts were reinforced by the
arrival of General Carl von Stutterheim, sent by Emperor
Francis precisely to allay Prussian fears about the Franco-
Austrian negotiation. [34]

But December 15 was also the day Haugwitz signed the treaty
of Schönbrunn. Now it was the Austrians who felt isolated, and
two weeks later they signed the crushing peace of Pressburg,
which removed them from the war. Frederick William, mean-

[32] Metternich, *Memoirs*, II, 88ff.
[33] Deutsch, *Genesis*, 409.
[34] Metternich to Cobenzl, 13 and 16 Dec. 1805, in Metternich, *Memoirs*, II,
99ff. and 105ff.

while, was doing his best in the midst of unprecedented confusion to cooperate with Metternich and Stutterheim, and with Alopeus too, despite the clearest indications that Russia would not contribute more than a token force. Without the news of Pressburg he might well have repudiated Haugwitz' treaty. As it was, left to face Napoleon alone, he ratified in February, 1806, an even worse agreement, one which added to the previous stipulations provision for a Franco-Prussian alliance.[35]

It has been fashionable to assign most of the blame for the debacle to the timidity of the Prussian monarch. This Metternich himself did not do. Although merciless in his judgment of Haugwitz as a man and naturally indignant at the treaty of Schönbrunn, he had acquired enough of "the physician's cold-bloodedness" to appreciate the part played by faulty communication; he had, moreover, the temerity to suggest to his government that it was the news of Austria's peace discussions which "has stopped all the King's measures toward bringing us direct help. . . ."[36] If he criticized the king at all, it was not on partisan grounds but as one statesman to another. As a matter of Prussia's own interest, he believed, the monarch should have *forced* his help upon Austria instead of waiting for a call that never came—never came because Austria's leaders too were irresolute. Such objectivity was not the mark of an amateur, and indeed Clemens Metternich was no longer that; the assignment in Berlin, the focal point of European diplomacy in those days, had made him a professional. "I have aged thirty years," he wrote to Gentz of his tenure there, and his main conclusion was that the real importance of July 14, 1789, was that it had led to Austerlitz.[37] Not the Revolution but the power of France was the supreme reality.

The treaty of Pressburg inflicted the heaviest losses Austria had yet sustained. Venice, Dalmatia, and Istria she ceded to the Kingdom of Italy; Brixen, Trent, Vorarlberg, and the Tyrol, including the Brenner Pass, she surrendered to the Wittels-

---

[35] *ibid.*, 410ff.; Lobanov-Rostovsky, *Russia and Europe*, 114–117.

[36] Metternich to Stadion, 10 Jan. 1806, in Metternich, *Memoirs*, II, 119.

[37] Metternich to Gentz, 21 Jan. 1806, in Friederich von Gentz, *Briefe von und an Friedrich von Gentz*, ed. by Friedrich Carl Wittichen and Ernst Salzer, III (Munich and Berlin, 1913), 4.

bachs, making Bavaria the supreme power in the Alps. The scattered Austrian lands in Swabia, so important to her bond with the Reich, were divided between Würtemberg and Bavaria. As compensation, it is true, she at last received Salzburg and Berchtesgaden, and the Grand Duke Ferdinand was indemnified with Würzburg. But the duke of Modena, who had in the Recess been given Ortenau and the Breisgau, now lost these two bastions on the Upper Rhine and received no compensation at all, though his right to it was acknowledged. Of some significance, however, was the assignment to Austria of the properties of the Teutonic Knights, along with the office of Grand Master of the order, which was to fall to a Habsburg. On the other hand, Bavaria and Würtemberg were recognized as sovereign and ambiguously referred to in the treaty as members of "the *Confédération Germanique*," even though the Reich was not expressly dissolved.[38]

Never before, at the storming of the Strasbourg city hall or the futile negotiations at Rastatt, had Metternich felt more dejected. "The world is lost," he moaned, "Europe is burning out, and only out of its ashes will a new order of things arise." [39] His despondence is understandable. His first important assignment had ended not merely in failure but in utter confusion; and, although it was hardly his fault, there was criticism enough from the Russophobes and neutralists in Vienna and from the perennial enemies of the Metternich family. To professional failure, moreover, were added personal barbs. With Austria's withdrawal from Swabia, the principality of Ochsenhausen faced imminent annexation to Würtemberg, while at Austerlitz Napoleon had chosen for his headquarters none other than Metternich's new home, Schloss Kaunitz—bed, library, linen, and all. Nowhere, it seemed, could the harried émigré escape the aggression of France.

For Austria as a whole the shock of the lost war was equally severe. Cobenzl and Colloredo resigned, as expected, and the post of foreign minister was given to Count Philip Stadion, the

[38] Text of treaty in Martens, *Recueil*, VIII, 388ff. Note especially Arts. VII and XIV.
[39] Metternich to Gentz, 21 Jan. 1806, *loc.cit.*

ambassador in St. Petersburg. Unlike Thugut and Cobenzl, who were Austrians, Stadion was a *Reichsgraf,* the first ever to hold a post responsible for all of Austria's diplomacy, inside as well as outside of Germany. Scion of a *reichsunmittelbare* family in Swabia, he was not yet a dispossessed émigré like the Metternichs, but he had deep material and emotional attachments to the empire, and his appointment signified the determination of the Emperor Francis to uphold the Reich as long as possible. Stadion hoped that even yet a new coalition might materialize to save Francis' Roman crown and Austria's vital recruiting rights in the Reich. Otherwise, he believed, Bonaparte would take the crown for himself and create a "Napoleonic Empire of the German Nation"—a course that Dalberg, the archchancellor, was then urging upon him.[40]

Metternich shared some of Stadion's hopes. To Gentz he conveyed his conviction that ultimately Napoleon's system must be overthrown. "I say *overthrown,*" he added, "for under the present circumstances *resistance* will never suffice." [41] He too hoped to reconstitute the coalition, adding Saxony to it and this time making sure of Prussia in advance by awarding her Hanover and establishing, not merely conventional alliances, but a permanent system of collective security with a coordinated defense establishment—the Confederation of the East he proposed to call it. But there the similarity with Stadion's outlook ended. In the short term Metternich's aims were purely defensive: to construct a counterweight to Napoleon's western bloc by uniting the eastern powers behind a line marked by the Weser River, the Thuringian and Bohemian forests, and the Inn and Tagliamento Rivers to the Adriatic. It was plain to Metternich that France had won the struggle for the third Germany and that Austria, driven both from there and from Italy, must accept the fact. "A federal system in the west of Europe, with France at its head, should not be opposed," [42] he said. A federal system —that was the language of the Pressburg treaty, and it meant

[40] Cf. Hellmuth Rössler, *Österreichs Kampf um Deutschlands Befreiung,* I (Hamburg, 1940), 196–218.
[41] Metternich to Gentz, 21 Jan. 1806, *op.cit.,* III, 54.
[42] "Metternich's Sketch of a Political Scheme, January, 1806," in Metternich, *Memoirs,* II, 121ff.

the extinction of the Reich. And so, instead of scrutinizing the treaty for loopholes that would permit the salvage of a few remnants of the old order, as Stadion intended, it was Metternich's idea to demand the territorial modifications necessary for his line of demarcation, offering in compensation "the abdication of the Imperial Roman crown, on condition of its perpetual extinction." [43]

These views, summarized in a memorandum of January, 1806, mark a new stage in his thought about the German question. Even though he had probably never shared his father's sentimental imperial patriotism, he had never doubted the importance of the Reich for both Austria and the immediate estates. Now, in the light of hard facts and cold reason, he was ready to abandon the principality of Ochsenhausen to whatever fate Napoleon's "federal system" should decree. At the time, to be sure, this was probably a matter of tactics, a means of effecting a temporary settlement free of nagging irritants, while preparing a counteroffensive, after which, circumstances permitting, the Reich could be restored. But even as a tactic, his analysis was a model of clear thinking, exhibiting an objectivity that few imperial aristocrats of his generation ever acquired and many even scorned. It also revealed, as matters turned out, that Metternich's intuition was far keener than Stadion's in divining the meaning of the phrase *Confédération Germanique* in the treaty of Pressburg.

Mention has already been made of Dalberg's efforts to preserve the petty estates (including his own office as archchancellor) by thrusting the crown at the Emperor of the French. Contrary to all expectations, however, Napoleon, who had sacrificed much popular acclaim in Europe for the sake of one imperial title, had no desire to take another. The French crown had won him friends among the dukes and electors of Germany; a German crown would lose them again. Unlike the Habsburgs, he was not bound by history to antagonize the strong by defending the weak, especially as he fancied that every castle in the unincorporated areas housed a secret Austrian agent. What he required above all in Germany were allies, bound to him by

[43] *ibid.*, II, 122.

self-interest, who could field whole divisions or even corps. For such purposes the imperial nobility, heroes in the past of many a cavalry charge, had long since become obsolete. Bonaparte needed the 30,000 or so troops that Bavaria could give him, the 12,000 from Würtemberg, the 8000 from Baden, and so on; and to get them he was willing to sacrifice the two main attributes of "empire": the crown and the hundreds of miniscule fiefs attached to it.[44]

Napoleon's solution of the problem was embodied in the institution known as the Confederation of the Rhine; and since this eventually became the starting point and model for Metternich's treatment of the German question, the Confederation— or *Rheinbund,* as it may more conveniently be called—deserves a brief examination. Essentially the Rheinbund was a league of sovereign states represented by diplomatic envoys in a central organ called the federal diet.[45] The diet was divided into two curia, one for the kingdoms, the other for states of lesser rank. In an ingenious compromise, designed to spare the feelings of the new kings of Bavaria and Würtemberg, no additional kingdoms were created, but Baden, Hesse-Darmstadt, and Napoleon's recent creation, Berg, sat in the royal curia with the rank of grand duchies. The presiding officer of the college of "monarchs" was to be the former archchancellor, now called the Prince Primate and appointed by the French Emperor. In this way Dalberg managed to preserve his position, though in a purely secular capacity. The main functions of the diet were to regulate relations among the members and to deal with Napoleon, who took the title, Protector.

The new titles were deliberately chosen; with the exception of Dalberg, all concerned wanted a clean break with the past. If the new league were construed as the juridical successor to the Reich, the precedence of state legislation over imperial law might even yet be challenged. Collectively and individually the member states were bound to France by a permanent offensive

[44] Cf. Hellmuth Rössler, *Napoleons Griff nach der Kaiserkrone* (Munich, 1957), *passim,* for the novel but unconvincing contention that Napoleon in reality sought the Roman crown.

[45] "Traité de confédération des états du Rhin," in Martens, *Recueil,* VIII, 480–492.

and defensive alliance which made each government answerable to Paris for maintaining its military contingent at required strength. In this way Napoleon could be sure that the foreign policies and military resources of the German states would always be in his hands even if the union were later reorganized or even dissolved.

Furthermore, Bonaparte was shrewd enough to see that by affording some protection to the mediatized houses he would have more control over the sovereigns than if he gave them everything at once. Hence, the price he exacted for the right to annex was the acceptance of federal norms in the treatment of the victims. In contrast to the ecclesiastical estates, which in 1803 had been physically sequestrated and added to the patrimonies of various secular princes, the mediatized domains were merely *placed under the sovereignty* of the ruling houses. Sovereignty was defined as the right of "legislation, supreme judicial authority; superior police power, and of military conscription, recruitment, and imposts." [46] It did not include a right to the revenues of the properties or the pre-emption of seignorial and feudal rights, such as local administration of justice or the regulation of manorial facilities: pastures, forests, mines, mills, and the like. As to taxation, the mediatized nobles were to be treated on the same basis as princes of the ruling house; and in criminal cases they were to be tried only by their peers. They were free to maintain residence wherever they pleased within the Confederation or the territory of its allies— a blow at such as Stadion and Metternich, though the latter was not affected as long as Franz Georg lived. And the statute at least gave some assurance that the revenue of Ochsenhausen would not be impounded.

There was a certain ambivalence in these arrangements. On the one hand, the operation appeared little more than a matter of subinfeudation, the rights of the emperor and the old *Kreis* assemblies being transferred to the new sovereigns but not greatly enlarged. On the other hand, the sovereign right of legislation could mean anything, especially as there was no mention of *Landstände* or diets to restrain the crown. What of serf-

[46] *ibid.*, Art. XXVI.

47

dom, for example, the most urgent problem of the time? Did it fall within the legislative competence of the ruler or was it an inviolable right of the manor? Later developments indicate that Napoleon intended the privileged status of the mediatized as a mere transitional step in the development of centralized, egalitarian institutions based on French models. His clients, however, wanted no external dictation and stubbornly resisted.[47]

Indeed, when the Rheinbund Act was suddenly presented as an ultimatum on July 12, it caused consternation. Ferdinand, brother of the Emperor Francis and the new duke of Würzburg, was in principle opposed to joining the Rheinbund, membership in which was not required of him in the treaty of Pressburg.[48] Frederick of Würtemberg and Max Joseph of Bavaria, having instructed their plenipotentiaries to sign, began to indulge in second thoughts. In the council of monarchs they had expected to be the joint leaders of the Confederation; now they must share their glory with the so-called grand duchies. Without full control of the mediatized lands territorial aggrandizement suddenly lost its appeal. Suddenly it dawned on Max Joseph that his key weapon, the ability to play France against Austria, was being bartered away in a contract which took foreign policy forever from his hands. Hurriedly he sent a new envoy to Paris, Baron Carl von Gravenreuth, with instructions to reject a federation which, he said, "made the lesser princes the judges of kings" and gave to the Protector a power "more extensive than the emperor of Germany had ever had." [49]

Never was a mission more futile. At Rastatt Gravenreuth met the courier bearing the Rheinbund Act with the first Bavarian signature back to Munich. In Strasbourg he was detained so long by French frontier guards that when he finally did arrive

---

[47] On Napoleon's motives and the resistance of the German sovereigns see Marcel Dunan, *Napoléon et l'Allemagne. Le système continental et les débuts du royaume de Bavière 1806–1810* (Paris, 1942), 222–223; Fritz Valjavec, *Die Entstehung der politischen Strömungen in Deutschland 1770–1815* (Munich, 1951), 350ff; and E. Hölzle, "Das Napoleonische Staatensystem im Deutschland," *Historische Zeitschrift*, Bd. 148 (1933), 279.

[48] Anton Chroust, *Geschichte des Grossherzogtums Würzburg 1806–1814. Die äussere Politik des Grossherzogtums* (Würzburg, 1932), 152–161.

[49] Quoted in Dunan, *Napoléon et l'Allemagne*, 30.

NORTH SEA

BALTIC SEA

(To Sweden)

P R U S S I A

MECKLENBURG

OLDEN
BURG

○ Berlin

GRAND D. of WARSAW

HOLLAND

A

L

WESTPHALIA

ANHALT

SAXONY

Oder

S

A

BERG

HESSE-DARMST.

W

Ss

T

FRANCE

NASSAU

FRANKFORT

WÜRZBURG

Mainz

B

○ Prague

AUSTRIAN EMPIRE

Rhine

An

BADEN

WÜRTTEMBERG

R

BAVARIA

Danube

H

Munich ○

Vienna ○

SWITZERLAND

**RHENISH
CONFEDERATION
1806-1809**

L — Lippe
S — Salm
A — Arenberg
W — Waldeck
Ss — Schwarzburg–Sonderhausen
H — Hohenzollern
R — Regensburg
An — Ansbach
B — Bayreuth
T — Thuringian States

Added to Confederation
1808 — 1809

Added to Confederation
1806 — 1807

Original members

Venice ○

in Paris, he deemed it inadvisable to deliver the king's new views of the matter. By then all the other princes had signed— the king of Würtemberg, their serene highnesses, the grand dukes of Hesse-Darmstadt, Baden, and Berg, the Archchancel- lor, and nine lesser princes. Even Ferdinand of Würzburg joined several months later, when it became apparent that he faced discrimination in the award of the mediatized territories. On September 25 he was admitted, with the title of grand duke, and given a seat in the college of monarchs. Only by such crude methods was Napoleon able at last to found the Confederation of the Rhine.[50]

Since Napoleon had carried out the negotiations with such secrecy, it is not surprising that Stadion too was hard pressed to ascertain French intentions. His first need was an experi- enced ambassador in Paris. The post was vacant, and even the chargé d'affaires, Baron Carl Vincent, was a general sent there originally on a routine military mission. Stadion's first choice, the able Philip Cobenzl, turned out to be *persona non grata* because of his role in wringing recognition of the Austrian em- pire. Napoleon, with an unmistakable allusion to Austria's former Francophile policy, requested instead someone from "the truly Austrian family of Kaunitz." [51]

Why he should believe that this former Rhinelander, whose fief at Ochsenhausen was about to be mediatized by the king of Würtemberg, would look at things as a "true Austrian" is still something of a mystery. At the time Metternich attributed the invitation to the intercession of his friend, Count Alexander de la Rochefoucauld, the French chargé d'affaires in Vienna.[52] Later he claimed that the personal courtesy he had shown the French ambassador in Berlin, Count Antoine de LaForest, a con- fidant of Talleyrand, was behind the appointment.[53] LaForest's reports confirm this, at least to the extent that they show Met- ternich making extravagant gestures of good will toward France

[50] *ibid.*, 30f; Chroust, *Geschichte Würzburgs,* 259f.

[51] Rössler, *Österreichs Kampf,* I, 221.

[52] Metternich to his wife, 25 June 1806, in Corti, *Metternich und die Frauen,* I, 90.

[53] Metternich, *Memoirs,* I, 64.

once the news of Pressburg had reached Berlin [54]—a behavior consonant with the aforementioned memorandum about the division of Europe written at this same time. Whatever the reason, the request was made, and Stadion, after calling Metternich to Vienna, gave him his choice: St. Petersburg, where Tsar Alexander, his colleague of Berlin days, had asked for him, or Paris, to placate the conqueror. Paris it was!

Metternich's decision was based primarily on two things: pride in having, as he boasted, "completely outstripped all my colleagues of my age," and the handsome annual emolument of 90,000 guilders, almost twice the sum the family had once derived from Winneburg.[55] In other respects, however, he felt a certain trepidation. In St. Petersburg he could have worked for the creation of the Eastern Confederation; in Paris he could only be a suppliant.

Gentz commiserated with him, though Metternich must have felt more amused than flattered by his friend's customary pomposity. "A soul so pure and lofty as yours," Gentz wrote, "ought never to have found itself in contact with the home of so much crime and horror." [56] And the new envoy could find little to admire in the instructions drafted for him. While offering Austrian friendship, he was to explain that any closer ties depended on proof of Napoleon's good faith—proof was to be literal observance of the treaty of Pressburg, which implicitly recognized the Reich and Austria's recruiting rights. But, if worst came to worst, so Metternich was told, he should know that the crown was for sale—though he was not himself to make any offers.[57]

Totally in the dark about Napoleon's intentions, Stadion and the emperor could hardly have acted decisively. Nevertheless, the ambivalence, the futile expressions of injured pride, the pleas for justice coupled with veiled requests for an offer—all this contrasted with Metternich's view that one must make a clean break with the past, not piously invoking the fine print of the treaty but candidly seeking rational and mutually ad-

---

[54] Missoffe, *Metternich*, 88–89.
[55] Quoted in Corti, *Metternich und die Frauen*, I, 91.
[56] Gentz to Metternich, 22 Sept. 1806, in Gentz, *Briefe von und an*, III, 45.
[57] Rössler, *Österreichs Kampf*, I, 221–223.

vantageous modification of its terms. To make matters worse, although the instructions had been drafted on July 8, he was kept waiting and did not leave Vienna until the 12th, the very day the Rheinbund pact was initialed. When he reached Strasbourg, moreover, he was detained as Gravenreuth had been, and for the same reasons: Napoleon wanted no outside interference with "the rapid movement imparted to the political machine in the last two weeks of July." [58]

In his memoirs, written long afterward, Metternich contended that the machinations Napoleon did not want him to witness concerned Franco-Russian affairs, that he feared Metternich's influence on the Russian envoy, the "inexperienced" Count Oubril.[59] The real issue, however, was the Rheinbund and the dissolution of the Reich. Napoleon probably did not know the details of Metternich's or Gravenreuth's instructions, but he could well have guessed that neither was authorized to recognize the Rheinbund, however different the reasons. True, the pact had been signed, but only provisionally and only under duress. The process of final ratification was scheduled for July 25 in Munich, and there was still time for the governments to disavow their envoys' signatures. On July 14, therefore, Napoleon closed the frontier to all foreigners coming from across the Rhine. On July 22 he told General Vincent that if Francis did not abdicate by August 10, French troops would cross the Inn. Only at the head of one's own army could one reply to such words, Vincent answered,[60] and it was a courageous rebuke even if essentially a private one. On July 25 the ratifications of the Rheinbund Act were exchanged at Munich. On the 29th Metternich was released from custody at Strasbourg, and on August 2 he finally arrived in Paris—to an icy welcome. Napoleon insisted on receiving him only as the ambassador of Austria and not, as his credentials certified, as the emissary of the Roman Emperor.

It was a shocking experience. True, the outcome was about

---

[58] Metternich to Stadion, 11 Aug. 1806, in Constantin de Grunwald (ed.), "Les débuts diplomatiques de Metternich à Paris (documents inédites)," *Revue de Paris, Année* 43, t. 4 (July–Aug., 1936), 497.

[59] Metternich, *Memoirs,* I, 66.

[60] Rössler, *Österreichs Kampf,* I, 225.

what he had expected, but to have been assigned at last a central role in the German drama only to be maneuvered off the stage at the climax of the action amounted to a professional humiliation which he felt keenly. The Paris embassy had always been a nightmare for "any man devoted to the interests of the service," he reported after a briefing by Vincent and the embassy staff, but "no other period ever offered less favorable opportunity to the representatives of our master, the emperor, than that of my arrival." [61]

Austria now faced the same painful decisions which had tormented the lesser states. In Vienna there was no such bravado as Vincent had displayed. Some wished to bargain further, seeking guarantees that the emperor's brother Ferdinand might annex some of the mediatized lands to Würzburg. Under the circumstances this was not bargaining; it was begging, and Stadion, to his credit, would have none of it. What he did insist upon, however, was that the emperor, in announcing his abdication, should also decree the dissolution of the Reich, lest Napoleon some day assume the crown or, worse yet, confer it upon the king of Prussia. In either case the Habsburgs would be reduced to vassalage, as Cobenzl had once feared. Another reason for this course was that the very illegality of a unilateral declaration would make it easier to annul some day. On August 6 Francis II, fifty-fourth emperor since Charlemagne and twentieth of the Habsburg line, laid down his Roman-German crown and ended the dynasty's adventure in political bigamy.[62]

The same fate which had placed Metternich in Dresden when the Recess was adopted, in Strasbourg when the Rheinbund was founded, and in Paris when the Reich was dissolved, kept him in the French capital when Germany's fate was being decided on the distant battlefields of Jena and Friedland. He had been in Paris hardly more than a month when Bonaparte was off to the front. He thereupon requested Stadion's permission to follow the French leaders as far as Mainz, but this was refused and he had to content himself with routine chores in Paris, viewing

---

[61] Metternich to Stadion, 11 Aug. 1806, in Grunwald, "Les débuts . . . ," *ibid.*, 497–499.

[62] Cf. Rössler, *Österreichs Kampf*, I, 221–228.

developments in Germany from afar for the better part of a year.

The crushing of Prussia at Jena completed the conquest of the third Germany, and Napoleon, still with a war on his hands, proceeded to reorganize the country. To make sure that his mastery was fully understood he peremptorily deposed the elector of Hesse-Cassel and the duke of Brunswick, the man who had led the attack on the Revolution in 1792. Their lands were occupied by the French until a year later they were added to the Kingdom of Westphalia. Of the remaining princes many were mediatized, and others, often for no other reason than good connections in Paris or liberality with their purses, were able to enter the Rheinbund as sovereigns.

The first to join was Frederick August of Saxony. He received the title of king, and assumed a military obligation of 20,000 men, second only to that of Bavaria. He was followed by the five houses of the ducal Saxon line (Saxe-Weimar, Saxe-Gotha, Saxe-Meiningen, Saxe-Hildburghausen, and Saxe-Coburg), which joined under similar terms except that they were to pool their military efforts so as to form a single contingent of 2800 men. In April of the following year many more princes joined: the three dukes of the House of Anhalt, the four princes of Reuss, the princes of Lippe-Detmold and Lippe-Schaumburg, the prince of Waldeck, and the princes of Schwarzburg-Sonderhausen and Schwarzburg-Rudolstadt. As with the Saxon duchies, the diminutive contingents of related lines were merged into common units. The new treaties also accorded equal status to Catholics, reflecting Bonaparte's desire to appease Catholic Europe and overcome the divisive heritage of the Reformation as the Rheinbund reached into the Protestant North.[63]

In the midst of these events Austria remained neutral, partly because of exhaustion, partly because of indecision in Vienna, where the disaster generated the heated debate that inevitably accompanies a profound shift in a state's external relations. On the surface the issue was Stadion's proposal for armed mediation in the northern war against Archduke Carl's insistence upon a

---

[63] Texts of accession treaties in Martens, *Recueil*, VIII, 552ff.

completely inert neutrality. Underneath, however, and but dimly apprehended at the time, a schism was developing between a pro-French school and a pro-Russian school. In an armed mediation Stadion really expected to aid the two eastern powers to liberate Germany. Carl, on the other hand, commander of the army and president of the *Hofkriegsrat,* feared Russian aggression in the Balkans and believed that in any case the three eastern powers could not collaborate in Germany long enough to exploit a victory over Napoleon even if they gained one.

Since the dissolution of the Reich Carl had become, like many another general, "Austrian to the core" in outlook—*stock-österreichisch,* to use the apt expression then becoming popular. He was almost relieved by the severing of the bonds which had stretched Austrian commitments too thin, even if they had also yielded recruits for the army. Carl was no Francophile, but he saw Russia as an enduring threat whereas French preponderance would be likely to vanish with the death of Bonaparte. In the meantime Austria's best course was to husband her resources and reform her military system, awaiting an opportunity to intervene with an overwhelming force independent of all other powers. It was pointless, he concluded, to challenge Bonaparte's mastery of Germany before Austria could be sure that she, rather than the northern powers, would dictate the reconstruction.[64]

Carl's suspicions on this score were soon confirmed. In a convention signed at Bartenstein in April, 1807, Russia and Prussia announced their war aims. Pointedly warning that the restoration of the Reich would be "a dangerous error," they declared their intention of establishing a "constitutional federation" under the direction of Austria and Prussia, each acting "within limits to be determined by agreement." [65] This meant partitioning Germany between Prussia and Austria. What Haugwitz had attempted under French auspices the new foreign minister, Hardenberg, meant to achieve with the aid of Russia. Henceforward, anti-Prussian feeling in Vienna was twofold: a com-

---

[64] Rössler, *Österreichs Kampf,* I, 246–269.
[65] Text in Martens, *Recueil,* VIII, 606–612.

pound of the traditional antipathy, which saw Prussia simply as a rival in Germany, and a more subtle concern, in which Prussia appeared as the instrument of Russia's ambitions in Germany.

For this reason the Bartenstein program only strengthened Austria's resolve to remain neutral, and thus paved the way for Napoleonic victory at Friedland in June, followed by the peace of Tilsit in July. Far from attaining hegemony over North Germany, Prussia was reduced to a second-class state with an army of 42,000, on a par with Bavaria. Her territory west of the Elbe River became the nucleus of an entirely new state, the Kingdom of Westphalia, ruled by Napoleon's brother Jerome; while her Polish lands (excluding West Prussia) were used to create the Grand Duchy of Warsaw, joined to the Rheinbund by personal union through the king of Saxony. A Polish state lived again, a standing threat to all the erstwhile partitioners, both militarily and in respect to the explosive potentialities of Polish nationalism. In other provisions Danzig became a free city with a French garrison, and Prussia was to suffer an army of occupation until an indemnity of 120,000,000 francs was paid. For the Hohenzollerns it was a truly shattering peace, and it might have been even worse but for a few concessions Napoleon was willing to make "in deference to his Majesty, the Emperor of all the Russias"—a phrase which Napoleon maliciously insisted upon inserting.[66]

Russia suffered no such injuries. Territorially she actually gained, annexing the Polish border district of Bialystok. In some ways Alexander emerged Napoleon's equal. The two emperors concluded a mutual assistance pact against third parties; and if Alexander undertook to make war on England unless she accepted French terms, Napoleon agreed to support Russian demands on Turkey. Russia's defeat was essentially strategic in nature, consisting in a general contraction of her influence beyond her boundaries: recognition of the Grand Duchy of Warsaw, withdrawal from the Dalmatian coast and the Danubian provinces in the Balkans, and recognition of the Rheinbund and all subsequent additions to it. If Russian influence was evident anywhere in Germany, it was in the duchies of

[66] Text in *ibid.*, VIII, 637ff.

Oldenburg, Mecklenburg-Strelitz, and Mecklenburg-Schwerin, all traditionally allied to Russia by dynastic bonds. Yet even they had to submit their ports to French control, and a year later they joined the Rheinbund.

The peace of Tilsit demonstrated once again the difference between the central powers and the flanking powers. Russia, though driven from Central Europe, could not, it appeared, be profitably invaded; therefore she could force Bonaparte to limit his hegemony, even if on terms far more favorable to him than in the days of the Imperial Recess. Austria and Prussia, on the other hand, were isolated. The line of the Weser and Thuringian forests, which Metternich the year before had advised holding at all costs, was breached and Austria's right flank fully exposed. Vienna was vulnerable to drives eastward down the valley of the Danube and southward through the Moravian Gateway. "The Confederation of the Rhine embraces us on both sides. Any war with France would begin at the same time on the borders of the Inn and the Wieliczka." [67] Such was Metternich's analysis of the peace of Tilsit when the news reached Paris toward the end of July, 1807.

A year later he was still pondering Austria's new predicament: "our situation is different from what it was before the last war with Prussia; we no longer go through the intermediate steps which formerly were necessary to precede the opening of a campaign. Napoleon has no preparations to make; he has two hundred thousand men in front of us, on our two flanks, and at our rear. He has not to pass the Rhine with new troops to fall on us. He can enter Galicia before we know at Vienna that he has made war upon us. . . ." [68] "Before we know"—that was the heart of the matter, for under the limits set by the technology of the time, adequate warning was possible only by means of buffer states. A great power could almost be defined as one which was usually able to fight its wars on foreign soil. Until Austerlitz that had been true of Austria. Now, except for Turkey to the southeast, she had no buffers, and the humiliating thought struck home that she herself had become one.

[67] Metternich to Stadion, 26 July 1807, in Metternich, *Memoirs*, II, 145.
[68] Metternich to Stadion, 23 June 1808, *ibid.*, II, 210.

CHAPTER III

THE WAR TO RESTORE THE REICH

For Metternich, Napoleon's triumphal return from Tilsit brought one welcome advantage: he was able to resume the normal activities of a diplomat, which had been interrupted by the emperor's prolonged absence from the capital. The main purpose of his mission had been to protect Austria's rights under the treaty of Pressburg and if possible to obtain favorable modification of the terms. With the proclamation of the Rheinbund some objectives had become manifestly impossible, such as the preservation of the imperial crown and recruiting rights. Other claims, however, were still negotiable—notably the determination of a firm boundary on the Isonzo River in Italy, the evacuation of French troops from Braunau, a town situated on the Austrian side of the Inn River, and above all the delivery of the Mergentheim dependencies of the Teutonic Order, which had been promised to a Habsburg prince. In the excitement attending the death of the Reich, there had seemed no urgency about comparatively routine details; then, in the absence of the emperor, torpor settled over Paris and there was little to be done.

Now, in August of 1807, the city was anything but dull. Champagny, a nonentity, replaced Talleyrand as foreign minister, and Metternich renewed his attempts to reach a settlement, without which normal relations between France and Austria could not be restored. Braunau was no longer a serious problem. The war with Russia ended, a military base east of the Inn had lost much of its value, and so Napoleon willingly relinquished it. The problem of the Isonzo was more difficult, and Metternich, throughout the month of September, fought stubbornly, breaking off the negotiations three times before acquiescing in a solution which destroyed Austria's last strong flank on the Adriatic. Particularly galling was the concession of a military route linking the Kingdom of Italy with Dalmatia. The agreements were incorporated in a convention which Metternich, almost under duress, signed at Fontainebleau on October 10.[1]

The question of Mergentheim, however, was not settled. The treaty of Pressburg had provided that the lands of the Teutonic Order, which were scattered throughout South Germany as dependencies of the capital of the order at Mergentheim, be transferred to a Habsburg prince to be named by the Emperor Francis. Francis had appointed his younger brother, Archduke Anton—a natural choice, since Anton had in fact been the Grand Master of the order all along. For good reasons the archduke chose to live in Vienna and thus put himself in a position analogous to that of Stadion and Metternich—an Austrian servant with property in the Rheinbund. The difference was that Anton was a sovereign prince and, so far as the treaty of Pressburg was concerned, under no obligation to join the Rheinbund. Nor did he desire to join, despite the example set by his brother, Archduke Ferdinand at Würzburg, who was a member in good standing. Yet it was precisely membership in the Rheinbund that Napoleon insisted upon, since he would tolerate "no foreign prince between the Inn and the Rhine." [2] That, at any rate, was what he said. However, the fact that he continued to cavil even after Stadion, on October 5, instructed Metternich to acquiesce,[3] suggests another purpose. It was the emperor's old game of keeping the dwindling supply of immediate lands in his own hands as long as possible in order to dangle further rewards before his German clients. Such, in any case, was the final outcome, for when war between France and Austria broke out again in 1809, the Protector decreed the dissolution of the ancient order, not merely mediatizing the lands but awarding them in fee simple to the personal domains of the sovereigns within whose boundaries they lay. The principality of Mergentheim itself went to Würtemberg.[4]

Napoleon's attitude was by no means a simple matter of ill-will toward Austria. The fate of Mergentheim was only one part

[1] See Metternich to Stadion, 12 Oct. 1807, in Metternich, *Memoirs*, II, 146–154.
[2] Quoted in Dunan, *Napoléon et l'Allemagne*, 620, note 77.
[3] Rössler, *Österreichs Kampf*, I, 294.
[4] Text of decree of 24 April 1809 in Martens, *Nouveau recueil de traités*, I, 201. (This series is a continuation of the previously cited title by Martens and will hereafter be referred to as *Nouveau recueil*.)

of the much greater problem of revising the Act of Confederation, which he had always regarded as a mere stopgap pending
the pacification of the continent. The pressure for reform was
considerable. While the Prince Primate importuned the Protector to transform the Confederation into a modernized German empire based on the lesser estates, French ideologists, led
by the chargé d'affaires at Frankfurt, Théobald-Jacques Bacher,
were flooding Paris, at the time of Napoleon's return from Tilsit, with copies of a plan to create a federal supreme court, a
permanent parliament, and a real "chief." [5]

Yet even at this stage of his career—in many ways its apogee
—Bonaparte did not feel strong enough to defy the princes to
whom he had solemnly promised "full and complete sovereignty" and who, by defecting, could one day draw all of Eastern
Europe into the fight again. One solution he considered for a
time was appeasing Bavaria, the most formidable opponent of
reform, by separating her from the Rheinbund the better to
crush the states that remained. In the end, however, he concluded that he must appease them all. Hence he abandoned for
the time being the attempt to reform the superstructure of the
confederation and concentrated instead on the internal order
within the states. On this level resistance to reform was at a
minimum, since most of the German monarchs and ministers
saw in revolutionary legislation the means of consolidating their
variegated territories and of shattering domestic opposition,
especially among the mediatized. Even so, they resisted external
compulsion, considering reforms so introduced almost as ob-
noxious as concessions wrested from them by rebellious subjects.
That is why Max Joseph, for example, Napoleon's severest critic
in the matter of tightening the Rheinbund, rushed to introduce
a constitution in Bavaria before the Frankfurt diet could impose one.[6]

In part copied from the constitution of Westphalia, in part

[5] Dunan, *Napoléon et l'Allemagne*, 222–225. On Bacher see *Dictionnaire de
biographie française*, ed. by M. Prévost and Roman d'Amat, IV (Paris, 1948),
1074f.

[6] Dunan, *Napoléon et l'Allemagne*, 222–225; and Erwin Hölzle, *Württemberg im
Zeitalter Napoleons und der deutschen Erhebung* (Stuttgart and Berlin, 1937),
31–34.

built on the earlier reforms of Carl Theodore, the Bavarian constitution provided for the abolition of serfdom, liberty of conscience, equality before the law, separation of the judiciary from administration, abolition of the nobility's tax exemptions, and the opening of government offices to men of talent. Administrative *Kreise* replaced the old provinces, all provincial assemblies were eliminated, and a national assembly was to take their place. "Sham constitutionalism" is what German jurists have usually called the system, because the promise of a parliament was never carried out. Nevertheless, the substance of what was attempted included much that in a later age was inscribed on the banner of liberalism.[7]

In other states similar results were obtained by means of undisguised absolutism. There were of course variations. In Baden Carl Frederick proceeded slowly, and with such tact that even the mediatized houses were to some extent reconciled. In Würtemberg, on the other hand, King Frederick inaugurated a harsh program of regimentation and was the only monarch who dared tamper to any great extent with the social and economic structure of the mediatized fiefs, even confiscating them on the slightest pretext. In the case of the Metternich and Stadion domains he invoked the residence requirements of the Rheinbund Act to impound their revenue. Only in the central and northern portions of Germany, where territorial exchanges were few and traditional ways of life less disturbed, did the old hierarchy of estates retain some vitality. The main exception was Saxe-Weimar, which in 1809 adopted a mildly centralistic constitution.[8]

But despite the variation in their problems and the difference in their techniques, the Rheinbund sovereigns—at least those of royal and grand ducal rank—had one aim in common: to consolidate their power within their boundaries, to do so in their own way and not necessarily by adopting French models, and to defend their sovereignty from encroachments by the federal apparatus. Bonaparte, on the other hand, though grati-

---

[7] *ibid.*, 100ff.; Huber, *Deutsche Verfassungsgeschichte*, I, 88–89 Cf. Valjavec, *Die Entstehung der politischen Strömungen*, 350f.
[8] *ibid.*, 352f.

fied at such reforms as could be obtained at the time, looked to a distant future in which all the member states would have virtually identical constitutions, patterned after that of France and enforced by a vigorous central authority at Frankfurt.[9]

Metternich seems not to have noticed these rifts, actual and potential, in the Rhenish Confederation. To him Napoleon's empire appeared an advancing juggernaut and Napoleon himself completely successful in subduing the German princes. The Protector had once told him, "I only want from the federation men and money." [10] For that reason Napoleon allowed the greater princes to oppress the lesser ones, and Metternich took him at his word. It was, Metternich concluded, Bonaparte's prerogative in return to oppress the greater princes, and each day brought new examples of his successful bullying: the way he dispensed with the federal constitution and raised troops by direct orders to the sovereigns, or the way he tried to charge the king of Bavaria for the costs of marching French troops over Bavarian territory. The French aim, Metternich reported, was "the extension by the protector of the rights of conscription, taxation, and customs to all the States of the confederation." [11] The Bavarian constitution, which was promulgated on May 1, 1808, seemed only the natural sequel to the marriage, in 1806, of Princess Augusta to Eugene Beauharnais, viceroy of Italy, and to decrees of December, 1807, which further strengthened the bonds between Bavaria and the Kingdom of Italy. One might just as well have had King Jerome ensconced on the banks of the Inn and Napoleon's codes in force on the Austrian frontier. "For none," Metternich bitterly remarked shortly after hearing

[9] Hartung, *Deutsche Verfassungsgeschichte*, 198–204; Huber, *Deutsche Verfassungsgeschichte*, 1, 87–91; Heinrich Heffter, *Die deutsche Selbstverwaltung im 19. Jahrhundert* (Stuttgart, 1950), 106–109; Valjavec, *Entstehung der politischen Strömungen*, 355–359; and Hölzle, "Das Napoleonische Staatensystem in Deutschland," *Historische Zeitschrift*, Bd. 148, 279ff.

[10] "Autobiographical Memoir," in Metternich, *Memoirs*, 1, 74. The occasion was one in which Napoleon was recounting to Metternich what he had told Dalberg. It is doubtful that Bonaparte was so blunt with the Prince Primate; but he might well have put the matter that way to Metternich to conceal the failure of his larger ambitions for the Rhenish Confederation.

[11] Metternich to Stadion, 13 May 1808, Vienna, *Haus- Hof- und Staatsarchiv, Staatskanzlei, Frankreich, Berichte*, Fasc. 289, No. 14 D. (Hereafter, the Haus-Hof- und Staatsarchiv in Vienna will be indicated by HHSA.)

of the Bavarian constitution, "would dare to describe as po-
tentates that rabble of crowned prefects who—having recently
become indebted to France for their very existence—now pay
for their doubtful and precarious privilege with the blood and
money of their subjects." [12] Here was none of the bland objectivity of the professional diplomat. Here was only a count-of-the-
empire's honest loathing for the wreckers of the Reich.

Metternich's political education was taking a new turn. He
had mastered the "coldbloodedness" of classical diplomacy only
to find that Napoleon did not play the game that way. The lust
for personal power, the Austrian now discovered, could be
every bit as demonic as the revolutionary fury against which he
had directed the fulminations of his youth. "Peace," he told
Stadion, "does not exist with a revolutionary system, and
whether Robespierre declares eternal war against the *châteaux*,
or Napoleon makes it against the Powers, the tyranny is the
same and the danger is only more general." [13] If the emperor
had really intended a permanent settlement, he would never, so
Metternich reasoned, have created the Duchy of Warsaw or
countenanced "the disappearance of one of the great inter-
mediaries." [14]

Nothing, however, shook Metternich more than the French
invasion of Spain in the spring of 1808, which brought about
the overthrow of the Bourbon ruling house and yielded another
throne for the Bonaparte dynasty. It all seemed part of a pattern: first brother-in-law Joachim Murat made duke of Berg;
then thrones for the brothers: Joseph in Naples, Louis in Holland, Jerome in Westphalia; now Joseph on the throne of Spain
and Murat moved to Naples. Nor could one ignore the second-
generation marriages, which brought Bavaria and Baden into
the network, and later Würtemberg—by means of Jerome's
marriage to King Frederick's daughter Catherine. The Habsburgs themselves had never so brazenly juggled provinces and
played the dynastic game. Metternich, convinced that Napoleon
meant to rear a system of European hegemony on "the establish-

---

[12] Quoted in Constantin de Grunwald, *Metternich*, Eng. ed. (London, 1953), 33.
[13] Metternich to Stadion, 27 April 1808, in Metternich, *Memoirs*, II, 205.
[14] Metternich to Stadion, 6 Dec. 1807, in *ibid.*, II, 174.

ment of members of his family on ancient thrones and those he has created," [15] made his estimates: the Habsburgs would be next, the empire would be partitioned, and the ancient provinces would be redistributed, perhaps to Napoleon's marshals. War was inevitable.[16]

The threat to the Habsburg throne was a recurrent theme of the Metternich-Stadion correspondence, and Stadion, in his presentations to the Emperor Francis, invariably explained the situation in this way, stating, for example, that "one has difficulty convincing oneself of the real interest of state which under the circumstances has caused the French emperor to overthrow a power already entirely subservient to him." [17] But such remarks must be assessed cautiously. It was only natural to stress the dynastic argument in addressing the emperor, and Stadion had already, in the previous autumn, instructed Metternich to incline his reports in this direction. "I desire," he had said then, "that your reports will keep us on the alert." [18] The real danger remained the presence of French troops in Poland and the Rheinbund.

Actually Metternich perceived clearly enough Napoleon's interests of state. As early as January, 1808, he had heard from Napoleon's own lips something of his bold plans for the Levant. It was not so mysterious that the French emperor should wish to drive toward Gibraltar and safeguard his rear before advancing against Turkey. An attack on the Porte, moreover, was in itself a grave danger to Austria: it threatened her last remaining buffer, it could involve her in war with Russia, or it could mean the march of a French army down the Danube. Metternich's own solution was an alliance with Russia and war against France—regardless of the Spanish question. "Our dangers are great—they are imminent," he concluded; "the fall of the last throne of the Bourbons does not augment them; it will have been an immense benefit if it arouses generally a feeling of in-

[15] Metternich to Stadion, 1 July 1808, in Constantin de Grunwald (ed.), "La fin d'une ambassade. Metternich à Paris en 1808–1809. Mémoires inédites," *Revue de Paris*, Année 44, t. 5 (Sept.–Oct. 1937), 510.

[16] *ibid.*, 510–511.

[17] Stadion's *Vortrag* of 13 April 1808, quoted in Rössler, *Österreichs Kampf*, I, 304.

[18] *ibid.*, 300.

dignation and with us in particular the conviction that peace with Napoleon is not peace. . . ." [19]

Metternich was now an intimate of the war party in Vienna, and in line with Stadion's instructions he made the most of every opportunity to incite to action. The unexpected resistance of the Spanish people, he argued, was both a drain on Bonaparte's strength in Germany and a lesson the Austrians themselves might follow. The Spanish guerilla fighters might not hold out for ever, but they were proof that "any government will always find, in moments of crisis, great resources in the nation; it must arouse and above all make use of them. . . ." [20] One way to do this was to set in motion a mighty propaganda campaign, on the one hand disseminating "the truth," on the other, censoring "false news." "Public opinion," Metternich had concluded, judging from the French example, "is the most powerful of all means; like religion, it penetrates the most hidden recesses, where administrative measures have no influence." [21] It was with such advice that he threw himself into the people's war, which Stadion, Archduke John, and Anton von Baldacci were preparing in Vienna no less assiduously than Stein, Gneisenau, and Scharnhorst in Berlin.

The key was Austria's military system, reform of which had been hotly debated ever since Austerlitz. The loss of important provinces by the treaty of Pressburg, the alienation of recruiting rights in Germany by the founding of the Rheinbund, and the diplomatic isolation of Austria had created new problems calling for drastic solutions. On May 12 the emperor authorized the creation of two reserve battalions for each German infantry regiment, and two weeks later he made Archduke John chairman of a commission to establish a *Landwehr* separate from the standing army and based on the principle of universal service. All men between eighteen and forty-five not otherwise in service were liable for active duty, and those from forty-five to fifty were assigned to auxiliary services. Soon recruits were streaming to the double eagle, and the hour of decision was set

[19] Metternich to Stadion, 27 April 1808, in Metternich, *Memoirs*, II, 202–208.
[20] Metternich to Stadion, 1 July 1808, in Grunwald, "La fin . . ." *loc.cit.* Cf. same to same, 23 June 1808, in Metternich, *Memoirs*, II, 212.
[21] Metternich to Stadion, 23 June 1808, in *ibid.*, II, 226.

65

for some time in the following spring. Before that time the army would be short of the planned maximum of 400,000; after it, as finance minister Count Joseph Odonell reiterated, the treasury could not stand the strain. Such was the cost of a mass army, such the price of a people's war![22] When Napoleon complained of the Austrian preparations, despite his own 200,000 men in Germany and Poland, Metternich, to the delight of the entire diplomatic corps assembled for a group audience at St. Cloud, coolly replied: "Be assured, Sire, that if you count our soldiers, we also count yours."[23]

Yet, while Metternich was scoring verbal points in Paris, Stadion was losing the diplomatic battle in St. Petersburg and Berlin. Alexander preferred for the time being to exploit Bonaparte's friendship rather than take advantage of his difficulties in Spain. It was safer, the tsar concluded, to conquer strong flanking positions in Finland and the Danubian principalities than to risk a premature showdown with the emperor of the West. Hence he not only accepted the latter's invitation to a conference at Erfurt, he also warned Stadion against provoking war and dissuaded Frederick William from joining one. It was his pressure more than Napoleon's that brought about the dismissal of Baron Stein in November, and drew Prussia back from the war of national liberation to which Stein and Stadion together had pledged their lives.[24]

The Erfurt congress, which took place in October, 1808, was another of those glittering diplomatic spectacles from which Metternich was excluded—this time because Napoleon desired to dramatize the contrast between Austria's isolation and his own omnipotence. The most he permitted was the participation of Baron Vincent as an observer, a low-ranking Austrian looking all the more insignificant beside notables like the poet Wieland and the great Goethe, who came in the retinue of Carl August

[22] Cf. Rössler, Österreichs Kampf, I, 318–330 and 375.
[23] Metternich to Stadion, 17 Aug. 1808, in Metternich, Memoirs, II, 240.
[24] Lobanov-Rostovsky, Russia and Europe, 183–184; Hellmuth Rössler, Reichsfreiherr vom Stein (Berlin and Frankfurt, 1957), 60–68; Rössler, Österreichs Kampf, I, 317–318; Albert Sorel, L'Europe et la révolution française, VII (Paris, 1906), 305–312; and Gerhard Ritter, Stein, eine politische Biographie, one-vol. ed. (Stuttgart, 1958), 339–353.

of Saxe-Weimar. Metternich's part was confined to private conversations with Talleyrand in Paris before the congress began.
The latter opposed Napoleon's course, and privately begged
Metternich to relay to Vienna the suggestion that were Francis
to appear majestically at Erfurt declaring that he had 400,000
men to throw into "the balance of justice," he could morally
disarm Napoleon and Alexander and keep the peace. Stadion
was indifferent to the idea, fearing that without an invitation
Francis would look like another of Napoleon's vassals.[25]

Outwardly the congress was a dazzling success, the pinnacle
of Napoleon's career. In public—on the ride with Bonaparte at
Weimar, at the theatre, at official receptions—Alexander did all
that was expected of him and Europe cowered. The German sovereigns outdid themselves to toast their protector, and
all believed that Austria was now so completely hemmed in
that peace would be preserved. A month before the congress,
Napoleon had conjured war clouds by demanding mobilization
of the Confederation army; [26] now he dramatically dispelled
them by ordering the troops back to quarters.[27] Behind closed
doors, however, it was different. The Rheinbund princes sensed
their importance to Bonaparte at this juncture and, more confidently than before, refused his entreaties to reform the Confederation. As a result he not only abandoned the attempt but
also met their demands for an early distribution of the lands left
over from the last war, a settlement he had hitherto withheld
as leverage for executing the federal reform plans.[28]

Alexander, too, was difficult. Napoleon had hoped to issue a
joint Franco-Russian ultimatum demanding that Austria disarm, recognize Bonapartist thrones in Spain and Sicily, and declare war on England. The tsar refused, agreeing merely to aid
France if war should break out. In fact he went out of his way
to assure Vincent that Austria's armaments were no concern of

[25] Metternich to Stadion, 14, 22, and 23 Sept. 1808, in Metternich, *Memoirs*, II,
265–274.
[26] Metternich to Stadion, 17 Aug. 1808, HHSA, *Staatskanzlei, Frankreich, Berichte*,
Fasc. 290, No. 24 D.
[27] Circular addressed by Napoleon to the confederate princes, Erfurt, 12 Oct.
1808 (copy), HHSA, *Staatskanzlei, Frankreich, Varia*, 1808.
[28] Hölzle, *Württemberg im Zeitalter Napoleons*, 34–35.

Russia's, and with both Vincent and Talleyrand he left the impression that his aid to France, if any, would be nominal.[29] "One truth very evident to me," Metternich reported after hearing these details from the treasonous Talleyrand, "is that the result of the Erfurt Conferences has not at all corresponded with the ideas that were taken there." [30]

In the month after Erfurt the news continued good. Metternich had frequent interviews with Talleyrand and Fouché, minister of police, both of whom yearned for pacification and stability, as did Armand Caulaincourt, the French ambassador in St. Petersburg.[31] Metternich was profoundly impressed. Only the central core of the army, he believed, and a few army contractors, still supported Napoleon. France, he said, is "like the residuum of an extinct volcano." [32] Even Stadion was skeptical of such a cheerful estimate and reprimanded his ambassador for his intimate relations with Talleyrand. It was one thing to pay the scoundrel, quite another to believe everything he said. In Paris—as once at Mainz in student days—Clemens Metternich was caught in the spell of his immediate surroundings.

Stadion's superior perspective, however, did not keep him from using Metternich's arguments in Vienna, where the emperor and Archduke Carl still needed to be persuaded. It was mainly for this purpose, in fact, that he recalled Metternich to Vienna for personal consultations. The ambassador was delighted, both to get away from Paris during the lull which came with Napoleon's departure for Spain, and also to have a direct chance to influence policy. For some time he had been Stadion's chief confidant; now he was to be almost a deputy foreign minister.

In Vienna, where he arrived in early December, he presented three memoranda which summarized his views. In the first he elaborated on his thesis that Napoleon had lost the support of the French nation.[33] In the second he argued that Russia would for all practical purposes remain neutral, adding that "the com-

[29] Lobanov-Rostovsky, *Russia and Europe*, 180–182; Sorel, *L'Europe*, VII, 312–322.
[30] Metternich to Stadion, 30 Oct. 1808, in Metternich, *Memoirs*, II, 288.
[31] Lobanov-Rostovsky, *Russia and Europe*, 184.
[32] Metternich to Stadion, 24 Sept. 1808, in Metternich, *Memoirs*, II, 284.
[33] Text in Adolf Beer, *Zehn Jahre österreichischer Politik, 1801–1810* (Leipzig, 1877), 516–525.

plete nullity of Russia relative to us . . . is worth more than mismanaged and little sustained assistance . . . and the day when it is clearly demonstrated will be equivalent to victory." [34] In the third memorandum he analyzed Napoleon's armies, coming to the optimistic conclusion that there would be no more than 206,000 available for a war against Austria, of which 99,000 would be allied troops of doubtful reliability—78,000 from the Rhenish Confederation and 21,000 from the Duchy of Warsaw. The total official strength of the Rheinbund was 118,050, he noted, but units from Berg, Westphalia, and the smaller states were already fighting in Spain and could thus be discounted.[35] With or without allies, therefore, Austria would have at least numerical equality; hence "we must seek the means of our salvation only in ourselves." [36]

To these arguments Stadion added his own unshakable belief in the ideological incompatibility between France and Austria, the doctrine best calculated to make a strong impression on the emperor and even on Carl. On the premise that war was inevitable in any case, the latter, though full of misgivings, was won over and asked only that a date be set for the attack. On December 10 Stadion outlined his course: diplomatic negotiations in Paris and St. Petersburg to be strung out until March and then terminated. Between the 15th and 20th of December Carl and Odonell settled their differences over paying the troops. On the 23rd Metternich received his instructions from the emperor. He was to assure Napoleon that Austria still desired peace but was ready for war—which of course had been the line of argument in Paris all along. Later he would be told when to adopt a sterner attitude. If Napoleon wanted war, he could have it. If he did not, Austria would force it upon him. If ever there was a conspiracy to wage aggressive war, this was it. Yet who would deny that it was morally justified? As Metternich put it on his return to Paris: for Austria "not to give herself up, feet and hands tied, not to expose herself to succumb

---

[34] Text of second memorandum in *ibid.*, 525–529.

[35] Text of third memorandum, which shows the gross figures, in *ibid.*, 529–535. The detailed breakdown of Rheinbund strength is given in annexes available in HHSA, *Staatskanzlei, Vorträge*, 1808, Fasc. 267.

[36] Second memorandum, Beer, *Zehn Jahre*, 528.

to the first blow, cannot be a crime." [37] And again to Rumiantzev, the Russian ambassador: "War does not date from the first
shot . . . a moral war precedes that of arms." [38]

But if the motive of the war was mere self-preservation, its
goal was more ambitious; it was the expulsion of the French
from Central Europe. On this point there was practically no
dissent. Even Carl's doubts stemmed mainly from consideration of what would happen once the Rhine had been reached.
There was no intermediate stopping point. A France extended
to the Inn and the Vistula was mistress of the continent, and
Austria was not free. Allied to Russia, she might for a time
help to effect an uneasy balance; allied to France, she might
contribute to a peace based on the sheer preponderance of one
side. But in either case she would be the servile junior partner.
At the moment, however, even these options were withheld
from her; she faced instead an alliance of the flanking powers
against the center, which, as Metternich told Rumiantzev, "is
against the peace of Europe because laws of the most simple
prudence may keep these same intermediate powers in a continual excitement. Peace and anxiety are two entirely opposite
ideas." [39] Only be restoring an independent center, then, could
Austria end her anxiety and Europe enjoy peace.

Metternich's remarks to Rumiantzev implied that Austria's
war aim was restoration of the European equilibrium. This
was the truth but not the whole truth. In Vienna the preparations acquired more and more the character of a campaign of
vengeance against the Rheinbund sovereigns. It could hardly
have been otherwise. A mere three years had passed since the
peace of Pressburg, two and a half years since the founding of
the Rheinbund, and less than one since the adoption of the
Bavarian constitution. Psychologically it was too early to recognize the permanence of the new social and political order in
Germany.

The yearning for revenge was natural enough considering
that in ever increasing numbers refugees from Napoleonic

[37] Metternich to Stadion, 2 Feb. 1809, in Metternich, *Memoirs*, II, 321.
[38] Metternich to Stadion, 1 Feb. 1809, in *ibid.*, II, 325.
[39] Metternich to Stadion, 25 Jan. 1809, in *ibid.*, II, 316.

Europe joined the Metternichs and the Stadions (Philip and his brother Friedrich) in the Austrian state services. Some were already veterans—Mathias von Fassbender, for example, a victim of the French conquest of Trier, and Anton von Baldacci, of Corsican extraction but a German nationalist nonetheless, who had been the confidant of emperors since the time of Joseph II. But the influx that came after the Imperial Recess and the mediatizations of 1806 was an entirely new phenomenon, and the newcomers found in Philip Stadion a kindred spirit, who saw to it that they received important posts. Two army officers, Stutterheim (Metternich's associate of Berlin days) and Baron August von Steigentesch, had begun their careers in the Saxon service, while a third, Count Ludwig Georg von Wallmoden, brother-in-law of Baron Stein, was from Hanover. Another officer, Count Maximilian von Merveldt from Westphalia, had served in 1808 as ambassador to Russia. Baron Andreas Merian von Falkach, the Austrian chargé d'affaires at Karlsruhe, and Baron Johann Philip von Wessenberg, the envoy to Cassel and later to Berlin, were from the Breisgau on the Upper Rhine. A Swabian, Baron Heinrich von Crumpipen, represented Austria at Stuttgart, and a Tyrolean, Baron Joseph von Buol-Schauenstein, was the Austrian chargé d'affaires at Dresden. Other Tyroleans were Count Anton von Thun and Baron Joseph von Hormayr, the latter serving as a court secretary.[40]

These German aristocrats were all relatively young, all had reason to hate Bonapartism, and all to some extent had discovered the "nation," which caused them to see fellow Germans as paragons of goodness and dignity, where formerly they had noticed only illiterate peasants, rude craftsmen, and other social inferiors. Like their imperial contemporary, Archduke John, the exiles were avid readers of Heinrich von Kleist, Max von Schenkendorf, Ernst Moritz Arndt, and the other patriotic poets of the day. In the romantic movement they found sophisticated reasons for denouncing the rationalistic innovations of the Rheinbund sovereigns and for restoring continuity

[40] *Hof- und Staats-Schematismus des Österreichischen Kaiserthums* (Vienna, 1808), 160–165; and *Allgemeine deutsche Biographie* (Leipzig, 1875–1912), *passim*.

71

with the past.[41] They welcomed the Prussian army expatriates, Otto Rühle von Lilienstern, Ernst von Pfuel, General Friedrich von Westphalen and, last but not least, Baron Stein, who spoke for them all when he said "that the coddling and indulgent treatment of the wretched German princes would be at variance both with justice and with healthy policy . . . and that in such an extraordinary war as this, one can promise himself success only by resort to extraordinary means." [42]

Stadion was in complete accord. As early as September of 1808 he had advised the emperor that a national war was necessary "not only for all the Austrian provinces but also for the people of Germany and the other lands which have been conquered by French usurpations." [43] It was in this spirit that plots were laid to foment uprisings in the Tyrol, in Electoral Hesse, in Brunswick and Hanover. The dispossessed duke of Brunswick, who maintained headquarters in Silesia, and the elector of Hesse, who had fled to Prague with a fortune amassed through years of dealing in mercenary troops, provided rallying-points. England, it was hoped, would supply money and would land amphibious troops. Friedrich Stadion organized a recruiting system for the day when Austrian armies entered the Rheinbund, and Austrian consulates at Ulm, Nuremberg, and Augsburg were already secretly enlisting volunteers. The Tyrol in particular was ripe for revolt, and Baron Hormayr, Archduke John's field agent, had no difficulty winning recruits, chief among whom was the Innsbruck innkeeper, Andreas Hofer. At a meeting of the three shortly after Metternich's return to his post in Paris, the final plans were laid and the date of the rising set for March 12.[44]

The campaign plans rested on two further assumptions. The first was the active participation of Prussia, which suddenly appeared certain on the basis of assurances given in January by a special emissary from Berlin.[45] The other was the neutrality of

---

[41] These activities are best summarized in Walter Consuelo Langsam, *The Napoleonic Wars and German Nationalism in Austria* (New York, 1930), 28–93.

[42] Quoted by Rössler, *Österreichs Kampf*, I, 500.

[43] Quoted *ibid.*, I, 380.

[44] Rössler, *Österreichs Kampf*, I, 406–422; Dunan, *Napoléon et l'Allemagne*, 235.

[45] Beer, *Zehn Jahre*, 357.

Russia, which Metternich at the Vienna conference had said was assured, and which a month later he regarded as "clear and mathematically proven." [46] To confirm these estimates, in February Stadion sent Prince Carl zu Schwarzenberg to St. Petersburg and Baron Wessenberg to Berlin. Russia, the tsar told Schwarzenberg, was willing to guarantee Austria against attack as she had guaranteed Napoleon, but he begged the Austrians not to be the aggressors, for in that case he must stand by his obligations to aid France. The only concession he made was the assurance that even if he had to declare war, he would, as Schwarzenberg reported it, do everything "humanly possible to avoid striking blows at us;" [47] he would move slowly and order his troops to avert any collision with Austrian forces. In Vienna this was considered guarantee enough, and Schwarzenberg's report was interpreted as victory, but in Berlin Alexander's attitude had the opposite effect. Shortly before his conversations with Schwarzenberg the tsar had given similar advice to Frederick William, and the latter had taken it to heart. Returning to Königsberg, the king announced his decision. "Without Russia I cannot do it," he said, according to the stunned and crestfallen Wessenberg,[48] who now concluded that the only hope was a direct appeal to the Prussian people.

Despite these jolts to his calculations, Stadion, convinced that there would never be a better time, was determined to have his war and have it in his own way. The mass army, infused with energy and faith in the justice of the cause, seemed an adequate substitute for allies. It had become the master of policy; it must either fight soon or be disbanded for lack of funds. Boldness and determination in Stadion's policy now verged on recklessness and fanaticism. Thus he left unexplored the tsar's offer of a treaty of guarantee, nor did he heed the broad hint that Russia might stay completely neutral if Austria was not the aggressor—he did not in fact even bother to find a pretext for

[46] Metternich to Stadion, 31 Jan. 1809 (in cipher), HHSA, *Staatskanzlei, Frankreich, Berichte,* Fasc. 292.

[47] Quoted by Beer, *Zehn Jahre,* 351, note 1.

[48] *ibid.,* 360. On the Wessenberg mission see Alfred Ritter von Arneth, *Johann Freiherr von Wessenberg, Ein österreichishcher Staatsmann des neunzehnten Jahrhunderts,* I (Vienna and Leipzig, 1898), 99–117.

the war.[49] When Austrian troops crossed the Inn on April 10, there was nothing new to be said. Carl's manifesto, written by Friedrich Stadion, could make no specific charges; it could only declare that "we fight to assert the independence of the Austrian monarchy, to restore to Germany the independence and national honor that belong to her." [50] Similarly, the more comprehensive statement written by Gentz and released two weeks later, though brilliantly argued, was more a catalog of longstanding grievances against Napoleon than a convincing demonstration of hostile intentions on the part of France.[51]

Against this headlong rush to war two voices were raised—neither of them Metternich's. The first was that of Archduke Carl, who doubted the efficacy of the plots, doubted that Russia could be trusted, doubted that Prussia would ever change course, and doubted that victory was possible unless she did. The other voice of caution was that of Gentz. Essentially, he favored a policy of appeasement toward the Rheinbund sovereigns, hoping to capitalize on the schisms that divided them from Napoleon. In a long memorandum composed in the fall of 1808 [52] he argued against any attempt to revive the old Reich. Instead the German princes should be told that Austria intended neither the restoration of the Reich nor any basic revision of the territorial *status quo* in Germany. It was no mere war propaganda that Gentz concocted. Almost alone in the Austrian service he busied himself with serious postwar planning, including in his memorandum the draft of a German constitution which provided for a defense league of sovereign states, joined in equality and governed by majority decisions.[53]

The document has been justly famous as a precursor to the

---

[49] Cf. Emil Lauber, *Metternichs Kampf um die europäische Mitte. Struktur seiner Politik von 1809 bis 1815* (Vienna and Leipzig, 1939), 20–22, who probably makes more of Stadion's carelessness on this score than is justified.

[50] Text of manifesto in Rössler, *Osterreichs Kampf*, I, 498–499.

[51] Text of manifesto, which was really a "white paper," in Eugen Guglia (ed.), *Friedrich von Gentz: Österreichische Manifeste von 1809 und 1813* (Vienna, n.d.), 1–17.

[52] "Gedanken über die Frage: Was würde das Haus Habsburg unter den jetzigen Umständen zu beschliessen haben, um Deutschland auf eine dauerhafte Weise von fremder Gewalt zu befrien." Text in Friedrich von Gentz, *Aus dem Nachlasse Friedrichs von Gentz*, II (Vienna, 1868), 109–158.

[53] *ibid.*, II, 134–139. Excerpts available in Ellinor von Puttkamer, *Föderative Elemente, im deutschen Staatsrecht seit 1648* (Berlin and Frankfurt, 1955), 68–70.

Act of Confederation of 1815 and a possible inspiration for Metternich's conduct of the war of 1813; [54] its original purpose, however, as a guide to Austrian strategy in 1809, has hitherto gone unnoticed. Missing was the hated Rheinbund statute regulating the rights of the mediatized houses; in its place was an explicit guarantee against interference in the members' internal affairs. Unlike Bonaparte, who was the external protector of the Rheinbund, Austria would be a member and partner in the new Bund, the "first among equals." At a time when Confederate armies were fighting in Spain and arming in Germany, Austria would be giving assurances (viz., in the provisions for majority decisions and the non-liability of the Bund for the extra-German lands of its members) that she would not drag her associates into alien wars. In short, for all but defensive purposes Austria would be content with the neutrality of the third Germany and would remain aloof from its domestic affairs. It is not known whether Gentz, in desiring to court the German states, consciously intended to outbid Alexander as well as Napoleon, but it is significant that this early plea for moderate treatment of the German states was coupled with extreme circumspection toward the eastern power. "Russia's inaction," Gentz advised, "is not merely a matter of no concern but actually desirable. All direct assistance from this power could weaken the confidence that Austria must above all acquire in Germany . . . and would open the way to dangerous pretensions." [55] Thus Gentz sided with Metternich against Carl in holding that Russia at the moment represented an acceptable risk.

Interestingly enough, Gentz, a Prussian, was not a mediatized nobleman. In contrast to his sober judgments, the exhortations of *Reichsgraf* Clemens Metternich became, if anything, more shrill, as he wholeheartedly adopted Talleyrand's advice that Austria must attack before the war in Spain was over.[56] What-

[54] E. g., Paul R. Sweet, *Frederick von Gentz, Defender of the Old Order* (Madison, Wis., 1941), 151ff.

[55] Gentz, *Nachlasse*, II, 128.

[56] Metternich to Stadion, 11 and 31 Jan. 1809. HHSA, *Staatskanzlei, Frankreich, Berichte,* Fasc. 293; and same to same, 27 Feb. 1809, in Prince Clemens Metternich, *Aus Metternich's nachgelassenen Papieren,* ed. by Fürst Richard Metternich, II (Vienna, 1880), 289–293. (This work, which is the German edition of Metternich, *Memoirs,* previously cited, will hereafter be referred to as *N.P.*)

ever justification a weak Austria had once had to remain on friendly terms with all-conquering France, a strong Austria could not tolerate Bonaparte's threat to the Habsburg dynasty. If the monarchy were again to lose, Bohemia would become "a tributary state like Bavaria," Austria would have a French marshal as governor, and Hungary could not remain "united as a single national body." [57] But Austria need not lose. Compared with conditions in 1805, France was now morally and financially weaker, Austria immensely stronger, and instead of following "the advice of a Cabinet [i.e. Russia] which has only too well proved that it does not know how to govern itself; we are now free to make our own calculations." [58] Not inferior armies but deficient leadership had caused the previous defeats. Now we face "the necessity of making war and making peace as he [the enemy] does." [59] So "let us, in a word, fight the enemy with his own weapons, let us send him back his own balls." Pressing the attack beyond the first cannon shot, not limiting our ambitions to local successes, "let us take advantage of our strength and never forget that the year 1809 is the last of the old or the first of a new era."

These were fighting words. Even when due allowance is made for Metternich's understanding of the value of propaganda and the bias that Stadion requested of his reports, there is no reason to doubt that he spoke from the heart. In his conviction that faulty technique had caused past defeats and that correct methods—Napoleon's own methods—would bring victory, he stood with the brothers Stadion, with the Archduke John, with the Gneisenaus, Scharnhorsts, and Boyens in Prussia, and above all with Stein. Did he also stand with them on the problem of Germany? It is a question of fundamental importance, for on it hinged Metternich's relationship to the heroes of the War of Liberation four years later. It is also, unfortunately, a question that cannot be definitively answered: the evidence is too meager. The reports from the Paris embassy in the early months of 1809 do not reveal a single significant conversation with the representatives of the Rheinbund courts,

[57] Metternich to Stadion, 3 Apr. 1809, in Metternich, *N.P.*, II, 296
[58] Metternich to Stadion, 11 Apr. 1809, in *ibid.*, II, 296.
[59] This and following from Metternich to Stadion, 3 Apr. 1809, in *ibid.*, II, 296–297.

let alone an effort to draw them over to the Austrian side. In view of the free hand Metternich enjoyed at his post and his intimate relationship with Stadion, silence on this score can only mean that he too considered the defection of Bonaparte's confederates improbable, perhaps even undesirable. It was not that he depreciated the German contingents; he had always reported faithfully on their numbers and movements, and his Vienna memorandum of December, 1808, which on the whole corresponded to the estimates of the *Hofkriegsrat*,[60] assigned them an important weight. On this evidence one can at least conclude that, like Stadion, he took it for granted that the Rheinbund troops would fight for France and made no effort to have it otherwise.

On the other hand, the reports make no reference to the conspiracies in Germany, and give no indication of how Metternich might have judged the prospects for successful insurrection or for forming free corps on German soil. The nearest allusion is a remark he quoted approvingly from Talleyrand—"all Germany will be with you"—by which Talleyrand meant the *people* of Germany, not the princes.[61] In a similar vein Metternich himself said, when the war began, that in contrast to the situation in 1805, "the cause of Austria is now that of all the peoples up to the banks of the Rhine." [62] From such random utterances, however, little can be inferred. Pro-Austrian public opinion would deserve mention even if it did no more than impair the enemy's efficiency, which is probably the most Metternich expected of it. When "rumors, true or false," of "popular tumults" in North Germany reached him, he seems to have regarded the events as spontaneous and incidental, worth noting because they interfered with his family's transit back to Vienna.[63]

But perhaps our demands for documentary certainty are too severe. The diplomatic pouches between Vienna and Paris were no place to discuss sensitive matters which lay outside Metternich's province. All other evidence links him too intimately

---

[60] See memorandum evaluating Metternich's figures in HHSA, *Staatskanzlei, Vorträge*, 1808, Fasc. 267.

[61] Metternich to Stadion, 11, Jan. 1809 (in cipher), HHSA, *Staatskanzlei, Frankreich, Berichte*, Fasc. 293, No. 1, I.

[62] Metternich to Stadion, 11 Apr. 1809, in Metternich, *N.P.*, II, 299.

[63] Metternich to Stadion, 18 Apr. 1809, in *ibid.*, II, 303.

with Stadion's program to leave doubt about the basic harmony of their thinking. Certainly the man who so eloquently promoted Austria's internal measures for waging a people's war could have had no scruples against revolutionizing Germany. If he did not explicitly approve the plots, neither did he criticize them. His postwar accusations were directed not at Stadion but at the skeptical Archduke Carl, who, in turn, ranked Metternich with the brothers Stadion as the chief culprits. Austrian foreign policy, Carl lamented later, was dominated by victims of Napoleon who "allied themselves with their fellow sufferers even from foreign lands." [64] They clung to "preconceived notions, avoided serious discussions, and put clever witticisms and mental twists in place of reasons. . . ." [65] All in all, it would be fair to conclude that, as often before, Metternich, though perhaps less doctrinaire and sentimental than the other German refugees, was nonetheless still one of them, full of a *Reichsgraf's* fervor for freeing Germany.

Because of Metternich's intimate association with the Austrian rising of 1809, it is of utmost importance to establish the exact nature of the movement. Some historians have seen in the Austrian war program a revolutionary crusade with genuine national and liberal ideals.[66] The thesis is supported by the radical talk of the war leaders—the praise of liberty, the promises of reviving and reforming state diets, the extravagant tributes to the virtues of "the people," and the subversive measures contemplated in Germany. Furthermore, it must be granted that the émigré nobles assembled by Stadion were a far more enlightened and energetic breed than their fathers, older brothers, and cousins who sulked on their estates and who, when their turn came in 1814, had nothing better to offer than a literal restoration with their rights minutely and exhaustively described.[67]

<hr />

[64] Carl von Österreich, *Ausgewählte Schriften*, VI (Vienna, 1894), 326.

[65] *ibid.*, VI, 327.

[66] Notably Rössler, *Österreichs Kampf*, I and II, *passim*; Heinrich Ritter von Srbik, *Deutsche Einheit, Idee und Wirklichkeit vom Heiligen Reich bis Königgrätz*, I (Munich, 1935), *passim*: and Langsam, *German Nationalism in Austria, passim*.

[67] Johann Friedrich Hoff, *Die Mediatisiertenfrage in den Jahren 1813–1815* (Berlin and Leipzig, 1913), 23–26. See also below, p. 318.

Any restorative movement, however, must be a reform movement to the extent that it must at least seek to remove the causes of the original catastrophe. How much reform was to be expected from men who had property and a way of life at stake, and who in any case were never in a position to redeem their pledges, necessarily remains problematical. In the first place, there was no real agreement as to what a nation was. Frederick Stadion, Stein, and Archduke John dimly perceived a German nation based on a common culture, but most people, including Philip Stadion and Metternich, considered the "nation" synonymous with the people—*das Volk*—of any state, as opposed to the government. For the rest, the so-called nationalism of the time was in reality either a kind of provincial patriotism generated in opposition to the centralistic and bureaucratic practices of Bonapartism or an intense nostalgia for the old Reich, an affection for institutions which had suddenly acquired a romantic glamor when they ceased to exist. It is difficult, for example, to make of Hormayr or Andreas Hofer anything but stalwart defenders of Tyrolean autonomy—latter-day William Tells. The German nationalism of this period, like the Polish variety, was mainly the credo of aristocrats who looked to the past, in the one case to 1803, in the other, to 1772; reformist though it may have been in certain respects, it had little to do with the ethnic nationalism and middle-class liberalism of a later generation. Few serious proposals were made to transform the corporately organized *Landstände* into modern parliaments, to abolish serfdom, or indeed to tamper in any way with the social and economic organization of the manor.[68]

By contrast, the utmost solicitude was displayed toward all grades of nobility, including even the reviled Rheinbund sover-

[68] These conclusions based primarily on André Robert, *L'Idée nationale autrichienne et les guerres de Napoléon* (Paris, 1933), 216–500; A. Berney, "Reichstradition und Nationalstaatsgedanke, 1789–1815," *Historische Zeitschrift*, Bd. 140 (1929), 57ff; Aira Kemiläinen, *Auffassungen über die Sendung des deutschen Volkes um die Wende des 18. und 19. Jahrhunderts* (Helsinki, 1956), *passim;* Valjavec, *Entstehung der politischen Strömungen,* 328–349; Helmuth Tiedemann, *Das deutsche Kaisergedanke vor und nach dem Wiener Kongress* (Breslau, 1932), *passim;* and Karl Wolff, *Die deutsche Publizistik in der Zeit der Freiheitskämpfe und des Wiener Kongress 1813–1815* (Plauen, 1934). Cf. Heinz Gollwitzer, *Die Standesherren: die politische und gesellschaftliche Stellung der Mediatisierten 1815–1918* (Stuttgart, 1957) 15–17.

eigns. Except for those patent interlopers, the duke of Berg and the king of Westphalia, all the princes were to keep at least their "hereditary lands," and some (like Austria herself) might retain the ecclesiastical awards of the Imperial Recess.[69] In this way the "legitimate" claims of Napoleon's wards could be reconciled with the restoration of the mediatized domains. Indeed the instructions which Wallmoden carried to London and Schwarzenberg to St. Petersburg, in 1809, declared explicitly that Austria's aim was "to restore every legal property owner to the possession of the lands belonging to him before the time of Napoleon's usurpations." [70]

As far as Germany is concerned, the conclusion seems inescapable that Stadion's aim was at bottom the restoration of the old Reich. Neither he nor anyone else of his general outlook ever prepared a plan for the future comparable in detail, say, to the one drawn up in a different spirit by Gentz. Why? Because in Austria one need not belabor the obvious; because in the Rhenish Confederation the announcement of an impending restoration would only have strengthened the sovereigns' bonds with Napoleon; because in Prussia it would only have increased the desire to remain neutral. As a result, the statements of the *Hofburg* were evasive and contradictory.[71] The war manifesto affirmed that the emperor would never "intervene in the internal affairs of foreign states or set himself up as the judge of their systems of government, their legislation, their administrative measures, or the development of their armed forces." [72] But it did not guarantee sovereignty or flatly disavow the intent to restore the Reich, as Gentz pleaded should be done. Instead, it listed the dissolution of the Reich as one of Napoleon's crimes, a cause of the war, and something in which Austria had only temporarily acquiesced.[73]

Napoleon never tired of telling the German sovereigns that the two causes of the impending hostilities were English gold

[69] Rössler, *Österreichs Kampf*, I, 499–504.
[70] Quoted in August Fournier, "Österreichs Kriegsziele im Jahre 1809," *Beiträge zur neueren Geschichte Österreichs*, December, 1908, Heft IV, 216–217.
[71] *ibid.*, 223–230. Cf. Beer, *Zehn Jahre*, 392.
[72] Text of manifesto in Guglia, *Österreichische Manifeste*, 1–17. This quotation from p. 16.
[73] *ibid.*, 5.

and the machinations of the imperial aristocrats in the Austrian service.[74] To some extent he was right; Archduke Carl, for one, agreed with him. But even if he had not been right, he made it ridiculously easy for the Rheinbund princes to choose between Stadion's ambiguous utterances and his own incisive deeds. On March 8 he urged the Rhenish confederates to enforce the statutes requiring mediatized princes, counts, and knights to reside within the Confederation; [75] and on April 24 the *Moniteur* announced the confiscation of the properties of those who remained in Austrian employ.[76] Also confiscated (though with compensations) were the properties of the Teutonic Knights, and Mergentheim, as already noted, was awarded outright to Würtemberg. A petty craving for revenge on Napoleon's part perhaps, but it signified something of importance in his predicament: in every European crisis he had to pass out gratuities to his German servants.

So once again the contest with Napoleon took a personal turn, and Metternich rushed to assure the emperor of his loyalty. "Issue of a family for centuries subject to the august House of Austria," he asseverated in reporting on Napoleon's action, "my offspring will never change masters. They can lose their fortune [but] they will never give in to crime." In these principles, he said, "I am rearing the only son that I have." [77] With this affirmation of allegiance he watched the war approach, the war which he had done so much to bring about. He ended his embassy in Paris with the same conviction he had brought there three years before—the belief that Napoleon's system must be overthrown, not merely resisted. He left France as he had arrived—the prisoner of Bonaparte.

[74] Dunan, *Napoléon et l'Allemagne*, 236–237; Rössler, *Österreichs Kampf*, I, 375.
[75] French note to Würtemberg, 8 March 1809 (copy), HHSA, *Staatskanzlei, Frankreich, Varia*, Fasc. 72, Folio 12.
[76] Text of decree in Martens, *Nouveau recueil*, I, 200–202.
[77] Metternich to Stadion, 17 March 1809, in HHSA, *Staatskanzlei, Frankreich, Berichte*, Fasc. 293, No. 14 F. The son was Victor, born 1803.

CHAPTER IV

WAR AND PEACE: THE MATURING

OF A FOREIGN MINISTER

But Metternich did not leave immediately—he was kept in Paris by Napoleon. Unlike his captivity at Strasbourg during the signing of the Rheinbund Act, this detention seems to have had no ulterior motivation. It was simply a matter of retaliation for his own government's arrest of several French diplomats in Vienna.[1] Because of such trifles he missed—in fact, he was ignorant of—developments which shaped the situation he was to meet on his return to Austria. But as these are basic to a judgment not merely of his part in negotiating the peace but also of his future German policy, one last digression is necessary.

On April 10, 1809, Archduke Carl sent the Austrian forces across the Inn and began the war. At Regensburg on the 22nd he was defeated—repulsed at the gates of the very town where once the Reichstag had sat. If one could not take Regensburg, how could one expect to restore the Reich? Indeed, the question soon became one of preserving Cobenzl's empire, for the French and their Rhenish confederates, in steady pursuit of the retreating Austrians, entered Vienna on May 13. In the face of this blow it seemed almost irrelevant that a small force commanded by Francis' brother-in-law, Archduke Ferdinand of Modena-Este, had meanwhile captured Warsaw.

No less disappointing was the failure of the projected Ger-

---

[1] The reasons for his captivity are not entirely clear. In his autobiographical memoir, N.P., I, 70–71, it was the detention of the French diplomats that brought about the French reprisal. In his official report, however, drafted shortly after his release, he laid his detention to "the Sherlock" affair, Sherlock being a French exile living in Vienna, who had been expelled at the approach of war but later was arrested as a spy. See Metternich to Stadion, 4 July 1809, in HHSA, Staatskanzlei, Frankreich, Berichte, Fasc. 293. Cf. Dunan, Napoléon et l'Allemagne, 634. The point is not important but whichever version is correct, the common contention—repeated most recently by Lauber, Metternichs Kampf, 24—that Metternich was held because he knew too much about the internal weaknesses of France, seems untenable.

man insurrections. For this Stadion blamed Carl's military reverses, but the fact remained that Austria's propaganda appealed primarily to aristocrats—"the men who make up what is called society," the French envoy to Munich called them [2]—and they were not the sort to risk their necks in treasonous enterprises. The conspiracies were also plagued by poor coordination and lack of discipline. Despite the efforts of that master of revolution, Napoleon, to represent them to the tsar as Jacobins,[3] the plotters remained at heart romantic amateurs —"inept enthusiasts and windy project makers," scoffed Gentz,[4] who had predicted the result. The one glorious exception was the Tyrol. There, where discontent with Bavarian rule reached the scale of a mass movement, the plotters were completely victorious and by June 1 ruled the province in the name of Austria.

A generation earlier, in the heyday of cabinet warfare, the loss of the capital would almost certainly have ended the war. This was no longer true. Napoleon had held Madrid for a year, but he did not control Spain. Now in Vienna, far removed from his bases, he knew that before he could dictate peace he must first destroy the Austrian army, which Carl had brought to a solid position on the left bank of the Danube near Vienna, after a masterly retreat. Over the protests of Stadion and the war party Carl awaited Napoleon's attack instead of launching one of his own. On May 20 it came, and in a brilliant counterattack, distinguished by Carl's personal bravery, Napoleon was defeated. Driven from the key towns of Aspern and Essling, he sought refuge on the Lobau, an island in the Danube.[5]

The immediate result of the victory was an upsurge of confidence. Aspern seemed the magic catalyst that would bring Prussia and Russia into the war and touch off the German revolution. Hopefully Stadion dispatched Colonel Steigentesch to Berlin, only to discover that the Prussians still demanded

[2] Quoted by Dunan, *Napoléon et l'Allemagne*, 234.
[3] Albert Vandal, *Napoléon et Alexandre Ier. L'alliance russe sous le premier empire*, II (Paris, 1893), 80–81.
[4] Quoted by Rössler, *Österreichs Kampf*, II, 64.
[5] Beer, *Zehn Jahre*, 385ff; Eduard Wertheimer, *Geschichte Oesterreichs und Ungarns im ersten Jahrzehnt des 19. Jahrhunderts*, II (Leipzig, 1890), 319–330. Cf. Vandal, *Napoléon et Alexandre*, II, 91.

hegemony over North Germany as their price and in any case would march only with Russian approval. This Alexander refused, even though his own attitude toward Austria had been more benevolent than Prussia's.[6]

True to his promises, the tsar avoided striking serious blows; indeed, he moved with such painful slowness that Archduke Ferdinand, as noted, was able to capture Warsaw and inflict several sharp defeats on a native Polish army commanded by Prince Joseph Poniatowski. The French were suspicious, angry, and exasperated, but Alexander, though he regretted Napoleon's wrath, feared a resurrection of a French-protected Poland even more. If Poniatowski succeeded in wresting Galicia from Austria, the Poles would almost certainly set up a clamor for the return of Russia's Polish provinces. Volunteers from Podolia and Volhynia already served with Poniatowski. The Polish question, often enough a bone of contention among the eastern powers, was also at times their common bond.

The truth was, however, that Alexander still hoped to conquer Finland and the Danubian Principalities under cover of the French alliance. Until the armies fighting there were free for action again in Central Europe, he had no desire to see the continent reorganized, by either France or Austria. The solution Alexander finally settled on was devious and inscrutable, even by his standards. He would occupy Galicia with his own troops, trying to interpose them between Ferdinand's Austrians and Poniatowski's Poles without, he hoped, having to fight either of them. From Cracow and the headwaters of the Vistula he could command the Moravian approaches to Vienna and adapt his next moves to ensuing events. The news of Aspern and evidence that Napoleon's patience was at the breaking point reached St. Petersburg in the first days of June. On the 4th the tsar ordered an army under General Prince Serge Galitzin into the disputed province.[7]

This development is scarcely what Stadion or Gentz or Met-

[6] Fedor von Demlitsch, *Metternich und seine auswärtige Politik* (Stuttgart, 1898), 13ff; Beer, *Zehn Jahre*, 388ff; and Rössler, *Österreichs Kampf*, 31–34.

[7] Vandal, *Napoléon et Alexandre*, II, 75–117; Beer, *Zehn Jahre*, 398ff; Demelitsch, *Metternich und seine auswärtige Politik*, 18–25; and M. Kukiel, *Czartoryski and European Unity 1770–1861* (Princeton, 1955), 89–90.

ternich—indeed, hardly anyone save perhaps Archduke Carl—
had anticipated when they had drawn their optimistic conclusions from Schwarzenberg's St. Petersburg reports a few short
months before. Then the assumption had been that, if Alexander intervened at all, it would be as their full-fledged ally
and that he would bring Prussia with him. They had not foreseen the possibility of an intermediate course, the Machiavel-
lian policy that Alexander actually pursued within the frame-
work of both his alliance with France and his commitments to
Austria. What made it all the more exasperating was that no
one could tell exactly what it portended of Russia's subsequent
policy.

Meanwhile, at the Austrian headquarters at Wolkersdorf, the
central question after Aspern was how best to exploit the victory. As time passed and the French did nothing, Stadion and
Baldacci, eager to utilize the psychological impact of Aspern,
grew impatient. They were further encouraged by the capture
of Dresden and Bayreuth early in June and the amazing success of the Tyrol rising, which spilled over into Vorarlberg.
One more victory, and Russia would turn on Napoleon, Prussia would declare war, and Germany would rise against the
Rheinbund—such was Stadion's hope. The real hero of Aspern,
however, Archduke Carl, once again advised negotiations. What
had been a polite disagreement with Stadion was now an open
breach, one that penetrated to every level of the civil and military services and deepened Carl's distrust of the German refugees. Despite this, it was he far more than Stadion who completed Metternich's education in statecraft.

Carl could list the military pros and cons as well as anyone,
and he used them, excessively perhaps, to support his arguments
for peace.[8] At bottom, however, his case rested not so much on
the *chances* of victory or defeat in battle as on their *consequences*. If the rewards of victory were great or the penalty of
defeat slight, one could dare much. But Carl held the reverse
to be true. Metternich had time and again reported from Paris

[8] Beer, *Zehn Jahre*, 401ff, and Lauber, *Metternichs Kampf*, 24–26, are the main
defenders of Carl; while Wertheimer, *Geschichte Oesterreichs*, II, 382–388, and
Rössler, *Österreichs Kampf*, II, 11–47, present the case against him, though not in
a hostile tone.

that Napoleon's target was the Habsburg dynasty; and Napoleon himself, from the gardens of Schönbrunn, had told the world he would partition the monarchy. "It is," said Carl in a memorandum to the Kaiser on June 23, "no longer a hyperbolic manner of speaking, it is literally true: the first lost battle is the death sentence of the monarchy and the present dynasty." [9] The army could not retreat because Galitzin's force was at its back and must, if Austria lost the battle, do everything to appease Bonaparte. Thus, while Napoleon risked nothing but a retreat into Germany, Austria risked everything.

Such were the consequences of defeat. The heart of Carl's case, however, the root of that pessimism which his critics attributed to battle-shyness, was his conviction that Austria could not exploit a victory. The reason again was Russia. Once before, in 1807, he had counseled neutrality mainly because he believed a coalition of Austria, Prussia, and Russia would fall apart before it had reached the Elbe, let alone the Rhine. He was, as previously explained, of the school which considered France the lesser of the two evils,[10] and nothing had happened since to change his mind. Alexander menaced Austria at the mouth of the Danube; and if for the time being he did not wage full-scale war, it was because he believed Austria was certain to lose anyway. When he responded to Austria's only victory by invading Galicia, Carl concluded that his hypothesis had been confirmed, that Russia, however amiable when presented with Austrian reverses, would never permit her to profit from victory. To defeat Napoleon once more would make a two-front war a certainty, and it was such a conflict, not merely a local engagement on the Danube, that Carl was sure the monarchy could not survive. "Austria has not the physical possibility of waging a Russo-Polish and a French-Italian-German war at the same time," he insisted.[11] With nothing to win and everything to lose, it was folly to give battle regardless of the military odds, especially as they were not quite so favorable as the foreign minister imagined. Stadion's arguments he called "be-

[9] Quoted by Wertheimer, *Geschichte Oesterreichs*, II, 358.
[10] See above, Chapter II, p. 55.
[11] Quoted by Rössler, *Österreichs Kampf*, II, 37.

neath contempt," [12] comprehensible only on the ground of the former *Reichsgraf's* personal interest in Germany.

In this frame of mind Carl set out as best he could to husband his beloved army, the last refuge of the state. Although no peace negotiation was started, he had his way about awaiting attack rather than launching one. On July 5 it finally came, reaching a climax the next day at Deutsch Wagram, where Napoleon was the victor. Whether a more expert performance by General Prince Franz Seraph Rosenberg on the left wing or the timely arrival of Archduke John's force from Hungary would have changed the outcome can be left to specialists in campaign autopsy. What matters here is that the result of the battle, as well as Carl's subsequent conduct, were at least in part due to his political predilections. His main purpose was to preserve the army, and he had planned his retreat as carefully as his battle deployment. Since the Russians commanded the passes into nearby Moravia and Hungary, he had decided to retire into Bohemia, a maneuver which, because of the greater distance, made it necessary to break off the engagement at Wagram sooner.

A week later (July 12), after further bloody battles near the Bohemian town of Znaim, Carl, on his own authority, concluded an armistice. By its terms France won the right to reoccupy Vorarlberg, the Tyrol, and parts of Styria. Otherwise the belligerents were to hold approximately what they then controlled. The duration of the truce was set at four weeks, with two weeks' notice necessary for terminating it. In this way Carl believed he had frozen the Russian force in its cantonments in Galicia, prevented its marching to join Napoleon, and gained time to withdraw his own army from the potential trap.[13] The price he paid was the relinquishment of every advantage over Napoleon which Austria then possessed in Germany. Carl even ordered Bayreuth and Dresden evacuated, though the terms did not expressly require it.

At imperial headquarters at Comorn in Hungary the armis-

---

[12] Carl to Duke Albert of Saxe-Teschen, 27 June 1809, quoted in Wertheimer, *Geschichte Oesterreichs,* II, 358.

[13] Wertheimer, *Geschichte Oesterreichs,* II, 380–381; Demelitsch, *Metternich und seine auswärtige Politik,* 28–29.

tice caused consternation. Carl might have been forgiven his interference in a political question, but the actual provisions were another matter. For the emperor the support of Andreas Hofer and his followers in the Tyrol was a point of honor; for Stadion it was, along with the retention of Bayreuth and Dresden, the *sine qua non* of a German revolution. These tangible assets Carl had bartered away with disconcerting alacrity, and all because he had no faith—or so it seemed to those who did not comprehend the deeper reasons for his action, who still operated on the original assumption that Russia awaited only an Austrian victory before joining her in battle. Under the circumstances the emperor, though he did not repudiate the armistice, was almost forced to discipline his brother, and he did so by relieving him of the supreme command. Carl replied by submitting his resignation from all posts, and on July 31 it was accepted.

In the stormy arguments that attended Austria's conduct of the war, Clemens Metternich, voice was missing—he was not permitted to return home until May 23. Ironically, by that time Vienna was in French hands, and he was sent there to be exchanged for the French diplomats. On May 26, accompanied by Prince Paul Esterhazy and other members of the embassy staff, he began the journey, impatiently looking for fresh news of the war. He had long since grown tired of reading the *Moniteur* and Napoleon's bulletins, which included personal attacks on him in their propaganda. At Châlons he talked with Austrian prisoners; at Lunéville he heard the first rumors of a great French defeat; at Strasbourg the victory at Aspern was confirmed by no less an authority than the Empress Josephine, who resided in the Alsatian city at the time. Buoyed by this news he continued the journey, arriving in Vienna on June 5.[14]

In Vienna the French made every effort to be gracious hosts, while Metternich was equally determined to play the role of prisoner. Denied the freedom of the inner city, he established residence at his mother's summer house in the suburbs, on a hill adjoining the grounds of Schönbrunn palace, where Napoleon

---

[14] Metternich, *N.P.*, I, 76–78; and Metternich to Stadion, 4 July 1809, *loc.cit.*

himself was lodged. At an interview on June 6 Champagny took pains to apologize for the personal insults contained in the bulletins, dismissing them as mere war propaganda and assuring the ambassador that he would again be welcome in Paris.[15] Nine days later General Savary paid a call. Broadly hinting at the possibility of peace negotiations, he suggested that Metternich would find Napoleon in a friendly mood were he to stroll to Schönbrunn for a visit. Metternich refused; he was a prisoner, he said, and "prisoners of my sort, if they understand their duty, must regard themselves as dead." [16] His stand was correct, politically as well as with respect to protocol. Ignorant as he then was of the actual military situation, he would hardly have taken it upon himself to inaugurate, however tentatively, a change of policy. Nevertheless he thought the feeler interesting and had no doubt that Napoleon himself had ordered it. Savary departed, and thereafter Metternich's contacts with the French were confined to the details of his transfer, which, after several false starts caused by delays from the Austrian side, was accomplished on July 2. The next day the Emperor Francis embraced him at Wolkersdorf.

Thus Metternich returned to headquarters on the eve of Wagram. The emperor he found determined, Stadion in despair, awaiting only the outcome of the battle before submitting his resignation. The battle itself he witnessed by the side of the emperor, happy to follow the action through a spyglass instead of from Napoleon's bulletins. The day after the battle Metternich met with Stadion and Francis to decide the next move. Actually the defeat had removed all doubt. Francis read a dispatch from Carl indicating that only 35,000 troops were at the moment fit for duty. Metternich contributed the notes of his interview with General Savary, which, though possibly obsolete as a result of Wagram, allowed some hope that Napoleon was still interested in peace. Accordingly they decided to send Prince Johann Liechtenstein, another hero of Aspern, to Na-

[15] Précis of conversation of 6 June 1809, HHSA, *Staatskanzlei, Frankreich, Berichte,* Fasc. 293.

[16] Metternich, *N.P.,* I, 78. Cf. Précis of conversation of 15 June 1809, in HHSA, *Staatskanzlei, Frankreich, Berichte,* Fasc. 293.

poleon's headquarters to hear his terms. It was quite a different decision from those reached at the decisive conference in Vienna seven months before. The following day at Znaim Stadion submitted his resignation; then and there the emperor offered the post to Metternich.[17]

The reason Stadion gave for his withdrawal was that his long identification with the policy of war would prejudice the peace negotiations.[18] Whether true or not, the explanation is typical of his ingenuous conception of politics: one first demonstrates his good faith and then endeavors to reach an honorable agreement. Metternich's reaction was also typical, indicating from the first moment that a fresh mind was in the ascendancy at imperial headquarters. In the first place, he said, there was no assurance that peace would come and, if the war continued, it was more important to inspire confidence in London, Berlin, and Constantinople than in Paris. For this purpose Stadion at the helm was indispensable. On the other hand, to dismiss Stadion at the outset would be a shot fired into the air; it would inflict no damage but would signal the enemy that Austria was ready to accept any terms. It would be far better to marshal all assets and prepare to resume hostilities. There would be time enough during the negotiation to demonstrate good faith; equivalents might then be gained for such concessions as the dismissal of Stadion. Interlarding the argument with copious avowals of his own unworthiness, Metternich convinced the emperor; and Stadion, sensing that he had an ally who would not permit unconditional surrender, acquiesced in a compromise plan. Officially he would remain foreign minister and, stationed at Archduke Carl's headquarters, would handle relations with Prussia, England, and the North German conspirators. Metternich, meanwhile, would remain with the emperor and deal with France. Although Metternich's motives were no doubt honorable enough, the unorthodox arrangement had its personal advantages for him, conferring as it did the gift that politicians dream of, power without responsibility. The sacrifices were all

[17] Metternich, *N.P., I,* 83f; Rössler, *Österreichs Kampf,* ii, 43; Wertheimer, *Geschichte Oesterreichs,* ii, 392–393; and Beer, *Zehn Jahre,* 422, who gives the date of the meeting as July 8.

[18] Stadion's *Vortrag* of 12 July 1809, hhsa, *Staatskanzlei, Vorträge,* Fasc. 269.

on Stadion's side—despite his title, he had been reduced to a pawn in the negotiation with France.[19]

No sooner had the bargain been sealed than the parties to it had to evacuate Znaim, Stadion proceeding to Carl's headquarters to the northwest, Metternich and the emperor riding off to Hungary, to the castle of Totis near Comorn. At Znaim there ensued on July 10 and 11 further bloody encounters with Napoleon's troops, on the 12th Archduke Carl's armistice, and there Prince Liechtenstein finally found Napoleon and heard his terms. These were shockingly severe: Francis must abdicate or the monarchy would be dissolved.[20] Liechtenstein, a forthright man inclined to take people at their word, was so incredulous that he withdrew briefly to his estate in Moravia. Nevertheless, he decided to try once more and proceeded to Vienna, whither Napoleon had returned. To his amazement he found the emperor in a friendly mood, willing to negotiate and no longer threatening to partition the empire. Territorially the French position now was that Austria must cede at least as much as at Pressburg, which meant between three and four million subjects. Liechtenstein was relieved, but his satisfaction could hardly have been as great as sometimes pictured,[21] since it is probable that Napoleon continued to insist on Francis' abdication.[22] The atmosphere, at any rate, was friendlier, and Liechtenstein was able to inform his monarch that a peace conference could be held.

At the same time, in a personal letter from Champagny and possibly through Liechtenstein as well, Napoleon declared his preference for Metternich as the Austrian plenipotentiary.[23] One may speculate interminably on his reasons but the most

[19] Metternich, N.P., I, 84–88. Cf. Metternich to his mother, 25 July 1809, ibid., I, 231–232. Also Demelitsch, Metternich und seine auswärtige Politik, 27–28, who provides confirmation from Stadion's side.

[20] Beer, Zehn Jahre, 423; Wertheimer, Geschichte Oesterreichs, II, 393.

[21] E.g., ibid., II, 393 and note 4.

[22] Beer, Zehn Jahre, 427. The sources disagree on this point, but the fact that Metternich, in his Vortrag of 20 July 1809 (Metternich, N.P., II, 306ff), explicitly excluded Francis' abdication from his list of acceptable terms, indicates that Napoleon made the demand to someone at that time. Indeed, he later contended that Napoleon had promised Liechtenstein not only the status quo ante but the Tyrol and another territory as well for Francis' abdication. Chroust, Die Geschichte . . . Würzburgs, 318.

[23] Metternich, N.P., I, 88; and Wertheimer, Geschichte Oesterreichs, II, 393.

prosaic is perhaps the best, namely that since his own spokes-man was to be Champagny, the foreign minister, the Austrians might respond by sending Stadion unless directed otherwise. Another possibility is that Napoleon, perhaps from impressions gained during Metternich's captivity, considered him the most sympathetic of all possible emissaries to a Franco-Austrian rapprochement. In any case, it was a needless request because Francis had no intention to the contrary, and Metternich doubt-less fancied the situation ideally suited to his talents, which it was. The only problem was a title, to give him official status, and this was solved, at his own suggestion, by making him simply a *Staats-Minister* without portfolio.[24] General Count Laval Nugent, a bluff soldier of Irish descent, was appointed as his military advisor.

In his handling of Stadion's attempt to resign, Metternich had demonstrated a knack for selling what others would have given away. He soon found that Napoleon worked in the same manner: if the Austrians wanted a peace conference, let them pay for it by accepting conditions. In announcing Champagny's appointment on July 22, the emperor laid down his terms: abolition of the *Landwehr*, reduction of the army by one-half, and the expulsion of the French and German émigrés in the Austrian service. The question of cessions was to be discussed on the basis of the *uti possidetis,* that is to say, the territories then occupied by the respective armies. The only way Austria could recover any of her lost provinces would be to surrender an equivalent from the portions of the empire she still held. It was a harsh demand, and caused dismay when the note con-taining it reached Comorn on July 25. The following day Met-ternich replied that Austria could not prejudge the issues that would arise at the peace conference and, accusing Napoleon of deliberate procrastination, proposed August 3 as the opening date. But Bonaparte did not reply until August 3 and even then, instead of suggesting another date, he made more difficul-ties, especially regarding Austrian disarmament. This time Francis sent his aide-de-camp, General Count Ferdinand von

[24] Metternich's *Vortrag* of 31 July 1809 and the emperor's note of 4 August in HHSA, *Staatskanzlei, Vorträge,* Fasc. 269.

Bubna, to explain once more that the French demands were suitable only for the agenda of a peace conference. At last the French agreed to a time and place, August 15 at Altenburg, but it was evident that they were in no particular hurry.[25]

Napoleon was indeed delaying, and for the simple reason that he actually did not know what terms to offer. Austria was only one factor in his grand policy, and it was difficult to decide what combinations would best fit the circumstances. In order to magnify the psychological impact of Wagram on Europe, he wanted Austria to sacrifice at least as much as at Pressburg. Because of his commitments to the Rheinbund sovereigns, Austria must cede more of her German territories. Because the Poles fought valiantly both in Spain and Poland, she must cede them all or most of Galicia. Because of the war with England, she must join the continental system and, to make it physically impossible for her to do otherwise, she must cede the Adriatic littoral with the ports of Trieste and Fiume.

Unfortunately each of these considerations brought complications. To take three to four million subjects, as the Pressburg formula required, would wound and infuriate Austria without killing her; and a vengeful Austria would be, like Prussia, a potential ally of Russia. Nor was it as simple as one might think to reward the Rheinbund sovereigns. Experience had shown the Protector that there would be no rest in Germany without a definitive territorial settlement. Yet to grant one would remove his last hold on his clients, his only real leverage for retaining their military services in Spain and Germany and eventually for executing his federal reform plans. In the meantime nothing that he could do would satisfy everybody, since one state's gain was another's disappointment. The same jealousies that he had exploited so successfully in conquering Germany were most unwelcome now that it was time to stabilize Germany. One may divide and conquer; one cannot divide and govern. The prospect of setting off anew the bickering and intrigue that had followed in the wake of Pressburg, Tilsit, and to some extent Erfurt, was disagreeable to contemplate, and

---

[25] Beer, *Zehn Jahre*, 428–429; Demelitsch, *Metternich und seine auswärtige Politik*, 32.

93

Napoleon was already getting a foretaste of it. Less than a week after the armistice was signed, special envoys of the South German courts began to appear in Vienna, all bearing letters and memoranda setting forth their masters' ambitions, many of which, not surprisingly, were mutually exclusive.[26] Metternich had been a more pleasant guest; his only demand had been to be treated as a prisoner.

Napoleon's main worry was Bavaria. Abutting Austria as she did, she should have been the easiest and the most important to reward. If she acquired Salzburg, Berchtesgaden, and the Inn and Hausrück districts, she would have the good frontier necessary to protect Munich from another Austrian occupation. In return, she might make cessions elsewhere in favor of other states. But this was not enough for the court in Munich. In a memorandum of July 29 Montgelas demanded the province of Southern Bohemia and, if cessions were required, Styria, Carinthia, and parts of Upper Austria. He took for granted the annexation of oft-promised Bayreuth and Regensburg.[27] These were towering demands, though perhaps not disproportionate to the booty that might be available if Napoleon actually carried out his threats to dissolve the Austrian Empire. Was it too much to hope that at last the Wittelsbachs were about to surpass the Habsburgs?

If Montgelas' demands represented a serious effort to convince Napoleon that Bavaria was the logical anchor of his system in the southeast, Napoleon was not impressed. For such a purpose he needed a government of unquestioned loyalty and proven military and administrative capabilities, and these tests Bavaria failed to meet. Although she fielded a somewhat larger contingent than the 30,000 the Rheinbund Act required, Napoleon considered her total performance mediocre. He found fault with her original deployment, which had given way too hastily before Carl's attack; he was critical of the generalship of Count Carl Wrede and Crown Prince Ludwig; and he was dumbfounded at the debacle in the Tyrol, which seemed to him

---

[26] Dunan, *Napoléon et l'Allemagne*, 260–261.
[27] *ibid.*, 261; and Michael Doeberl, *Entwicklungsgeschichte Bayerns*, II (Munich, 1912), 375.

an indication of political incompetence and called into question the Wittelsbachs' ability to govern any new provinces they might acquire.[28]

Similar doubts could be raised about Bavaria's loyalty. The crown prince, who had once considered defecting, was now, on the eve of the peace conference, dickering with Metternich about a plan whereby he would marry Archduchess Louise of Habsburg and rule the Tyrol and Vorarlberg as parts of the Austrian Empire.[29] Montgelas and King Max Joseph were not actually treasonous, but hardly exuded faith. Before the war had even begun, they had sought "special guarantees" in St. Petersburg only to have Rumiantzev reply that Russia did not wish to challenge the Protector's monopoly in this respect. During the war they instructed their envoy to Russia, Count Bray, in case of reverses, "to engage this power not to remain aloof from the fate of Bavaria and to insert stipulations in her favor in the separate peace that she would make. . . ." [30] Even when basking in victory they continued to appeal to the tsar to support their peace demands. How much Napoleon knew of these intrigues is a matter of conjecture, but he usually learned what was going on, and must have had his doubts about Ludwig, whose Austrian sympathies were an open secret. All in all, it was clear that however much he might in the end have to reward Bavaria, he would not do so out of gratitude or because she deserved it. Würtemberg, to take a contrasting example, furnished a contingent of 25,000, more than twice her assigned quota; conducted a skillful campaign in Vorarlberg; and had never boggled at the Protector's peacetime levies.[31]

While the German problem, in Napoleon's planning, consisted of swarms of minor difficulties, the Polish question boiled down to one crucial issue, the fate of Galicia. Nothing would have pleased Napoleon more than to act in concert with Alexander, to demonstrate again the vitality of the Tilsit alliance. For that reason his first move after the armistice had been to

[28] Chroust, *Geschichte . . . Würzburgs*, 314; Dunan, *Napoléon et l'Allemagne*, 232–275.
[29] Metternich to Francis, 16 Aug. 1809, HHSA, *Staatskanzlei*, *Vorträge*, Fasc. 269.
[30] Quoted by Dunan, *Napoléon et l'Allemagne*, 264.
[31] Hölzle, *Württemberg im Zeitalter*, 37–39.

invite the Russians to the peace conference, which, as allies, they had a right to attend. Through Caulaincourt, his envoy in St. Petersburg, he also urged them to offer their own solution. But Alexander was evasive. Since anything he proposed would antagonize either France or Austria, he preferred to leave the initiative to Napoleon, to force him to divulge spontaneously which really came first in his plans: Russia or Poland. Communication was slow, and one month after the armistice Napoleon was still in the dark not only about Russia's preferences regarding Galicia, but even about her attending the conference. Here then were the causes of the long delay about which Metternich complained.[32]

While he waited, Napoleon hit upon a compromise solution. He would divide Galicia, adding four-fifths to the Duchy of Warsaw, one fifth to Russia. If Russia objected to even this much expansion of Warsaw, he would leave part of Galicia to Austria and seize more from her elsewhere. Once more the German question and the Polish question merged. Reluctant as he was to take the initiative, Napoleon finally decided he could wait no more and on August 12 instructed Caulaincourt to sound out the Russians on this plan. Since an answer would probably not arrive in less than twenty days and the Altenburg conference was to begin in three, the prospects for fruitful discussion between Champagny and Metternich seemed slight.[33]

In the meantime the French emperor pondered two radically different ways out of his dilemmas. The first was the possibility of actually partitioning the Habsburg monarchy as he had frequently threatened. With so much territory to distribute he would have no trouble finding something for all his friends, including even his marshals. There was one formidable deterrent: it would mean a war to the finish, a war that would be neither popular at home nor assured of success. Wagram was not Jena and, unlike Stadion, Napoleon rather admired Archduke Carl's skill in preserving the army, which would have to be destroyed before France could impose unconditional surrender. There

[32] Vandal, *Napoléon et Alexandre*, II, 112f.
[33] *ibid.*, II, 120–126.

was moreover no telling what upheavals would ensue from the sudden creation of a power vacuum in Eastern Europe, how Russia would react, or Turkey, or the inhabitants themselves. For these reasons it was a course better held in reserve, in the event Austria refused his terms.[34]

More tempting in the long run, therefore, was the opposite alternative, making Austria herself the southeastern anchor of his system. Instead of rendering her impotent he would win her by making no demands at all, with the possible exception that she might cede Galicia against compensation. In return she would enter an alliance with France and join the continental system. In this way he could avoid many invidious choices in Germany, bypass unreliable Bavaria, and in Poland either maintain the *status quo* or change it, at his convenience rather than Alexander's. This, in essence, was the reasoning which led to his offer, first broached to Liechtenstein and repeated many times thereafter, to restore the *status quo ante* provided that Francis abdicate.

But why demand the abdication? Because he could risk a strong Austria only if he had complete trust in her rulers, and only if a generous peace appeared to Europe an expression of strength rather than weakness. He must demonstrate that if he took no provinces, it was because he preferred to unseat an emperor. Austria must acknowledge her defeat and pledge her allegiance by deposing the man who had turned on France. And what more appropriate successor than Ferdinand of Würzburg, the man who had once befriended the young French artillery officer in Tuscany, who had proved a loyal member of the Rheinbund, who had obeyed every mobilization order, and who had never had anything to do with the conspiracies? [35]

There is no need to question Napoleon's seriousness.[36] The plan was not only plausible; it was perhaps his only way out should Alexander prove adamant in regard to Poland. In short, when Napoleon demanded the abdication of Francis, when he

---

[34] *ibid.*, II, 114.
[35] *ibid.*, II, 141–145; and Chroust, *Geschichte . . . Würzburgs*, 257–292.
[36] As Chroust, *ibid.*, 321, does and many others.

insisted upon the expulsion of French émigrés (among whom he included the refugees from the Rheinbund), he was not staging tantrums; he was seriously trying to gauge Austria's interest in such a solution. It was really a variation of the Rheinbund formula: territorial benefits in exchange for unswerving political devotion. In 1806 he had considered a similar policy toward Prussia; perhaps he regretted that he had turned to Saxony instead.

While Napoleon juggled the many combinations open to him, Metternich used the time to survey his own pitifully circumscribed situation. The coming negotiation, difficult under any circumstances, was the more so because of his long isolation from the main stream of events. "Three months' interruption in world affairs have made me a stranger to them," he wrote his mother on July 25. "I am stranded between all the old affairs and the current problems." [37] His first step was to take an exhaustive inventory of Austria's assets and liabilities. Politically, he was appalled by what he found. Napoleon had said that the peace must be at least as severe as that of Pressburg. Yet in 1805, when that treaty was signed, Austria's flank and rear had been protected by Russia and Prussia and the status of France in Germany had still been that of usurpation and "could have been revealed as such by a single successful battle." [38] Austria herself had still been large enough so that the cession of territories would merely weaken her, not destroy her. This time it was different. Prussia was "destroyed," Russia was the ally of France, France the master of Germany, and the Rheinbund, in the form of its appendage, the Duchy of Warsaw, had "recently appeared at the back of the Austrian state outfitted with revolutionary capabilities." [39] Already weakened by Pressburg, the monarchy was now in a position where "every cession strikes at the political existence of the state." [40]

Equally discouraging were Austria's internal circumstances. Financially she had strained to the utmost to train and arm the

[37] Metternich to mother, 25 July 1809 in Metternich, *N.P.*, I, 232.
[38] Metternich's *Vortrag* of 20 July 1809, HHSA, *Staatskanzlei, Vorträge*, Fasc. 269. Also given, with some deletions in Metternich, *N.P.*, II, 306ff.
[39] *ibid.*
[40] *ibid.*

mass army. In the occupied provinces Napoleon exacted further tribute to support his armies, a policy which meant that the armistice was at Austria's expense on both sides of the line. To add insult to injury he had guaranteed Dutch bankers that their loans to Austria would be paid. More serious yet was the breakdown of government itself, at least at the top levels. In comparison with the smooth functioning of an efficient bureaucracy obedient to a genius, which Metternich had observed for three years in Paris, the spectacle at Comorn was chaos: a government living out of trunks and packing crates, a bitter feud between the commander-in-chief of the armies and the foreign minister, the pernicious influence of assorted dilettantes whose right to be in the imperial presence stemmed from the relationships of a feudal past rather than a talent for solving present problems. Which was worse, an Archduke Rainer pleading for abject surrender, or a Baldacci, with his shrill demands for a fight to the finish? Like Archduke Carl, Metternich knew that what was missing was firm centralized direction, and he littered his memoranda to the emperor with scarcely veiled entreaties to take hold. "It is up to the monarch alone to choose among divers evils and dangers," he told Francis. "No one but Your Majesty can decide between peace and war." [41]

In listing these weaknesses Metternich said nothing that Carl had not said many times before. Similarly his list of assets included most of the items Stadion had used in his presentations to the emperor. Within the monarchy the disposition of the peoples had never been better. The same was true of other peoples. Spain fought on, inspired anew by a British victory over Marshal Soult. In Germany and Italy the population was ripe for revolt. "The descent of twenty-five or thirty thousand English on the Weser" might already have taken place.[42] Turkey, though still neutral in the Franco-Austrian war, made serious difficulties for the Russians in Moldavia and Wallachia.[43] As for the Russian troops in Galicia, they seemed to have gone as far as they ever would; at least Russia "has up to the present

---

[41] *ibid.*
[42] Metternich to his mother, 25 July 1809, *loc.cit.*
[43] Metternich's *Vortrag* of 19 July 1809, HHSA, *Staatskanzlei, Vorträge,* Fasc. 269.

served our cause more than that of France." [44] If there was any danger in Galicia, it was from the Poles, who threatened Austria's rear with "an army of 60,000 fanatics." [45] In all this Metternich sounded more optimistic than Stadion, if that was possible. But there was a difference: where Stadion was giving reasons for continuing the war, Metternich was explaining why there was hope for a tolerable peace if Austria handled the negotiations properly. His points related more to French vulnerability than to Austrian strength.

The same direction was evident in his thinking about the monarchy's main asset, the army. "The finest army in the world," he called it and put its strength at 250,000.[46] The estimate was astonishingly high in comparison with Carl's figures; indeed, it seemed the kind of fatuous optimism that led the archduke to include Metternich among the dilettantes at court, differing from the others, he said, "only in [having] more cunning and flexibility." [47] Yet flexibility is no mean virtue, and Metternich, whose mistakes of enthusiasm may have contributed to bringing on the war, was now the convinced and energetic advocate of Carl's own policy, which was to use the army for negotiating peace. For this purpose it was perfectly permissible to include potential strength in the estimates, since that is what the enemy would have to reckon with. In any case Metternich knew as well as anyone that the better an army is for fighting, the better it also is for bargaining, and so he continually urged the emperor to prepare for the resumption of hostilities. As a result he often seemed more bellicose than Stadion and continued to be classed as a member of the war party.[48] Nevertheless, the negotiation remained the main thing; as he

[44] Metternich's memorial, "Coup d'oeil sur la situation politique et militaire de l'Autriche et de la France au commencement des négotiations en août 1809," HHSA, Staatskanzlei, Vorträge, Fasc. 269.
[45] ibid.
[46] Metternich to his mother, 25 July 1809, op.cit., I, 232. Same figures used in Vortrag of 20 July, loc.cit.
[47] Archduke Carl, Schriften, VI, 327.
[48] Rössler, Österreichs Kampf, II, 56–61, corrects the older view (represented, among others, by Wertheimer, Geschichte Oesterreichs, II, 392ff.) that Metternich set an extreme pacifism against Stadion's fanaticism, but by taking Metternich's sometimes militant statements at their face value, he completely misses the subtlety of his position—as did Stadion.

confided to Stadion, "the more critical the state of our affairs [and] the more we need to conclude for the time being a peace which presents us with chances for repose, the more we are compelled to call to our rescue effective material capabilities." [49] If he had any grievance with Carl, it was the ineptitude with which the armistice had been negotiated. He rightly guessed that Napoleon's main reason for agreeing to a truce had been the chance to regain control of the strategically vital Tyrol. The armistice conceded this; it removed the key province from Austria's "trading potential" even before the negotiations had begun, and this was "culpable shortsightedness." [50]

The place of Prussia in Metternich's ingenious efforts to scrape together trading potential, as he called it, is difficult to establish. After the misleading Goltz mission of February and Steigentesch's disillusioning talks with Frederick William in June, there was every reason for caution, and Metternich nowhere listed Prussia among Austria's assets. Nevertheless, when still another emissary from Berlin, Colonel Carl Friedrich von dem Knesebeck, arrived at Comorn on August 8, Metternich seems to have been impressed. In an excess of zeal, which carried him beyond his orders, Knesebeck declared that Austria could count on Prussian aid even if Russia stood by France. In return, to enable Prussia to deploy without arousing Napoleon's suspicions, Metternich agreed to have Wessenberg in Berlin protest Prussian preparations as if they were aimed at Austria. Then he reported to the emperor his opinion that Knesebeck was "so candid and definite" that "I see no reason to doubt his statements." [51]

Was Metternich being duped? Again the answer depends on the difference between preparing a peace negotiation and preparing for war. For the former purpose even the appearance of Prussian support could be useful, and Metternich himself would have been "culpable" if he had not pursued every lead. He would hardly, however, have risked war on the chance that

---

[49] Metternich to Stadion, 2 Aug. 1809, HHSA, *Staatskanzlei, Frankreich, Berichte,* Fasc. 293.

[50] Metternich to Stadion, 31 July 1809, *ibid.,* Fasc. 293.

[51] Metternich's *Vortrag* of 8 Aug. 1809, HHSA, *Staatskanzlei, Vorträge,* Fasc. 269. Cf. Beer, *Zehn Jahre,* 436f.

Prussia would come in, especially as the longer Knesebeck stayed in Austria the clearer it became that Prussia was less interested in a military convention than in winning equality in Germany. "The emperor of Austria and the king of Prussia," so read one article of a draft convention the colonel submitted, "declare themselves to be . . . the dominant powers and directors of German affairs in such manner that Austria shall become the dominant and directing power of the South of Germany and Prussia of the North." [52] When Knesebeck departed on September 25, Frederick William was still neutral.

With regard to Russia Metternich's calculations were equally devious. Because he understood the tension between the alliance partners of Tilsit he knew that Galitzin's army in Galicia was not necessarily hostile; his own guess was that it would march no farther. Still, according to his earlier contention, so excruciating to recall now, that Russian neutrality had been "mathematically proven," [53] Galitzin's army should not have been in Galicia at all. It had already caused a precipitate armistice, and its weight during the peace negotiation was bound to be on Napoleon's side. No one but Alexander could end the guesswork. Metternich therefore favored one more approach to St. Petersburg, and on July 30 dispatched a personal letter to Alexander over the emperor's signature, expressing the hope "that the interests of Austria would never become alien to those of Russia." [54] Unlike some of the military, however, such as Archduke Ferdinand who favored yielding all Galicia to the Russians, Metternich expected nothing. "I have no illusions," he wrote to Stadion in sending him a copy of the letter, "My report of July 20 shows where I stand" [55] (that was the document in which he had dwelt on Austria's total isolation). Hence, unlike his adversary at Altenburg, who had to mark time while awaiting news from St. Petersburg, Metternich had reason, other

[52] Quoted by Rössler, *Österreichs Kampf*, II, 532. For a more sympathetic version of Prussia's intentions, see Wilhelm Oncken, *Oesterreich und Preussen im Befreiungskriege*, I, (Berlin, 1876), 112ff.

[53] See above, Ch. III, p. 73.

[54] Francis to Alexander, 30 July 1809, in Napoléon Ier, *Correspondance de Napoléon Ier*, XIX (Paris, 1864), 409–410.

[55] Metternich to Stadion, 2 Aug. 1809, HHSA, *Staatskanzlei, Frankreich, Berichte*, Fasc. 293.

things being equal, to launch into serious discussions imme-
diately: as long as there was doubt about Russian intentions,
Napoleon must treat Austria with some consideration. The
Russian factor therefore, it is worth repeating, was a matter of
French weakness rather than Austrian strength.

Weighing all the components, Metternich concluded that
Austria's assets were too limited to enable her to obtain the
status quo ante and too great to justify a capitulation. Sacrifices
there must be, but in determining them the negotiations must
start from the basis of the prewar extent of the empire, and not
the *uti possidetis* as Napoleon had demanded. In this way Austria could systematically sacrifice immediate advantages to long-
term strength. If it must come to cessions, Metternich would
first yield West Galicia, because it had the least economic and
military value and would perhaps aggravate the friction between France and Russia. Salzburg or the Inn District, high in
strategic value but low in yield of revenue, he would cede ahead
of the littoral, which he regarded as essential to Austrian commerce. In no case would he cede all four of the areas. To meet
Napoleon's disarmament demands he would reduce the standing army, which was too expensive to maintain anyway, and
preserve the *Landwehr,* reservoir of future strength. The very
last thing he would acquiesce in was an indemnity, and he
would insist that the indebtedness of ceded provinces be assumed by the new owners.[56] In the final instructions which the
emperor gave Metternich on August 14 the concessions were
modified, in that West Galicia was to be ceded only in exchange
for the Tyrol, Istria, or Dalmatia. The importance of ascertain-
ing Russia's intentions was also stressed.[57] Whether the modifications originated with Metternich or other advisors, or with
Francis himself, cannot be established. In any case, though not
identical with Metternich's known recommendations, they were
not incompatible, and it may be that they were added because
he wanted a less conciliatory document to show Champagny as
proof of Austria's firmness.

Among the reports that Metternich submitted to the emperor

[56] Metternich's *Vortrag* of 20 July 1809, *loc.cit.*
[57] Text in Metternich, *N.P.,* II, 313–314.

shortly before the peace conference was one of August 10, in which he discussed the postwar situation of the monarchy.[58] Austria, he said, could no longer assume the European responsibilities that had been hers as a great power; she could no longer seek her own freedom and security by working for the general well-being of the continent. "Whatever the stipulations of the peace may be," he concluded, "the result will be the same, namely that we can seek our security only in adapting ourselves to the triumphant French system." Austria must join the continental system and recognize the usrpation in Spain. Repugnant as it might be, she must develop the art of "tacking, evading, and flattering"; there was no quarreling with necessity. "Without Russia's aid no resistance against the general oppression is thinkable," he added, and one could only hope that "seeing us as an eager rival" for French favors, the great eastern power might at last change her fickle ways.[59]

The memorandum, long available in Metternich's published papers, is justly famous as a candid—one might even say, the classic—statement of his course from 1809 until Napoleon's invasion of Russia in 1812. Except for the Habsburg-Bonaparte marriage, everything is here adumbrated: the alliance with France, participation in the continental system, the displacement of Russia as Napoleon's chief support, and even the change that finally came about in Russian policy. And yet the really important thing about the document is the date. In the first place, it shows that even then Metternich shared Archduke Carl's anti-Russian orientation, though not perhaps Carl's immediate concern about Galitzin's army. In the second place, the pessimism the document suggests, and the abject surrender it implies, are entirely at variance with Metternich's known views at that time. It was indeed an odd moment to choose for setting down fatalistic reflections about postwar conditions.

The answer is that once again Metternich was trying to sell something that others might have given away, in this case a mortgage on Austria's future. If alliance with France was desir-

---

[58] Text in HHSA, *Staatskanzlei, Vorträge,* Fasc. 269; also in Metternich, *N.P.,* II, 311–312.
[59] *ibid.*

able in any case, why not throw it into the bargaining while there was still a chance to gain a return on it? A strong Austria should be a more desirable ally than a weak one. The idea was by no means fantastic. Because of it Alexander kept silent about Galicia; because of it Frederick William sent Knesebeck to Comorn. It might even have been mentioned by Champagny or Savary when Metternich was their prisoner in Vienna, although there is no record of it in those talks. At any rate, Napoleon himself had offered to spare the empire if Francis abdicated, and Metternich knew that the offer was dictated by solid, well-calculated French interests. That being the case, an Austrian offer of alliance in exchange for territorial integrity stood a good chance of success. It was permission to make such an offer that he sought in the report of August 10—on the surface a document of despair, in reality an expression of audacious optimism. In it, for example, he spoke of closing Austria's harbors to England—in the peace she ultimately signed Austria had no harbors to close.

There was one obstacle: the abdication. For this reason the utmost delicacy was required. On the one hand, one had to be careful how the project was broached to Francis; on the other, one was dealing with Napoleon's prejudices, and prejudices are always more difficult to discuss than interests. It must have occurred to Metternich, therefore, that the abdication would actually be the easy way out. Yet, at least in the early stages of the negotiations, he was always forcefully against such a step, partly because he thought he could carry the negotiation off without sacrificing his master, partly because he believed an abdication would forfeit Napoleon's respect and place the monarchy on a level with the toadying states of the Rheinbund. *Mutual* security through alliance and disarmament was to be his case at Altenburg, not an ignominious, one-sided sacrifice by Austria.[60]

How then guarantee Austria's good behavior? Part of the pledge would be the alliance itself, but beyond that Metternich

---

[60] Metternich's *Vortrag*, "Points de vue sur la marche à suivre dans la négotiation qui va s'ouvrir à Altenbourg, août 1809," submitted 11 Aug. 1809, HHSA, *Staatskanzlei, Vorträge*, Fasc. 269.

hoped that Napoleon would be satisfied with the banishment of the war party. Seen in this light, his treatment of Stadion's attempts to resign acquires added significance: the foreign minister would be sacrificed in place of the emperor. When Stadion on July 22 submitted his resignation a second time, Metternich raised strenuous objections and again dissuaded the emperor from accepting it.[61] "If I succeed in getting Stadion to stay in office," he wrote his mother shortly afterwards, "I shall be the happiest man in the world." But, he cautioned her, "do not breathe a word of all this to anybody, either the family of Stadion or any other individual; the negotiation itself would suffer from it." [62] On the face of things the resignation of a minister and the abdication of an emperor were hardly commensurable. But Metternich, who grasped Napoleon's problems almost as well as Napoleon himself, apparently believed that it would be enough to show him that Francis had repudiated the French and German émigrés, that Austrian policy henceforth would be made by men who accepted the new order. One of his tasks at Altenburg, therefore, would be to convince Napoleon that he was one of those men, despite his *reichsgräfliche* background, despite his part in the coming of the war. Indeed, he might turn that background to his advantage. Who could better symbolize the new attitude in Austria than one who had lost his ancestral estates to France, yet counseled forgiveness and a fresh start?

No one was very much surprised that Champagny arrived at Altenburg two days late or that his first move, when the conference opened on August 18, was to demand acceptance of the *uti possidetis* as the basis of negotiation. According to Napoleon's plan, Metternich should then have made a counteroffer, inaugurating a give and take discussion which would end with a rough estimate of the total population and area that Austria should cede. This gambit had the advantage of consuming time, yet making some progress while awaiting news from Alexander, which would indicate the particular territories that could be

[61] Rössler, *Österreichs Kampf*, II, 56.
[62] Metternich to his mother, 25 July 1809, *op.cit.*, I, 232.

named.[63] Instead, Metternich seized the initiative. Did the *uti possidetis*, he asked, include the territory held by Napoleon's allies? Champagny said it did, the Russian occupation of Galicia included. "We do not know we are in a war with them," the Austrian replied, then added that if France was authorized to speak for the Russians, why did Champagny not show his plenary powers to that effect? [64] Champagny's silence was more important than any reply: Franco-Russian relations were as uncertain as Metternich had believed. The way was clear to work for Austria's main objective, and not to haggle about separate provinces.

Why, Metternich continued, should Austria have to accept such a cruel basis when a defeated Russia had gained at Tilsit both territory and an alliance? Austria was tired of being a third person in a room with two others who were continually flirting; that, he said, was "the true cause of the present war." Austria would make a more reliable ally than Russia: "let us enter your system and you could be sure of us." [65] Who first mentioned the word alliance cannot be determined. In his reports to Napoleon Champagny quotes himself as saying at this point: "You speak of alliance, M. de Metternich, but before we can think of that we must first conclude a peace treaty." [66] According to Metternich, however, Champagny asked *him* if Austria desired an alliance, whereupon he replied: "The word alliance is premature . . . before peace has even been made; but such ought to be the result of it." [67] On the surface this was nothing but a matter of claiming credit for a witty rejoinder. Underneath, however, the contradictory reports revealed a fundamental issue: whether, as Metternich hoped, the offer of alliance could be used to ameliorate the peace terms; or whether, as Champagny implied, Austria would be driven to

[63] Vandal, *Napoléon et Alexandre*, II, 126.

[64] Metternich to Francis, 18 Aug. 1809, HHSA, *Staatskanzlei, Frankreich, Berichte,* Fasc. 293.

[65] Quotations from Champagny's report of 18 Aug. 1809 in both Vandal, *Napoléon et Alexandre*, II, 132–133; and Wertheimer, *Geschichte Oesterreichs*, II, 398.

[66] Quoted *ibid.*, II, 398.

[67] Metternich to Francis, 18 Aug. 1809, *loc.cit.*

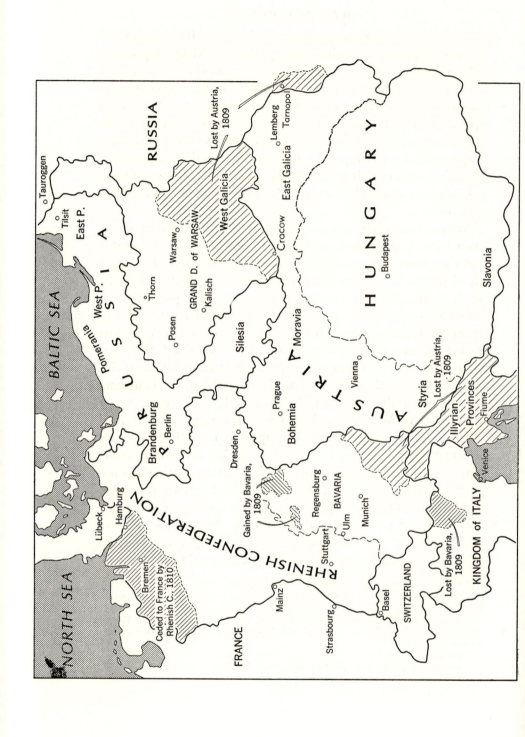

alliance with France regardless of the peace terms. Which it would be still depended in large measure on Russia and the problem of Galicia.

To strengthen the French case in St. Petersburg Bonaparte now demanded that a detailed record or *procès-verbal* be kept of the proceedings, hoping by suitable editing to make France appear magnanimous in her demands. Metternich was furious at the protocols Champagny presented of the early sessions but finally acquiesced, provided that he be allowed to insert retroactive rejoinders to his opponent's fictitious statements. "The respective ministers have not come together to write a novel," he complained, and cautioned Francis to consider the protocols "entirely null as to what was said." [68] For the rest, Champagny continued to ask, on the basis of the *uti possidetis,* what provinces Austria was willing to exchange to regain Vienna, and Metternich continued to insist that the emperor could not trade one of his provinces for another that was already rightfully his. What Bonaparte really wanted to know was how Austria rated Galicia in her system of priorities and, to find out, he finally authorized Champagny on August 25 to suggest informally Salzburg and Upper Austria to the Enns for Bavaria, leaving it to Austria to make the next move. Again Metternich refused to speak out. Although he was reasonably sure that West Galicia, which he considered Austria's most expendable province, was scheduled to be added to the Duchy of Warsaw, he would not consent to its loss until he knew the fate of the parts of Galicia held by Galitzin—whether they would go to Russia or would be used to give Russia, as he put it, "the honor of having worked for the aggrandizement of Poland." [69] Hence he clung to his original position: France must first present her total demands; then Austria would make her counterproposals.

In the meantime he turned his attention to the growth of the ever present third force in Galicia, the "fanatical" army of Poniatowski. When Austrian intelligence officers estimated its strength in mid-August at 60,000 against the 55,000 of Galit-

---

[68] Metternich to Francis, 21 and 23 Aug. 1809, HHSA, *Staatskanzlei, Frankreich, Berichte,* Fasc. 293.
[69] Metternich to Francis, 25 Aug. 1809, *ibid.*

zin's army, Metternich concluded that even were Alexander to reply favorably to Francis' letter, it would take all his energy merely to pin down the Poles. "To come to our aid in any other way lies outside its possibility," he said of the Russian force.[70] That was the best that could happen; the worst was that Russia might conclude she had no choice but to appease Bonaparte and cooperate with the Poles after all. Indeed. according to the reports of General Mohr, sent by Francis on August 19 to treat with the Russian commanders in Galicia, the latter eventuality seemed the more probable. Most Russian officers continued to express sympathy for Austria but said their orders were to enter Hungary while the Poles fell upon Moravia and Bohemia.[71] In either case cultivation of the Poles was indicated.

This was the background for another remarkable memorandum which Metternich placed before the emperor about August 23.[72] In it he raised the possibility of winning the Poles to "the common Austro-Prussian cause," both to "eliminate a great advantage to Napoleon" and to be able to turn them loose on the Russians in Galicia. This would mean the abandonment of all Galicia save for what was necessary to a good military frontier, but, he pointed out, Austria already did without the resources of the province, and "a conquest of the same is not thinkable without very successful blows at the great French army." To interest the Poles he offered a six-point program: Prussia to renounce her claims to Warsaw; Austria to do the same for Galicia; Poland to be restored under a Polish king; an alliance concluded between Austria, Prussia, England, Turkey, Spain, Portugal, and Sicily; Austria to be compensated for Galicia in Germany or Italy; and the Polish army to come immediately under Austrian command.

For obvious reasons this plan has usually been considered sheer fantasy, a kind of momentary delirium in the head of a

---

[70] Undated *Vortrag* in HHSA, *Staatskanzlei, Vorträge*, Fasc. 270.

[71] Demelitsch, *Metternich und seine auswärtige Politik*, 35.

[72] The memorandum is undated (see note 70 above). This guess at the date is based on the fact that the document is appended to an order from Francis to Stadion of August 24. Internal evidence precludes any date more than a week earlier. Both the memorandum and Francis' order are in turn appended to Stadion's critique of the plan which is dated Sept. 1. HHSA, *Staatskanzlei, Vorträge*, Fasc. 270.

normally sober diplomat.[73] Stadion thought of it mainly as a means to put pressure on Russia, despite Metternich's statement in the memorandum itself that it was too late for that kind of manuever. Actually there is nothing mysterious about the plan. In order to play France and Russia against each other, it was desirable to be in contact with the third party over which they disputed. Hitherto Metternich had at most been in a position to use Napoleon's solicitude for Poland to goad Russia; contact with Poniatowski would enable him to translate any concessions Napoleon might make to Russia into provocation of the Poles. To establish contact the main thing was to have a program that would gain their ears; it was not necessary that the program be in all details compatible with Austria's other relations—those with Prussia, for instance, which could hardly be described as constituting a "common Austro-Prussian cause." What Metternich really expected from Poland was about what he expected from Prussia, a tentative, potentially amicable relationship that might be used as trading material with Napoleon. If Poniatowski responded favorably, well and good; if he did not, Napoleon would hear of the offer and would have objective evidence that Austria, unlike Russia, posed no obstacle to a Polish restoration. Metternich was often to return to such a solution in the years ahead, though never with success. Regrettably, the evidence regarding his motives is slight. But the project must have had more to commend it to Francis than the seemingly bizarre surface features; in a secret mission of Prince Dietrichstein to the headquarters of Poniatowski it was undertaken and was actually in progress when the first opportunity came for making use of the contact.[74]

On September 1 Count Alexander Chernyshev, a Russian colonel, dismounted in Vienna, bearing two messages from the tsar. One was a note to Napoleon to the effect that Russia, instead of attending the peace conference, would leave her interests in French hands. The other was a reply to the Austrian

---

[73] Cf. Demelitsch, *Metternich und seine auswärtige Politik,* 39, who calls it "fantastic"; Beer, *Zehn Jahre,* 434–435, who calls it "peculiar"; and Rössler, *Österreichs Kampf,* II, 58, who, with Stadion, considers it "psychologically false."

[74] On the Dietrichstein mission see Emil Kipa, *Austria a sprawa Polska w r. 1809* (Warsaw, 1952).

note of July 30, and said simply that Russia considered the French position compatible with the interests of Austria and Russia. Essentially it was a refusal of aid and cast a shadow over imperial headquarters at Comorn, where Chernyshev delivered it on September 3. Yet Napoleon was disappointed too, since the tsar had still not defined the Russian interest in Poland. There was nothing to do now but hope that Caulaincourt's next dispatch would clarify the matter. In the meantime, fearing that Austria would brook no further delays, he ordered Champagny to reserve the question of Galicia but accelerate the discussion of Salzburg, Upper Austria, the littoral, and several districts in Bohemia. If successful in these regions, France could demand less in Galicia and thus reduce the risk of antagonizing Alexander.[75]

Metternich was ready for the new turn and saw advantages in it. He correctly surmised that it was "the result of news from St. Petersburg" and that it signified an intent to appease Russia.[76] The omission of Galicia from the day's protocol, he told the emperor on September 5, offered "a great *point d'appui* for the Polish negotiation," [77] and gave Austria the chance to hammer on the province as a wedge between France and Russia. When Champagny informally called Galicia "a secondary matter" and promised that it would never mean the restoration of Poland, Metternich jauntily replied that a Polish king, far from worrying Austria, might be "a certain and useful ally." [78] Accordingly, the Austrian counterproject, which he introduced on September 9, contained a voluntary offer of West Galicia. As for the non-Polish provinces, Austria refused to cede the littoral and the Bohemian districts under any circumstances, and agreed to the cession of Salzburg and the Inn district only against indemnification in the Tyrol—preferably by annexation but, if necessary, by awarding the province to Archduke Anton, who was still due the compensation denied him when Mergentheim was joined to Würtemberg. To lend

[75] Vandal, *Napoléon et Alexandre*, II, 134–140.
[76] Metternich to Francis, 5 Sept. 1809, HHSA, *Staatskanzlei, Frankreich, Berichte*, Fasc. 293.
[77] *ibid.*
[78] *ibid.*

force to Austria's position Metternich requested the emperor's permission to threaten the termination of the armistice.[79]

At Comorn, meanwhile, Napoleon's demands created an atmosphere of desperation. On the surface all was determination. Stadion was summoned back to headquarters. On September 3 Napoleon proposed an extension of the armistice and Francis rejected it. On the 10th Friedrich Stadion urged a war to the finish, advising the emperor that all South Germany should be annexed to Austria.[80] News of the British landing and the myth that Russia withheld aid solely because of Austrian timidity were grounds for hope, but by this time the enthusiasm was forced. Under the supreme command of Prince Liechtenstein the army was even less warlike than under Archduke Carl. Before, the war party had been naïvely confident; now it was consciously clutching at straws, driven on, as Stadion put it, simply because Napoleon offered only a choice between immediate destruction and slow strangulation.[81]

Under the circumstances the emperor can hardly be blamed for his next move. Before taking the final plunge into war he decided to have one more try at an honorable peace, this time sending General Bubna to plead personally with Napoleon. The latter regarded the mission as an attempt to convince him that Austria would be a trustworthy ally even if Stadion remained foreign minister. Hence, at the first interview on September 10, he took pains to deny this hypothesis. Francis, Napoleon said, always listened to his last advisor, who was usually Stadion, and Stadion listened to his "turbulent brother." Ferdinand and Carl, he added, were more trustworthy.[82] Nevertheless, he did not explicitly demand Francis' abdication as the price of alliance, and though he refused to change his territorial demands, he expressly withdrew the *uti possidetis* as the negotiating base. His position was noticeably softer.

It did not remain so. On September 12 the long-awaited re-

[79] Metternich to Francis, 6, 7, 9, and 11 Sept. 1809, HHSA, *Staatskanzlei, Frankreich, Berichte,* Fasc. 293.

[80] Friedrich Stadion's memorandum of 10 Sept. 1809, HHSA, *Staatskanzlei, Kriegsakten,* Fasc. 488.

[81] Rössler, *Österreichs Kampf,* II, 62.

[82] Napoleon to Champagny, 10 Sept. 1809, in Napoléon, *Correspondance,* XIX, 446–448.

port from Caulaincourt arrived, containing the information that Alexander had at last agreed to allow something to the Poles, though he still refused to say whether he would be satisfied with a share smaller than theirs. Meager as the information was, Napoleon decided to go ahead. In his final interview with Bubna on the 15th he gave Austria her choice: a peace without cessions if Francis abdicated in favor of Ferdinand, or a peace with territorial losses equivalent to those of Pressburg—2,000,000 souls in Germany and the littoral, to be reassigned at his discretion, and an equal number from Galicia to be divided between Russia and the Duchy of Warsaw. This meant a reduction of Napoleon's population demands to 4,000,000, which corresponded to the Pressburg formula.[83] While Bubna carried the new offer to Comorn, Napoleon dispatched it to Champagny at Altenburg, instructing him to present the territorial demands officially as a "moderate ultimatum." As for the abdication, he told his envoy to be sure Metternich understood "that if the present emperor wanted to leave the throne to the Grand Duke of Würzburg for any reason whatever, I would leave the monarchy intact."[84] Even gout, he suggested, could be adduced to make Francis' exit less humiliating.

For Metternich the week of the Bubna mission was a wretched one. At the very time he was trying to heighten the pressure on Napoleon the undertaking betrayed weakness and canceled the psychological effect of Stadion's return. More important, it took the initiative out of his hands just when the prospects of gaining a French alliance were unusually promising. It was, in short, both a personal affront and a tactical blunder, and Metternich made little effort to hide his feelings. "I see with pain," he told the emperor on seeing the first reports, "that the Count Bubna does not sufficiently keep himself on guard against the phrases that one makes to him." Besides, he added, there was no reason to change procedure since "our course up to the present time has been perfectly correct."[85]

[83] Vandal, *Napoléon et Alexandre*, II, 149–153.
[84] Napoleon to Champagny, 15 Sept. 1809, in Napoléon, *Correspondance*, XIX, 474f.
[85] Metternich to Francis, 12 Sept. 1809, HHSA, *Staatskanzlei, Frankreich, Berichte*, Fasc. 293.

So far as his own role was concerned, he did not change course. The so-called moderate ultimatum he considered a trick, warning that the reduction of population demands was meaningless unless the exact territories, with their varying military and economic assets, were specified.[86] He also continued to urge more strenuous military efforts, and this time his advice was heeded. Angered by the harsh ultimatum, the Emperor Francis ordered him to reject it and to announce the termination of the armistice. Metternich, however, unlike Baldacci and Stadion, who really meant to fight on, continued to think of military pressure primarily as a means of promoting his true objective, territorial integrity in exchange for alliance. That this was also Napoleon's first choice was now more evident than ever. There remained the abdication question, and on this Metternich wavered for the first time. On September 18 he apparently told Champagny that the emperor was noble enough to abdicate, provided that the *independence* as well as the *integrity* of the monarchy was respected. Interpreting this as a plea that Austria should not be required to join the Rheinbund, Napoleon immediately instructed Champagny to give the necessary assurances.[87] The trouble was that Metternich lacked orders to speak for the emperor, and on an issue of such delicacy he believed that no mere minister could offer advice. Hence, when the matter came up again four days later, he simply commented on its anti-monarchical implications; [88] more he could not do until a decision had been reached at Comorn. There, on September 25, at a conference attended by Stadion, Liechtenstein, Bellegarde, and the emperor, the decision was made. There would be no abdication. Instead, Prince Liechtenstein would proceed to Vienna to accept the ultimatum as the basis of negotiation, but within its somewhat vague terms he would fight for amelioration.[89]

Although it was not Francis' intention to remove Metternich from the negotiation, the Liechtenstein mission had that effect.

<hr />

[86] Metternich to Francis, 15 Sept. 1809, HHSA, *Staatskanzlei, Frankreich, Berichte,* Fasc. 293.

[87] Napoleon to Champagny, 21 Sept. 1809, in Napoléon, *Correspondance,* XIX, 435f.

[88] Chroust, *Geschichte . . . Würzburgs,* 318–319.

[89] Rössler, *Österreichs Kampf,* II, 72–75.

Pausing at Altenburg on his way to Vienna, the prince informed Metternich of the plenary powers he carried and instructed him to return to Comorn, without however dissolving the congress. The *Staats-Minister* was dumbfounded. Ranting that no one at Comorn understood the situation, he predicted the mission would fail and wrote Francis that, regardless of Austria's intentions, Napoleon would surely recall Champagny. In this he was right. Subjecting Liechtenstein to one of his famous outbursts of temper, Bonaparte declared the congress ended and insisted that if peace was not signed at Vienna it would not be signed at all. Francis, meanwhile, impressed by Metternich's opinion, ordered Liechtenstein to say that Austria considered the congress merely transferred to Vienna. Napoleon answered that he would treat with Metternich no more, and branded him one of the authors of the war.[90]

It was a surprising turn, considering his previous regard for the *Staats-Minister* whose presence at Altenburg he had specifically requested. Some have held that the reason for the change was Napoleon's desire to remove such an able opponent; others, including Metternich himself, explained it as a clever ruse to keep Liechtenstein, the head of the army, from properly attending to military preparations.[91] It is more likely, however, that the *volte face* was simply a natural consequence of Francis' decision not to abdicate. Since Austria had opted for the harsh territorial peace, it was only logical to deal with someone closely identified with that solution. Conversely, having dropped the project of alliance, Napoleon also dropped its most consistent advocate. Indeed, it is not too much to say that ever since the days of captivity in Vienna Metternich's relationship to Napoleon had been governed mainly by that one idea. Upon its repudiation, the *Staats-Minister* found himself excluded from all further participation in the negotiation. In this way, ironically, he met the same fate he had envisaged for Stadion: he was sacrificed to appease the enemy.

As far as Metternich's personal interests were concerned, it was probably just as well. His skillful maneuvering at Alten-

---

[90] Wertheimer, *Geschichte Oesterreichs*, II, 422–423.
[91] *ibid.*, II, 423; Metternich, *N.P.*, I, 93; and Lauber, *Metternichs Kampf*, 31.

burg had depended on several cards that could no longer be played: the possibility of war, the possibility of abdication, and for a time Napoleon's uncertainty about Russia. Liechtenstein's performance must be judged in this light. The peace he initialed on October 14 at Schönbrunn met virtually all Napoleon's demands. The German lands that Austria ceded were Salzburg, Berchtesgaden, the Inn district, and part of the Hausrück district. These were given to Napoleon "in order to be made part of the Rhenish Confederation and to be disposed in favor of the sovereigns of the Confederation." [92] In this way Napoleon served notice on the king of Bavaria that his acquisition of the provinces depended upon his making cessions elsewhere to sovereigns who could not profit directly from the booty. Strategically the cessions ruined Austria's defenses toward Germany and moved the border of the Rheinbund perilously close to Vienna. Galicia was partitioned according to the formula previously discussed. West Galicia, with Cracow, was added to the Duchy of Warsaw while Russia's share, the Tarnopol district, one-fourth as large, was taken from East Galicia. The remainder of East Galicia as well as a half-interest in the salt mines at Wieliczka remained with Austria. In the region nearer the Adriatic Görtz, Carniola, Villach, Croatia, the Austrian littoral with Trieste, and the Hungarian littoral with Fiume, were ceded to Napoleon to be made into the Illyrian Provinces under direct French rule.

In other provisions Austria renounced Archduke Anton's claims to Mergentheim; recognized the suppression of the Teutonic order and the other property confiscations in the Rheinbund; permitted Napoleon to finish collecting the taxes he had already levied in the occupied provinces; and accorded a complete amnesty to the Polish rebels in the unceded portions of Galicia. In return Napoleon granted a similar amnesty to the rebels of the Tyrol. A series of secret articles continued the dismal story. An indemnity of 85,000,000 guilders was imposed in addition to the heavy indebtedness already incurred. Austria's military strength, including all types of militia, was

---

[92] Text of treaty in Martens, *Nouveau recueil*, I, 210ff. Secret articles given in full in Demelitsch, *Metternich und seine auswärtige Politik*, 70–72.

limited to 150,000. Finally, perhaps the most humiliating provision because it infringed sovereignty, though not the most oppressive, required the emperor to dismiss from his service all those who had been born in old France, in Piedmont, or Venetia, and even to deport them upon request from Paris. Altogether the monarchy lost about 3,500,000 subjects, and provinces with lucrative revenues, as well as all its maritime commerce, including the trade with England.

Despite the severity of Napoleon's demands, during the negotiations he surprisingly returned to a practice of flattering the Austrians and even broached the possibility of a marriage at some level of the Bonaparte and Habsburg family hierarchies.[93] This solicitude had its painful side, for it showed how much Bonaparte still valued a rapprochement, and thereby supported Metternich's thesis that a peace without cessions had been within reach. Nevertheless, it also implied that there was room in the postwar world for advocates of Franco-Austrian collaboration, and this is undoubtedly why Napoleon did not protest Metternich's appointment as foreign minister. It may also explain why natives of the Rhineland were not included among the officials whose dismissal was required in the treaty. Thus the former *Reichsgraf* had salvaged something from the Altenburg congress after all: his personal dissociation from the war party. That he could win a certain measure of confidence from Napoleon despite all he had done to bring on the war was a tribute to his imaginative planning. That at the same time he was spared the opprobrium that went with negotiating the cruel peace was sheer chance, a piece of luck which, owing to his smug belief that he could have done better, he never fully appreciated. On October 6 Stadion officially resigned and two days later Metternich became foreign minister. The years of apprenticeship were over, climaxed by the kind of ordeal few diplomats ever have to undergo—a struggle for the very existence of the state.

[93] *ibid.*, 48–49.

CHAPTER V

1809–1812: THE CONTEST SUSPENDED

With the advantage of historical perspective it is natural to view the intervals of peace in the Napoleonic epoch as periods of preparation for the next war. Yet the men who lived through that era usually thought of themselves, at the end of each conflict, as living in a postwar world. This was especially true of Austria in 1809, since both the scale of the war effort and the harshness of the peace were beyond anything hitherto experienced. The mood was akin to that of the American South in 1865, of France in 1871, or of Germany in 1919. It was a mood of despair for the future and recriminations about the past. It could almost be argued that the army had not been defeated but rather betrayed at the conference table, though this was the contention of the civilian war party rather than that of the generals. Both a large war debt and a heavy indemnity had to be borne by an economy at least thirty per cent weaker than before the war and, until the first installment was paid, an army of occupation would remain on Austrian soil.

As for future payments, they could be made only by extraordinary tax levies that would antagonize the separate provinces, and call into question the loyalty of the lands joined by the Pragmatic Sanction. Here was the Achilles' heel of the old dynastic state of Austria: that the centralized, efficient institutions required by the times could not be introduced without risking the defection of the historic political entities. That had been the lesson of Joseph II. That is what Stadion meant when he said that the treaty amounted to slow strangulation as opposed to immediate destruction. That is why Metternich held the treaty to be a device whereby Bonaparte hoped to bring about the partition of the monarchy which he had failed to achieve by arms. This fear of impending dissolution, as it turned out, proved to be exaggerated, but it was genuine; it was the minister without portfolio at every state conference; and its appreciation is just as fundamental to understanding

Metternich's policy in the interlude between the wars as it was in assessing Cobenzl's course after the Imperial Recess.

The crown was further diminished in prestige by the clauses of the treaty which touched on honor: Austria must discharge and perhaps deport a group of loyal servants while extending forgiveness to disloyal subjects in Galicia. To be sure, Austria's followers in the Tyrol were likewise entitled to amnesty, but as no means existed to enforce the right, there was nothing the emperor could do when, for example, Andreas Hofer was executed in Mantua early in 1810. Externally Austria was more isolated than ever, for the peace treaty, while requiring her to join the continental system against England, neither provided an alliance with France nor canceled the Franco-Russian alliance of Tilsit. As for Germany, Napoleon had obviously won, and nothing but his death or some unforeseen catastrophe could make resumption of the contest possible.

Such was the melancholy situation which awaited Metternich as he took up his new duties in the *Ballhaus*, and his personal position was hardly better. Some, like Archduke Carl and Prince Liechtenstein, knew him only as a principal instigator of the catastrophe; others, like Baldacci, deplored his pro-French proclivities; and gossips on all sides spread the rumor that he had schemed his way into office behind Stadion's back—a view which Stadion, to his credit, did not share. In diplomatic circles he was known as a clever manipulator but, in comparison to Stadion, a man with little strength of character. Even his old friend Gentz was critical, deploring the seeming levity with which the new foreign minister approached his grave responsibilities. To all appearances, therefore, Metternich's acceptability to the Emperor Francis was even more of a wonder than his acceptability to Napoleon.[1]

There were good reasons for Francis' choice. Except for the discarded ministers of the past—some even wanted to recall Thugut from retirement—Metternich was the most experienced diplomat available, a professional in an age that commonly gave diplomatic assignments to generals. His service

[1] Rössler, *Österreichs Kampf*, II, 89ff.; Demelitsch, *Metternich und seine auswärtige Politik*, 76ff.; and Oncken, *Oesterreich und Preussen*, II, 52ff.

antedated not only the acts of mediatization of 1806 but also the Imperial Recess of 1803, and his marriage with the house of Kaunitz did much to blur his identification with the German émigrés, whom Napoleon and Carl alike blamed for the war. During the peace negotiations, moreover, when Stadion, for example, had at least broached the possibility of Francis' abdication, Metternich had remained discreetly silent, exhibiting a personal loyalty and an equally important sense of propriety that the emperor could not but appreciate. It is also just possible that Francis turned to Metternich simply because he preferred his program to any other that was offered.

To a remarkable degree Metternich's program was that already outlined in the memorandum of August 10, just before the Altenburg conference. If "adapting ourselves to the triumphant French system" had been the part of wisdom for the intact and relatively strong Austria which he had envisaged at that time, it was all the more necessary now that the monarchy was weak and Napoleon openly distrustful of its rulers. The first need was a period of repose which would allow Austria to straighten out her finances, reorganize the army, and unify her chaotic internal administration. Only Napoleon could guarantee a respite from external threats, and only he could provide relief by moderating the terms of the treaty. It was also possible that the considerations which had once inclined him to offer the integrity of the monarchy still played a part in his plans. Hence the dominant theme of Metternich's postwar policy was rapprochement with France, and to this end he bent every effort, inside and outside the country. He kept the Russian colony in Vienna under constant police surveillance and expelled the Russian diplomat, Count Carl Pozzo di Borgo, Napoleon's most formidable Corsican foe. The diehards of the old war party in Austria he endeavored to remove from the vicinity of the emperor, and he issued a directive to all state officials forbidding public airing of their political views.[2]

As for public opinion, Metternich discovered that it was more difficult to dispel the spirit of chauvinism than it had been to generate it. Within weeks of assuming office he was

[2] Rössler, *Österreichs Kampf*, II, 109f.

forced to make a decision. In late November anti-French dem-
onstrations were evoked by a play at the *Theater an der Wien*
and were quickly reported in Paris, where they caused angry
speeches against Austria in the *Corps législatif*. Determined
that nothing must disturb Franco-Austrian relations, Metternich ordered a tight censorship of the theater, forbidding any
allusions to current politics. Even Schiller's *Wilhelm Tell* was
edited so as to eliminate possible parallels with the Tyrol.[3]
A trifling episode perhaps, but it started Metternich on what
was certainly the most odious practice of his career, the suppression of free expression in the interests of foreign policy.

It would be unfair to judge the Rhenish nobleman by the
standards of a society with long traditions of freedom in such
matters—not merely in the sense that he could not be expected
to take the issue so seriously, but also because he knew that a
government which *could* legally suppress certain sentiments and
did not would be judged abroad as approving them. As an
absolute monarchy Austria did not enjoy the peculiar advantage of the established liberal society, in which an unfettered
and diversified public opinion often serves foreign policy by
throwing up a smoke screen of babble which bewilders the
enemy. Napoleon, himself a practiced manipulator of public
opinion, was certain to regard anti-French outbursts as reflections of the government's attitude and not of mere private
opinion. If Austria was not actually at war, her situation was an
abnormal one, her very existence, in Metternich's view, perhaps
depending on the success of his diplomacy. The same reasoning
that had originally prompted the propaganda campaign now
dictated its suppression.

The first great victory of Metternich's foreign policy was the
marriage of Francis' daughter, Marie Louise, to Napoleon.
Although Napoleon's principal motive was to acquire an heir,
there is no doubt that political alignment ran fecundity a close
second in his appraisal of a bride. When he had rejected Austria
in favor of Russia, on signing the treaty of Schönbrunn, he also
initiated a suit at St. Petersburg for the hand of the Grand

[3] Demelitsch, *Metternich und seine auswärtige Politik*, 110–111.

122

Duchess Anna Pavlovna, sister of the tsar.[4] As a hedge against failure, however, he had to consider alternatives. Any of the Rheinbund princes would have jumped at the chance, but in a union of that kind there were no political advantages, but rather the very real disadvantage, always inherent in Rheinbund dealings, of antagonizing all the sovereigns not favored. One possible exception, the House of Wettin in Saxony, which had a European status of sorts because of the Duchy of Warsaw, would be certain to rekindle Alexander's fears about Poland. The only real alternative to a Russian princess was therefore an Austrian one, and Napoleon dropped hints to that effect throughout the fall of 1809.[5]

To Metternich the advantages of such a marriage were so obvious that he would no doubt have pressed the cause in any circumstances, but the knowledge that Bonaparte's first choice was Anna Pavlovna left him no option: he must forestall an act that would perpetuate the Tilsit partnership. Just as the nation must sacrifice liberty on the altar of foreign policy so must the emperor sacrifice his daughter. With the aid of his wife, the *Gräfin* Eleanor, who had remained in Paris during the war, Metternich launched a campaign of backstairs intrigue and conventional diplomatic negotiation that was finally crowned with success. When Napoleon, on February 7, 1810, announced his decision in favor of Marie Louise, Metternich's successor in Paris, Prince Schwarzenberg, made haste to initial the pact without waiting for Francis to approve.[6] The project was too important to allow the father of the bride to interfere, and to make doubly sure that all went smoothly, Metternich himself escorted the princess to Paris to meet her husband.

Although the marriage was undoubtedly a personal triumph for Metternich, its importance lay more in what it prevented than in what it achieved. It averted a Franco-Russian dynastic union and, by linking Napoleon's power to the unsteady Austrian throne, helped to restore Francis' authority over lands

---

[4] Srbik, *Metternich*, III (1954), 47.
[5] Vandal, *Napoléon et Alexandre*, II, 167–198; Demelitsch, *Metternich und seine auswärtige Politik*, 146.
[6] *ibid.*, 165.

which the war had brought to the verge of dissolution. Then and ever afterwards Metternich's thesis was that the Austrian emperor needed Napoleon's prestige just as much as Napoleon needed the Habsburgs' ancient lineage.[7] The positive results of the marriage, however, were meager. The main purpose of Metternich's visit to Paris was to exploit the nuptial atmosphere to obtain modification of the onerous peace terms. Nowhere did he succeed conspicuously. Napoleon granted some privileges to Austrian merchants in the Illyrian provinces, but he would not restore the territory to Austrian sovereignty. Payments on the indemnity were made easier, and some of the installments were deferred, but Austria had to pay the extra interest charges, and the total amount remained at the figure stated in the treaty, 85 million. A commercial treaty Metternich initialed was regarded so unfavorably in Vienna that it was never ratified. Despite the celebrated marriage, Napoleon, it was clear, was determined to uphold the treaty he had imposed. Rapprochement and revisionism were not the same thing.[8]

Oddly enough, on one matter which had nothing to do with the peace treaty itself, Metternich scored a substantial victory, one "infinitely more complete than one could have expected," as he called it.[9] This was the restitution of the properties seized in April, 1809, from the mediatized nobility in the Austrian service. In a convention signed August 30, 1810,[10] Napoleon rescinded the confiscation order on condition that the owners recognize the sovereignty of the respective Rheinbund rulers and agree to transfer their estates to another member of the family should they decide to remain in Austria. Although the conditions were nothing more than a restatement of the provisions of the Rheinbund Act in this regard, they were especially convenient to the Metternich family, for as long as Franz Georg lived, Clemens could serve Austria without jeopardizing the family title to Ochsenhausen. For Stadion, however, the results

[7] See Metternich's important *Vortrag* of 17 Jan. 1811, in *N.P.*, II, 411–412.
[8] Demelitsch, *Metternich und seine auswärtige Politik*, 175 and 204ff.; Rössler, *Österreichs Kampf*, II, 94.
[9] Metternich to the Emperor Francis, 5 Sept. 1810, *N.P.*, II, 394.
[10] Text in Philipp Anton Guido von Meyer (ed.), *Corpus Juris Confoederationis Germanicae*, I (Frankfurt, 1858), 117–118.

were less satisfactory. On the specious grounds that the Stadion fief at Chodenschloss had always been a Würtemberg dependency and therefore never *reichsunmittelbar,* the king of Würtemberg refused to restore the property. Napoleon did nothing, possibly because he desired to make an example of Stadion as he had once made an example of the duke of Enghien. Metternich protested, and the Emperor Francis retaliated by impounding certain assets of Würtemberg in Austria, but to no avail. Stadion continued to reside in Bohemia as a ward of the emperor.[11]

With respect to the revenue involved, the convention of restitution was almost a detail, having no bearing on Austria's financial burdens, and Napoleon probably viewed it as a technicality. Its political overtones, however, were more significant, for even as a gesture it signified that Austria had a certain ascendancy over the Rheinbund states in Napoleon's system, almost as if the Habsburgs were once again able to protect the old *reichunmittelbare* aristocrats against the greater *Reichsstände.* It came, moreover, at a time when a new crisis was brewing in Napoleon's relations with his German clients.

Immediately after the war no one had been more popular in the Rheinbund than the great conqueror with his bag of provinces to distribute. Stopping at Munich, Stuttgart, and Karlsruhe on his return from Vienna in October, 1809, he had made lavish promises. In November and December the sovereigns followed him to Paris, partly to plead their cases in person but even more to keep an eye on each other.[12] The ensuing negotiations were painful; they took place during the first few months of 1810, and required Napoleon to make many invidious distinctions. His first difficulty came when he decided that the Tyrolean passes were too important to be returned to Bavaria alone, and so divided the South Tyrol between the Kingdom of Italy and the new province of Illyria. The Bavarians thereupon resisted the surrender of Swabian territories to Würtemberg, and Franconian lands to Würzburg and Saxony, to which

[11] Rössler, *Österreichs Kampf,* II, 98–99.
[12] Hölzle, *Württemberg im Zeitalter,* 40–42; Doeberl, *Entwicklungsgeschichte Bayerns,* II, 375f.

they had previously been resigned. In the end Bavaria ceded 170,000 souls, receiving Bayreuth and Regensburg as compensation, in addition, of course, to Salzburg, Berchtesgaden, and the Inn and Hausrück districts from Austria.[13] The transfer of Regensburg in turn necessitated an indemnity for the Prince Primate, Dalberg, which was provided by giving him Fulda and Hanau and, as an extra fillip, elevating his territory at Frankfurt to the rank of a grand duchy.[14]

All regular petitioners sooner or later learn that requests must always be far in excess of expectations, and in this art no one excelled King Frederick of Würtemberg. Having fielded a contingent double the size Napoleon had assigned, he thought himself entitled not only to generous portions of Bavarian Swabia and Franconia, but also to the two sovereign Hohenzollern principalities and the entire state of Baden. The grand duke of Baden could be transferred to Hanover, which had not yet been awarded. Though never intending favors of such magnitude, Napoleon had nevertheless mentioned at Stuttgart a very generous gain of 200,000 inhabitants; but after the South Tyrol decision he had to back down. In April, 1810, he forced the king's plenipotentiary, Count Taube, to sign a treaty by which Würtemberg received 155,000 subjects from Bavaria and ceded 45,000 to Baden—a net gain of only 110,000. Final title to Mergentheim was explicitly granted, but otherwise the naming of particular territories within those population limits was left to the states concerned to work out—an astute procedure whereby Napoleon could remain aloof from the fiercest local disputes. In this fashion, a settlement with Bavaria was made in May.

Negotiations with Baden, however, were interrupted by Napoleon, who intervened to veto the transfer of the important Strasbourg-Schaffhausen military road from the docile grand duke to the truculent king of Würtemberg. Frederick, already smarting from Napoleon's broken promises regarding population totals, resisted, forcing the emperor to unsheathe the su-

[13] *ibid.*, II, 375–376.
[14] August Fournier, *Napoleon I. Eine Biographie*, III (Vienna and Leipzig, 1913), 56.

preme weapon reserved for such cases: the threat of reforming the Rheinbund and imposing French law codes. A definitive treaty between the two states, by which Baden received 45,000 subjects from Würtemberg and ceded 15,000 to Hesse-Darmstadt, was not concluded until October 2. It could well be, therefore, that Metternich's convention of August 30 regarding the mediatized properties owed less to his own efforts than to Napoleon's desire to discipline the king of Würtemberg.[15]

The main crisis in Napoleon's relations with the Rheinbund, however, came in North Germany, and it arose not from the booty made available by the Austrian war but from the continuing war with England. After the treaty of Tilsit in 1807 Bonaparte had hoped, with Russian assistance, to make peace with the great sea power, for which reason he had not made a final disposition of Hanover. However, by the end of the Austrian war he had abandoned this hope and decided to stake everything on that extraordinary experiment of boycott and blockade known as the continental system. Hanover thereupon became part of the territorial surplus available for distribution; it was awarded to the kingdom of Westphalia by a treaty signed on January 14, 1810, along with the entire North Sea coast between the Weser and the Elbe, with the proviso that French officials could police the ports and customs frontiers as necessary to enforce the blockade.[16]

In the summer of 1810, however, while Metternich was still in Paris, Napoleon concluded that stronger measures were necessary to prevent illicit traffic through the great German and Dutch ports, which were the most immediate sufferers from the system. The problem was the same as in the Adriatic Ports, and he solved it in the same way—by annexing the territory to France.[17] In a senatorial decree of December 13, which ratified the annexations, the new French boundary was vaguely described as following a line from Wesel on the Rhine (hitherto the *only* right-bank territory of France) to Lübeck.[18]

With the exception of Holland, Lauenburg, and the Hanse-

[15] Hötzle, *Württemberg im Zeitalter*, 40–43.
[16] Text of treaty in Meyer, *Corpus Juris*, I, 107–108. See especially Art. x.
[17] Edouard Driault, *Napoléon et l'Europe*, IV (Paris, 1924), 191.
[18] Text in Meyer, *Corpus Juris*, I, 105.

atic towns, the provinces within the line were not listed by
name, because Napoleon had not yet decided what to do with
the Rheinbund sovereigns affected: the princes of Salm-Salm
and Salm-Kibourg, the duke of Arenberg, and the duke of
Oldenburg. To absorb into the monolithic structure of French
law and administration several of his old accomplices, whose
protector he was and whose sovereignty he had personally
guaranteed in the Act of Confederation, would shake his system
in Germany to its foundations. Three of the states, it is true,
were minute entities, and if they had merely been mediatized
by a larger Rheinbund member, many would have said that
Napoleon was acting within the spirit of the Imperial Recess
and the legislation of 1806. But the spectacle of a parent de-
vouring his children is always abhorrent, especially to the other
children. On this ground alone the Protector had reason to
pause.

The real cause of his indecision, however, was the case of
Oldenburg. Not only was this a duchy of considerable size, but
its ruling house was a branch of the family Holstein-Gottorp,
related to Alexander of Russia. Indeed, Alexander was both the
nephew of Duke Peter, who ruled as regent for his mentally ill
cousin, and the brother-in-law of Peter's son George, who had
married Grand Duchess Catherine after Ludwig of Bavaria had
withdrawn his suit. The tsar was already incensed by the annexation of the North German ports, which hurt Russian as
well as British commerce. Small wonder, then, that Napoleon
hesitated to seize a territory which Alexander regarded as a fief
of the Russian crown.[19] At the same time the prospect of permanent enclaves within French territory was intolerable, and so
the emperor conceived the idea of a territorial exchange. The
house of Holstein-Gottorp, Oldenburg branch, should be moved
to Erfurt, a Thuringian principality only one-sixth the size of
Oldenburg, but more fertile and more productive of revenue.

He put his proposition both in Oldenburg and St. Petersburg: the duke could choose between staying where he was
under French sovereignty or remaining sovereign at Erfurt. To
Napoleon's astonishment Duke Peter chose the first option,

[19] Fournier, *Napoleon*, III, 45; Vandal, *Napoléon et Alexandre*, II, 526–527.

holding that as regent he had no right to dispose of the ancestral home. In the meantime an army of French officials, expecting the opposite decision, had already descended on the duchy and was taking over its administration. It was a blunder, but Napoleon, convinced that softness would have a more unsettling effect on the Rheinbund than a harsh demonstration of his mastery, decided to go through with the annexation. On January 22, 1811, a decree of the senate ratified the exchange of Erfurt for Oldenburg but, as a concession to the tsar, permitted the duke to keep his private domains in Oldenburg until the transfer was actually effected.[20]

Alexander reacted with the vehemence of a wounded boar, moving troops to the Warsaw frontier and trying to enlist the aid of the Poles by a plan to proclaim a Russian-protected Kingdom of Poland.[21] Whether, given a favorable response, he would actually have made a *casus belli* of the Oldenburg affair, is a matter of conjecture. As it happened, the Polish reaction was cool, and so he confined himself to dispatching a circular letter of protest to the European courts. "This state . . . cannot be destroyed without violating all justice," the letter [22] read, and went on to assert that Russia could not recognize an annexation which violated half a dozen treaties dating back to 1766. There was a special flavor of resentment in the tsar's protest. On all political issues he had long since conceded the exclusive influence of France in Germany, yet here was Napoleon brutally and without provocation proceeding against a member of the family, and making the German question again a factor in Franco-Russian relations. The fate of Oldenburg was not the main cause of the great war of 1812 but neither was it the least. Within three months of Alexander's protest Napoleon ordered the Rheinbund states to put their contingents on a war footing.[23]

The senatorial decree which ratified the annexation of Oldenburg provided a similar settlement for the duke of Arenberg and the two princely houses of Salm; they retained their

[20] *ibid.*, II, 526–529; Driault, *Napoléon et l'Europe*, IV, 193–194.
[21] Kukiel, *Czartoryski*, 94; Fournier, *Napoleon*, III, 45.
[22] Text in Meyer, *Corpus Juris*, I, 105, note 2.
[23] Fournier, *Napoleon*, III, 45 and 55.

private domains and, for the loss of their sovereignty and vassals, received titles as French princes. Within months the whole of the annexed area was organized into departments, placed under French law codes, and designated as the 32nd military district, a name suggestive of its real purpose. Significantly, the man Napoleon chose as governor of the district was Théobald-Jacques Bacher, one of the architects of the Rheinbund and, since its founding, the French minister to the court of the Prince Primate.[24] With Bacher's transfer, France ceased to be represented at the Rheinbund as such, and henceforth acted only through the envoys accredited to the separate governments. It is certainly an exaggeration to say, with Edouard Driault, that thereby "the Confederation found itself in truth dissolved." [25] But the fact remains that for Napoleon's immediate purposes the separate treaties of alliance, which he had had the foresight to write into the Act of Confederation, had become the key to his dealings with Germany. And it was plain to the remaining Rheinbund members that there was no longer any safety in the Act of Confederation, but only in individual bargains with Napoleon.

It might appear that the time had come for the German sovereigns to turn to Austria, but nothing of the kind occurred. On the contrary, most of the Rheinbund courts interpreted the Austrian marriage of their Protector as introducing a potent new rival for his affections, a rival all the more formidable because she was not tied hand and foot to the French system by covenants like the Rheinbund Act. Their reaction therefore was to cling more closely than ever to France and not to risk the slightest suggestion of infidelity.

Furthermore, if there was any natural alternative to Napoleon, it was not the Emperor Francis and his *reichsgräfliche* minister but Tsar Alexander, although none but the arrogant king of Würtemberg dared to act on this assumption. Almost simultaneously with the dispatch of Alexander's letter of protest regarding Oldenburg an envoy from St. Petersburg, Baron Maximilian Alopeus, arrived in Stuttgart to attempt to restore

[24] See above Chapter III, p. 60.
[25] Driault, *Napoléon et l'Europe*, IV, 145.

Alexander's former influence at the court of his South German relatives. Perhaps he and King Frederick feared that with the opening of a Franco-Russian war Würtemberg would meet the fate of Oldenburg. At any rate, within the narrow limits open to him, Frederick began to make his plans against the day when Napoleon's oppression should become intolerable. The plotting did not amount to very much, but it was, as we shall see, the small beginning of an alignment that for years to come lay close to the heart of Metternich's difficulties in Germany.[26]

But whether the German states looked to Paris or St. Petersburg, it is certain that they eyed Vienna with the deepest distrust, particularly the states which had actually acquired Austrian territory. After the war Metternich did his best to restore normal, friendly relations with Bavaria but to no avail. His first envoy to Munich, the legation councilor Dohle, was unacceptable to the Montgelas government and was quickly sent home. His overtures to effect minor rectifications in the new Austro-Bavarian frontier were rebuffed; and his efforts to enforce the property rights of Austrian patriots in the ceded provinces, as provided by the peace treaty, resulted only in tedious negotiations that were still in progress at the beginning of 1811. In the spring of that year Baron Wessenberg was transferred from Berlin to Munich, but he had no more success than his predecessors. Indeed, by that time the impact of the Habsburg-Bonaparte dynastic union was fully felt; to Montgelas, who believed that a political alliance went with it, it appeared that Austria had replaced Bavaria in Napoleon's system. In fact, the Bavarian minister-president actually welcomed the Protector's demand to send a small force to reinforce the French garrison at Danzig; it showed that Napoleon still had some use for Bavaria after all. Only Crown Prince Ludwig exhibited sympathy for Austria, but then he had never been one of Napoleon's favorites, and now, after the fate of Salm, Arenberg, and Oldenburg, he feared that he would never inherit the Bavarian crown.[27]

With Saxony Metternich's relations were only slightly better.

[26] Hölzle, *Württemberg im Zeitalter*, 43–45.
[27] Demelitsch, *Metternich und seine auswärtige Politik*, 88–89 and 492–494.

In Dresden the Austrian marriage seems not to have aroused the same jealousy as in Munich, but as long as King Frederick Augustus, as grand duke of Warsaw, held West Galicia, he had to regard Austria as a rival. Furthermore, since the duchy made him both a target for Alexander and a mortal foe of the Polish national movement represented by Poniatowski, which Napoleon could reactivate at any time, he was totally beholden to France. Indeed, the court adopted French fashions and cleared everything with the resident French minister in a way that was almost ludicrous. Austrian diplomatic notes were dutifully forwarded to the French foreign office and, in regard to the birth of the king of Rome, an event that concerned Austria at least as much as France, only the French minister received an invitation to the celebration held in Dresden.[28]

The Saxon attitude toward Austria, however, was determined more by duress than animosity, and negotiations on substantive disputes proceeded amicably enough though hardly with great success. These included such thorny subjects as the joint administration of the salt mines at Wieliczka, the demarkation of the Bohemian enclaves ceded to Saxony, the drawing of a boundary around the region of Cracow, and the status of the two duchies, Upper and Lower Lusatia—whether with the dissolution of the Reich they fell to Saxony or whether, as fiefs of the Bohemian crown, they still belonged to Austria. The discussions dragged on for months, but the only decision reached concerned the salt mines: Austria won the right to administer them exclusively for a period of eight years.[29]

These were typical of the problems left by almost all of Napoleon's peace treaties, and one suspects that, as with the intra-Rheinbund negotiations, he deliberately left many loose ends to keep the other governments of Europe busy with harmless details. Metternich, on his part, realizing Austria's disadvantages, displayed patience and objectivity in dealing with the German states; he neither pressed for quick decisions in Austria's favor, nor capitulated in the futile hope of making friends where none were to be had. "The princes," he told the emperor,

[28] *ibid.,* 495.
[29] *ibid.,* 312–314 and 495–498.

"completely carried away by their private interests and all too profitable compromises, are no longer to be brought into any kind of combination against France as was the case in former times." [30] It was not his intention, of course, to antagonize the German states, but rather than risk alienating Napoleon by a premature resumption of the contest for Germany, it was better to regard the situation as the Rheinbund states themselves regarded it, as a competition with Austria for the conqueror's favor. The only German state that did seek Austrian advice and support was Prussia, not a member of the Rheinbund. But with her, too, Metternich was disinclined to take chances. Weak as she was, she had nothing to offer Austria now that the war was over.[31]

Actually, of course, Austria was more important to Napoleon than were the Rheinbund states. The Austrian army of 150,000 allowed by the peace treaty was about as large as the Rheinbund and Prussian forces combined, figuring the former at approximately 110,000 and Prussia at 42,000 men. An army of that size meant that Austria still had to be regarded as a great power, and so Metternich, determined to retain this advantage in spite of worry about financial problems, was frequently at odds with finance minister Odonell and his successor Count Joseph Wallis over maintaining a respectable military establishment. And since Austria was the strongest of the so-called neutrals, Metternich was able to serve France in ways not open to Napoleon himself. Thus, for example, he influenced Denmark to abandon her plans for a neutral Scandinavian union and ally with France instead. Again, when Napoleon's marshal, Jean Jules Bernadotte, was elected Prince Royal of Sweden, Metternich was among the first to recognize him. Similarly, when required by the peace treaty to recognize Napoleon's brother-in-law Murat as king of Naples, Metternich did so with alacrity and entered upon a friendly relationship well beyond the requirements of duress, a relationship which in the long run served him much better than it did Napoleon.[32]

---

[30] Metternich's *Vortrag* of 17 Jan. 1811, in *N.P.*, II, 407f.
[31] Demelitsch, *Metternich und seine auswärtige Politik*, 305–312.
[32] *ibid.*, 315–325 and 502–507.

Outwardly Metternich's policy appeared one of fawning self-abasement, and he himself confessed that it resembled the antics of a Rheinbund state more than the dignified and independent course of a great power. Yet he had solid, well-calculated objects in mind, and there was some substance to the boast that "among the European powers we are almost the only one which has the possibility of a choice." [33] If he influenced other states to join the French cause, it was because he believed the formation of an anti-French coalition would only speed the onset of war. Since he was convinced that such a war would inevitably end in another Napoleonic victory, it would be disastrous not only for Austria but for the whole continent. That his policy at bottom was one of independence is best illustrated by his handling of the Eastern question, which had always had a bearing on Austria's posture in Germany and, as matters then stood, presented Metternich with problems on the Danube analogous to those he would one day face on the Rhine.

The reopening of the Eastern question was mainly the work of Alexander. In 1810 he brought his war with Sweden to a successful conclusion with the annexation of Finland, and turned with redoubled strength to the prosecution of his campaign against Turkey, hoping to consolidate his left flank while Napoleon was occupied in Spain and while Austria was still too weak to resist. His minimum goal was the conquest of the Danubian Principalities. This, as always, was a threat to Austria, but for Metternich it was complicated by other concerns. His first fear on becoming foreign minister had been the possibility of a Franco-Russian agreement to partition Turkey, and one of the purposes of his mission to Paris had been to prevent it.[34] In Paris, however, as his stay dragged on at Napoleon's insistence, he found the real danger was not Austria's exclusion but her forced participation in the plots of the Balkans. Napoleon, unable to spare troops from Spain, and bound by his Erfurt promise to allow Alexander to take the principalities, hoped that Austria could be used to stop the Russian advance. Declaring to Metternich that he would never

---

[33] Metternich's *Vortrag* of 17 Jan. 1811, in *N.P.*, II, 406.
[34] Demelitsch, *Metternich und seine auswärtige Politik*, 107–108.

tolerate a Russian foothold south of the Danube, he urged Austria to seize Serbia herself. He repeated the blandishments after Metternich had returned home.[35]

In Vienna the problem brought out once more the differences between Russophiles and Francophiles. The former generally regarded Russia's policy as defensive and hence no lasting threat to Austria. In the main this group consisted of the German imperialists and nationalists, since the ultimate purpose of a common course with Russia would be the eventual liberation of Germany. They were also bound to Russia by a common fear of Poland. One of the chief advocates of allowing Russia to take Serbia, incidentally, was that unreconciled old *Reichsgraf,* Franz Georg Metternich.[36] The Francophiles, on the other hand, including most of the army,[37] regarded the German question as settled for the foreseeable future and looked to the Balkans for opportunities to redress Austria's losses—a course such as Bismarck urged on the Austrians in the 1860's. Since this was necessarily anti-Russian, anti-Turkish, and anti-British, it implied a collaboration with Napoleon well beyond the requirements of the peace treaty or of simple duress.

In Metternich's opinion both groups were wrong, because they both put specific regional interests ahead of Austria's larger interest in the pattern of continental alignments. To seize Serbia, as Napoleon urged, would make the monarchy dependent on France in future, and would probably eliminate forever the possibility of restoring a continental balance based on an independent center. Yet to ally with Russia, or even tacitly to acquiesce in her Balkan conquests with or without an alliance, would compel Bonaparte to take countermeasures. These would not only bring on the war which Metternich believed France would win, they would also channel the fighting to the southeast, virtually assuring that Austria would be a battleground, either as Napoleon's ally or as his first victim. Hence, though the foreign minister shared his father's view that the Russian occupation of Serbia would in itself be no

[35] Metternich's *Vortrag* of 28 July 1810 from Paris, in *N.P.,* II, 377–389. Cf. Lauber, *Metternichs Kampf,* 39–40.
[36] Demelitsch, *Metternich und seine auswärtige Politik,* 276ff.
[37] *ibid.,* 524.

real threat, he knew that its ultimate consequences could be fatal. His Balkan policy therefore had one single object: the preservation of the Ottoman Empire exactly as it was, as a buffer against all the contending parties.

It was totally incomprehensible to Metternich that Alexander did not also adopt this solution, that he persisted instead in waging both a conventional war and a campaign of subversion against the Porte by inciting the Serbs to rebellion. Apart from the inherent folly of Alexander's policy, it also indicated how little he was willing to sacrifice to obtain an Austrian alliance. It was "unprecedented blindness," Metternich told the emperor, for Russia to choose "as objects of aggrandizement . . . the states of harmless peaceloving neighbors . . . and to destroy one after the other the bulwarks of her own security." [38] Thus the foreign minister was convinced that the tsar was digging his own grave and Austria's as well.

The main cause of Metternich's belief in Russia's impending downfall, however, was Poland, where Napoleon seemed to have all the advantages. Poland in truth was the principal cause of the war then in the making, for Napoleon could not convince Alexander that he would let the matter rest where the treaty of Schönbrunn had left it.[39] As a result the tsar turned to the Poles himself, in December, 1810, in connection with the Oldenburg affair, and offered a Polish kingdom to his old friend and admirer in Warsaw, Prince Adam Czartoryski. But the Poles remained cool to Alexander's overtures, both then and in the months to come. Poniatowski reaffirmed his allegiance to Napoleon, and in the end even Czartoryski had to break with his friends in St. Petersburg.[40]

It is improbable that Metternich knew all the details of the diplomatic tug-of-war over Poland, but he did not have to. It was obvious that Napoleon's appeal, on grounds of sentiment as well as of realistic calculation, was greater than Alexander's. Hence Metternich regarded Poland as Napoleon's secret weapon,

[38] Metternich's *Vortrag* of 17 Jan. 1811, *op.cit.*, 410.
[39] Vandal, *Napoléon et Alexandre*, II, 163ff.
[40] Fournier, *Napoleon*, III, 38–39; Kukiel, *Czartoryski*, 94–101.

ready to be exploded when needed; he fully expected that the war would begin with the proclamation of a Polish state, followed by a massive rising in Russia's Polish provinces that would at the outset eliminate the acquisitions of half a century and provide new manpower to overwhelm the long and relatively thinly-manned Russian frontier. A force of 200,000 German confederates and Poles, combined with 80,000 Frenchmen, he said, "will spread the fire of rebellion into the farthest corners of the old frontiers of Poland." [41] That would still leave, by his estimates, 300,000 French troops elsewhere in Europe, "more than enough to hold Germany and Italy in check and smother any popular movement at its birth. . . ." [42] Thus numerical superiority as well as the advantages of utilizing subversive techniques were all on Napoleon's side. This was Metternich's answer to those who believed that the outbreak of war would "be the signal for a general uprising and thus the harbinger of Russian victories." [43]

Believing both that war was inevitable and that Russia did not have "the remotest prospect for success," [44] he saw Austria's alternatives limited to neutrality or alliance with France. In the short term neutrality was preferable and possible: though Austria could not prevent a war, she might postpone it for a time by a firm and candid attitude toward France and Russia. Each must be assured of Austria's peaceful intentions toward the other; in this way at least war would not be precipitated by the fear of a hostile coalition, or by overconfidence in Austria's assistance. In the long run, however, neutrality was impossible. It would neither suffice to defeat Napoleon nor would it prevent the loss of Galicia, certain to result from his victory. One would have to ally with France, not only to avoid the victor's reprisals but also in the hope of being compensated for the loss of Galicia. Galicia, Metternich estimated, should be worth the return of the entire Illyrian province ceded in 1809 and, with luck, the return of the Inn frontier against Bavaria. A part of

[41] Metternich's *Vortrag* of 17 Jan. 1811, *op.cit.*, II, 417.
[42] *ibid.*, II, 417.
[43] *ibid.*, II, 416.
[44] *ibid.*, II, 414.

Silesia was also a possibility, but only in the event that Prussia was dismembered, an eventuality which Metternich also believed probable.[45]

This advice constituted a memorandum from Metternich to the emperor in January, 1811, during the crisis over Oldenburg. It showed him again the master of making the most of a bad situation. It also shows the degree to which the experiences of 1809 had changed him. Rashness and overconfidence had turned to caution and pessimism. Then he had had confidence in Russia —now he trusted her not at all, neither her policy nor her intentions toward Austria, nor her capacity to wage an intelligent, let alone a successful campaign. The popular movements in Germany and the assistance of Prussia, which he had thought were good risks in 1809, in 1811 he considered forlorn prospects. The temptation is strong, therefore, to say that he had swung too far in the opposite direction, especially as his central postulate, the defeat of Russia, proved to be as fallacious as his "mathematical proof" of Russian neutrality in 1809. Yet the wrong guess was not as important as it appears, since—whatever the outcome—there was little else Austria could do. Metternich knew that Alexander planned to fight a defensive war and could not render assistance to his allies. Austria, weak as she was, as an ally of Russia would be destroyed at the outset, regardless of later developments. It could even be argued that Austria served Russia best by allying with France and keeping her army intact for a happier day—a point Metternich made later in assuring Alexander that Austria would not strike serious blows.[46] It sometimes happens that the most intelligent of appraisals are belied by events while uninformed, arbitrary guesses accidentally hit the mark. The best the responsible minister can do is to play the odds and, where several possibilities exist, so act that even if the less probable should occur, it too can be accommodated.

A more fundamental deficiency in Metternich's analysis was his harsh judgment of Russian policy: it showed how much he had the preconceptions of an ordinary continental statesman,

---

[45] *ibid.*, II, 417–420.
[46] Demelitsch, *Metternich und seine auswärtige Politik*, 539–541.

even when trying to solve Alexander's problems for him. He thought Russian policy fickle because it inconvenienced the *Ballhaus* not to have a steady reference point for its own devious and shifting maneuvers. He did not understand that St. Petersburg saw the jagged little peninsula of Europe as a mosaic of relatively small states filled with ideological protest movements of one kind or another; that the task of Russian policy, therefore, was to find the best combination of these at any given time. In 1811 Alexander, having decided on a defensive war in the interior of Russia, needed above all solid flanking positions, and these he won with the conquest of Finland and, in 1812, the peace of Bucharest with Turkey.

That he could do this and at the same time keep Sweden and Turkey neutral was a diplomatic accomplishment of no mean proportions. A defensive war, moreover, made alliances with a weak Austria and an almost insignificant Prussia desirable, perhaps, but not something for which to sacrifice his Balkan position, as many Austrians demanded, or to make rash commitments for the future as the Prussians, as usual, demanded. Alexander sometimes forgot that what to Russia was a mere tactic, to the lesser European states was often a matter of life and death, but this is not capriciousness. Metternich thought the Russian rulers fickle in the way that ministers usually thought their monarchs irresolute: because they did not steadily follow the advice of a single man. Only after Russia's victory did Metternich seem to recover that appreciation of the tsar's many options which he had first realized in Dresden exactly ten years before.

Fortunately Metternich's station was not on the Neva but on the Danube, where his prejudices, if belying his universality, were appropriate to his responsibilities. During 1811 neutrality became increasingly difficult. The rival emperors courted Austria and Prussia, and though Metternich knew where he stood, he had constantly to fight off the Russophiles, who were not without influence on Francis. In August he recalled Schwarzenberg from Paris to bolster his position, exactly as Stadion had once recalled him. Throughout that year and the next he was plagued by numerous conspiracies involving Tyrolean patriots, former army officers, agents from the North German resistance movement, and the usual sprinkling of West German refugees. Significantly, one of the broadest plots was led by a *Reichsgraf,* Christian von Leiningen-Westerburg, was financed by England, and coordinated with similar movements in Germany by the Russian embassy in Vienna.[47] Financially, the condition of the monarchy went from alarming to desperate. In January, 1811, a reform plan calling for vastly increased land taxes had been decided upon, but, owing to a successful boycott by the Hungarian magnates, it never went into operation. By the end of the year the situation was so critical that Metternich could not obtain funds from the finance ministry to assemble a modest observation corps of 60,000, which he wanted in order to increase his bargaining power.[48] Indeed, he now believed alliance with France was unavoidable, if for no other reason than the chance of obtaining a subsidy and forestalling an attempt by Bonaparte to revolutionize tax-shy Hungary.[49]

Then, in November, two new dangers brought matters to a head. The first was a decisive Russian victory over the Turks, which raised anew the specter of a French attack through Austrian territory. The other was a crisis in Prussian policy. Originally Metternich had assumed that Prussia would fight with a small force on the French side simply to avoid destruction,[50] and indeed Hardenberg did his best to gain favorable terms from Napoleon. But the French emperor proved recalcitrant, refusing to accept any of the Prussian proposals for safeguards and postwar guarantees, because Prussia, in Napoleon's plans, if she survived at all, would have to submit to a new territorial distribution. How else, for example, could the king of Saxony be compensated for the loss of Warsaw to a new Poland? Napoleon's final offer to Prussia, therefore, was a choice between joining the Rheinbund with her existing territories—in itself a dubious guarantee after the Oldenburg-Salms-Arenberg incidents—and taking her chances in an offensive-defensive alliance

[47] Rössler, *Österreichs Kampf,* II, 109–110 and 118.
[48] Demelitsch, *Metternich und seine auswärtige Politik,* 399.
[49] Metternich's *Vortrag* of 28 Nov. 1811, in *N.P.,* II, 433–434.
[50] *ibid.,* II, 434.

with no guarantees whatsoever.[51] Frustrated in Paris, Hardenberg turned to St. Petersburg and, much to Metternich's astonishment, tentatively decided to ally with Russia.

In Metternich's opinion, for Prussia this was tantamount to suicide; for Austria it gave new urgency to the question of Silesia, which in any hands but Prussia's would be a grave danger, a mortal one in fact if Galicia were lost to a Polish kingdom. An accommodation with Bonaparte could be delayed no longer; neutrality must be abandoned. On November 28 the foreign minister put his case to the emperor. An alliance with Russia was excluded for reasons long since understood; neutrality was theoretically possible, but only at a cost in armaments as great as alliance with France would entail, and with no gains, whoever won the war. Therefore Schwarzenberg in Paris must be instructed to offer the aid of an army corps against compensation in Silesia, Illyria, the Inn district, and Salzburg. It was taken for granted that Galicia would be lost. The emperor approved the new course, and Metternich had won a crucial skirmish with his enemies in Vienna.[52]

There remained the external struggle, and this was again complicated by Prussia. The reason the government in Berlin had not fully committed itself to Russia was Alexander's candid admission that he could offer no military assistance, beyond a force of 12,000 to defend Königsberg, until *after* he had driven Napoleon from his country. Accordingly Hardenberg made a final decision contingent on Austria's participation, and in early December sent General Scharnhorst to Vienna—an unusual choice, since Scharnhorst was the very soul of the Prussian reform party, a pro-Russian, and a member of the so-called *Tugendbund,* which was linked to the underground movements.[53]

Nevertheless, Metternich formed a better impression of the emissary than of his mission and told the general that Prussia had Austria's sympathy but nothing more. He added, however,

---

[51] Demelitsch, *Metternich und seine auswärtige Politik,* 485.

[52] Metternich's *Vortrag* of 28 Nov. 1811, *op.cit.,* II, 435ff.

[53] Demelitsch, *Metternich und seine auswärtige Politik,* 486ff.

that he could not advise Prussia about her own course, a remark which has led several writers to claim that Metternich deliberately tried to nudge Prussia over to the Russians in order to assure her destruction at Napoleon's hands and thereby acquire Silesia.[54] The thesis is untenable, partly because it imputes malice to a position that was in fact scrupulously correct, and partly because it mistakenly assumes that Metternich valued the acquisition of Silesia above the survival of Prussia. Such a notion would have been contrary to the spirit of his entire policy, which was to keep afloat as many of Bonaparte's potential enemies as possible. In the aforementioned argument to Francis on November 28 it is clear that Silesia was added to the list of possible indemnities only as a consolation prize should Prussia be partitioned.

Whatever Metternich's intentions, the actual effect of his statements was to convert Hardenberg to a French alliance after all, even though the terms made Prussia a complete captive. The alliance was signed on February 24, 1812. Three weeks later (March 14) Austria also entered into alliance and, under the circumstances, the terms were relatively advantageous. She agreed to provide a corps of 30,000 men, only half of what Napoleon had originally demanded; and, unlike the Prussian corps, which was placed unreservedly at Napoleon's disposal, it was not obligated to fight in Spain or against England. To emphasize the limited commitments, the unit, at Metternich's insistence, was called an "auxiliary corps," not a contingent like the Rheinbund contributions. The corps was subject to Napoleon's orders but to no other French general, and the immediate commander was to be an Austrian. Originally Napoleon had requested Archduke Carl for this post and Metternich had agreed, but when Carl refused, Schwarzenberg became commander. He was a man of extensive political experience, which Metternich valued well above military ability for that particular assignment.

In the territorial provisions Austria fared even better, being

[54] Fournier, *Napoleon*, III, 63–65; and more recently W. Rohr, "Scharnhorsts Sendung nach Wien Ende 1811 und Metternichs Politik," *Forschungen zur brandenburgischen und preussischen Geschichte* XLVIII (1930) 76–128. See refutation in Srbik, *Metternich*, III, 50f.

guaranteed possession of Galicia even if a Polish kingdom was created, but acquiring the right to exchange the province for Illyria at her own volition. She was also to receive additional territory, over and above payment for her sacrifices in the war —a reference to Silesia or the Inn district, which Metternich did not want named lest postwar circumstances make their acquisition impossible, inadvisable, or perhaps embarrassing. All in all, the treaty of alliance was such that, though Metternich still expected an easy French victory, he would not be caught off balance should the unforeseen occur.[55]

Now that the contractual foundations of his coalition had been laid, Napoleon's next task was to complete the military preparations and instill awe, if not enthusiasm, into his allies. For this purpose he summoned them to the Saxon capital of Dresden, as four years earlier he had called them to Erfurt. Once more he treated Europe to a spectacle of grandeur, and as before his allies outdid themselves in their efforts to please. The king of Saxony was a generous host, straining the resources of his kingdom, and perhaps the last revenue he would ever receive from Warsaw, to provide Italian opera, illuminated fountains, sumptuous balls and dinners, and salvos of cannon fire to greet the arriving dignitaries. Cavalry escorts awaited the visitors in the outlying towns, and *chaises de poste,* with plumed footmen, whisked them through lovely parks.[56]

Napoleon, with headquarters at the Marcolini palace, maintained a heavy schedule of formal conferences, intimate chats, official dinners, and gala receptions, here affectionately patting the back of a dour grand duke, there outrageously flattering a vain minister. The Emperor Francis and the Empress Louise arrived on May 19, and on them he lavished special attention. At Erfurt he had been, for all his titles, only a Bonaparte; now he was the father of a Habsburg prince who could inherit most of Europe. Was it this he had in mind when he expressed his disappointment at the absence of poor, ailing Ferdinand, Francis' unstable son and heir, who was the only rival? Was this the

---

[55] Terms of treaty in Demelitsch, *Metternich und seine auswärtige Politik,* 516ff. Cf. Metternich's *Vortrag* of 15 Jan. 1812, in *N.P.,* II, 438ff.

[56] This and the following based on the classic account in Vandal, *Napoléon et Alexandre,* III, 401ff.

reason he kept the Bonapartes in the background, why Prince Eugene had orders to join his troops before the congress began, why King Jerome must remain at his post on the North Sea coast, and why King Joachim Murat of Naples, on his way to Poland, was routed so as to avoid Dresden? With what presumption did Napoleon refer to Louis XVI as "his poor uncle," without whose weakness everything might have been so different? No matter; it was enough that Bonaparte came to Dresden not merely as the Protector of the Rheinbund princes, but as their social superior.

The meeting of the monarchs, however, was more than an expression of Napoleon's vanity, and he was the first to sense an air of impending doom. Years of the continental system had taken their toll. Merchants and entrepreneurs, who once had welcomed army contracts and emancipation from feudal business restraints, now surveyed with anger and dismay their shrunken markets, their empty warehouses, or their unsold surpluses. Intellectuals who once had admired rational uniformity in the abstract, now regarded as tyrants the bureaucrats who made it concrete reality. Posterity has tended to exaggerate the practical effects of these dissenting voices, but the Rheinbund sovereigns heard them and half-way agreed. The men and money extracted from them for the Russian campaign were the most yet demanded, and the campaign itself promised to be the most difficult. The possibility of defeat could not be discounted, and even Napoleon spoke of the imponderables that could easily upset the best-laid plans.

But what of victory? At Erfurt Napoleon's allies could look forward with confidence to territorial rewards at Austria's expense. This time there was nothing left from the old victories and little to be expected from the new. Poland was to be reconstituted; about that there was no doubt after Bonaparte ordered the king of Saxony to decree the autonomy of the Duchy of Warsaw, and delegate his sovereign powers to a Polish council of ministers.[57] For Frederick August that meant either an outright loss or compensation elsewhere—if the latter, some other prince would have to suffer, probably the king of Prussia

[57] *ibid.*, III, 432f.

by trading Silesia for some of Russia's Baltic territory. Yet even Russian territory could not be taken for granted since Napoleon was anxious to avoid commitments that could increase the difficulties of making peace in the future. For this reason he decided to make the restoration of Poland as much as possible a Polish affair, leaving the question of revolutionizing the Russian provinces to the Poles themselves, and reminding them that Galicia, being guaranteed to Austria, was out of bounds.[58]

The paucity of political discussion at Dresden has been noted by many observers, including Metternich. The reason is that Napoleon knew that his policy of buying allies by means of territorial awards was approaching bankruptcy; that only a total victory over Russia or a mammoth reorganization of the Austro-Prussian-German world could extricate him from his difficulties. In the meantime, his clients would have to be satisfied with the medals and decorations and flattery which he handed out so lavishly at the Marcolini palace.

As the only ally possessing a written guarantee of reimbursement for its services, the Austrian delegation might have enjoyed the extravaganza. It did not. Francis was ill at ease throughout and, though Metternich reported that he got on well with his son-in-law,[59] most observers (including those who did not have Metternich's personal interest in making the emperor appear enthusiastic about the French alliance) thought the relationship strikingly cool.[60] The empress, the proud, the intelligent, the cultivated Louise of Este, spurned all her son-in-law's advances and maintained an icy calm, melted only by the tears she shed in refusing the jewelry offered by her young and naïve step-daughter. Finally there was Metternich, whose uneasiness was not the result of wounded pride but of worry about the future. In a victory for Russia he did not believe. In a victory for France he saw the elimination of the one force on the continent which checked the conqueror and compelled him to show some consideration for his allies. The guarantee of

[58] ibid., III, 433; Demelitsch, Metternich und seine auswärtige Politik, 535.
[59] Metternich to Josef von Hudelist, 23 May 1812, in Fournier, Napoleon, III, Beil. II, 415f. In his "Autobiographical Memoir," however, Metternich says the relationship was correct but cool. N.P. I, 123.
[60] Demelitsch, Metternich und seine auswärtige Politik, 534.

Galicia could easily become a scrap of paper should the Poles insist on having the province. The only thing that Bonaparte seemed to prize was the *alliance de famille,* but his evasiveness regarding a subsidy and a more precise agreement about Galicia, the two goals Metternich had set himself at Dresden,[61] demonstrated anew that the dynastic tie did not automatically translate into political advantage.

On this note the congress broke up at the end of May. Napoleon set forth to join his army, and Metternich returned to the *Ballhaus* in Vienna, each to prepare in his own way for the mighty events to come.

[61] *ibid.,* 536ff.; Metternich to Hudelist, 3 June 1812, in Fournier, *Napoleon,* III, 416.

CHAPTER VI

THE GRAND MEDIATION ATTEMPT

Anyone who relishes the ironies of history cannot do better than reflect, as contemporaries did, on the presence of the Emperor Francis at Dresden in place of Alexander. The roles of Austria and Russia were reversed; and Metternich's policy in 1812 was a facsimile of Alexander's in 1809. At first the Austrian minister kept his alliance with France secret, still hoping, as an independent, to delay the war. But when the news leaked out he made the most of it, assuring Count Stackelberg, the Russian ambassador in Vienna, that the Austrian contribution would never exceed the auxiliary corps required by the pact, that Austria would remain on the defensive unless Russia forced her to do otherwise, and that even yet Russia, if she earnestly negotiated with Napoleon, would have a friend at the French court. Later, when Stackelberg requested a written pledge to that effect, Francis declared it impossible, no doubt recalling the treatment Schwarzenberg had once received in St. Petersburg. Oral assurances, however, he gave with great solemnity, and on the strength of these Alexander withdrew his troops from the Austrian frontier. In this way the Austrians not only helped Russia; they also spared their own troops and diverted the fighting to the North.[1]

Despite the alliance of March 14 and Napoleon's invasion on June 25, Metternich still sought a way to negotiate peace, and maintained contacts with all powers regardless of their position in the struggle. With Russia he did not break diplomatic relations and with Great Britain he was in contact both through General Nugent, who resided in London as a private person, and Count Ernst Münster, former minister-resident of Hanover, who was represented at Vienna by the astute observer, Count Ernst Hardenberg, a cousin of the Prussian chancellor. The channels were different but the message was the same:

[1] Demelitsch, *Metternich und seine auswärtige Politik*, 540ff.; and Oncken, *Oesterreich und Preussen*, II, 93–95.

147

Austria was independent; she wanted peace; and she served Napoleon's foes better this way than by exposing herself to immediate annihilation.

On September 4 Hardenberg of Prussia, brooding over Napoleon's omnipotence if he won in Russia and his exorbitant demands if he lost, turned to Metternich in a personal letter. A month later the Austrian minister replied. France, he agreed, was insufferable, but Russia was equally to blame for Europe's misery. Weak and vacillating, she was not predictable enough to form the basis of Austrian policy. "We must seek the instrument of our salvation in our own resources," he concluded; "we cannot gamble our existence on a single card." [2] Austria accordingly intended to make peace overtures in London, Paris, and Moscow, and she could only hope that Prussia would support her efforts. Knowing that Hardenberg must fear the rebirth of the Kaunitz tradition in Vienna, which equated a French alliance with animosity toward Prussia, he was giving assurance that his program was Austro-Prussian collaboration against East and West. Those, at any rate, were his views on October 5, when the reports from Russia showed Napoleon at the peak of his success. Would they be the same when the gods had shifted their favors, when the remnants of the Grand Army were chased out of Russia?

The question presented itself to Metternich with chilling suddenness. On October 14 Napoleon evacuated Moscow; on November 11, the first blizzards of the Russian winter swept down on his fair-weather troops; on December 3 he released the famous twenty-ninth bulletin announcing the rout of the Grand Army. By the end of the year the Russian army, sweeping forward on all fronts, stood at the river Niemen, ready, if need be, to enter East Prussia. Suddenly the central powers faced an altogether different situation; suddenly Russia had recovered all of her old options and more. She could attempt to make peace, with terms at least as favorable as those of Tilsit, or she could move into Central Europe, hoping to pursue the dragon to his lair. If she wanted peace, she could treat directly with Napoleon, although that would be in violation of her treaties with

[2] Metternich to Hardenberg, 5 Oct. 1812, in *ibid.*, I, 17–18.

Sweden and England; or she could strive for a general pacification that would include England. If she elected to continue the war, she could attempt to seduce Napoleon's allies by conventional diplomatic means, with the hope of assuming his place in their political life; or she could try to incite revolution among the peoples of Central Europe.

These diverse possibilities were open to Alexander because almost alone he had had faith in the outcome. Despite the defensive character of his military planning, his political preparations from the very outset had anticipated a campaign beyond Russian frontiers. With the disclosure of the Franco-Austrian and Franco-Prussian alliances in the spring of 1812 he had perforce to look at the Austro-Prussian-German world much as Stadion had in 1809. Whatever the prospects at a later time for winning over governments, the only immediate hope for support in Central Europe lay with the resistance movement. Indeed, even if he had not desired it, he had, as it were, inherited the leadership of the movement.

The role of the Russian embassy in Vienna in Count Leiningen's conspiracy has already been noted. This project continued and was powerfully aided in the fall of 1812 by Archduke John's adherence. A similar conspiracy in North Germany was represented in Prague by a Prussian *Staatsrat*, Justus von Gruner, who received orders from St. Petersburg. A migration of patriots took place from the Austrian and Prussian services to the Russian—such men as Merian von Falkach, previously mentioned, and the generals, Baron Carl von Tettenborn and Baron Ferdinand von Winzingerode.[3] In May, 1812, the tsar invited Baron vom Stein himself to St. Petersburg to head a committee for a free Germany, and Stein in turn summoned his brother-in-law, General Wallmoden, to organize a German legion. In the Russian capital the Germans joined the representatives of other national groups—the Corsican Pozzo di Borgo, whom Metternich had recently expelled, the Greek nationalist, Count John Capo d'Istria, the French émigré the duke of Richelieu, who served the tsar as governor of Odessa, and the Swiss *philosophe* Frederick Caesar La Harpe, Alexander's old

[3] Rössler, *Österreichs Kampf*, II, 104–107.

tutor, to name the most important. Conspicuously absent was Czartoryski, but the tsar had good reason to believe, in view of their past relations, that he would return to the fold once Napoleon's grip on Poland had been broken.

Most of these men came in time to think of Alexander in the way Metternich did, as erratic and inconsistent, but that was largely because, however similar their interim goals, their ultimate purposes seldom coincided with his. They saw him as the indispensable, if not necessarily benevolent, executant of their national aims; he saw the national movements as instruments of Russian power, as a "formidable weapon of which France should be deprived," to use the language of the Grand Design of 1804. His support of any national movement was always subject to modification in the light of other interests and alternatives. The thesis that Alexander, perhaps because of a trauma induced by the campaign of 1812, was incorrigibly unpredictable, given to fits of enthusiasm now for this cause, now for that, implies that he was easily influenced by his advisers. Actually the initiative was usually his; in the case of Stein, for example, one must never forget that it was Alexander who summoned *him*, not Stein who insinuated himself into the tsar's favor. Once this is understood, his policy emerges as one of rational calculation with a continuity fundamentally uninterrupted by the campaign of 1812. His policies, like those of Metternich, who began his diplomatic career the year Alexander became tsar, derived from the grueling experiences of the decade of Napoleon's ascendancy.

Alexander's ambivalent relationship with his non-Russian advisers was especially marked in the case of Stein. The latter, the great emancipator of Prussia's serfs, genuinely desired a mighty national rising such as he and Stadion had attempted in 1809, a people's war sustained by expectations of social reform and ignited by the sparks that flew from Arndt's verse, Fichte's speeches, and Friedrich Ludwig Jahn's gymnastic rallies. In this upheaval he imagined Prussia in the vanguard, the Prussia of Scharnhorst, Gneisenau, and von Boyen, his former comrades in military reform. Basically he desired to restore the Reich, but with greater cohesiveness and vitality. A reformed Reich, he hoped, would instill in the people "a feeling of dignity," banish "preoccupation with petty territorial affairs," and curb the Rheinbund princes, those "cowards, who sold the blood of their people in order to prolong their miserable existence." [4] He did not necessarily call for the overthrow of the Rheinbund sovereigns, but, like the Stadion brothers in 1809, he believed they should be reduced to their territorial holdings of 1802, an operation which would have released most of the mediatized properties. As alternatives, albeit unattractive ones, to a comprehensive German empire, he envisaged either a partition of Germany between Austria and Prussia or a "federal relationship" between Prussia and Austria and the larger secondary states. "I have only one fatherland," he proudly wrote to his friend, Count Münster in London; "that is Germany." [5]

Alexander, too, had but one fatherland, and that was Russia. He was the ruler of a great power which had what it considered to be legitimate interests in Germany, namely to recover the direct influence it had once exercised in certain states—Oldenburg, Mecklenburg, Würtemberg, Baden, and Bavaria in particular—and to regain a voice in the German question in general, such as Russia had had in the days of the Imperial Recess. At that time the weakened condition of Prussia and Austria had reduced the earlier four-way struggle for Germany to a two-way contest between France and Russia, and that is the way Alexander continued to conceive it. To him, Austria and Prussia were simply part of the vast Central European area which was disputed by the two superpowers: it followed that if one of the disputants was seriously weakened, the other would be in a strong position to impose its hegemony. Napoleon had done it, and there was no inherent reason why Russia could not do the same, seizing the Duchy of Warsaw and assuming a protectorate over the Rheinbund, some of whose members had already shown pro-Russian propensities. In the long run it was this option of courting Napoleon's allies that set limits to the tsar's collaboration with Stein in German affairs.

[4] This and following from Stein's "Denkschrift ueber Deutschlands künftige Verfassung," 18 Sept. 1812, in G. H. Pertz, *Aus Stein's Leben*, 1 (Berlin, 1856), 536–539.
[5] Stein to Münster, 1 Dec. 1812, *ibid.*, 1, 587.

In the short term, however, while Napoleon's armies were deep in Russia, the only real possibility open to Alexander was to give unstinting support to the resistance movements. In September he endorsed a memorandum incorporating Stein's ideas on the German problem and allowed it to be dispatched to London and Stockholm as an official Russian proposal.[6] Although it did not include Stein's idea about undoing the acts of mediatization, Alexander for the time being at least was committed to the restoration of a German empire. By thus putting his weight behind Stein, by flooding the Illyrian provinces with agitators, by dispatching General Wallmoden to provide military advice to the conspirators in the Tyrol, by allowing Stein a free hand to stir up the population of East Prussia and cooperate with the jubilant members of the *Tugendbund* in Prussia, the tsar kept open his options to carry the war beyond the Russian frontier, and to do so by means of almost unbearable pressure on the governments of Austria and Prussia. "You will place yourself, Sire," Stein pleaded with him, "at the head of Europe's powers. The exalted role of benefactor and restorer is yours to play" [7]—benefactor and restorer, be it noted, not liberator.

As the reports of Napoleon's steadily mounting reverses trickled into Vienna—on the average, about two weeks after the events—Metternich's reaction was neither the panic of the Francophiles, who regarded the dynasty's fortunes as indissolubly bound with those of France, nor the jubilance of the Russophiles, who believed the time was approaching to drop the mask and turn on the tyrant regardless of whose son-in-law he was. What concerned the foreign minister was simply the growing uncertainty of the situation, an uncertainty that stemmed equally from lack of information on the magnitude of Napoleon's defeat and a serious question as to Russia's ability to exploit the victory. The possibilities ranged between two extremes. If the Grand Army was annihilated and Napoleon himself was killed or captured, only Russia could capitalize on the ensuing chaos; her mastery of the continent would be virtually assured. If, on

[6] Gerhard Ritter, *Stein. Eine politische Biographie*, II (Stuttgart and Berlin, 1931), 190.

[7] Memorandum of 17 Nov. 1812, in Pertz, *Aus Stein's Leben*, I, 583.

the other hand, Napoleon escaped and the Russian army reached its frontiers in a state of exhaustion, a new Tilsit was a possibility too ominous to ignore. The only safe course, the only course open to the responsible minister, as Metternich saw it, was to redouble his efforts to negotiate a peace, or at least to maneuver Austria into a more or less neutral position where she could not be compromised whatever happened. "The first, the most inalterable of all Austrian interests," he said, "is independence." [8]

His first move came on November 4, shortly after he had learned of a peace feeler put out by Napoleon. Fearing Austria's exclusion from a negotiation between France and Russia, he hastened to offer his services as go-between.[9] In St. Petersburg and London his dispatches stressed the objectivity and relative independence of the centrally located power. In Vilna, where French headquarters were located at the time, his argument stressed the advantage to Napoleon of having peace proposals come from a third party and not from France.[10] On December 9, when the full scope of the catastrophe was becoming apparent, he made his second move. This time he approached France alone, to obtain permission to establish official contact with the other powers. The *Ballhaus,* he said, was not fooled by French bulletins. It knew and Europe knew what had happened in Russia and, if Napoleon was unreasonable, it would be impossible to hold the peoples of Central Europe in check.[11] Several more appeals of this kind followed, as well as a personal letter from Francis to his son-in-law on December 20, and an interview on December 31 between Napoleon and the Austrian ambassador in Paris, Count Bubna. Finally on January 7, 1813, Napoleon authorized a negotiation to be initiated by Austria. The treaty with France remained, but Austria had won *de facto* independence.[12]

Prussia's position meanwhile was almost the opposite. Since

[8] Metternich to Floret, 3 Jan. 1813, in Oncken, *Oesterreich und Preussen,* I, 80.
[9] Demelitsch, *Metternich und seine auswärtige Politik,* 146–147.
[10] Oncken, *Oesterreich und Preussen,* I, 29ff.
[11] *ibid.,* I, 35ff. Cf. Constantin de Grunwald, "Metternich et Napoléon," *Revue des deux Mondes* Series 8, XLI (Sept.–Oct., 1937), 610–613, which provides, for the spring of 1813, corroborative material from the French archives.
[12] *ibid.,* I, 57–82.

the fighting, partly because of Metternich's previous maneuvering, had taken place in the north, it was Prussia's border that the tsar's armies reached first. Then, on December 30, the commander of the Prussian corps, General Hans David Yorck von Wartenburg, on his own initiative, signed an armistice which opened East Prussia to the Russians. Scenting victory and glory, Stein set foot once more on Prussian soil, convoked the East Prussian *Landtag*, seized control of administration in the provinces, and began to organize a militia. He also caught a glimpse of the darker side of his dependence on the Russians, for they treated the occupied zones as conquered territory and spoke openly of annexation. Nor was this idle gossip. The tsar already had Sweden's consent, and many Russians, especially in the army, believed that the acquisition of East Prussia and the Duchy of Warsaw would be ample reward—one might just as well end the war there.[13]

The government at Potsdam was now on the verge of panic. As a breach of discipline the action of General Yorck was painful enough, but, as Hardenberg put it, "that is the least of my worries; the main thing is not to be compromised with France too early, and General Yorck has knocked the bottom out of the barrel."[14] Russia was too strong to be resisted and too weak to be trustworthy. If she should threaten further invasion, Prussia would have to enter an alliance with her no matter what terms were offered; but once committed, there was no assurance that Russia, in her momentary exhaustion, would protect her from Napoleon, who still controlled most of Prussia outside of Silesia. In this dilemma Hardenberg and the king turned once more to Metternich, and sent General Knesebeck secretly to Vienna, where he arrived on January 12.

Ideally, what Hardenberg wanted was an alliance with Austria good for all purposes. If the Russians should remain quiet long enough, the central states would join in the mediation which Metternich was so anxious to undertake. The operation, Hardenberg believed, should be an *armed* mediation, and should require a French withdrawal from Italy and Germany. The Rhein-

---

[13] Ritter, *Stein*, II, 169–171.
[14] Quoted by Oncken, *Oesterreich und Preussen*, I, 130–131.

bund states, with the exception of Westphalia, were to be kept intact, and Napoleon's role was to be taken over by Prussia and Austria, on the basis of that perennial Prussian plan for Prussia's pre-eminence in the North and Austria's in the South. If, however, the Russians should threaten Prussia with invasion, then Austria should join her in shifting sides and in this way enable the central states to bargain on equal terms, in particular to obtain for Prussia her pre-Jena domains, including East Prussia and her former Polish provinces. If Austria refused an alliance, then Knesebeck was to try, at the very least, to obtain her approval of a bilateral Prussian-Russian pact. This last sounded harmless enough, in fact little more than a courtesy, but it was the very core of Knesebeck's mission. In the eyes of the Prussians Austria's approval would mean her assumption of responsibility if Prussia signed such a pact; Austria would be obligated not only not to strike at Prussia herself, but to come to her rescue if Russia failed to do so.[15]

Thus the Knesebeck mission presented Metternich with a dilemma. Normally he would have welcomed Prussia's bid to join the meditation effort, which at the moment carried all his hopes. Here was the state, which since the peace of Basel had stood on every side but Austria's, now begging for an Austrian alliance, defending the policy of the independent center, proposing to reorganize Germany without interference from France or Russia, and even offering to place her troops under Austrian command. All that was tempting. And yet Metternich clearly understood that the same emergency which prompted the offer must deter him from accepting it. Hardenberg's talk about the common interest of the two central powers was not entirely accurate. Time was running out for Prussia faster than it was for Austria. That is why Hardenberg insisted that the central powers state their terms and back them with their armies, whereas Metternich, having just received Napoleon's permission to act, still saw a long and tedious negotiation ahead. The mediation could not fairly begin before Austria would be dragged into alliance with Russia. Metternich therefore rejected an Austro-Prussian alliance out of hand. He sensed a similar danger in the proposal

[15] *ibid.,* I, 119–129.

merely to approve Prussia's change of sides, and for that reason he was very careful officially to withhold his approval even while indirectly conveying his personal belief that Prussia had no choice. The emperor himself expressed the same opinion to Knesebeck. Indeed, by this time the danger was that if Frederick William did not assume leadership of the disgruntled officers, student volunteers, and other outraged citizens, Stein and the tsar would do so. When Knesebeck left Vienna on January 30 he returned to Potsdam empty-handed.[16]

Hardenberg now had no choice but to turn to Russia and make the best bargain he could. Metternich, therefore, was in a sense instrumental in bringing about the notorious treaty of Kalisch which, like a neglected rook, was to become increasingly dangerous to Austria as the game progressed. Negotiated by Knesebeck and signed on February 28,[17] the treaty promised to Prussia "the actual strength that she had had before the war of 1806," territorially, financially, and in population, but not necessarily with the same provinces. Her existing provinces, including East Prussia, were guaranteed to her, but in Poland she was to receive back only "a territory which, both militarily and geographically, shall connect [East Prussia] to Silesia"—a vague statement that could have meant anything from the relatively extensive regions of Kulm, Bromberg, and Posen to just a fringe of them. In compensation she was to receive territories "in the northern part of Germany with the exception of the former possessions of the house of Hanover," and with "the compactness and contiguity necessary to constitute an independent political whole." Saxony as such was not named as the object of compensation but, in view of the need to restore Hanover and to spare the tsar's relatives in Mecklenburg, no other territory could reasonably have been intended, and Alexander gave Hardenberg oral assurances to this effect.[18] In other provisions, the signatories were enjoined not to sign a separate peace, Russia was to field an army of 150,000 and Prussia one of 80,000, supplemented by a "national militia."

Although the treaty was Prussia's second choice, it did not

[16] Mission treated in great detail in *ibid.*, I, 110–157.
[17] Text in Meyer, *Corpus Juris*, I, 135–137.
[18] Oncken, *Oesterreich und Preussen*, II, 248.

enslave her as had her pact with France the year before; it even had advantages. It eliminated the mortal threat to East Prussia, guaranteed what she then held, and pledged Russia to remain in the war until Prussia's pre-Jena extent and the security thereof were assured. In Napoleon's heyday Prussia's aspirations had been directed toward Hanover; now they were directed toward Saxony—actually a considerable improvement, in that Napoleon had only temporarily delivered Hanover whereas Alexander had to make good his promise in order to acquire Prussia's former share of Poland. The treaty said nothing about Prussian hegemony in North Germany, but this goal stood greater chances of attainment with Russian backing than it ever had with Austrian. With Russia behind him Hardenberg could talk to Metternich as an equal. There was one condition, the same condition Metternich had perceived in his courting of Napoleon: to harvest the fruits dangled by the alliance, to be safe in the arms of the strong power, the weak one must be absolutely unswerving and devoted in its loyalty. No one in Berlin understood this better than Frederick William, and to this course he stubbornly clung for the next two years, at times over the pleas of his own ministers and of most of Europe.

The treaty of Kalisch was also a turning-point for Alexander. It marked the irrevocable decision to carry the war into Germany. The guarantee of East Prussia meant sacrifice of an attractive local gain for the sake of grander objectives, partly revealed in the refusal to restore Prussia's Polish lands. At that very time, in fact, the tsar was again in correspondence with Czartoryski, offering to restore Poland.[19] The treaty also complicated to some extent his policy of working through the resistance movements of Central Europe. It was a conventional state treaty; it implied a cabinet war rather than a people's war. The clause about a national militia pertained to Prussia alone. In reference to other states it spoke only of ushering in "the great epoch of the independence of all the states which want to use it to free themselves from the yoke that France has imposed on them for so many years." [20] About the liberation, freedom, or unity of Germany it was silent. It did not even revive

[19] Kukiel, *Czartoryski*, 103–104.
[20] Preamble to treaty, Meyer, *Corpus Juris*, I, 135.

the allusion to the "constitutional federation" which the Bartenstein convention of 1807 had envisaged.[21] Once Prussian troops were committed to Russia there was no point in further undermining the Prussian government. Frederick William was under sufficient pressure at home to summon his people to arms, and this he did in several proclamations a month later.[22]

Thus in the public clauses of the treaty, insofar as it was possible to do so, Hardenberg and the tsar seem to have taken pains to reassure the other German states and encourage them to follow Prussia's example. Yet there was one ruler of whom such an action could not be desired—the king of Saxony, the man both Russia and Prussia had to eliminate in order to obtain the booty they had promised each other. What if he should suddenly declare himself in the allied camp? Would it be politically, let alone morally, possible to go through with the plan? Fortunately for the new allies Frederick August and his Francophile minister, Count Senfft, frittered away precious time in futile attempts to hang on to Warsaw by appeasing the Poles.[23] Fortunately too, Napoleon had withdrawn into Saxony, so that the king could hardly defect if he wanted to. But, depending on the military situation, there was always the chance of an eleventh-hour shift which would force the Kalisch partners either to accept him as an ally or, by seizing his territories, to commit themselves to war aims based on nothing more than the right of conquest—an unwelcome choice, since the king of Saxony would be first in the allied armies' line of march, and thus a test case for the treatment the other Rheinbund sovereigns could expect. If, however, he resisted to the bitter end, all embarrassment could be avoided and the situation turned to advantage, by representing his fate as the penalty any prince must expect for resisting too long. The problem was how to discourage the king of Saxony from making a precipitate capitulation without alienating the rest of the Rheinbund.[24]

Baron Stein's answer was to deny the need for distinctions, to

---

[21] See Ch. II, p. 55.

[22] On March 7 and March 17. Text in Meyer, *Corpus Juris*, I, 147ff.

[23] Oncken, *Oesterreich und Preussen*, II, 245ff.

[24] Cf. *ibid.*, II, 248. See also Karl Griewank, *Der Wiener Kongress und die Neuordnung Europas 1814/15* (Leipzig, 1942), 24.

treat all alike and all harshly. As the allied armies approached the Saxon frontier in March, he proposed a stringent occupation program and implored Alexander to assume the leadership of a German revolution. The tsar, he said, should appeal to the German people to rise against their princes and actually overthrow those who delayed joining the movement for a united German empire.[25] What was finally done, however, reflects the tsar's desire to keep both his options open: the leadership of Europe's resistance movements, and freedom to deal with established governments.

On March 19 he approved a harsh occupation statute, mainly inspired by Stein and Hardenberg, which established a central administrative council with "unlimited powers" over the military and financial resources of the conquered areas, and empowered to divide all occupied territory into five districts irrespective of state boundaries.[26] But when one of the tsar's own relatives, the duke of Mecklenburg, refused to join the coalition on these terms, when even Count Münster, who was to occupy one of the four seats on the council, complained, Alexander changed his mind. On April 4 the power of the council was reduced to supervising the negotiation of voluntary agreements between the allied powers and the rulers of the occupied states. This pertained both to the latter's participation in the war and the future status of their lands. The amendments were a blow to Stein: he eventually became chairman of the council and, under the first plan, would have been almost a dictator. It was already good fun at headquarters to refer to him as "the Emperor of Germany." [27]

Meanwhile his efforts to have Alexander try to launch the German revolution also misfired. On March 25 the Russian commander-in-chief, General Count Michael Kutusov, issued an appeal, not to the German people alone but to "the princes and peoples of Germany," exhorting them to accept the protection of the tsar and "from the innermost spirit of the German people" create a renewed Germany joined in unity.[28] The

---

[25] Ritter, *Stein*, II, 195–196.
[26] Text in Meyer, *Corpus Juris*, I, 138–139.
[27] Ritter, *Stein*, II, 194 and 196.
[28] Text in Meyer, *Corpus Juris*, I, 146–147.

proclamation addressed no ultimatum to the princes but only suggested that, if they refused their cooperation, they would "deserve destruction by the strength of public opinion and the might of righteous arms." The Rheinbund was described as an "insidious fetter . . . which can no longer be tolerated," and its dissolution made a principal allied war aim.

It was an ingenious document. It made the tsar appear the friend of national aspirations without actually unleashing a national rising. It proclaimed that thrones were not necessarily secure because they were legitimate, nor were they doomed because of any revolutionary intentions of the allies. And by demanding the dissolution of the Rheinbund it implied that the fate of the king of Saxony in no way affected the other princes if they acted in time. In the final analysis the Kutusov proclamation meant that neither legitimacy nor revolutionary nationalism was basic to the Russian conduct of the war, but rather that everything depended on individual diplomatic bargains.

Unfortunately for Alexander, the gambit was too subtle. True, the king of Saxony did not defect, but then neither did any of the other sovereigns, most of whom were thoroughly alarmed by the manifesto. It was months before the worst effects wore off and Alexander was never able to restore complete confidence in his intentions. The appeal undoubtedly stimulated voluntary military enlistments in North Germany and useful ground-swells of discontent with Rheinbund rule, but these were no substitute for the disciplined contingents of the established governments. In the meantime the man who profited most was Metternich.

It has been a favorite thesis of the Prussians, not only of Hardenberg and Knesebeck but of their historians as well, that Metternich, even after the failure of the Knesebeck mission, could have prevented the worst features of the treaty by timely support at Kalisch. On leaving Vienna Knesebeck believed it was only a matter of time before Austria would ally with Prussia, and his orders at Kalisch were to collaborate "as closely as a heart and its soul" with the Austrian emissary there. But the latter, Baron Ludwig von Lebzeltern, did not arrive until several days after the treaty was signed, and even then the only reference to Prussia in his orders was the matter-of-fact remark that her part in the struggle had probably already been decided.[29] Hardenberg in particular was disappointed, for he had assumed that, if nothing else, Alexander's Polish plans would force Metternich to help save Warsaw for Prussia. "We were *both* very wrong," he said some time later when Metternich was reproaching him for his pro-Russian policy, "we were both very wrong not to make our conditions with Russia on this subject before entering into the coalition with her." [30] How much greater would Hardenberg's distrust have been had he known that Metternich, weeks before the Kalisch talks began, had gained full knowledge of Alexander's plans through intercepted correspondence between him and Czartoryski.

The question about Metternich's motives arises from the provincial outlook typical of Prussia in those days. It is true that Austria and Prussia had a common interest in preventing the resurrection of Poland, and in other fields as well. But common interests are not necessarily interests of equal import. Prussia, as things then stood, was not a great power, and only the acquisition of her former territory or its equivalent could make her one. Her chief concern therefore was rightly with territorial expansion. Austria, however, even if far from her former glory, still had the resources of a great power. Metternich was as covetous as anyone, but, with an insight as little understood in Vienna as in Berlin, he saw that there were some things more important than territorial gain: namely, the over-all organization of Europe and Austria's place in it. He was convinced, moreover, that a rare opportunity had been presented to do something about it. The Russian campaign had unexpectedly weakened both France and Russia, at least temporarily. "Austria," he told Floret in one of his numerous dispatches to Paris, "sees herself at the beginning of the year 1813 strong through the weakness of the two other imperial courts, and the emperor is without doubt responsible before his people

[29] Metternich to Lebzeltern, 8 Feb. 1813, Oncken, *Oesterreich und Preussen,* I, 421.
[30] Zichy to Metternich, 12 Aug. 1814, in August Fournier, "Zur Vorgeschichte des Wiener Kongresses," *Historische Studien und Skizzen* (Vienna and Leipzig, 1908), 322.

and before posterity not to let slip away the advantages that the present state of things offers to him." [31]

That meant mediation as an independent force, not a hasty alliance with Prussia and Russia, even if on better terms than Prussia alone received. Thus when Lebzeltern, after an extremely dilatory journey, finally arrived in Kalisch on March 5, it was to sound out Russia on the prospects of making peace, not to determine the conditions of entering the war.[32] This is not to say that Metternich took lightly the double threat to Saxony and Galicia, which later caused him so much grief. But he hoped that what he could not then prevent he could later eliminate, in the course of his mediation effort. In the meantime the best use he could make of the incriminating intercepted correspondence was to forward it to Paris.[33] In this way he could make a show of loyalty to Napoleon, discourage any hopes the emperor might entertain of a separate peace with Russia and, what was most important, demonstrate that if France was asked to make sacrifices in the interest of peace, the eastern powers also had ambitious plans they would have to drop.

The same parochial outlook the Prussians displayed in regard to Poland determined their attitude toward the German question. Again they assumed that a similarity of interests (which, as a matter of fact, was much less obvious than in the case of Poland) implied an equality of status. That is the inference to be drawn from the fact that in 1813 Knesebeck took to Vienna virtually the same plan he had taken in the summer of 1809, when the bargaining power had all been on Prussia's side. Both times he proposed a Prussian sphere of influence north of the Main River and an Austrian sphere to the south, and both times the Austrians had backed away. The Prussians thereupon concluded that it was Austria's abiding aim to restore the hegemony over Germany that she had exercised under the Holy Roman Empire.

This was the natural assumption to make in view of Metternich's role in the restorative crusade of 1809. But it did not

[31] Metternich to Floret, 3 Jan. 1813, Oncken, *Oesterreich und Preussen*, I, 80.
[32] Metternich to Lebzeltern, 8 Feb. 1813, *op.cit.*, I, 421f.
[33] Oncken, *Oesterreich und Preussen*, I, 219–220.

take into account his flexibility, his capacity to learn from experience, and his unsentimental attitude toward the Reich, which even in 1809 had subtly distinguished his outlook from that of Stadion. Whatever had been his views before, now he no longer considered Austria strong enough to impose a meaningful imperium over states that under Napoleon had become accustomed to sovereignty, and had uprooted many of the old institutions within their borders which had nourished the Reich and given it a *raison d'être*. Even an Austrian-led federation such as Gentz had proposed in 1808 he considered premature; too many prerequisites were still undetermined— notably the acquiescence of Prussia, and European alignments such that the lesser German states could not lean on France or Russia.

The latter consideration was the most important of all. For in contrast to the Prussian cabinet, which thought of the German question mainly as the rivalry of Austria and Prussia, Metternich conceived it primarily as a struggle between Austria and France or, potentially, Russia; and in this scheme of things Prussia could not be rated as more important than the Rheinbund. In fact, Metternich even saw a certain advantage in Prussia's alliance with Russia, since it all but eliminated the possibility of a Russian withdrawal (which he still feared as late as February 8, when he drafted Lebzeltern's instructions),[34] and it tended to create a more adequate counterweight to the France-Rheinbund combination. In any case, it was much too early to commit oneself to an ultimate solution of the German problem—that could only be considered in the light of Austria's other interests.

In the spring of 1813 the function of Germany in Metternich's policy was to aid in the mediation between France and Russia, and this he made perfectly clear to Knesebeck, who reported verbatim the Austrian minister's case: "To reach this goal the Austrian cabinet desires that all the powers utilize the moment of French weakness and can shift from a condition of dependence to one of independence; and it hopes that they will voluntarily join Austria and that in this way a great voluntary

---

[34] Metternich to Lebzeltern, 8 Feb. 1813, *op.cit.*, I, 422.

union [*Verbündung*], through us and with Austria, will arise in the center of Europe and rest on the principle of the independence of states and the security of property; that a system of justice will be formed to take the place of the system of forced union . . . and to resist all lust for conquest and aggrandizement *regardless of which power these might emanate from.*" [35] One might have expected more literary grace in a statement which Metternich edited, in order to be sure Knesbeck quoted his correctly, but the main ideas come through: voluntary union, independence of states, and security of property, the last-named referring to the territorial integrity of the Rheinbund states.

On all counts the program conflicted with Prussian aims, especially after the treaty of Kalisch put the Hohenzollerns on the side of despoliation. Yet the alternative to Prussian hegemony was not Austrian hegemony but a neutralized Germany. The most that Metternich expected was that Austria might become the rallying-point for all states which feared Prussian encroachments and were willing to settle for the sociopolitical *status quo.* His policy was not one of conservatism or restoration, but rather of non-interference in the internal affairs of established governments. This he hoped would have the widest appeal: to the Rheinbund states, *including the purely Napoleonic creations of Berg and Westphalia,* to Murat in Naples— yes, to Napoleon himself if he would give up his domination beyond the Rhine.

The loss of Prussia was a serious blow, of course, for a Central European union could not materialize without her, but there was no help for it save to try to break up the Russo-Prussian front as part of the mediation effort, or perhaps to convert both powers to Metternich's German program at the outset. That is why Lebzeltern was ordered to try to influence the manifesto the allies were preparing. The allies should declare, so Metternich suggested, "that the states of the second and third rank should lose nothing of their present strength, rather that one desires to see them enjoy all the rights of sovereignty with the greatest independence. This talk will have . . . more effect on

[35] Knesebeck's report of 14 Jan. 1813, in Oncken, *Oesterreich und Preussen,* I, 143. Italics mine.

the courts of the South than any conceivable negotiation." [36]
Such a statement of course would have annulled the treaty of
Kalisch—as Metternich well knew—and so the Kutusov declaration was issued instead. From that time on Metternich's
fear was no longer that Russia would withdraw prematurely
from the war but that, through the medium of Prussia, she
intended to impose her hegemony to the Rhine.

Furthermore, as Metternich saw the situation, Russia had
powerful allies in Germany besides Prussia. One was the patriotic movement inspired from Russian headquarters. Another
was the grand conspiracy headed by Archduke John, which
aimed at revolutionizing the Tyrol, Illyria, and Carinthia, and
which, had it succeeded, would have dwarfed York's defection
at Tauroggen. Finally there was the war party of 1809, Metternich's old comrades, who believed that the time had come to
strike again, and further that there was much merit in a partition of Germany such as Hardenberg proposed. [37] Stein, of
course, was out of reach except through diplomacy, and about
the last group there was little Metternich could do since it included such prestigious figures as Stadion and Baldacci. The
same was also true of the conspiracy, but as its menace was of
an altogether different magnitude, Metternich finally decided
to act. On the night of February 25–26 his agents ambushed the
conspirators' English courier on his way to St. Petersburg and
seized his papers, which provided the evidence needed to expose
the plot a few weeks later to an incredulous emperor. The
Barons Hormayer and Roschmann, among the heroes of 1809,
were captured in the provinces, and Archduke John was placed
under house arrest in Vienna. [38] It was a daring move on Metternich's part, one he would never have made had he not thought
the exaltation of a war of liberation would fatally dissipate
Austria's bargaining power, and would place her in Prussia's
position in a war to the finish against Bonaparte.

Such decisive measures were not possible in dealing with the
allies. Toward them Metternich continued his attempts to

[36] Metternich to Lebzeltern, 23 March 1813, Oncken, *Oesterreich und Preussen,*
I, 357.
[37] Srbik, *Metternich,* III, 54–56.
[38] *ibid.,* I, 151; and Robert, *L'idée nationale autrichienne,* 505–520.

mediate without appearing still to be the lackey of Bonaparte. He began to fill the diplomatic pouches with long and often tiresome disquisitions, in which he sought to reassure the allies that his mild peace proposals and seemingly interminable negotiations with Napoleon were only a sham. The sham was necessary, according to Metternich, to gain time for Austria's military preparations and to convince Francis, the French people, and the rest of Europe of Napoleon's intransigeance. At the same time it was safe, his argument ran, because Napoleon would not accept a peace that was acceptable to anyone else. The entire picture he drew was one of scheming to extricate Austria from her alliance with France, gracefully and with due regard for the claims of legitimacy; and since this is the course events actually took, Metternich's prophecies have often been taken for his intentions.[39]

This view rests heavily on the assumption that Metternich was pro-allied from the start and wanted only to assure himself that the allied campaign would not be waged in the name of national revolution. Moreover, it harmonizes with the French picture of Metternich as an underhanded traitor,[40] and the liberal picture of him as above all the foe of revolution. Yet actually, as we have seen, Metternich feared both sides equally and, after the treaty of Kalisch and the Kutusov proclamation, possibly he feared Russia even more than France.

It was not that the tsar was niggardly in his offers. On the contrary, impatient at Austria's studied indifference, he told Lebzeltern that Austria might expect the return of all her former possessions, the independence of Prussia, the removal of French influence in Germany, and perhaps the restoration of the Reich. Several weeks later, on March 29, he even proposed a free hand for Austria in South Germany.[41] These were generous terms, comparable to the territorial inducements Napoleon

[39] Cf. Sorel, *L'Europe*, VIII, ch. II, of the older scholars; Kissinger, *World Restored*, ch. V, Edward Vose Gulick, *Europe's Classical Balance of Power* (Ithaca, N.Y., 1955), ch. IV, and Rohden, *Die klassische Diplomatie*, 105, of the more recent writers.

[40] See especially Sorel, *L'Europe*, VIII, 84.

[41] Kissinger, *World Restored*, 55–56. Cf. Lauber, *Metternichs Kampf*, 100–101.

had so often offered, and they had great appeal to both the Austrian school in Vienna and the German nationalists. But Metternich was axiomatically opposed to territorial aggrandizement if it in any way interfered with the creation of a balanced European order. When the tsar, in granting Austria carte blanche in South Germany, added the proviso, "the allies reserving to themselves to act in the north of Germany," [42] it was evident that the offer was simply a reaffirmation of Hardenberg's plan for the partition of Germany.[43] The task remained the same: to break French control east of the Rhine and Russian influence west of the Vistula.

This task would have been much simplified had Metternich been able to obtain the help of Great Britain. Early in February he sent Wessenberg to London to explain Austria's hesitations, and to offer her mediation in the war with France. "If England consults the interests which connect it with the continent," Metternich pleaded, "if it appreciates the value . . . of a European equilibrium, it will wish to preserve the one power which can contain the ambition both of Russia and of France." [44] The unofficial British reply was the offer of 20,000 pounds sterling to finance the conspiracy in the Tyrol. The official reply, presented toward the end of March after further correspondence, was a rejection of Austrian mediation.

It was a sobering lesson, for Britain continued to be Metternich's most maddening problem. A continental peace was impeded by Napoleon's understandable hesitation to surrender important military positions while there was still the English war to be fought. A general peace, on the other hand, was hindered by Britain's determination to remove France from Spain, Holland, and the Rhine, objectives which Metternich deemed neither necessary to equilibrium nor conducive to bringing Napoleon to terms. One thing was certain; the problem could not be solved by an abstract discussion of the European equilibrium, the only thing Metternich had to offer at the time.

[42] Quoted in Sorel, *L'Europe*, VIII, 72.
[43] Kissinger, *World Restored*, 56, on the contrary regards the Russian offer as a complete capitulation to Austria.
[44] Quoted in *ibid.*, 53.

And so he was thrown back on his own resources. Denied an Anglo-Austrian entente that might dictate to both France and Russia, he must now in a very literal way attempt to use France and Russia to check each other.

England's attitude therefore compelled Metternich to reduce his demands in negotiating with Bonaparte. When a new French ambassador, Count Louis de Narbonne, arrived in Vienna to try to persuade Austria to join her French ally in war, Metternich pointedly excluded Spain and Holland from the negotiations. These, he assured Narbonne, were matters between France and England. In return Metternich pleaded for assistance in setting up "the barrier of the East" by enlarging Prussia with the Duchy of Warsaw. He also demanded that Austria receive the Illyrian provinces, that France withdraw from the Hanseatic cities and relinquish her protectorate over the Rheinbund.[45] Narbonne was only too happy to break up the Russo-Prussian plans of Kalisch, but in his own way. He countered with an invitation to Austria to join in the annihilation of Prussia. Austria would receive Silesia while Saxony and Westphalia would share in the rest.

If Metternich had really coveted Silesia, as has been claimed,[46] here was an opportunity even more attractive than that of the year before. Yet in the interest of Central European solidarity he refused. "What is necessary for us is that the Confederation of the Rhine not extend from the Rhine to the Niemen," he replied. "Austria cannot fight to preserve France's protectorate of the Confederation of the Rhine." [47] This was on April 7. A few days later a special Austrian envoy, Prince Schwarzenberg, who had relinquished command of the Austrian corps, was saying the same thing in Paris and adding reassurances about Austria's own motives. "We are," Metternich had instructed him to say, "far from striving to reinstitute the old order of things in Germany, for neither the imperial crown nor a constitutional supremacy under any other title could promise it

45 Sorel, *L'Europe*, VIII, 90.
46 See above, p. 142 and note 54.
47 Quoted in *ibid.*, VIII, 88–89. Cf. Grunwald, *Metternich*, 95.

to us." [48] There the matter rested except for one thing: Metternich, professing to regard Napoleon's bid for aid as exceeding the terms of the Franco-Austrian alliance, declared the alliance void and Austria a free agent.[49]

Metternich, the armed neutral, had now appraised the rival sides. The allies could be counted upon to remove French influence from Germany, without giving up their plans for Poland and Saxony. France was eager to frustrate the Kalisch arrangements but only in order to extend the Rheinbund to the Russian frontier. The time had come to work for a peace conference, where the rivals might be induced to forego their respective positions in Central Europe. Bilateral negotiations led not to peace but only to bargaining for Austria's collaboration in war. At a conference concessions might be mutually and simultaneously made and Austria's weight as a mediator would be at a maximum. To bring the two sides together at such a conference and to appear there himself with the greatest possible following from the states of the central area, which was the main point of contention—this was now Metternich's immediate objective.

As the allied armies moved forward and carried the fighting into Germany, the need for a rapprochment with the Rheinbund states became greater than ever. On March 26, the day after the Kutusov proclamation was delivered, the Prussian general, Gebhard Blücher, entered Saxony. Denouncing the king as a tool of Bonaparte and calling for popular support, he made doubly sure that Frederick August would not embarrass everyone by declaring for the allies. Instead the king fled to Austria, where he found both sympathy and more tangible comfort. On April 20 at Prague he obtained from Metternich a treaty in which Austria promised her fullest protection against annexation by Prussia or the establishment of a Prussian protectorate.[50] The treaty of Prague for all practical purposes nullified allied administration in Saxony. The provisional govern-

[48] Quoted by Alfred Greulich, *Österreichs Beitritt zur Koalition im Jahre 1813* (Leipzig, 1931), 18.
[49] *ibid.*, 25.
[50] Srbik, *Deutsche Einheit*, I, 199-200.

ment, an *Immediat-Kommission* which had been taking orders from Stein's Central Administrative Council, now made all further compliance with allied directives dependent on the approval of the absent king.[51] That the allied leaders overruled Stein's advice to invoke the law of conquest, and thereby passed up the tempting opportunity of seizing Saxony for Prussia then and there, only proved more conclusively than ever the non-revolutionary character of the Kutusov appeal. More important, their failure to act demonstrated to all how effective Austria's protection could be.

Bavaria too, the very backbone of the Rheinbund, felt the tremors of approaching allied armies and the pressure of a Prussia bent on obtaining, from her association with Russia, the maximum advantage in Germany while that was still possible. Bavaria was not, like Saxony, faced with annihilation, but she had her own negotiating weakness in the form of her Frankish provinces. These included numerous mediatized estates and the former Prussian possessions of Ansbach and Bayreuth, where public opinion resembled the patriotic transports of the North more than it did the lingering pro-French tradition of "old Bavaria." [52] King Max Joseph's difficulties were increased, moreover, as were Metternich's in Austria, by the presence of a patriotic German party led by the Crown Prince Ludwig, a group which would have emotionally so committed Bavaria to the allies that she would have had nothing left with which to bargain.

On April 5 the blow fell; the Prussian envoy to Munich officially threatened to seize the territories unless Bavaria immediately changed sides. The king and Montgelas now found comfort where the king of Saxony had found it, in Austria. When Schwarzenberg, on his way to Paris, stopped in Munich, he brought not demands but requests, and these the very soul of cool reason and moderation. Metternich asked only that Bavaria evade Napoleon's demands for new levies, keep her army neutral, and support Austria's own peace efforts, and he sent the same message by Schwarzenberg to Stuttgart and Karlsruhe, the capitals of the other South German states. On

---

[51] Huber, *Verfassungsgeschichte*, I, 492–493.
[52] Doeberl, *Entwicklungsgeschichte*, II, 537–538.

April 25 Bavaria declared her neutrality and early in May prepared to enter an alliance with Austria.[53]

So far Metternich's program was developing favorably. The two pivotal states of the Rheinbund were no longer at Bonaparte's disposal, and they had even more reason than Austria had to frustrate the Russo-Prussian plans. Meanwhile, Austria's own strength continued to grow. In April Metternich, Stadion, and Baldacci joined in a rare show of unison to bypass finance minister Count Wallis, and force through a new issue of notes which anticipated the next twelve years of land-tax revenue from the crown lands. At the same time the emperor ordered the assembling of 64,000 men in Bohemia, and brought the level of all forces up to 160,000 by the end of the month.[54]

Meanwhile Metternich turned his attention once more to Prussia. One of the two main objects of a peace conference was to abrogate the treaty of Kalisch, in spirit if not in letter, and when this should be accomplished and Prussia freed from her obligations to Russia, she would have to be dealt with as a potential member of the central bloc. "The stronger and larger Prussia is, the greater will our satisfaction be," Metternich was frank enough to tell the Bavarian ambassador in Vienna toward the middle of April; "we cannot allow Prussia to become the victim of the party that has seized her, her preservation is for Austria a political necessity." [55] Again, it was not so much the political philosophy of the popular movement as its complete dependence on Russia that worried the Austrian foreign minister.

Even with a realist like Hardenberg he made little headway, however, for the danger in the Russian alliance lay in the future while its advantages were present and concrete: only by means of the alliance could Prussia face Austria as an equal, and as an equal Hardenberg regarded the partition of Germany as the only sensible and honorable basis for rapprochement with Austria. That is why he still smarted from the treaty of Prague, which had snatched Saxony almost from his grasp. Despite Met-

[53] *ibid.*, II, 539–541.
[54] Rössler, *Österreichs Kampf*, II, 132–133.
[55] Quoted in Srbik, *Metternich*, I, 156.

ternich's disavowals, he viewed it as an unwarranted incursion into Prussia's rightful North German sphere of influence.[56] The Prussian minister was not unmoved by the knowledge, conveyed from Vienna, that Metternich had refused Napoleon's offer of Silesia, and he accepted the principle that both German and Polish affairs required Austro-Prussian collaboration "without the slightest loss of time." But he always insisted on bringing Russia into the negotiations—just as Stein was wont to do. When Hardenberg on April 11 proposed a secret conference of himself, Metternich, and Nesselrode, Metternich declined, announcing that he would simply send Stadion on a special mission to Russian headquarters.[57] He was not ready to give Napoleon the impression that he was part of a hostile interallied cabinet.

Discouraging as the Prussian stand was, it was hardly surprising. Far more serious were two military successes of Napolean, at Lützen on May 2 and at Bautzen on May 20. These were unexpected, they regained Saxony for Bonaparte, and they created new dangers for Metternich. One was the possibility of a separate peace between France and Russia. The fact that a new Tilsit did not occur, despite Napoleon's overtures, is further evidence that Alexander from the outset resolutely set his sights on objectives greater than merely expelling the enemy from Russian soil. Instead the tsar referred Napoleon to Vienna, almost certainly in the hope of intimidating the Austrians into dropping their diffident attitude toward the coalition.

The other danger actually materialized: namely, the collapse of the central bloc that Metternich was building to add weight to his mediation efforts. With Saxony cleared of allied troops and Bonaparte again making his headquarters in Dresden, the king of Saxony was quick to repudiate his treaty with Austria and rejoin his former protector. The king of Bavaria dropped his plans to ally with Austria, and the king of Würtemberg, remembering his troubles with Austria over the imperial knights of Swabia, was all the more inclined to stand by his former benefactor.[58] Any peace conference now would have to be

[56] Srbik, *Metternich*, I, 155.
[57] Sorel, *L'Europe*, VIII, 86.
[58] Doeberl, *Entwicklungsgeschichte*, II, 541.

brought about by Austria's influence alone. Only war-weariness on both sides and respect for uncommitted Austria's flanking position produced an armistice, signed at Pläswitz on June and scheduled to last until July 26.[59]

In order to progress from an armistice to a peace conference Metternich calculated that the allies must be convinced that their Kalisch plans would be respected while France would be required to retire at least beyond the Rhine, surrendering the German territory she had annexed east of the Rhine, dissolving the Rheinbund, and evacuating Italy. On the other side Napoleon would have to be convinced that he might retain influence in Germany and Italy while neither Russia nor Prussia nor Austria would be, from the French point of view, dangerously augmented. As the two conditions were contradictory, both sides would have to be somewhat misled, not necessarily by devising compacts that Metternich intended to violate, but by luring the rivals into a situation where, their expectations proving illusory, they might make mutual concessions under the threat of Austria's joining the other side if one or the other should refuse. This is the red thread running through the complex, often bewildering negotiations that led to Metternich's famous meeting with Napoleon at Dresden in June. It was the last chance to solve the Rheinbund and Saxon-Polish problems at the same time and to Austrian advantage.

To impress the allies Metternich chose as the bearer of the Austrian program not the regular envoy, Lebzeltern, but Count Stadion, the one man who commanded confidence in St. Petersburg and who could be counted on to give Metternich's directions the strongest and most bellicose interpretation. It was also an advantage for Metternich to remove this firebrand from Vienna and the immediate vicinity of the emperor. Employing the hero of 1809 in this fashion had in fact been Metternich's plan since the first of the year, but Stadion, refusing association with a policy of appeasement, had steadfastly declined all assignments until Metternich should prove his determination to fight. The required proof was the mobilization of the army. Since that had now been ordered, Stadion eagerly accepted his appoint-

---

[59] Cf. Lauber, *Metternichs Kampf*, 75–76, who gives Metternich much credit for bringing about the armistice.

ment, the more so as he might now more effectively oppose a peace, which he no less than Metternich believed Napoleon might accept.[60]

The instructions that Stadion carried to allied headquarters in early May contained the outline of what Metternich called a "good" peace.[61] Except for demanding the return of Austria's former share of the Duchy of Warsaw and a vague reference to the restoration of Prussia to her former status in North Germany (points one and two), Metternich's program gave the impression that he desired nothing less than Russia and Prussia did—which in many respects was true. He proposed, in order: (3) the surrender of all territory annexed by France east of the Rhine; (4) the independence of Holland; (5) the surrender of all provinces annexed by France in Italy; (6) the restoration of the pope; (7) the return to Austria of all territory taken from her after the peace of Lunéville; (8) "the cessation of Napoleon's supremacy in Germany"; and (9) the removal of Italy from French protection. This would be a *good* peace, Metternich suggested, one that he would be willing to strive for at a parley. He added, however, that to induce Napoleon to attend a conference more moderate terms would be necessary, for which reason agreement must be reached on a *minimal* program. The latter Metternich divided into two parts, Austria's own minimum terms and those minimum claims of the other powers which she recognized and would support. The Austrian minimum consisted of the recovery of Illyria, a new frontier with Bavaria, and the dissolution of the Duchy of Warsaw. The other minimum included the return of South Prussia to Prussia, Napoleon's renunciation of all territory east of the Rhine, and his "renunciation of the Confederation of the Rhine at least in part or with modifications."

Never had Metternich chosen his words with such care. The dissolution of the Duchy of Warsaw implied, but did not absolutely necessitate, a repartition of the country so that Russia could not acquire the duchy intact—which was Austria's main

---

[60] *ibid.*, 69; and Rössler, *Österreichs Kampf*, II, 129–134 and 145.

[61] This and following from Instructions for Count Stadion, 7 May 1813, Oncken, *Oesterreich und Preussen*, II, 644ff.

concern. The reference to South Prussia suggested but did not explicitly state that Prussia's fair share of Poland was limited. Most ingenious, however, was the provision about the Rheinbund. The Kutusov declaration had emphatically called for its dissolution, among other reasons, in order that Saxony could be dealt with differently from the other states. But this is precisely what Metternich wanted to avoid; and in addition Napoleon was not likely voluntarily to surrender his German position as long as the war with England continued. Metternich hoped, apparently, that the allies, and possibly Stadion himself, would construe Napoleon's "renunciation of the Confederation of the Rhine" to mean its dissolution. Hence in Stadion's instructions he did not explain the somewhat different plan he intended to offer the French. At any rate, when Stadion met with Nesselrode and Hardenberg at Goerlitz on May 13, Nesselrode gained the impression that Austria would demand nothing less than the dissolution of the Rheinbund and the reconstruction of Prussia on a basis consistent with the treaty of Kalisch.[62]

While Stadion was presenting Austria's case at Goerlitz, Count Bubna arrived at Dresden with Metternich's proposals for Napoleon.[63] Again the Austrian minister called for French surrender of her right-bank departments, the return of the Illyrian provinces and the dissolution of the Duchy of Warsaw. This time, however, he made it explicit that dissolution of the duchy meant repartition, "the use of its present domains for the reinforcement of the intermediate powers." Another change was that the frontier adjustment toward Bavaria which had been requested of the allies was shifted to an adjustment in Italy, presumably because, if the Rheinbund was not dissolved, Metternich would not violate his own principles by taking territory from it.

As for the Rheinbund itself, Metternich insisted that Austria did not wish to challenge Napoleon's protectorate for her own ends but that the allies were bound to bring the matter up, and

---

[62] Sorel, *L'Europe*, VIII, 115–116; Rössler, *Österreichs Kampf*, II, 134–137. That Stadion was also misled on this point has been conclusively demonstrated by Greulich, *Österreichs Beitritt*, 2ff.

[63] Instructions for Count Bubna, 11 May 1813, Oncken, *Oesterreich und Preussen*, II, 645ff.

so he might as well state his position: namely, the conviction that "the independence of the German states under the guarantee of the great powers would offer, both to France and to the rest of Europe, real advantages for the chances of tranquility which such an order of things would establish. In admitting the incontestable principle that nothing would better assure the repose of the great empires than the interposition of another political body suited to diminish the natural friction between great masses, we pronounce the fate of Germany." [64]

There it was—the intermediate plan. Napoleon would renounce his exclusive protectorate but retain influence in Germany through an *international* protectorate. The Rheinbund would remain intact, not as the instrument of any power but to secure the repose of all the powers. Prussia would abandon her designs on Saxony, and Austria would forego her slice of Bavaria. Here and there "modifications" could be made as mentioned in Stadion's instructions, but basically this was Metternich's solution of the German problem.

For the moment, however, neither camp was interested. On May 16 both Hardenberg and Nesselrode, who were now involved in negotiations with England, insisted that the independence of Italy, Holland, and Spain be added to the minimal program, and made it clear that the terms pertained only to a preliminary, not a definitive peace. They also rephrased Metternich's minimum to remove all doubt about "the dissolution of the Rheinbund, the independence of Germany, and the return of the annexed provinces in North Germany." [65] On the other side Napoleon, whose military position appeared to be improving and who in any case could hardly believe that allied and Austrian demands would remain fixed, once more rejected Austria's offer of mediation.

If Metternich's purpose had been merely to expose Bonaparte's intrasigeance, he could simply have published his terms. In fact, so far as the effect on Emperor Francis was concerned, the knowledge that Napoleon had refused even to attend a con-

---

[64] *ibid.*, II, 647. Cf. Sorel, *L'Europe*, VIII, 115–117; Rössler, *Österreichs Kampf*, II, 138–139; and Srbik, *Metternich*, I, 157, none of whom understood the issues.
[65] Text in Oncken, *Oesterreich und Preussen*, II, 318.

ference on such terms should have been more convincing than his rejection of the conditions at the conference itself. Since Metternich, however, genuinely desired both a peace conference and a peace without actually using Austria's armed forces, he continued his efforts. Under the sobering influence of the battle of Bautzen, he now went to the extremity of offering Napoleon a chance to approve in advance peace terms which Austria might then officially demand of him. Were such an accord reached, Metternich said, Austria would back it with her full military strength.[66] Toward the allies, on the other hand, his attitude stiffened, and Stadion was able to induce Hardenberg and Nesselrode to accept a program milder than Austria's previously proposed minimum and considerably more compatible with what Bubna had first suggested to Napoleon.

The trick was turned by dividing the project into two parts, a *sine qua non,* which Austria was prepared to support with her army, and a set of terms for which she would plead but not fight. In the first group there remained of the previous minimum the award of Illyria to Austria and the dissolution of the Duchy of Warsaw. A third point mentioned the aggrandizement of Prussia "resulting from this dissolution"—an obvious effort to undermine the Kalisch pact although the phrase did not literally contradict the treaty.[67] The fourth point concerned the trans-Rhine territory of France known as the 32nd military district. In all previous propositions the entire area was to have been unconditionally ceded by France. In the new formula this was true of only Hamburg and Lübeck, the remainder of the area being reserved as the subject for "a possible agreement" at a general peace conference. Thus the only immediate goal in this regard was to disrupt the continental system and satisfy Russia's demand for freedom of commerce in the Baltic.[68]

Such were the terms *sine qua non.* The two points which

---

[66] Greulich, *Österreichs Beitritt,* 4.

[67] Srbik, *Metternich,* I, 159, interprets the agreement as a categorical abandonment by Russia of her Polish ambitions. More cautiously, Lauber, *Metternichs Kampf,* 81 and 87, takes a similar view. The wording is ambiguous, however, and in any case the allies were not committed beyond the preliminary peace. Cf. Heinrich von Treitschke, *History of Germany in the Nineteenth Century,* I, English ed. (New York, 1915) 573, who comes closer to the mark on this point.

[68] Text of note of June 7 in Greulich, *Österreichs Beitritt,* 25f.

Austria would support but not to the point of breaking up the conference were the clause about the Rheinbund, and the reconstruction of Prussia "as much as possible to her dimensions of 1805." But note: since the fate of the Rheinbund no longer represented an Austrian commitment, Metternich was now willing to adopt phrasing more congenial to the allies. Hence, for the first time he expressly mentioned not only the abolition of Napoleon's protectorate but also "the dissolution of this confederation." In this context, of course, the concession meant nothing. Should a peace conference materialize, he could easily offer as a compromise his plan for preserving but neutralizing the Rheinbund, and this maneuver continued to be the basis of his appeals to France.

There was one other problem. The allies at that very time were putting the final touches on a treaty of alliance with Great Britain, which was in fact signed on June 15 at Reichenbach. It provided for British subsidies and a guarantee of Prussia's 1805 extent. In return Britain was promised the restoration of Hanover and, above all, that no separate peace would be signed. Therefore even if Hardenberg and Nesselrode had not required it as a simple matter of precaution, their obligation to England now made it necessary to apply the terms of mediation to a *preliminary* rather than a final peace. This Metternich himself was willing to do, not only because the terms of the preliminary peace fell short of his major goal, the concomitant withdrawal of France and Russia from Central Europe, but also because England would now be implicated in any future peace conference. British participation had, to be sure, the disadvantage that England would probably insist on the liberation of Holland and Spain,[69] but it would also give Metternich one more chance to establish an entente with the island empire and interpose a truly formidable force between Napoleon and Alexander. With great Britain in attendance the conference would have been a veritable "Congress of Vienna" a year ahead of time, and with

[69] Actually England at the time was not this demanding, Castlereagh being willing to omit Holland. C. K. Webster, *The Foreign Policy of Castlereagh 1812–1815* (London, 1931), 146.

Napoleon's headquarters still in Dresden the Saxon-Polish question could hardly have taken the form it later did.[70]

With several minor modifications the program concerted by Stadion, Hardenberg, and Nesselrode was finally endorsed by Alexander when Metternich personally interceded with him at Opotschna on June 19. It was formalized in the treaty of Reichenbach on June 27: if by July 20 Bonaparte had not accepted the four *sine qua non* points as the basis for a preliminary peace, Austria would join the allies, declare war, and accept the broader allied peace proposals of May 16 as "the program of the peace to be striven for in common." [71] The last proviso was subject to various interpretations, as we shall see.

Napoleon, meanwhile, impressed by, or at least curious about Metternich's visit to the tsar, extended an invitation for a similar interview at Dresden. Metternich has left two accounts of the meeting. One, written many years later and stressing the confrontation of two philosophies, the clash between the man of balance and the man of limitless ambition, exploited the poetical possibilities to the utmost.[72] The other was a terse report composed at the time for the information of Francis,[73] which corroborates, so far as it goes, a much fuller account given from the French side by Caulaincourt, with whom Napoleon discussed the meeting immediately afterwards. Essentially Metternich represented Austria as the loyal ally "ready to range herself at [Napoleon's] side with all her forces," if only he would listen to reason.[74] Admitting the poor prospects of a general peace, he stressed the advantages of the continental terms Aus-

[70] Cf. Austrian declaration of war against France, Prague, 12 Aug. 1813 in *British Foreign and State Papers*, I:1, 819. Metternich's indifference toward England in these negotiations, noted by Webster, *Castlereagh*, 146–150, and Kissinger, *World Restored*, 85, pertains to excluding England from the preliminaries, not the general peace conference.

[71] Text in Fedor Fedorovitch Martens, *Recueil des traités et conventions conclus par la russie avec les puissances étrangères* (St. Petersburg, 1874–1909), III, 105–111.

[72] Metternich, "On the History of the Alliances, 1813–1814," in *Memoirs*, I, 185–192.

[73] Metternich to Francis, 28 June 1813, in Metternich, *Memoirs*, II, 540.

[74] Armand Caulaincourt, "Conversation de M. le Comte de Metternich avec l'empereur Napoléon, telle que S. M. me l'a raconté" (ed. by Jean Hanoteau), *Revue d'histoire diplomatique*, XLVII ((1933), 430.

tria offered. Italy and Spain were not even to be subjects for discussion, he reminded the emperor, while the renunciation of the protectorate over Germany would cost him "a mere title, without depriving him of the natural influence that his position and his power would preserve for France." [75]

On the surface Bonaparte was scornful, calling the sacrifices Metternich demanded worse than the effects of four lost battles, and too high a price to pay for the Austrian alliance. He took special delight in refusing to cede Illyria and maliciously intimated that the entire mediation maneuver was a bluff designed to extort the province from France. His real estimates, however, were different. Illyria, he told Caulaincourt, would only be the beginning. Austria "wants something else; she wants to reconquer her influence in Germany, then in Italy; she wants the protectorate of Germany." [76] Metternich's repeated efforts, through Schwarzenberg and Bubna, had been in vain after all: Bonaparte still would not believe that Austria would be satisfied with a *neutral* Germany.

There was only one way for Napoleon to test his assessment of Austrian intentions, and that was to see where an assent to negotiations might lead. Hence he at last recognized the neutrality claimed by Metternich and agreed to Austrian mediation, without, however, committing himself to the Reichenbach conditions. An official convention of June 30 confirmed the mediation, provided for a peace conference to open at Prague on July 5, and extended the armistice to August 10. Metternich undertook to make this last acceptable to Prussia and Russia.[77]

Since the extension of the armistice violated the Reichenbach agreement, Metternich had once more to brave the fury of Alexander, Frederick William, Stein, and the rest of the allied camp, whose trust in the Austrian minister now receded from levels that were already near rock bottom. The usual flurry of dispatches and letters from Metternich ensued, on the one hand stressing the need of convincing the Emperor Francis of his son-in-law's recalcitrance, on the other voicing confidence that the

[75] *ibid.*, 429.
[76] *ibid.*, 438.
[77] Text in Martens, *Nouveau Recueil*, I, 586.

negotiations were only a formality and had not the slightest chance of "succeeding."

Yet what Metternich represented to the allies as hopes were in reality his fears. So great was his determination to convince Napoleon of his peaceful intentions that even at this late date he was preparing a revision of the Reichenbach conditions in Napoleon's favor. He realized that he could not further strain the patience of the allies by tampering with the terms that directly concerned them, but he reasoned that they could not object to dropping the one purely Austrian stipulation in the minimal program, the claim to Illyria, key to the empire's commerce. "The Powers might certainly lay claim to Illyria as a *conditio sine qua non*," he advised Francis as he made ready for the conference at Prague, "but no one can compel your Majesty to go into a war against your Highness's judgment, for a sacrifice which concerns the monarchy alone." [78] Metternich had no intention of renouncing Illyria forever, since he hoped to obtain the territory later when it was a question of a general, rather than a preliminary peace; but in order to bring about the latter he was resolved to accommodate Bonaparte even on his spiteful vow at Dresden that Illyria was out of the question. To this course Francis agreed, but instructed Metternich to make the concession only "after you have exhausted all other means." [79]

Metternich arrived at Prague on July 12, where he was joined by Baron Johann von Anstett of Russia and Wilhelm von Humboldt of Prussia. The sojourn was a steady succession of disappointments. Metternich found it more difficult than he had supposed to carry out his promise of persuading the allies to accept an extension of the armistice. Since Austria was already committed to enter the war if the armistice expired with the mediation conditions unaccepted, he had no real bargaining power, the more so as news of the great English victory at Vittoria in Spain was just then heartening the allies to resort to

[78] Metternich to Francis, Brandeis, 12 July 1813, in Metternich, *Memoirs*, II, 544.
[79] Francis to Metternich, 18 July 1813, *ibid.*, II, 546–547. Kissinger, *World Restored*, 80, cites this same dispatch as evidence of Francis's timidity, entirely overlooking Metternich's initiative in the matter.

arms again. To meet the situation Metternich was compelled to throw in his last reserves. Only by acceding to Alexander's demand that if no peace was signed by August 9 the Russian army would be free to cross the Austrian frontier into Bohemia on the 10th, did he win consent to the extension of the armistice.[80] The last bridge was burned. If France did not acquiesce, there must be war.

Not until the extension had actually been signed (on July 26 at Neumark)[81] did Napoleon send an emissary to Prague. The emissary was Armand Caulaincourt and, when he arrived on July 28, he brought, alas, neither a program nor plenary powers but only instructions to sound out the opposition. Nevertheless, the conversations had a constructive side. Although averring in later years that he disdained all discussion until Caulaincourt's credentials arrived, Metternich in fact heard the Frenchman out. Caulaincourt, who personally favored a compromise peace in much the same spirit as did Talleyrand and Fouché, contended that two considerations caused Napoleon's adamant stand. One was the confident belief that Austria, whether from cowardice or from the eastern danger, would under no circumstances fight France; at the most she would remain neutral. The other was the equally firm conviction that the program of the minimum was only the beginning of ever increasing allied demands that would make final peace terms much harsher than those so far broached. Caulaincourt, as a man of peace, implored the Austrian foreign minister candidly to state all his terms, immediately and with sufficient force to convince Bonaparte of Austria's determination to fight. "Demand all that is just and especially whatever contains an idea of a genuine basis of pacification," Caulaincourt urged, and "you will obtain that more easily than a trifle because Napoleon will say: Austria has decided on war rather than a truce; if you ask little of him, he will not make any sacrifice for the peace and he will believe he can make arrangements with you at the expense of the belligerent powers. . . ."[82]

[80] Sorel, *L'Europe*, VIII, 161.
[81] Martens, *Nouveau Recueil*, I, 587.
[82] Quoted by Sorel, *L'Europe*, VIII, 164–165.

The most striking feature of Caulaincourt's advice was Metternich's complete willingness to follow it. First he stood firm on the armistice, assuring Caulaincourt on July 30, in an oblique allusion to his agreement about the transit of the Russian army, that "beyond the 10th nothing could get the armistice prolonged." [83] The firm stand was apparently successful, for on August 6 Caulaincourt presented a "secret inquiry" from Napoleon himself, who demanded to know "what Austria understood by peace" and whether, in the event that he should accept her terms, Francis would join him in war or merely remain neutral.[84]

The moment for decision had arrived. Austria must now divulge her entire peace program and state her position for or against Napoleon—or risk a separate peace between the flanking powers. A quick trip to Brandeis brought the emperor's approval, and on August 8 Metternich confronted the French emissary with an ultimatum. The first four terms were still the *sine qua non* portion of the Reichenbach pact, to which Austria was irrevocably pledged. But with respect to the two contingent points concerning the Rheinbund and Prussia's restoration, Metternich continued to hedge. Napoleon need only renounce his protectorate, "in order that the independence of all the present sovereigns of Germany be placed under the guarantee of all the powers." The Rheinbund, in short, would not be dissolved. As for the restoration of Prussia, this was to take place "with a tenable frontier on the Elbe," and no mention was made of her 1805 dimensions. These terms Austria was prepared to back with her full military power, Metternich said, and demanded an answer "yes or no" by August 10.[85]

In the meantime Metternich had learned from Bubna at Dresden that Napoleon had drafted new instructions for Caulaincourt, containing some concessions but no full consent to any of Austria's demands. But even these had not arrived by August 10 nor had Caulaincourt received his credentials. Anstett and Humboldt, their eyes fastened on the clock, their faces

---

[83] *ibid.*, VIII, 166.
[84] Text in Greulich, *Österreichs Beitritt*, 111.
[85] Texts in *ibid.*, 112–114.

registering the smiles of vindicated prescience, did not wait a minute beyond the stroke of midnight to declare their powers expired. Metternich pronounced the congress dissolved. Whatever his hopes and purposes, he now had no choice but to declare war. Any other course would have cost him his personal prestige, forever impaired his ability to negotiate, and invited a Franco-Russian peace at Austrian expense. Besides, the Austrian army had completed its preparations: it was now ready to play its part. Some idea of what that part would be was indicated on August 6, when Stadion wrested from Alexander a final concession: Schwarzenberg, not the tsar, would command the combined Bohemian army.[86] On August 12 Austria declared war on France.

Metternich devoted but one paragraph in his memoirs to the Congress of Prague—was it a painful experience better minimized for posterity? It is easy to see why it has been commonly described as a farce, a pantomime in which two irreconcilable doctrines, French imperialism and balanced European order, clashed in predetermined futility. Particularly suspicious, of course, was Metternich's sudden *volte face,* which at the last minute added the two contingent Reichenbach terms to the mere *sine qua non* conditions. Superficially the shift gave every appearance of being intended to make peace impossible once Austria's military preparations had been completed—a version that Metternich himself wanted the allies to accept.

Yet this view is outweighed by contrary evidence. First, Metternich proceeded to Prague with the emperor's permission to reduce the terms, not stiffen them, by dropping Illyria from the minimum. Second is the extraordinary similarity between Caulaincourt's advice on July 28 and Metternich's new demands of August 8. Not only were the latter more severe than before, to convince Napoleon of Austria's firmness; but they went beyond the preliminaries to a presentation of Metternich's central ideas for a permanent settlement, no doubt to reassure Bonaparte (again as Caulaincourt advised) that there was a moderate and definable limit to future demands. In this connection the core of the problem continued to be the status of Germany. Even at

[86] Srbik, *Metternich*, I, 161, note 6.

this late hour Metternich was practicing his guile, offering Napoleon a neutralized Rheinbund under international guarantee while assuring the allies, through Stadion, that he had demanded its dissolution. Similarly, he led them to believe that Prussia's 1805 extent had been demanded.[87]

Did this plan, with its insistence upon "the independence of all the *present* sovereigns of Germany," include Jerome Bonaparte, king of Westphalia? There is no question about it; it was largely for this reason that Prussia must be confined to "a tenable frontier on the Elbe." Thus Metternich's final offer, far from intending to sabotage peace negotiations, was actually a sincere, last-minute plea. It met Austria's own needs. It adumbrated the program he would have pursued at a general peace conference if one had come about: the preservation of the Rheinbund *in toto* to frustrate the Kalisch plans of Prussia and Russia, and the neutralization of the Rheinbund to remove France from Germany and end her European hegemony.

The new formula, like the Kutusov proclamation from Russian headquarters the preceding spring, was non-ideological. Whether a throne was "legitimate" or the fruit of usurpation was of little moment, provided that the territory it ruled was not disposed of contrary to Austria's strategic interests. Only if its system of government made a state the probable pawn of a hostile power did ideological considerations enter Metternich's calculations. This is not to say that he was indifferent to usurpation, that he took revolution with a light heart. He was indeed a conservative. Every man has his political philosophy, more or less articulately worked out, the sort of thing he extolls when addressing his fellow citizens, exhorting his subjects, musing in his study, or giving advice to his son. But in explaining historical causation it is a hazardous leap from abstractions and generalities of this kind to the mainsprings of practical action. With a gifted and complex personality like Metternich the

---

[87] Greulich, *Österreichs Beitritt*, 43f., 70, and 114. Greulich concludes from these discrepancies that Metternich really intended to break with the allies and join Napoleon. I cannot agree. Both logic and consonance with the over-all structure of Metternich's policy favor the conclusion that Metternich was making a last desperate effort to bring about a peace conference. The stronger the allies thought Austria's ultimatum was, the more difficult it would be for them to boycott a peace conference if Napoleon agreed.

linkage between belief and action is especially devious and tenuous. Throughout his entire career he had to work with slender resources, and he seldom enjoyed the luxury of doing exactly what he willed or willing what he emotionally and morally approved.

In the long years since his flight from the Rhineland Metternich had gradually come to the conclusion that policy and social philosophy operate on two different planes and intersect only at fortuitous intervals. Without panic or overconfidence, without despair or exaltation, he learned how to appraise the new forces abroad in Europe. He learned how to label and catalog them, accept them as facts to be faced, dangers to be met, tools to be used when trying to influence others, and he learned how to relate them to the old system of international rivalries. Metternich the thinker possibly saw liberalism, democracy, and nationalism as evils; Metternich the diplomat and guardian of Austria's interests saw them only as giving a new dimension to war and diplomacy. The "classical" diplomacy of the eighteenth century had been modified, not invalidated, by the revolutionary age.

CHAPTER VII

RIVAL PLANS FOR GERMANY

"War is a mere continuation of policy by other means." With these famous words the Prussian general, Carl von Clausewitz, gave the classic definition of the nature of war. And yet, as often happens with reflective men, Clausewitz found it easier to make a definition than to apply it. Though he himself was in the thick of the War of Liberation (the name itself implied a political objective), in assessing the Austrian war effort he could do no better than repeat the clichés of his day. Schwarzenberg's cautious tactics he compared unfavorably to "the enterprising spirit" of Blücher, and he added derisively that in fighting Schwarzenberg one did not need such strong ramparts as when fighting Napoleon.[1] Caught up in the highly charged atmosphere of the Prussian headquarters, he did not notice that it was the Austrian camp which produced the supreme masters of the principle that "policy therefore will permeate the whole action of war and exercise a continual influence upon it." [2] One was Archduke Carl, who had retired. The other was Metternich.

To be sure, it was Schwarzenberg who actually commanded armies in the field, and it was the Emperor Francis who had ultimately to approve military and diplomatic decisions. But with the latter Metternich generally had his way, far more often actually than he was willing to admit to his allies, while with the general he enjoyed an efficacious relationship that owed much to Schwarzenberg's diplomatic service. Next to Metternich himself no one in the Austrian service had had as much experience in blending diplomacy and war. As special envoy to St. Petersburg in the spring of 1809, he had had a part in delaying Russia's intervention. As Metternich's successor in the post of ambassador to Paris from 1809 to 1812 he had gained in-

---

[1] Carl von Clausewitz, *On War*, tr. by C. J. M. Jolles (New York, 1943), 100 and 375.
[2] *ibid.*, 16.

187

timate knowledge of Napoleon. As commander of the Austrian corps attached to the Grande Armée in 1812 he had skillfully executed the assignment, always distasteful for a general, of merely pretending to fight. Husbanding Austrian manpower, he had avoided serious combat with the Russians without unduly arousing the suspicions of Napoleon, who was always ready to see cowardice rather than method in Austria's lackluster battlefield tactics.[3] There were no military laurels to be won in this way, only the knowledge of a duty done and some appreciation from one's superiors. For in contrast to Frederick William, who stood in constant fear of his Gneisenaus and Blüchers and could not even trust them to obey orders, Francis was in perfect control of his troops, and Metternich delighted in the boast that his armies "started and stopped at a nod from the emperor."[4] Such was the happy relationship that existed between Austria's leaders—a vast improvement over the divided counsels of 1809.

Under the discreet direction of the Metternich-Schwarzenberg partnership Austria's entry into the war took place without the fanfare that had marked the crusade of 1809. Then Metternich's dispatches from Paris had been ardent calls to action; now he demanded caution and discipline. Missing were the drum rolls and trumpet blasts, the *Landwehr* battalions and rousing manifestos. Even the formal declaration of war expressed pain rather than anger and was more an essay on the European equilibrium than a denunciation of villainy. In this way Metternich avoided permanent commitment; belligerency was but another step in a complex maneuver, a continuation of his previous policy by other means.

Even now he managed to carry on the negotiation with Bonaparte. Austria had declared war because pledged to do so if no peace had been signed by August 10, but it had been agreed that hostilities were not to begin for another week. On August 11 Caulaincourt's new instructions arrived in Prague. These contained substantial concessions but left unsatisfied the main points regarding Germany: the cession of Hamburg and Lübeck, a "possible arrangement" for the 32nd military district, and the

[3] Hugo Hantsch, *Die Geschichte Österreichs*, II (Graz-Vienna, 1950), 288.
[4] Quoted in G. H. Pertz and Hans Delbrück, *Das Leben des Feldmarschalls Grafen Neithardt von Gneisenau*, v (Berlin, 1880), 20–21. Cf. Gerhard Ritter, *Staatskunst und Kriegshandwerk*, I (Munich, 1954), 107ff.

surrender of the protectorate over the Rheinbund. Metternich was unmoved. Having issued an ultimatum, he could accept nothing less than its complete fulfillment. Nor could he risk the final disillusionment of the allies, which could easily lead to another Tilsit. Nevertheless, his advice to Caulaincourt—dictated orally so that Napoleon would not have a compromising document to show the tsar—was that any time the emperor decided to accept *all* the Austrian conditions, he should address the three allies jointly, as provided by the Reichenbach treaty. In that event Austria would support his efforts "with the greatest zeal" and "with all our credit," and peace could be concluded "in 60 hours." [5] In this vein the conversations continued for the remainder of the week. Caulaincourt was "disconsolate at the course of events," but Napoleon would not yield. "The last attempt has failed," Metternich reported on August 16, "and Caulaincourt departs tonight" [6]—this was five days after the declaration of war.

On August 18 the French foreign minister, Bernard Maret, Duke of Bassano, replied with an offer of a general peace conference but again evaded the Austrian demands, charging that the mediation had been nothing but a blind to cover Austrian military preparations.[7] The reproach contained a kernel of truth, inasmuch as the Austrian mobilization had in fact been completed during the protracted negotiations—a point that Metternich made the most of in trying to justify his policy to the allies and to the Russophiles in Vienna. But the record is plain. Metternich's dealings with Napoleon contained none of the misrepresentations directed toward the allies. His ultimatum of August 8, the heart of which was a neutralized Rheinbund, had been laid down in good faith and must now be adhered to, if Napoleon was ever to realize that Austrian collaboration was not to be had cheaply. Convinced that military force alone could bring the Protector to relax his hold on Germany, Metternich repulsed Maret's overture. The allied armies must march to the Rhine, and Austria's contingent with them.

Having reached this conclusion, Metternich was forced to

[5] Greulich, *Österreichs Beitritt*, 99ff.

[6] Metternich to Baron Hudelist, 16 Aug. 1813, in Corti, *Metternich und die Frauen*, I, 390.

[7] Greulich, *Österreichs Beitritt*, 103.

modify his German policy. To achieve the neutralization of the Rheinbund without the weight of France on Austria's side was probably impossible. For one thing, there was no way to negotiate with the Confederation collectively except through the Protector, in whom all foreign and military powers were vested. For another, Austria's relations with her allies were for the moment governed by the Reichenbach agreement, which mentioned "the dissolution of this league." Technically this clause was not part of the *sine qua non,* but Metternich had, as we have seen, already led the allies to believe that it had been included in his ultimatum to Napoleon. Practically as well as morally it was no longer feasible to attempt to preserve the Rhenish Confederation.

The important question now was if he could save the German sovereigns individually; and this aim became the one constant in his policy throughout the war. The reasons are plain. Since the main purpose of the march to the Rhine was to induce Napoleon to negotiate, it was imperative to salvage as much of the existing order as possible, to do nothing that would be incompatible with the eventual neutralization of the third Germany. The sovereignty of the Rheinbund rulers must be preserved and the less said about their future union the better. Furthermore, there was no assurance that Napoleon would ever negotiate, and if he would not, then the Rheinbund sovereigns were all the more necessary to counter Russo-Prussian influence. With the decline of their protector, they would gravitate toward the power which offered maximum protection at minimum cost. Metternich was determined that Austria should be that power.

His reasoning recalls Gentz's advice of 1809 that the only feasible approach to the wards of Bonaparte was appeasement. There was, however, an important difference. Gentz's purpose at the time had been largely military; he believed that Austria, fighting alone, needed the disciplined Rheinbund contingents on her side. Metternich's motive, on the other hand, was political: to form under Austrian leadership a central bloc that might hold the balance between East and West regardless of what Napoleon should do. To be sure, Metternich was not indifferent to the military value of the German troops against Napoleon—a point he broached over and over again in his meetings with allied leaders. But if the campaign against France had been paramount in his thinking, he would not have rejected out of hand the kind of war he had advocated in 1809. The defeat of that year he had always attributed to poor leadership, not to the ineffectiveness of revolutionary means. If he now insisted on a cabinet war rather than a national war, if he now sought to appease the Rheinbund sovereigns rather than punish them, the reason was not dread of revolution or German "unity" but rather fear of the limitless ambitions of Russia.

The difficulty with Metternich's position, as with Gentz's earlier, was that it was out of tune with the psychology of the moment. To criticize one's allies at this juncture seemed a mark of rank disloyalty, to talk moderation an expression of cowardice. So far Alexander's official demands could all be construed, if one was eager to think the best, as reflecting the legitimate aspirations of a great power bent on future security, or the understandable excesses induced by the traumatic experience of the Napoleonic invasion, or the natural swagger of a conquering hero, who could later be checked if he proved dangerous. How defend a policy that seemed at once timid toward the French tyrant and disgustingly indulgent toward his puppets? How explain misgivings that were based not so much on overt signs of Russian malevolence as on the common prudence gained from twelve years' experience with public affairs? Politics is the art of the possible, not only in sensing what can be attained but also in appreciating the full range of what can happen. Theory is fundamental. Without it one is constantly being surprised by events. Just as Metternich distrusted enthusiasm in politics so did he shrink from gambling the future of the state on a mere intuitive assessment of personality, on gauging someone else's motives. He had had enough of that in 1809. Instead he reckoned with *all* potentialities, not just those selected in the light of proven intentions; he considered what was intrinsically possible, not merely what intelligence reports held to be imminent. Having been granted the rare privilege of surviving his early errors, he had learned the central lesson of statecraft— that capabilities take precedence over intentions.

At first no questions were asked—in the prevailing intoxication the reserve with which Austria had joined the coalition went almost unnoticed. To Alexander it appeared that Austria had fallen into line as Prussia had. Gone was the need to coddle and cajole, to supplicate the vacillating court at Vienna. The bonfires which blazed forth in the mountains of Bohemia to alert the army were beacons lighting the way to Paris. And, for Metternich, the German question had reached a critical and dangerous phase.

The first crisis in the young and untried coalition was precipitated by Alexander. The agreement of August 6 to give Schwarzenberg supreme command of the allied armies had been a bitter pill to the tsar. If there had to be an Austrian commander, he would have preferred the more "enthusiastic" Archduke Carl, who had built the mass army of 1809—a preference which showed how little the tsar really understood Carl's negative policy during the war itself. Now that the march to the Rhine had begun Alexander reminded his allies that the monarchs had never ratified Schwarzenberg's appointment. On August 17, the very day hostilities began, he demanded the post for himself. Moreau and Jomini, Napoleon's former comrades-in-arms, were to be his deputies. Hence, at the very outset of the campaign Metternich was forced to use his ultimate weapon, the threat of deserting the allies. His threats, benefiting from Maret's peace feeler of the 18th, had the desired effect. Metternich was able to save Schwarzenberg's command, but he could not prevent the mercurial tsar from continually interfering in military matters and dealing directly with Russian and Prussian armies over Schwarzenberg's head. The best Metternich could do to ease the general's burden was to order him to let Lebzeltern and Stadion handle all disputes with Alexander.[8] The tsar for his part displayed the resilience of a man with many different cards to play. When Moreau was shot down at his side a few days later, he observed to Metternich: "God has uttered his judgment. He was of your opinion."[9]

[8] Pertz, *Steins Leben*, I, 687; Srbik, *Metternich*, I, 164; Lauber, *Metternichs Kampf*, 96; and Rössler, *Österreichs Kampf*, II, 146–151. Cf. Treitschke, *History of Germany*, I, 573.
[9] Quoted by Metternich in "Autobiographical Memoir," Metternich, *Memoirs*, I, 207.

If the Austrian declaration of war refurbished Alexander's vision of himself as the great liberator and pacifier of Europe, it encouraged Baron Stein to similar fantasies regarding the restoration of the Reich. As chief of the Central Administrative Council, the indefatigable knight-of-the-empire was not the mere onlooker he had been the year before when dreaming of a rejuvenated Hohenstauffen Reich. Now he was in the midst of the action. Soon he and his council would move in and rule the conquered areas. "The thirty-six petty despots," he said, had forfeited all right to consideration; their continued sovereignty would be "ruinous for the civil liberty and moral fiber of the nation." [10] If he could somehow satisfy Prussia and Austria while pre-empting most of the third Germany to his own enterprises, he could proceed to integrate at least this much of the fatherland under unitary institutions. "It is the greatest opportunity in the world," he wrote toward the end of August in a new memorandum on the German constitution.

In this plan he dropped his earlier idea of a single German empire in favor of a tripartite arrangement. Mecklenburg, Holstein, and Saxony were to be removed from the existing Rheinbund to strengthen Prussia; Austria would regain the territories she had lost since 1805 and place a Habsburg archduke at the head of the province of Ansbach. For the remainder of Germany, although Stein did not altogether rule out the formation of two federal states under Austrian and Prussian leadership respectively, he left no doubt that he hoped to create a third entity, enjoying its own quasi-parliamentary organs unencumbered by association with "backward" Austria and east-Elbian Prussia.[11] The third Germany was to have a central authority with power over war and peace, foreign and military affairs, coinage and tariffs. There was to be a supreme court (a revival of the *Reichskammergericht*) and a reconstituted Reichstag,

---

[10] This and the following from Stein's memoir, "Ueber eine teutsche Verfassung," Prague, August, 1813, in F. von Ompteda (ed.), *Politischer Nachlass des hannoverschen Staats- und Cabinets- Minister Ludwig von Ompteda aus den Jahren 1804 bis 1813*, III (Jena, 1869), 224–231.

[11] Treitschke, *History of Germany*, I, 574–576, ignores the trialistic feature entirely, while Rössler, *Reichsfreiherr vom Stein*, 97–98, says nothing of dualism. Ritter, *Stein*, II, 224–226, though more comprehensive, is not altogether clear on the relationship of the two concepts but seems to dismiss the comments on dualism as peripheral.

members of which would be uninstructed representatives, not mere diplomatic envoys. The mediatized estates and communes were to be restored and given a large representation in the Reichstag, while on the state level diets were to be established with control of the purse and a voice in legislation. There was to be a Habsburg emperor, but the connection with Austria would be that of personal union only. The three parts—Austria, Prussia, and "Germany"—each with a population of about ten million, were then to be bound together in a perpetual defense alliance. It was an early form of the idea that was often to appear throughout the century under the name of trialism.

Stein's plan, with its sharp divorcement of the third Germany from Austria and Prussia, has generally been a source of dismay to German nationalists, hardly justifiable in their eyes even as a desperate concession to political reality. Conversely, it should have had, as Stein intended, much appeal to the Habsburgs, who would have worn two crowns again without subordinating their Austrian provinces to the legislation of a German central authority. On ideological grounds, moreover, both the dynasty and the foreign minister—assuming that Metternich would be swayed by personal interests—might have welcomed the restoration of the mediatized estates to a position of honor and influence. But these observations only emphasize that the animosity between the two imperial aristocrats was less a matter of German unity or German power than of strategy in Europe. Stein's project was more explicit than Stadion's inhibited statements on the eve of battle in 1809, but its intent was the same: to restore as much of the old Reich as was then possible. If it prevented an accommodation with the Rheinbund states, if it meant a fight to the finish against Bonaparte, so much the better. *Reichsfreiherr* vom Stein would return to his ancestral estates in Nassau as governor of Germany. Thus, in his effort to mollify Austria, Stein had in reality thrown down the gauntlet. Henceforward Metternich did everything possible to limit Stein's authority on the Central Administrative Council and the Council's authority in Germany.

The Austrian attitude was disappointing but not unexpected. Stein had drafted his plan to refute Metternich, not to convert him, and it was only through Stadion that the foreign minister heard of it at all. More discouraging and perplexing was Alexander's coolness. In the Kutusov proclamation and in the Russian endorsement of his previous German plan (September, 1812) Stein had taken it for granted that he had the tsar's mandate to re-establish a German empire. Technically the assumption was correct. Yet for Alexander the term "Reich" brought to mind not the era of Frederick Barbarossa but the satisfying days of the Imperial Recess and the Franco-Russian mediation. With Bonaparte destroyed, Alexander would be the sole mediator in a German Reich and could resume his former role as protector of uncles, cousins, and in-laws in the middle states. If, as he had originally supposed, the Habsburgs wished to recover the imperial title, he would be content to be the power behind the throne; but the issue of Reich *versus* Bund was not in itself vital to Russian interests. What was important was the recovery of his following in the third Germany without the competition of Bonaparte and without driving Austria from the coalition.

Stein was therefore becoming a liability to the tsar: it was clear that instead of courting the Rheinbund states he intended to conquer them. As chief of the Central Administrative Council he had already attempted to make a test case of the two dukes of Mecklenburg, who had been the very first to desert Napoleon. Although they had confidently expected to be treated as allies, Stein refused to write guarantees of their territory and sovereignty into the treaties of accession, in the meantime treating their lands as conquered territory. By August, even before Austria had joined the coalition, the dukes had appealed to Metternich for protection and received sympathetic reassurances.[12]

Alexander had deliberately accepted certain handicaps in appealing to Napoleon's wards: the despoliation of Saxony, for example, his agreement with Sweden to seize Norway from Denmark,[13] and his pledge to restore Hanover to England, which would necessitate the dissolution of Westphalia. But to lose in-

---

[12] Huber, *Deutsche Verfassungsgeschichte*, I, 491–492; Ritter, *Stein* (1958 ed.), 442ff.
[13] Cf. Ompteda to Münster, Prague, 5 Oct. 1813, in Ompteda, *Politischer Nachlass*, III, 216–217.

fluence with his own relatives and former protégés in Mecklenburg demonstrated all too painfully that the course inaugurated by the Kutusov proclamation was approaching a point of diminishing returns, or even bankruptcy. Having failed to gain control of the allied armies and to plunge Austria into a headlong crusade of revenge against the Rheinbund, the tsar must now strive to undo the damage.

He disclosed his new course, in the Mecklenburgs, by supporting Metternich's protests of Stein's policies and by withdrawing the governor, a Russian diplomat, from Stein's service.[14] In south Germany, the area in which Alexander had all along promised Austria a free hand, he showed the new line in his Bavarian policy. Now that Prussia and Austria were in the war, Bavaria, the next in line, had to be approached with either a threatening ultimatum or a concrete inducement. Alexander chose the latter, inviting the king of Bavaria to join the allies in a note of August 31, and promising compensation for any cessions Bavaria might be asked to make. That the king and Montgelas were still suspicious and insisted on more precise guarantees of independence does not diminish the force of the *volte face;* it only proves the urgency of a fresh approach to the Rheinbund states.[15]

The new course was, in effect, a repudiation of Stein's German program, and the wonder is that the two men avoided a complete break. Yet Stein was still of value to the tsar—for his crusading zeal, for his fanatical following among Prussian chauvinists, and for his implacable hatred of Bonaparte, which made him a leading advocate of a march to Paris and the overthrow of the tyrant. At the Rhine Stein might be more important than ever, an indispensable source of energy and determination for the crowning of Alexander's European ambitions. Thus, it was Stein's European views rather than his German program that constituted his bargaining power with the tsar and account for the somewhat presumptuous role the Central Administrative Council was permitted to play in German af-

---

[14] Huber, *Deutsche Verfassungsgeschichte,* I, 492.

[15] Hans W. Schwarz, *Die Vorgeschichte des Vertrages von Ried* (Munich, 1933), 89–90. Cf. Doeberl, *Entwicklungsgeschichte,* II, 541; Rössler, *Österreichs Kampf,* II, 157; and Lauber, *Metternich Kampf,* 106.

fairs.[16] In the meantime, if the imperial knight needed reassurances about Russian policy, the concessions to the Rheinbund states could be explained as temporary expedients necessitated by the malevolence of Metternich, the man whom Stein by this time regarded as a traitor to his class.

In Stein Metternich faced a sincere Reich restorer, in Alexander a sham one. The third of his major opponents, Baron Hardenberg, was neither of these; he was a Prussian statesman. As a last resort he might concede to the Habsburgs a purely ceremonial crown devoid of institutional significance, but an empire with organic vitality he opposed with all his might. Nor did he, either by family background or intellectual conviction, particularly sympathize with the mediatized estates. Inside of Prussia Stein's reforms had promoted local self-government through the *Stände* and municipalities; Hardenberg's, on the other hand, favored centralized administration based in part on Napoleonic models. His affinities, in short, were for the Josephinists in Austria, for the state-building ministers in Karlsruhe, Stuttgart, and Munich—and, in foreign affairs, for the methods of Metternich.[17]

Hardenberg's hostility to the Rheinbund princes was a matter of Prussian *Staatsraison*. If he demanded the reduction of Napoleon's allies, it was not to right the wrongs done the mediatized but to clear the way for the aggrandizement of Austria and Prussia and facilitate the partitioning of Germany between the two powers. His aim was essentially that advanced in the Bartenstein convention of 1807 and in the projects Knesebeck had several times taken to Vienna. By restoring the Habsburgs' former territories and reducing Bavaria, Baden, and Würtemberg to weak dependencies, Austria could establish her hegemony in the South. At the very time Stein was trying to minimize Austrian aggrandizement in the third Germany, Hardenberg was pleading with the Austrians to help themselves. Prussia,

---

[16] See below, Ch. VIII, pp. 225ff.
[17] On the differences between Stein and Hardenberg: Rössler, *Stein*, 78–79; Huber, *Deutsche Verfassungsgeschichte*, I, 122–125; Heffter, *Deutsche Selbstverwaltung*, 84–110; and Griewank, *Wiener Kongress*, 89–92. Cf. Hans Hausherr, *Die Stunde Hardenbergs* (Hamburg, 1943), *passim;* and Walter M. Simon, *The Failure of the Prussian Reform Movement 1807–1819* (Ithaca, N.Y., 1955).

meanwhile, was to do the same in the North, annexing, besides Saxony, most of Berg and those portions of Westphalia not required for the restoration of Hanover and Brunswick. In this way Prussia would dwarf all the other North German states territorially. To implement her hegemony Hardenberg envisaged a federal union, which under the circumstances would amount to an indirect extension of Prussian power without having all of North Germany counted as Prussian population gains. As for the mediatized houses, Hardenberg favored their restoration as far as possible: as in the old Reich, they would doubtless lean on the dominant state and thus subtract from the power of the middle states. Technically the Prussian proposals implied that the federal system would encompass Austria and South Germany as well, creating a kind of *Mitteleuropa*. But as the emphasis was not on a joint Austro-Prussian direction of the whole, but rather on a regional division of authority, the net result would have been the partition of Germany which Hardenberg had so long and so sedulously pursued.[18]

Hardenberg's program was ambitious. To raise Prussia from almost the status of a German middle state and make her the equal of Austria—this was a goal attainable only by unstinting effort and a willingness to accept allies where one could find them. But Hardenberg did not always seem capable of unstinting effort. His indolence, his frivolity, his pliability, now before the king, now before Metternich or the tsar, his love of high living, which was less than Metternich's only in measure as he was twenty-three years older—all these traits were legendary, and his contemporaries noted them again and again. They were the same complaints made of Metternich and for the same reasons —personal spite or, more often, plain ignorance of a foreign minister's problems.

The fact was that Hardenberg's methods were adapted to his situation. This was, if anything, more circumscribed than Metternich's, but required the same caution, the same flexibility, the same *sangfroid*, the same veiling of motive behind an ap-

[18] Griewank, *Wiener Kongress*, 91–92 and 115–116; Treitschke, *History of Germany*, I, 576.

pearance of unconcern, at which his younger counterpart in Vienna was so adept. Hardenberg, almost alone in Prussia, perceived the danger of the Russian alliance. He envied Metternich the greater freedom of action he had won for Austria—by his consummate skill, to be sure, but also because it was the Prussian border, not the Austrian, that the Russian army had reached first. Without the alliance Prussia could not really contest Austrian influence in Germany, yet the time would come when Prussia must make a break if she was ever to recover her liberty. But even assuming that the king and the reform party could be so persuaded, a rupture would be possible only if in the meantime Prussia had attained her objectives in Germany and could deal with Austria as an equal. Only then could the two central powers close ranks to block the Russians—as Hardenberg had wished to do before taking the road to Kalisch. The Russian alliance, then, though it did not exactly carry a time limit, was a temporary expedient, a check that would have to be cashed promptly so that the payee could transfer his account.

In opposing the restoration of the Reich, Metternich has been criticized for meekly disavowing Austria's rightful heritage. In resisting a partition of Germany, on the other hand, he has been pictured as arrogantly asserting an obsolete claim to hegemony over *all* of Germany, in however attenuated a form.[19] Metternich was not so doctrinaire as that, nor was he, as time would tell, among those who regarded the independence of Saxony an *absolute* requirement of Austrian security. As usual, it was the total European situation that dictated his course. Napoleon would reject the Prussian plan because it left no room for France to exercise the "natural influence" in German affairs that Metternich had proffered at Dresden and Prague. England must be wary because Prussian dominance over the North would weigh most heavily on Hanover, the one state in the area large enough to aspire to independence. Count Münster, in fact, was already bombarding the *Ballhaus* with reminders that the Prince Regent "would never consent" to an Austro-

[19] E.g., Griewank, *Wiener Kongress*, 116–117.

Prussian protectorate.[20] The British foreign minister, Castle-reagh, wished "to keep clear of the German internal politics as much as possible and only to interfere in extraordinary cases," [21] but what could be more "extraordinary" than the absorption of Hanover's military forces into the Prussian army?

Opposed by both France and England—to say nothing of the German states themselves—the Prussian program was enforce-able, if at all, only with the unreserved support of Russia. This condition, repugnant as it was, Hardenberg had to accept, but Metternich did not. It was one thing to appease an independent Prussia, another to strengthen a Russian satellite, especially as there was every reason to believe that Alexander did not really intend Austria to exercise an effective protectorate over the South German courts. For that matter, there is no evidence that the tsar, once the war was over, would have granted Prussia a free hand in the North either, considering the solicitude he had previously shown for his uncle in Oldenburg and his cousins in Mecklenburg, and the interest he had always manifested in the maintenance of freedom of trade in the Baltic. All in all, though in the abstract it had undoubted merits even from Metternich's Central European point of view, Hardenberg's design depended on many chance factors over which neither minister had con-trol. "The difference in the position of the cabinets is this," Metternich explained, "that Russia orders Prussia about at her pleasure while we intend to and will manage Russia." [22]

Hardenberg's main hope was to gain his ends before the latent opposition could coalesce. In May and June he had tried in vain to incorporate provisions for a federal union in the Reichenbach conventions.[23] Now, with Austria in the war, with France momentarily excluded as a factor, and Britain not yet wielding her maximum influence, the chancellor redoubled his efforts. Despite his reservations, he welcomed Stein's August

[20] Münster to Count Hardenberg, 1 Sept. 1813, in Ompteda, *Politischer Nach-lass*, II, 233.

[21] Castlereagh to Aberdeen, 21 Sept. 1813, in Charles K. Webster (ed.), *British Diplomacy 1813–1815. Select Documents Dealing with the Reconstruction of Europe* (London, 1921), 98.

[22] Metternich to Hudelist, 1 Oct. 1813, quoted in Corti, *Metternich und die Frauen*, I, 599.

[23] Rössler, *Österreichs Kampf*, II, 163.

memorandum because it at least put Germany on the agenda again. He also dropped his objection to a Habsburg crown [24]— though of course this was almost meaningless in view of his institutional plans. Added encouragement came from the battle-field. Those same unruly generals whose politics Hardenberg so heartily distrusted were giving an account of themselves which filled everyone with pride, diminished Prussia's dependence on Russia, and augmented her moral claim to parity in Germany. At Grossbeeren and on the banks of the Katzbach, at Kulm and Nollendorf and Dennewitz Prussian troops were triumphant, nullifying Napoleon's defeat of Schwarzenberg at Dresden. Europe began to hear the names of Bülow and Kleist and Blücher. The heat of the battleground warmed the cold blood of the chancelleries and powder smoke for the moment blurred the sharp outlines of policy. With half a million men on each side maneuvering into position for a military decision, Hardenberg again pressed for a political decision on the future organization of Germany.

The diplomatic situation following the Austrian declaration of war was full of ambiguities. With the failure of the mediation, both the *sine qua non* terms of the Reichenbach pact and the Austrian ultimatum of August 8, which had gratuitously added the provision for neutralizing the Rheinbund, had lost all binding force. Interallied relations therefore were governed by the remaining terms of the Reichenbach agreement. By these Austria (which, incidentally, was not spoken of as one of the "allied courts"), though barred from a separate peace negotiation, was not barred from simply dropping out of the war. This was the loophole Metternich had used in the dispute over the supreme command. As for war aims, Austria now recognized the Russo-Prussian program of May 16. Besides the restoration of Austria and Prussia to the scale of 1805, and the liberation of Holland, Spain, and Italy, this included a relatively weak clause about Poland ("The Duchy of Warsaw expires with respect to name and the form of its constitution"), and a relatively strong one about Germany ("Dissolution of the Rheinbund, independence of Germany, and return of the annexed provinces in North

[24] *ibid.*, II, 164.

Germany").[25] These seven points constituted "the program of the peace to be striven for in common," but whether a preliminary or a definitive peace was meant was still an open question. If the former, Austria was forbidden further negotiation with Napoleon until he had accepted what amounted to frontiers of the Rhine, the Alps, and the Pyrenees as the condition of a peace conference. If the latter, the provisions would become determinate only upon the convoking of a general peace conference; in the meantime they would possess the somewhat academic status of Metternich's "good peace" of May and leave open the possibility of a new approach to Napoleon. For this purpose, however, there was no interim program to serve as the basis of negotiation. Without one, the seven points would serve as a minimum, and this Metternich wished to prevent at all costs.

To head off the seven-point program Metternich wanted a new *sine qua non*. To clear the way for Prussian hegemony in North Germany Hardenberg wanted formal agreement to a future German federation. To bind Austria to the coalition as Prussia was already bound, Alexander wanted a guarantee that she would remain in the war. They all had reasons to fashion new agreements, and to this end, after Napoleon's victory at Dresden had been safely contained, the three men met at Teplitz early in September—not quite a year after the burning of Moscow.

The Teplitz treaties, signed on September 9, 1813, consisted of three bilateral pacts, each with a public section which could be freely shown, and secret terms incorporating the irreducible demands of the three allies.[26] The dexterous hand of Metternich was evident throughout. Since he still intended to negotiate with Bonaparte, his first consideration was to see to it that, outwardly at least, the treaties should have a completely defensive character, containing, as he said, nothing that even slightly

[25] See above, Ch. VI, pp. 176 and 179.
[26] Texts of the public terms in Martens, *Nouveau recueil*, I, 596–607. Full texts, including secret clauses, in Fedor Fedorovitch Martens, *Recueil des traités et conventions conclus par la russie avec les puissances étrangères* (St. Petersburg, 1874–1909), III, no. 70, 117–126. If the present study contributes nothing else, I hope it distinguishes clearly between these two indispensable but separate collections. The latter will hereafter be cited as Martens, *Traités par la russie*.

touched upon the tangible interests of France.[27] Hence the published section was no more than a defensive mutual assistance pact, almost devoid of concrete references to the current war. In it the allies guaranteed each others' territories and promised, in the event one of them was attacked, to intervene "in the most efficacious manner," to contribute 60,000 men, and to abstain from a separate peace. The solemnly pledged solidarity of the allies was the stick Metternich would use on his stubborn adversary, but to it he attached an olive branch, in the form of a war aim moderately defined as nothing more than "the reestablishment of a *juste équilibre* of the powers."

The importance Metternich attached to this clause is shown by the fact that it appears only in the two treaties involving Austria; the Russo-Prussian treaty, by contrast, referred simply to "the mutual interests" of the signatories and reaffirmed their previous commitments.[28] Since this is the only difference in the texts, it must have been the reason for drafting separate pacts instead of a single collective one. The net effect, in any case, was to reiterate across the battlelines Metternich's previous message: there was no chance of dividing the allies, but Bonaparte, should he agree to negotiate on Austria's terms, would find that there were differences among his enemies which would leave him an important voice in the proceedings.

Metternich's devious maneuvering is further evident in the secret clauses of the treaties. These too were divided into two parts. In the first the allies removed their mutual anxieties about a separate peace, each agreeing to keep an army of 150,000 in the field until the end of the war. As war aims they agreed to restore Austria and Prussia "as closely as possible" to their dimensions of 1805; to restore Hanover; and to settle the future of the Duchy of Warsaw by "an amicable arrangement among the three courts." Finally and most important, they agreed to "the dissolution of the Confederation of the Rhine and the entire and absolute independence of the intermediate states be-

[27] Metternich to Hudelist, 9 Sept. 1813, in August Fournier, *Der Congress von Chatillon. Die Politik im Kriege von 1814* (Vienna and Prague, 1900), 7 note 1.
[28] Cf. Jacques-Henri Pierenne, *La sainte-alliance. Organisation européenne de la paix mondiale*, 1 (Neuchâtel, 1946), 31–32, who surprisingly mentions only two treaties.

tween the frontiers of the Austrian and Prussian monarchies, reconstructed according to the scale mentioned above, and the Rhine and the Alps on the other." At first glance the states referred to in these crudely drafted lines appeared to be only those left by the dissolution of the Rheinbund. In the second secret section, however, a different interpretation was given. To impart to the clause "all desirable precision," the additional article read, "the two courts agree to concert their efforts" to: (1) bring about "the restitution of the 32nd military district to Germany;" and (2) to restore "the German provinces now under French princes."

The question naturally arises: why was the last article inserted separately from the others? Records of these events are unusually scarce since the principals were then in close personal contact with one another,[29] and so the answer must rest on circumstantial evidence. But this is overpowering. What else could the device have signified than another stage in the evolution of Austria's program of mediation, with its division into a *sine qua non* and the points for which Austria would plead but not necessarily fight? On this hypothesis Metternich's reasoning at Teplitz emerges as follows. If Napoleon reacted favorably to the oblique inducement tendered him in the public part of the treaties, the terms to be shown him as a new *sine qua non* would be those in secret section I: those regarding Prussia, Austria, Hanover, Warsaw, and "the intermediate states." Austria was now pledged to fight and to enter no negotiation until these were fulfilled. If Napoleon accepted this base and a peace conference materialized, then secret section II regarding the 32nd military district and the French princes in Berg and Westphalia would come into play. On these points Austria was not totally committed, for in regard to them the allies had merely agreed "to concert their efforts."

What Metternich sought by this arrangement was room to maneuver, leverage for enforcing his own esoteric interpretation of the article. Let us recall that Napoleon's counterproposal presented by Caulaincourt on August 11 had refused even to

[29] See F. von Martens, "Russland und Preussen während der Restauration," Teil I, *Deutsche Revue*, XIII:2 (April–June, 1888), 292f. Cf. Metternich, "Autobiographical Memoir," *Memoirs*, I, 172–173.

discuss the cession of the 32nd military district. This was reason enough to drop the issue from the *sine qua non,* where Metternich had hitherto listed it, at least so far as Napoleon could tell. Let us also bear in mind that the restoration of Hanover would have to come about mainly at the expense of Westphalia. Would it not be a reasonable compromise to remove the French princes, King Jerome and Grand Duke Napoleon Louis, from the defunct Rhenish Confederation and compensate them in the 32nd military district? In this way Napoleon would retain at least indirect influence there, yet the area would be "restored to Germany," and Berg and Westphalia would be returned to their former rulers or otherwise used to indemnify German princes. There would still be room, moreover, for restoring Oldenburg and the Hanseatic ports, whose independence was commercially vital to Russia. Nowhere in the Teplitz treaties was provision expressly made for the expulsion of the French princes from Germany.

The nuances of Metternich's phraseology would scarcely have been apparent to anyone who had dismissed the possibility of negotiating with Bonaparte and was bent on his destruction. Thus, while Napoleon was to be lured to a peace conference thinking that the 32nd military district had been removed from the basis of negotiation, the allies took it for granted that the area would be returned to Germany and the French princes expelled.

In comparison with this colossal dissimulation, the chicanery with which posterity has usually charged Metternich seems almost trivial. This concerns the meaning of the words "the entire and absolute independence" of the German states. It has commonly been held that Metternich here scored a smashing victory over the gullible Prussians, persuading them that the phrase meant merely immediate liberation from Napoleon and not, as he really intended, lasting independence from a future central authority.[30] The charge is not entirely unfounded, but it arises from a distorted conception of the situation.

In arguing against a German-union clause at this point, Met-

<hr/>

[30] Treitschke, *History of Germany,* I, 578–579; Ritter, *Stein,* II, 229; and Griewank, *Wiener Kongress,* 113, to name a few, all in varying degrees regard the wording as intentionally deceptive.

ternich probably did call it inopportune rather than intrinsically wrong, and maintained that the wording finally adopted simply kept the issue open. But this was his honest opinion. Since the article in question was secret, it represented a private understanding among the allies, not a solemn pledge to the German states. Metternich was not in principle opposed to a German union of some kind, at least not to a common defense league, which is all that Hardenberg and Humboldt proposed at the time; [31] and he actually kept open such a possibility in the accession treaties which he concluded with the South German states in the coming months. If one must have a culprit, Alexander will do as well as Metternich. Stein had frequently complained of the *Schutzverhältniss* of the tsar to the South German courts, and he was reminded of it again when Humboldt wrote somewhat apologetically from Teplitz several weeks later: "The Emperor Alexander is indeed very much for a union to be created in the future, not however for mentioning it now." [32]

Nor should one overlook the high price Metternich paid for his victory—if victory it was. "An amicable arrangement among the three courts" regarding Poland was not only the weakest statement he had yet agreed to, but for sly evasiveness it rivaled anything ever hatched in the *Ballhaus*. The same was true of Hardenberg's use of "the scale of 1805" as a euphemism for Saxony. Much that favored Austria in the treaties depended on eccentric interpretations which would decline in plausibility as the armies moved forward, and perhaps in the end prove to be no match for *de facto* military occupation. On the surface the Teplitz pacts were compatible with Hardenberg's program of dualism in Germany. Actually the constitutional question was subordinate to the territorial, and the chancellor no doubt

[31] Bruno Gebhardt, *Wilhelm von Humboldt als Staatsmann* (Stuttgart, 1899), II, 6–7. Cf. Heinrich Ulmann, *Geschichte der Befreiungskriege 1813–1814* (Munich and Berlin, 1914–1915), II, 104.

[32] Humboldt to Stein, Teplitz, 4 and 5 Oct. 1813, in Heinrich Friedrich Karl vom Stein, *Briefwechsel, Denkschriften, und Aufzeichnungen* ed. by Erich Botzenhart (Berlin, 1931–37), IV, 428. Cf. K. Waliszewski, *La russie il y a cent ans. Le règne d'Alexandre Ier*, II, (Paris, 1924), 200, who says of Alexander's performance at Teplitz that "it was well played." The attitude of the Russian generals, who are perhaps the main source of the legend about Metternich's ascendancy in the coalition, is suggested in *ibid.*, II, 200f. and Martens, *Traités par la russie*, III, No. 70, 116–117.

thought of the treaties as essentially delineating spheres of influence: Prussia to have a free hand in the North, Austria in the South, and Russia in Poland.

Metternich's greatest victory at Teplitz consisted of relegating to the background the seven-point Reichenbach program. Italy, Holland, and Spain were not even mentioned. Previous engagements, to be sure, were collectively reaffirmed,[33] but the very existence of new accords gave to the old an air of remoteness which made them, as Metternich wished, the desired *results* of a peace conference rather than the conditions for holding one.[34] His main goal continued to be peace with Bonaparte, but the new situation also served him in another way. If the Corsican should still prove intransigeant, Metternich now had "trading potential" with Great Britain. By avoiding all immediate commitments outside of Germany he could hold out for British endorsement of his goals in Central Europe before giving Austria's consent to the liberation of Spain, Holland, and Italy, three of the principal British goals on the continent. Whether the next approach to Napoleon would be based on the larger program, or on the limited one embodied in the secret articles of the treaty, would depend to a considerable degree on Metternich's relations with England. The important thing, however, was that he was free to choose. That is why the Anglo-Austrian treaty of alliance, which he concluded on October 3, was largely a matter of regulating subsidies; on the question of war aims it said less than the Teplitz pacts.[35]

Austria's immediate objectives, meanwhile, required first and foremost a settlement with the Rheinbund governments. The states that mattered most were Saxony and Bavaria, each of which presented its peculiar difficulties. Saxony, as a North German state, was in the sphere of influence allotted in the Teplitz agreements to Prussia and Russia, and Metternich did not feel strong enough at the moment to contest the matter. Until England's support could be enlisted or until the Rhine was reached and the weight of France was once more thrown into the bal-

---

[33] Articles séparés et sécrets, Art. II.

[34] See Castlereagh's complaints on this score. Castlereagh to Aberdeen, 5 Nov. 1813, in Webster, *British Diplomacy*, 106f.

[35] Text of treaty in *British and Foreign State Papers*, I:1, 104–105.

ance as a party to the negotiations, he had to live with the limitations he had already recognized. Above all he must not irrevocably alienate the Prussians, whose cooperation was essential to any Central European system. Only in this way can one explain Metternich's failure to issue another unilateral guarantee to the king of Saxony, as he had done the previous April, or for that matter his relatively mild reaction to the Russian occupation of the country after the battle of Leipzig. Already he was pondering the possibility that he might some day have to concede Saxony as the price for Berlin's support against St. Petersburg. Rather than stake everything on the Saxon question, it would only be prudent to endeavor to arrange things in Germany so as to offset the worst effects of Saxony's loss if that proved inevitable.

The Bavarian problem was different. Unlike Saxony, whose aggrandizement had come about mainly at Prussian expense, Bavaria feared Austria herself. Whereas Saxony's logical point of support, assuming the collapse of Napoleon's system, was Vienna, Bavaria's most natural refuge was St. Petersburg, where she had found assistance from the peace of Teschen in 1779 through the Imperial Recess of 1803. She had also, as we have seen, applied to the tsar for protection in 1809, as a precaution against the possibility that Austria would win the war and wreak her vengeance [36]—which, under the brothers Stadion, she would indeed have done. Metternich's problem, therefore, was how to win over to the allies this main beneficiary of the French system, but without driving her into Alexander's camp. The tie to Napoleon would no doubt be severed eventually by military defeat, but the tie to Russia, slender and tenuous at the moment, was likely to become firm with the presentation of Austria's territorial demands. The Russian note of August 31 had offered the king full compensation for any territorial cessions he might be asked to make. Metternich's bid must be at least as high.

But the list of Austria's claims was long. The Teplitz yardstick alone—the territorial extent of 1805—implied the return of Salzburg, Berchtesgaden, and the Inn and Hausrück districts

[36] See above, Ch. IV, p. 95.

lost in 1809, as well as the Tyrol, Vorarlberg, Brixen, Trent, and many smaller territories in Swabia, ceded to Bavaria at Pressburg. Would Austria insist on her claims? Almost everyone believed she must. In spite of all Metternich's efforts, the spirit of 1809 was abroad in the land, and though it demanded revenge on all the Rheinbund states, Bavaria, as Austria's immediate neighbor and the cause of her greatest humiliations, was the main target. With the possible exception of Gentz, whose attitude even in 1809 had been hard to classify, Metternich was the only one of the old war party who had fundamentally changed. Baldacci, the emperor's confidant, was still, like Stein, pleading for the unleashing of the German revolution.[37] Archduke John and Baron Roschmann, despite their setback in the spring, were at it again, still trying, with the aid of English money, to duplicate their Tyrolean triumph of 1809. They had believed ever since that only Archduke Carl's faintheartedness and Tsar Alexander's aloofness had deprived them of permanent success. Now Carl was out of the picture and Russia was in the war. What reason could there be for sparing Bavaria?

Even the moderates, the men who generally supported Metternich, demanded stern measures. Stadion, though not so sanguine about Russia as in the old days, still demanded the drastic reduction of the South German states to make way for a mammoth Austrian restoration in the region, while the Emperor Francis was sentimentally attached to the Breisgau, the ancient Habsburg outpost on the upper Rhine. The generals, meanwhile, led by Schwarzenberg, who was already angered by what he regarded as Metternich's weak stand on Saxony, rendered their sober judgment that, regardless of all other considerations, Salzburg, the Inn and Hausrück districts, and Passau were indispensable for a strong military frontier vis-à-vis Germany, while the Tyrol was required for access to Italy through the Brenner Pass.

Inside Austria, then, as well as outside, it was fully expected that the monarchy would present a heavy bill of damages. If Metternich did not do so, if he added to his concessions regarding Saxony a treaty incorporating gentle terms for Bavaria, he

[37] Rössler, *Österreichs Kampf*, II, 126–127.

stood a good chance of being dismissed as foreign minister, although finding a successor would have been difficult indeed. His German policy faced its most serious crisis. Accordingly he tried by every means to pry concessions from the realistic Francophiles in Munich. In the spring he had brought King Max Joseph and Montgelas to the verge of neutrality only to lose them again when Napoleon's military fortunes improved. Three more months of bargaining yielded no better results. Whatever Metternich might *say*, there was no proof that he could check Stein and his sponsors and annul the Kutusov proclamation. In August Montgelas finally proposed that Bavaria and Austria jointly declare their neutrality.[38] Coming at the moment when Austria was pledged to war if Napoleon did not give in, the offer was more a move to support Bonaparte's diplomacy than a concession to Austria.

England, meanwhile, continued to pour money into the Tyrol, and this time Metternich did not feel strong enough to oppose the conspirators openly. Instead he allowed preparations for the insurrection to continue, hoping that he might at least exercise some control over them. Whether he seriously intended to permit the project to succeed is doubtful. Probably he simply wanted to reinforce his pressure on Bavaria and curry favor with the British. At any rate, when the signal was prematurely given on August 17, he held back, saying that the Austrian army must first march to restore order and only then call for a popular rising. It did neither, and the revolt died.[39] With Napoleon's victory at Dresden on August 26 Bavaria's attachment to France, her ancient advocate against the Habsburgs, seemed as certain as ever.

Suddenly, on September 5, the Bavarian chief-of-staff, Colonel Anton von Rechberg, arrived in Munich bearing Alexander's note of August 31. The note did not, as we have seen, allay all misgivings, and the promise of compensations for any cessions that might be asked required further refinement, but Russian intercession created an entirely new atmosphere.[40] For the tsar

---

[38] *ibid.*, II, 156.
[39] *ibid.*, II, 154–155.
[40] Schwarz, *Vorgeschichte des Vertrages von Ried*, 90–91.

could do what Metternich could not do, namely, repudiate—
or authoritatively interpret—the Kutusov proclamation and
guarantee any commitments made. When, shortly thereafter,
the Teplitz treaties specified "entire and absolute independence," and the tsar referred all other matters to Vienna, Metternich's continuing difficulties lay less with Bavaria than with the
annexationists in Vienna. If anything, the pressure was on
Bavaria to make the change while she still had something to
offer: the passes into Italy and a strong flanking position on
Bonaparte's right wing. Up to this point the diplomats, Count
Carl Hruby for Austria and Prince Oettingen for Bavaria, had
been the principal agents. Now the rival military commanders,
whose forces were marking time in the Inn district, took up the
negotiations, Count Carl Wrede for Bavaria and Prince Henry
of Reuss, commander of the army of the Danube, for Austria.[41]
It was they who finally signed the treaty of alliance on October 8 at Ried.

By the treaty of Ried [42] Bavaria agreed to withdraw from the
Confederation of the Rhine, to join the allied cause with an
army of at least 36,000 men, and to sign no separate peace. In
return she was guaranteed by the Austrian emperor, "in his own
name as well as in the name of his allies," freedom of action and
"full and entire sovereignty," her army to be part of the grand
army of Austria but under the immediate command of a
Bavarian officer and operating as an indivisible unit. Territorially Bavaria accepted the fact that cessions would have to be
made "to assure to the two states a suitable military line," but
in no fewer than three different articles was she promised "the
most complete indemnity . . . at the convenience of Bavaria
and in such manner as to form with her a complete and uninterrupted contiguous whole." She was expected to open up the
Tyrol to the Austrian army, but otherwise she need not surrender any territory at all until the end of the war and then only
by common agreement. War aims were defined as the dissolution of the Confederation of the Rhine and the independence

[41] Ompteda to Münster, Prague, 24 and 26 Sept. 1813, in Ompteda, *Politischer
Nachlass,* III, 204–210.
[42] Text in Martens, *Nouveau recueil,* I, 610–614.

of Bavaria "in such a way that she, disengaged and placed out-side of all foreign influence, shall enjoy the plenitude of her sovereignty." [43]

These terms were a consequence of the treaty of Teplitz, though not in the way usually supposed. With the dissolution of the Rheinbund, the way was clear for wholesale territorial ex-changes and, although Metternich had not welcomed these, he was determined to profit from them as much as his opponents did. If Russia meant to get the king of Saxony out of the way, transfer him, say, to the Duchy of Berg, in order to indemnify Prussia, Metternich envisaged a similar function for the states in the strategically important area of the Rhine-Main con-fluence. Ferdinand of Würzburg could be returned to Italy, while Dalberg in Frankfurt and the prince of Isenburg could conceivably be transferred to the North or even expropriated. In this way Metternich could offer Bavaria full compensation, not merely statistically as the tsar had done but also in con-tiguous areas. He could do this and at the same time satisfy to some extent the demands of the "Austrian" group in Vienna. Moreover, since only the Austrian claims were hinted at in the treaty, Bavaria received what amounted to a guarantee of Ansbach and Bayreuth. Both features—retention of the Frank-ish provinces and expansion well north of the Main—would, if realized, constitute a blow to Prussia's aspirations comparable to the threat to Austria inherent in the Saxon question. On these grounds alone Hardenberg had reason to feel cheated by the treaty. It sounded better, however, to attack the sovereignty clauses.

None of these arrangements was rendered explicit, of course, any more than Saxony was mentioned by name in the Kalisch pact. By avoiding specific territorial references, by keeping mat-ters on the level of abstract principles—compensation, con-tiguity, etc.—Metternich avoided for the moment the wrangling that Alexander and Hardenberg had expected. In later years, however, when Prussian resistance thwarted Metternich's efforts to deliver the compensations exactly as promised, the court in Munich turned imploringly to St. Petersburg for assistance. It

[43] *ibid.*, Secret Art. I.

could hardly have worked out better for Alexander had he planned it that way.

From Berlin, from Vienna, and most of all from Commotau, where Baron Stein first heard the news, came angry protests. This was no minimum or *sine qua non;* this was a real peace treaty. Hardenberg's and Humboldt's efforts to bind Bavaria to a future German constitution had come to naught. The dreams of traditionalists for restoring a Habsburg Reich were all but shattered. Territorial cessions, since they were not specified by name, faced a questionable future. So vehement were Stadion's objections that he had to be withdrawn from his assignment.[44] But again, as at Teplitz, the cries of outrage came from literal-minded men who were not yet initiated into the mysteries of Metternichean nomenclature.

The crucial clause this time was Article I of the secret section, which provided that sovereignty and independence were to be achieved in such a way that Bavaria would be "disengaged and placed beyond all foreign influence." To the Bavarians, as to the Prussians, this suggested liberation from France followed by full independence. To Metternich, on the other hand, it meant a neutral status, either as a separate state or as a member of a German league neutralized under guarantee of the great powers. In either case Bavaria would not control her own military and foreign policies. Later, at the Congress of Vienna and after, he carried the inference much further, arguing that all manner of ordinances, from the establishment of a federal army to the introduction of censorship, were necessary to place the German states "beyond all foreign influence." Conversely, restrictions imposed by the German Confederation itself were admissible because they were not foreign. Thus the treaty of Ried was not quite so devoid of commitments to Germany as Stein and Hardenberg claimed. There was perhaps a bit of trickery in Metternich's phrasing, but the victim was Bavaria, not Prussia.

Trickery? Or was the phrase sheer chance, its implications only a later inspiration of the ever-resourceful Austrian foreign minister? The answer can perhaps be found in Metternich's dealings with another of the German states, Hanover, or rather

---

[44] Rössler, *Österreichs Kampf*, II, 156.

with the Hanoverian minister, Count Münster, since the state itself had not yet been restored. With Münster Metternich took special pains to explain his position, partly because he needed Münster's advocacy in London, where Austria's prestige and his own were so low, and even more because the Hanoverian was the one middle-state minister who desired to restore the Reich in some form. For this reason Münster is usually classed with Stein, Stadion, and the rest of the patriotic imperial school. Yet his main concern was to avoid subordination to Prussia, and his differences with, say, Montgelas in Bavaria, Baron Carl von Reitzenstein in Baden, or Count Georg von Winzingerode in Würtemberg can be traced to corresponding differences in Hanover's situation. Because the old Reich had not saved Hanover from destruction, Münster attached more importance to a common defense system. Because Hanover had not existed during the Rheinbund period, it had not developed the entrenched bureaucracy and centralized administration which elsewhere were the main obstacles to restoring the mediatized princes and promoting the interests of the aristocratic assemblies against the sovereign. And because Hanover traditionally had an absentee liege lord (at this time the ailing George III of England), there was no central source of energy for state-building in the South German or Westphalian manner; ministers like Münster were more inclined to identify themselves with the Hanoverian nobility, and hence to welcome an agency that might shore up the rights of the *Stände*.

The kind of Reich Münster advocated ministered to these special conditions.[45] Its main function would be, *among* the states to organize a permanent military defense against France, and *within* the states to regulate the rights of the *Stände*. The German princes must therefore give up their sovereign rights to enter alliances, make war, and govern their lands without restraint. The empire would exist "under an hereditary chief," preferably a Habsburg, but the chief or "emperor" would not so much as supervise the imperial army; that function would be-

[45] Münster's memorandum of late October, 1813, "Sur l'état futur de l'Allemagne," in W. A. Schmidt, *Geschichte der deutschen Verfassungsfrage während der Befreiungskriege und des Wiener Congresses 1812 bis 1815* (Stuttgart, 1890), 93–99.

long to a diet representing the states and working through a commander-in-chief of its own choice. One need not add that, as an appendage of a great power, Hanover could always count on having a powerful voice in imperial affairs. Thus the emperor was to be no more than a figurehead, and interstate affairs, confined to matters of defense, were to be handled by the deputies of the states themselves. That much cohesiveness any league or confederation would have to have; indeed the Rheinbund had more. Once again it is borne out that the champions of empire meant by the term more the rights of the *Stände* than German unity *per se*.

Since Münster was at bottom a defender of Hanoverian *Staatsraison*, Metternich stood a chance of converting him. At least it was not like dealing with the mediatized nobility, whose way of life depended on a restoration. It was rather a matter of semantics, of convincing Münster that the old imperial nomenclature was dangerous, that everything he desired in the superstructure of an empire could also be had through the Austrian approach, while his desires about the interior structure, though proper enough for Hanover, could be extended to all the German states only at the risk of losing everything. Metternich's rooms at Prague were frequently open to Münster's emissary Count Hardenberg, to whom he presented his case. Four days after the conclusion of the treaty of Ried Hardenberg reported in detail on the Austrian's views, providing perhaps the clearest statement there is of Metternich's German policy.[46]

In the interviews Metternich was perfectly candid. Even if the princes themselves offered a crown to Austria, he began, he would advise the emperor not to accept. It was not that he opposed German solidarity and strength, but that any institution which imposed a higher authority on the states would miss its mark, would create impotence and dissension. The Prussians would resist an empire because they desired an equal division of power between North and South. The other states would resist because their most prized possession was their sovereignty,

[46] This and the following from Hardenberg to Münster, Prague, 12 Oct. 1813 in Charles William Vane, Third Marquess of Londonderry (ed.), *Correspondence, Despatches and other Papers of Viscount Castlereagh* (London, 1850–1853), IX, 60–67.

and even though under Napoleon they were not really free, they had the appearance of sovereignty; for this they would prefer all the inconveniences entailed in standing by their benefactor to the risks inherent in a German Empire. "With positive laws for restricting sovereignty at present . . . one would only make secret friends of France." [47] Even Napoleon, for all his advantages—the belief in his invincibility, the territory he had to distribute—had had his troubles. Would not a German emperor have less chance to keep order and maintain a strong front against a common foe? In fact, Metternich added menacingly, Austria would be forced to ally with France to keep the malcontents in line.

As for internal affairs, Metternich pleaded that he was not insensible to the repression that might come from the exercise of unlimited sovereignty but, because of the above-mentioned difficulties, one could only rely on the pressure that restrains all despotic governments, namely public opinion. In a flash of stark self-revelation he added: Austria deals only with governments, not peoples.

How then could one avoid chaos and intrigue, prevent the lesser states from banding together to seek outside help? How could one promote the common welfare? First, Metternich said that one could not leave the states of "the third and fourth rank" (i.e., those smaller than Hanover) absolutely free—a statement which Hardenberg took as a hint that further mediatizing would be in order. Beyond that, as Hardenberg reported it, "the count Metternich believes that the sole means of avoiding this last inconvenience [i.e., chaos and intrigue] and at the same time of obtaining the great results that one vainly expects from a constitution . . . or at least the best remedy for all this, would be found only in a very extensive system of treaties and alliances among the German princes, by which each sovereign prince would undertake with the other princes, individually and thereby generally with all, the necessary engagements not to enter into ties with *foreign powers* directed against Germany; to guarantee reciprocally their estates and their sovereignty; to make common cause against all *foreign* aggression, and similarly

[47] *ibid.*

216

against any hostile aggression by a German prince inside of Germany." [48]

Here, in the interviews with Hardenberg, Metternich clearly used the terms *foreign* influence, *foreign* powers, to refer to non-German connections only; they were not mere redundancies underscoring the independence of the German states from each other. Why, then, should one doubt that he used them the same way in the treaty of Ried? Münster himself must have construed Metternich's explanation in this way, for in a memorandum written in late October (and hence just after he should have received Hardenberg's reports) he raised this same question.

"How can one achieve unity, when one begins by guaranteeing the absolute independence of the states of Germany? One dares to hope that this absolute independence stipulated in the secret article of the treaty signed on September 9, 1813 [i.e., the Teplitz pact] between Austria and Russia for the states of Germany is supposed to signify only the independence from every *foreign* [49] power, and that it is this meaning that one should try to give to the treaty of October 8 by which Bavaria has stipulated her accession to the alliance." [50] What Münster "dared to hope" is precisely what Metternich intended. Actually this use of the term "foreign" was nothing new; it was used that way in the Rheinbund Act too.

The main difficulty in describing Metternich's plans for Germany is that he was more concerned with procedure than with fixed goals. Whatever was to be done must be attempted with the voluntary cooperation of the German states. Otherwise they would seek foreign protection—in Paris if France remained strong, otherwise in St. Petersburg. In either case the minimum requirements of a German union must be pledges to abstain from extra-German alliances and intra-German aggression. The former would remove the third Germany from European politics, the latter would provide Austria a broad front against Prussian encroachments in Germany.

Beyond this minimum, however, Metternich was by no means

[48] *ibid.* Italics mine.
[49] Italics Münster's.
[50] "Sur l'état futur de l'Allemagne," *op.cit.*, 95.

dogmatically opposed to a large measure of centralism so long as it was negotiated, not dictated. In this connection he regarded Austria as the mediator between the strong particularism of the middle states and the strong and equally self-serving centralism advocated by Prussia. In any case, it is clear that when Metternich spoke of sovereignty, he did so in the spirit of a lawyer repudiating the hierarchical structure, medieval juridical concepts, and feudal social order of the Holy Roman Empire, not as the foe of German unity. Discussing the German question in terms of sovereignty, one could, he believed, reason with the Rheinbund states; but if one talked about the Reich they would instantly suspect the intent to restore the mediatized princes and the *Landstände*.

Had Metternich addressed his words to a Stein or a Gneisenau instead of to the emissary of a middle-state court, there would have been a ready answer: *écrasez l'infâme!* Crush the Rhenish princes and France too. *Nach Paris!* This philosophy, the doctrine of the national rising, of unlimited war aims and ideological slogans, was still in the air. Indeed, despite Reichenbach, despite Teplitz and Ried, it evoked new enthusiasm as the allied armies converged on Leipzig.

CHAPTER VIII

SAVING THE GERMAN SOVEREIGNS

"As long as the years roll by, as long as the sun shines high, as long as the rivers flow to the sea, remote generations will honor thee, oh battle of Leipzig." So sang (approximately) the troubadour-patriot Ernst Moritz Arndt of the clash on the upper Saxon plain, where "came the peoples from all the world to drive the Frenchmen out—the Russians, the Swedes, the intrepid Prussians, and those who strove to glorify the name of Austrians." [1] Few things stir us less than the myths of others, the heroes they worship, the imagery that sensitizes their feelings. Yet Arndt was not mistaken. The clamor of Leipzig *did* echo through the years, in song and story, in truth and fiction. The French *did* retire to the Rhine. The warriors of the nations *did* free Germany. Whatever disappointments there were yet to be, modern Germany was born:

> Born midst shot and shell
> 'twixt ecstasy and hell,
> Born with the aid of burghers' purses,
> Born to the bark of sergeants' curses,
> Born between the East and West
> Destined thus to know no rest.

With apologies to Arndt, we thus pay our homage to the glory of that hour.

Although not moved to similar transports, Metternich too had reason to rejoice. Victory brought problems; of that no one was more aware. But defeat would have meant unmitigated disaster. Russia would no doubt have left the war. Prussia would have been reoccupied, perhaps destroyed forever. Austria would have survived by virtue of the marriage bond, but diminished and enfeebled, her leaders left to torment themselves with the nagging remorse which comes from choosing wrongly. For once Schwarzenberg's cautious strategy derived not

---

[1] "Die Leipziger Schlacht," lines 17–21 and 38–42.

from circumspection regarding the Russians but from an in-
nocent desire for victory.

Only after the battle did the Austrians resume the dilatory
practices that so enraged their allies. Whether a complete rout
of Napoleon's army was possible is debatable. Schwarzenberg's
campaign can be defended on military grounds, but his pursuit
was notoriously slow. He was under standing orders from the
emperor to err on the side of caution, and he himself believed
that the war should end at the Rhine.[2] "History will be his
witness that he spared nothing at that moment to save the
Emperor Francis' son-in-law," [3] Metternich said years later. Now
that the French army no longer controlled Europe there was no
pressing need to weaken it further, and there was even less reason to expose Austrian forces to needless risk. Only Alexander
would gain from a bloody struggle that wrecked Austrian and
French armies alike. After Leipzig Schwarzenberg was promoted
to field marshal and Metternich was made an Austrian prince.
That was glory enough for a while.

Until the battle of Leipzig the problem of Europe and the
problem of Germany had been one. Breaking Bonaparte's hold
on the continent required the freeing of Germany, and both
operations required the joint efforts of the three eastern powers.
Those purposes were now accomplished. The new situation was
more complex. If the allies elected to end the war on the basis
of the *status quo,* which now presented a rare, perhaps a fleet-
ing, consonance between war aims and the actual military situation, then Russia would no longer need Austrian aid. But the
existence of a strong France would still prevent the tsar's controlling Germany. On the other hand, if the war continued,
Russia would still need Austria to defeat France, but in that
case Austria could conceivably make her aid contingent on
having her way in Germany.

Alexander's choices were divergent. He could accept a peace
of equilibrium and give up his dreams of continental hegemony,
the course which many a weary officer indeed advised; or he
could carry the war on until France was not merely weakened

---

[2] Lauber, *Metternichs Kampf,* 125.
[3] Quoted by Waliszewski, *Le règne d'Alexandre Ier,* II, 202.

but impotent, in which case his mastery of the continent would be a fact so overwhelming that a few concessions to Austria in Germany would not matter. Such speculation undoubtedly shaped his attitude toward the treaties of Teplitz and Ried, and consoled him for having to tolerate Schwarzenberg as allied commander. Here lies the cause of the ambivalence in Alexander's character so often noted by contemporaries: the immense divergence of his alternatives, the one calling for daring self-assertion, the other for meek withdrawal. No wonder he was tortured with doubts and anxieties.

Metternich's options, on the other hand, were convergent, for he aimed at nothing but a European balance. Now that the Teplitz aims had been attained, a separate peace was again possible, and with this as leverage he could insist on trying to negotiate with France. Or, if Napoleon's own folly prevented this and exposed France to destruction, Metternich could take the more hazardous course of attempting to construct a composite counterweight, substituting Great Britain for France (though not excluding France altogether), adding a number of the lesser states and, with luck, Prussia. One thing was certain: he could not agree to continue the war until he had some assurance of acquiring leadership in the German states. This was the least Alexander would have to pay if he wished to pursue his European aspiration beyond the Rhine.

By leadership Metternich did not mean coercion but rather a kind of cooperative system, comparable, one might say, to the relationship that the wiser twentieth-century powers have endeavored to establish with their former colonial dependencies. Neither did he mean a bond based on ideology or the similarity of domestic institutions. French-style centralized administration of varying degrees, Napoleonic codes, and written constitutions, existing or in the making—all that was alien to Austria. Indeed, Metternich was sharply critical of the emperor's own desire to centralize administration and rule the variegated provinces of the empire under uniform statutes.[4] No, leadership meant respecting sovereignty, eschewing revenge, and suppressing all

---

[4] See Arthur Haas, "Kaiser Franz, Metternich und die Stellung Illyriens," *Mitteilungen des österreichischen Staatsarchivs*, Bd. XI (Vienna, 1958), 387ff.

desires to indulge in ideological preaching or reform. It was not simply a question of ingratiating oneself with the Rheinbund courts; Alexander could do that too. More fundamentally, Metternich needed a following of governments which, like his own, made *Staatsraison* the basis of their decisions and in external matters acted with calculation, not enthusiasm. Metternich could lead only if his followers too had the option of joining the war, and then leaving it; only if their armies too could "start and stop at a nod from the Emperor." [5] Such governments were the existing regimes in the Rheinbund states; if anything, their dexterity was greater than that of Austria, as they had proved over and over again. The regimes Stein sought to install were not. They could be instruments of Russia and their goal the capture of Paris.

After Leipzig, therefore, Metternich's diplomacy moved on two levels. On the European level he again took up the question of renewing peace negotiations. On the German level he endeavored to control allied occupation policy so as not to endanger the regimes on which he must rely should peace negotiations fail—or even if they did not fail. Bonaparte's own overtures—one of August 18, another of September 26, and a last feeler, of October 17—Metternich had not followed up, convinced that only the demonstration of allied superiority at arms could give conversations a constructive turn.[6] Now the situation was reversed. Napoleon stood on the Rhine, not the Oder. If he accepted a peace offer on this basis there would be reason to rejoice. But even if he did not, it was important to confront Alexander with a choice between appeasing Austria and risking her defection. Now that the Teplitz war aims had been achieved, Austria had regained her former freedom. She was engaged but not committed. Indeed, Schwarzenberg's conduct of the war left some doubt that she was even engaged.

As the allied entourage moved from the battlefield of Leipzig to the new headquarters being prepared at Frankfurt, Metternich had ample opportunity to develop his plans. Francis and Alexander were in the party. Hardenberg, Nesselrode, and Met-

[5] Quoted previously, Chapter VII, p. 188.
[6] Kissinger, *World Restored*, 98.

ternich himself made up an itinerant conference of foreign ministers. Lord Aberdeen, Castlereagh's ambassador to Austria, was also present, together with Sir Charles Stewart, accredited to the Prussian court, and Lord William Cathcart, England's emissary to Russia. Metternich pleaded with Francis that only a timely peace could save the emperor's son-in-law from his own madness. To Alexander he professed to believe that there was no more chance of Napoleon's acquiescence now than there had been at Prague. To Aberdeen he gave assurances that British maritime rights would be protected. To the entire company he revealed the means he proposed to use. Dramatizing his stand that the continuity of negotiation should never be disrupted by mere military events, he insisted that the allied proposals should take the form of a reply to Napoleon's last offer, made October 17, before Leipzig. The agent he would use was St. Aignan, the French minister to Saxe-Weimar, whom he had recognized in a group of prisoners taken at Weimar on October 24. On October 29 Metternich, the tsar, and Aberdeen adopted the plan in principle, agreeing to offer France her "natural frontiers," and to issue a manifesto affirming the allies' desire for peace. There the matter rested until they arrived in Frankfurt.[7]

Under the cover of these controversies Metternich meanwhile turned his attention to Germany, where the problems, if not so magnificent in scope, were more immediate and acute and in the long run fully as decisive for grand policy. The third Germany was a vacuum. Only Bavaria had obtained a settlement, and even she had not yet secured Russian and Prussian signatures for her treaty. In the rest of the Rheinbund and in the 32nd military district only the controversial clauses of the Teplitz agreement stood between the sovereignty of the states and the ambitions of Baron Stein.

Stein, as we have noted, had staked everything on becoming ruler of the conquered areas, and with a minimum of interference even from his sponsors. As long as his Central Administrative Council was a two-power organ, with the Baron himself

---

[7] Aberdeen to Castlereagh, 29 Oct. 1813, in Webster, *British Diplomacy*, 107, note 1; Fournier, *Congress von Chatillon*, 8–9; Sorel, *L'Europe*, VIII, 200–205; and Kissinger, *World Restored*, 100–101.

as president and his old Prussian associates, Schön and Rehdiger, and the Russian Count Kotschubey as the other members, his influence was great.[8] But when Austria joined the coalition and demanded a seat on the council, he resented the intruder in what he considered his own house. To keep Austria out he argued that she should be content with her South German sphere and leave the North to the council[9]—thus he was one of those who gave Austria a free hand in the South, only to complain later because Metternich was not so greedy as they thought he should be.

Now Stein saw a chance not merely to salvage his position, but to strengthen it. Pointing out to Alexander that the addition of Austria would end Russian preponderance on the council (he counted himself as a Russian), he proposed replacing the council with a single minister. The minister would be responsible to the allied sovereigns but would receive direct orders from a committee of allied ministers empowered to act. The directing minister would also be a member of the committee.[10] The plan was audacious, even overweening. For the first time since 1808 Stein would have ministerial status. On the committee he would be the equal of Hardenberg, Nesselrode, and Metternich. Outside the committee he would be the direct governor of the occupied provinces and in a position to play the assembled ministers against the unassembled monarchs. At both levels Austria would be in the minority. Stein, in truth, still heard the cheers of the Prussian volunteers ringing in his ears. He, who had once forced the king of Prussia to join the war at the head of his aroused subjects, was confident that he could do the same in the Rheinbund states. It would no longer be such a good joke to call him the Emperor of Germany.

Certainly Metternich was not inclined to laugh. The occupation issue was the principal cause of the violent and fruitless arguments that shook allied headquarters in the weeks just preceding the battle of Leipzig. Metternich fought to keep the occupation director off the committee of ministers, to limit his

---

[8] Martens, *Nouveau recueil*, I, 566–567.

[9] Ritter, *Stein* (1958 ed. in one volume), 429.

[10] Stein's memorial for Alexander, Teplitz, 25 Sept. 1813, in Stein, *Briefwechsel*, IV, 422.

authority to routine problems of supply, and to obtain representation for the secondary states that joined the allies.[11] Then
came the victory at Leipzig. On October 19 the allied monarchs
and their retinues triumphantly entered the city. For the first
time Metternich met Stein face to face, and on the 21st they
came to terms.

The Leipzig convention [12] was largely the work of the scholarly Humboldt, acting as mediator between Stein and Metternich. Stein gained his point that the occupation apparatus
should have a single director acting under orders of an allied
ministerial committee, and possessing broad powers to appoint
regional governors and create ancillary organs as needed. Over
Metternich's protests Stein himself was named to the post.[13]
His main duty was to raise money and troops for the common
cause, but he was expressly forbidden to appeal directly to the
population or the state assemblies, as Humboldt had proposed.
This last limitation was of course Metternich's gain. In addition the Austrian managed to scatter his enemies by enlarging
the ministerial committee and excluding the director from
membership. True, he was unable to obtain a seat for Bavaria
or the other Rheinbund states soon to join the allies, but it was
a genuine relief to have at least Hanover and Sweden added.
Sweden, like Hanover, opposed Prussian expansion, since she
was anxious to find compensations for the king of Denmark the
better to justify her seizure of Norway. With Russia and Sweden
defending their mutual interests in northern Europe, with the
moderate Count Münster scheduled to join the committee, and
with Stein eliminated altogether (though he acquired the title
of minister), it was only fair that Hardenberg be rewarded for
his isolation by receiving the chairmanship.

But Metternich saw the deliberations drifting toward the exclusive spheres of influence he so dreaded. In his efforts to
vitiate the powers of the directing minister he succeeded only
in obtaining a dubious compromise, giving the Central Administrative Council varying degrees of authority in different

[11] Ritter, *Stein* (1958 ed.), 459–460.
[12] Text in Martens, *Nouveau recueil,* I, 615–619.
[13] Metternich, *Memoirs,* I, 212.

places.[14] In the former territories of Austria, Prussia, Hanover, and Sweden, as well as in the Grand Duchy of Würzburg (because of the Habsburg connection), Stein's department was to have no authority at all. In all the Rheinbund states that went over to the allies it was to have whatever jurisdiction the treaties of accession prescribed, with the proviso that it must operate through agents accredited to existing state authorities. In the completely sequestrated territories, the "masterless" lands, it was to exercise full and direct sovereignty. The compromise formula, to be sure, did not explicitly mention spheres of influence, but in practice it would tend to have that effect. The territory destined for the third category was almost all in the north: Saxony by right of conquest; Berg, Westphalia (minus the lands consigned to Hanover), Dalberg's Grand Duchy of Frankfurt, and the 32nd military district by the Teplitz terms. Conversely, the states most likely to fall into the second category were in the south, where Metternich, exercising his mandate to speak for the allies, could expect to win Würtemberg and Baden to the allied cause and extend to them the protection of treaties modeled on that accorded Bavaria.

What profound irony there is in the fact that the one thing Metternich and Stein had in common at this time was an aversion to the north-south partition which seemed to come a step nearer with each successive compromise. Both saw the third Germany as a whole, linked in some way to an Austria and a Prussia situated more to the east than either Stadion or Hardenberg desired. Both looked beyond the narrow limits of the unimaginative *Staatsegoismus* which had been Germany's undoing in the past generation. Both desired an end to Austro-Prussian rivalry, and both thought this could be accomplished, *in extremis*, by awarding Saxony to Prussia, at least the portions of it east of the Elbe. Their differences stemmed mainly from their opposing assessments of Russia. Trustingly Stein counted on the tsar to humble France and the Rhenish princes, and to play

[14] The contention of Lauber, *Metternichs Kampf*, 111, and Wilhelm Oncken, "Die Krisis der letzten Friedensverhandlungen mit Napoleon I," *Historisches Taschenbuch*, 6. Folge, v (1886), 1–53, that Metternich scored a major victory here in gaining recognition of the principle that conquered lands were the joint property of the allies seems exaggerated and forced to me.

the passive role of godfather to the new Germany. Suspiciously Metternich feared the tsar meant to become a real father to Germany, and a stern one, and hence refused to weaken France and the Rheinbund states, whose military forces were essential to the continental balance.

Considering all that had gone before and the preconceptions in the minds of both men, the first meeting between Metternich and Stein could hardly have been a warm one. Yet it was perhaps not the least of Germany's tragedies that these two scions of the old imperial nobility had the time to discuss only the urgent, concrete problems of the impending occupation. Had there been leisure for long walks and intimate dinners, had Metternich been able to instruct the baron in the realities of international politics, had Stein been able to convince Metternich that his intimate contacts with Arndt, Jahn, Gneisenau, and the other "Jacobins" meant little in comparison with his essential *altständisch* conservatism, they might have achieved at least a *modus vivendi*.[15] Two years later, indeed, Metternich, with his incomparable gift for keeping personal feelings out of politics, invited Stein to become Austria's first presidial envoy to the diet of the German Confederation. But by then the old baron was so disgusted, not merely with Alexander's ambitions but with all politics, that he preferred to return to his ancestral estates in Nassau.[16]

And so instead of settling their differences, the two adversaries parted at Leipzig quietly aware that the stakes were higher than ever, each determined in his own way to ignore the line of the Main. No sooner had the diplomatic corps left Leipzig, bound for the new headquarters at Frankfurt, than Stein, who had stayed behind to direct the occupation of Saxony, found a loophole in the agreements. Since the Leipzig convention contained no deadline by which the Rheinbund states must go over to the allies, he urged Hardenberg and Alexander to declare the time limit expired then and there. Even Würtemberg and Baden, he insisted, should be treated as conquered

---

[15] Ritter, *Stein* (1958 ed.), 467, takes the opposite view, regarding Stein and Metternich diametrically opposed in almost every way.

[16] Rössler, *Stein*, 103, who takes Metternich at his word; Ritter, *Stein* (1958 ed.), 522, who doubts Metternich was in earnest.

territories. "In order to execute to the fullest the plan for developing and utilizing Germany's resources," he pleaded, "it is necessary to place governors in charge of administration in the states, to suspend the powers of the princes . . . until the peace, and to banish the princes from the land until then." [17] It was an astonishing proposal—and a trifle underhanded. It raised the somber prospect that neither Teplitz nor Ried nor Leipzig made much difference after all. The Kutusov declaration was still very much alive.

If so, there was ample evidence of it in Stein's activities in Leipzig. There he had already acted as if the proposal were official policy. Saxony he intended to be a model for the occupation elsewhere. Almost ignoring the local governor-general, the Russian Prince Repnin, he doubled the financial requisitions and manpower levies Napoleon had imposed, gave the police extraordinary powers over security, and introduced martial law—all with a harshness that dismayed even his friends. This part of his program was still within the latitude allowed him by the Leipzig convention, but his next act was not: the extension of the Saxon military government to all the nearby states of Thuringia and Anhalt.[18]

Thuringia, in medieval times a duchy of some importance, was now merely the regional name given a cluster of dynastic fragments, some eleven tiny duchies and principalities lying south and west of Saxony and partially enveloped by her. In the Reich they had been part of the *Kreis* Upper Saxony, and many of them (Saxe-Weimar, Saxe-Gotha, Saxe-Meiningen, Saxe-Hildburghausen, and Saxe-Coburg) represented collateral lines of the royal House of Wettin, which had once ruled the entire region. The other states were the principalities of Schwarzburg-Rudolstadt, Schwarzburg-Sonderhausen and four principalities of the House of Reuss. Anhalt, lying northwest of Saxony and adjoining Prussia, consisted of three duchies ruled by different branches of the Anhalt family. The petty states

---

[17] Memorial of 30 Oct. 1813, in Stein, *Briefwechsel*, IV, 452.

[18] Huber, *Deutsche Verfassungsgeschichte*, I, 506, note 2. This and succeeding references to this factually rich but ill-digested compendium based largely on the Botzenhart collection of Stein's papers, apply to the data only, not the interpretation. Generally Huber praises Stein where Ritter belittles him.

were militarily weak, their quotas for Napoleon's armies having totaled no more than 4000 troops, but their strategic importance was great. They were part of the corridor of small entities in central Germany which formed a buffer between the larger states to the north and south, and in their center stood the fortress town of Erfurt, which Napoleon had annexed to France to provide a base for his armies in the heart of Germany.

When the inevitable showdown on the Saxon question came, these states were bound to be involved. At best their intimate association with Saxony might facilitate an extension of the area within which exchanges could be made and compromises more easily reached. At worst, if the kingdom should fall to Prussia, their independence would be all the more important to provide a shield for Bavaria and to keep Prussia as much as possible east of the Elbe. In either case, pending a final settlement, their inviolability was a basic requirement of Austrian policy. The Anhalt duchies were probably beyond rescue, but the Thuringian states could still be saved—if possible by treaties guaranteeing sovereignty, but at a minimum by transferring them to Austrian governors. So great was Metternich's distrust of Stein's and Alexander's machinations in this region that even in nearby Würzburg, which the Leipzig convention explicitly assigned to Austria, he took the precaution of stationing an Austrian general. His presence, Metternich wrote to Grand Duke Ferdinand on October 31 "is of the most urgent necessity to give the estates of yr. imp. highness the greatest possible protection from unjust pretensions." [19]

The question of occupation policy was the cause of acrimonious debate among the ministers and monarchs as they traveled to Frankfurt. Nesselrode, the Russian foreign minister, was also, interestingly enough, a mediatized count-of-the-empire, and he shared Stein's assumption that conquest would be normal, treaties of accession exceptional—or at any rate drafted in such harsh terms as to call for the appointment of governors, not the mere diplomatic agents prescribed in the Leipzig convention. His own list left only Bavaria and Würtemberg beyond the direct control of the administrative department, but even

---

[19] Quoted in Chroust, *Geschichte des Grossherzogtums Würzburg*, 398, note 1.

more ominous was the way in which he wanted to divide occupation duties. Not only Saxony and Thuringia, but Fulda, Frankfurt, Hesse-Darmstadt, and Nassau he proposed to place under Russian control, grouping them into two districts, each with a Russian governor. The arrangement would have made Alexander master of a wide belt straight through the center of Germany. To the north Nesselrode envisaged two districts under Prussian governors and to the south a single district, composed of Baden and Würzburg, for Austria. For the immediate future Nesselrode no doubt meant to provide the Russian armies with a secure line of operations from Russia to the Rhine, preparatory to the invasion of France. For the distant future who could tell? Even the patriots might ask why Russia need appoint any governors at all, let alone two of them—as many as Prussia named and one more than Austria. Stein himself, when he heard of the plan, advised the assignment of Hesse-Darmstadt and three of the Saxon duchies to Austria.[20]

Fortunately for Metternich, or possibly because of his own skill in timing, the issue of the Russian occupation corridor arose just when he and Aberdeen and the tsar were grappling with the problem of St. Aignan's mission to Napoleon. Information about these interviews is scanty. But in view of Metternich's conviction that Austria could not even contemplate remaining in the war unless she had her way in Germany, it is reasonable to suppose that he tied both issues together and relied once more on his ultimate weapon, the threat of a separate peace. He had one more advantage. Since he was in earnest about negotiating with Bonaparte, he knew that the occupation arrangements could soon become the basis of a final settlement and might, under Austrian guidance, be a force to help bring about peace. Alexander, on the other hand, had no intention of allowing the peace negotiations to succeed, and viewed any plans now made for Germany as alterable in his favor once France had been beaten. In any case, we do know that on October 29, when the allied leaders had reached Meiningen, the tsar agreed to renewing talks with Napoleon,[21] and on the

[20] Pertz, *Steins Leben*, I, 716.
[21] See above, this Chapter, p. 223.

30th Nesselrode dispatched a revised occupation plan to Stein.[22]

The new plan confined the Russian zone to the kingdom of Saxony, two of the Saxon duchies, and Fulda, adding the remainder to Austria's sphere. It did not appreciably change Prussia's zones. The plan also abandoned the system of consolidated districts, advocated by Stein and Nesselrode, in favor of separate administrations for each individual state, thus countermanding Stein's merger of Saxony and Thuringia and forestalling similar consolidations elsewhere. Lest there be any doubt about it, Nesselrode's covering letter reminded Stein that in dealing with the princes his job was administration; allied headquarters would handle the accession treaties. At Metternich's suggestion Nesselrode also ordered Stein to come to allied headquarters as soon as possible. The publicized reason was the need to draft regulations for the joint war effort; the unexpressed reason was the desire to keep an eye on him. At Frankfurt Metternich intended to sign treaties with allies, not to impose governors on conquered provinces.[23]

Three days later he scored two more triumphs. One was a military convention with Hesse-Darmstadt by which the grand duke left the Rheinbund and joined his troops to the Austro-Bavarian corps, thereby averting the possibility of being dragooned into the Russo-Prussian system.[24] The other victory was the long-awaited treaty with Würtemberg, negotiated with King Frederick's foreign minister, Count Zeppelin, and signed when the allied caravan reached Fulda on November 2.

In Zeppelin, Metternich did not find the nonchalance that the Bavarians had exhibited on a similar occasion. Bavaria's shift of sides could, in the eyes of a generous observer, pass as a diplomatic maneuver; Würtemberg's was plainly the penalty of defeat. In the very nature of things Würtemberg lacked the bargaining power of her stronger neighbor. Even without the increments of the Napoleonic period the Wittelsbachs had counted for something in Germany, but this could not be said for the House of Würtemberg, whose lofty status depended on

---

[22] Pertz, *Steins Leben*, I, 716.
[23] *ibid.*, I, 716.
[24] Text in Martens, *Nouveau recueil*, IV, 96–97.

retaining most of the ecclesiastical estates, mediatized properties, and former free cities in which the realm abounded. There were many states weaker than Würtemberg but hardly any so vulnerable, and this condition guided her conduct. If gross presumption was the hall mark of Bavarian policy, stealth characterized the court at Stuttgart.

Metternich's negotiations with Würtemberg had been long and tortuous. After a brief springtime flirtation he had seen the king scurry back to the familiar protection of Napoleon, and with Austria's declaration of war even diplomatic relations had ceased. Yet he persevered, and after making sure, at Teplitz, of his authority to reach a settlement with the South German courts, he used his former envoy to Stuttgart, Baron Franz von Binder, to renew the invitation to join the allies. The reply, secretly conveyed past Bonaparte's spies in a letter from the publisher Johann Friedrich Cotta, was encouraging but did little more than restore communication. A second letter, written October 6 by Count Zeppelin himself, was held up in Bavaria— perhaps the first hostile act committed by that state against her erstwhile allies after signing the treaty of Ried.[25]

The defection of Bavaria was the needed catalyst. Stunned by the news, the king of Würtemberg made haste to send a private subject, the banker Kaulla, to allied headquarters to seek terms similar to those in the treaty of Ried. The tsar, eager to have a hand in the impending success, on October 14 proposed to Metternich that he intercede as he had in the case of Bavaria. It was not Metternich's intention, however, to allow Alexander a second time to interfere in South German affairs, and to make it appear in Stuttgart that St. Petersburg rather than Vienna was responsible for a generous offer; he replied that no invitation was necessary as Würtemberg had already accepted. The statement was premature, if not an outright lie. Actually, Kaulla was delayed—again by action of the Bavarians—and did not reach headquarters until October 20, *after* the battle of Leipzig, and even then he was not empowered to act. In the meantime, however, the king's composure had been further shattered by the approach of the Bavarian army of the Danube com-

[25] Hölzle, *Württemberg im Zeitalter*, 159–160.

manded by General Wrede. Although under Austrian orders to proceed directly to Bamberg and threaten Napoleon's line of retreat, Wrede had taken a detour which brought him near the Würtemberg border and enabled him to threaten the king with conquest and expulsion; Stein himself could not have spoken more menacingly. It was to avoid invasion that King Frederick signed an armistice on October 23 and a week later sent Zeppelin to Fulda, instructing him to join the alliance only if neutrality would not be possible, but at all events to insist on territorial guarantees and recognition of sovereignty.

In tone the treaty of Fulda [26] catered to these sensitivities. Like that of Ried, which it followed in many respects, it was generously sprinkled with references to sovereignty and indemnities. Yet in cold fact it attached modifying clauses to both principles which could nullify them. Würtemberg was to enjoy sovereignty "under the guarantee of the political conditions which will result from the arrangements to be made at the time of the future peace for the purpose of restoring and assuring the independence and liberty of Germany." [27] A fine mess of verbiage, as Treitschke has pointed out,[28] but definitely more explicit than the restraints barely hinted at in the treaty with Bavaria. As to territorial integrity, only "the ancient Würtemberg possessions" received unconditional guarantee; the rest were subject to transfer if the "liberty and independence of Germany" required it. Indemnities were promised in contiguous areas and at Würtemberg's convenience, but only "insofar as possible," and always provided that "the masses of disposable objects at the peace will permit it."

The treaty of Fulda does not deserve the sinister reputation it soon acquired as an impediment to German unity. To be sure, it threw another spadeful of dirt on the grave of the Reich, with its hierarchy of estates culminating in a Habsburg emperor, but it set virtually no limit on the unity that might be obtained through a federal arrangement, which even Hardenberg and Humboldt regarded as the only possible or desirable

[26] Text in Martens, *Nouveau recueil*, I, 643–648.
[27] *ibid.*
[28] Treitschke, *History of Germany*, I, 610.

pattern for Germany. What the opponents of the treaty really deplored was the fact that it saved the dynasty, dashed the hopes of the mediatized houses, and kept the land free of Stein's control. For the treaty did not so much as mention the central department, let alone define Würtemberg's relationship to it, as the Leipzig convention implied should be done. In consequence Würtemberg, like Bavaria, Hanover, and the great powers, avoided the nuisance of having a supervisory agent of the department on the premises. It is in this sense that the treaty was a triumph for Metternich.

In another sense, however, Metternich did not succeed. Frederick, whose opinion is surely germane here, never ceased to regard the treaty as another step in a plot begun at Ried by Metternich and Montgelas, to deliver parts of Würtemberg to Bavaria and subordinate the remainder to a South German union under Wittelsbach leadership. "In one day," he lamented, "has been destroyed what I worked fourteen years to build." [29] Before signing the treaty he had taken care to assure his French protector that, were the fortunes of war to change again, "he could show his unchanged feelings for the Emperor." [30] His course after the treaty was in the other direction: not toward Metternich, however, but toward the tsar, who in January formally offered his protection [31] and a year later gave his sister in marriage to the crown prince. As often before, Metternich had bested Stein but not Alexander.

Arriving in Frankfurt on November 4, two days ahead of the emperor, Metternich found the proud old city as sophisticated as ever, serenely conscious that it stood at the center of Germany's commerce, her rivers and highways, and her history. The Prince Primate had fled, and the territory that made up the grand duchy fell within the authority of Stein's department. On hand to greet the allied monarchs were the emissaries of the Rheinbund princes, come in haste to plead for the inviolability of their states. There was not a Bonapartist among them, to judge from the tales they told of the Protector's tyranny and

[29] Quoted in Hölzle, *Württemberg im Zeitalter*, 160.
[30] *ibid.*, 161.
[31] See below, Ch. x, p. 307.

of their own intrepid criticism, voiced behind his back over the years. Politically they favored the *status quo,* and only hoped that they would fare as well as their colleagues in Munich and Stuttgart, though none had such large military contingents to contribute and some were hard pressed to muster so much as a single infantry squad.

These last, the very smallest of the Rheinbund states, faced an especially precarious future. In several cases they had acquired sovereignty because of some chance circumstance, perhaps a good connection in Paris, which might now be held against them. They were neither morally acceptable to Stein nor, with some exceptions, militarily important to Metternich. Of what use were the 29 soldiers of Prince von der Leyen or even the tenfold greater army (291) of the prince of Isenburg? [32] Some possessed strategic importance, like the Thuringian principalities, but this only involved them more deeply in the plots of the larger states. The danger of falling under the central department as conquered territory was scarcely more than the danger inherent in the treaties that Metternich hoped to sign at Frankfurt with the larger states. Guaranteeing indemnities for ceded territories worked two ways. One state's compensation was another's loss, and it was difficult to see how the claims of the great powers and the middle states could be met, and old entities restored, out of the sequestrated territories alone. Every redistribution from the treaty of Basel to the Rhenish Act of Confederation had brought more mediatizing. Even under the Rheinbund the small states had been threatened with it when they displeased the Protector. Now, at Frankfurt, the temptation to settle disputes among the great by sacrificing the small would be almost irresistible, particularly if the war ended at the Rhine and no left-bank territory was available to relieve the pressure. Legally the petty sovereigns had the same status as the great; politically, although they did not immediately perceive it, their interests lay closer to those of the mediatized. Hoping for the best but fearing the worst, they came to Frankfurt filled with anxiety.

The mediatized, on the other hand, both the princely houses

[32] Figures from d'Arenberg, *Les princes du St-Empire,* 162.

and the old imperial cities, were jubilant at the turn of events. They did not control a single squad among them, but they were numerous and had inexhaustible reserves of hate to contribute to the fight. They came from their castles and manor houses, from their guild halls and *Rathäuser,* cursing the upstart sovereigns and telling horrendous stories of encounters with arrogant prefects and surly bureaucrats. They carried ancient charters and deeds, and itemized bills of damage compiled during the many idle moments they had enjoyed since the collapse of the Reich. Filled with sweet memories of the old empire—the sweeter for being dim and inaccurate—they half expected the allies to resurrect the *Reichskammergericht,* and imagined they could already hear its avenging judgments. More realistically, they tied their hopes to their official representative, Geheimrat von Mieg,[33] and to Baron Stein, their peer and fellow sufferer, and the renowned fighter for municipal autonomy.

These victims of the Rheinbund came more as a noisy crowd than as a phalanx organized for effective action. They shared a vague hope of restoring the empire but their particular problems were varied. In Baden the mediatized enjoyed many of their old rights under the mild and enlightened rule of Carl Frederick.[34] In Würtemberg they had been all but dispossessed, as the tsar's sister Catherine could testify—she reported seeing the Stadion family crest on the king's dinner napkins.[35] The mediatized, moreover, stemmed from different levels of the feudal hierarchy, a divisive circumstance among men bred to appreciate the differences between princes, counts, barons and mere knights. And, to make matters worse, some of the later victims who now came to Frankfurt had to look in the eye lesser nobles they themselves had earlier absorbed. The duke of Oldenburg and the duke of Arenberg, for example, and the several princes of Salm, had been charter members of the Rheinbund, only to be overthrown in 1810 when Napoleon, in

[33] Gollwitzer, *Die Standesherren,* 23.

[34] Heffter, *Deutsche Selbstverwaltung,* 107f.

[35] Catherine to Alexander, 16 Jan. 1814, in Grand-Duc Nicholas Mikhailowitch (ed.), *Correspondance de l'Empereur Alexandre avec sa soeur la Grande-Duchesse Catherine* (St. Petersburg, 1910), 161–163.

creating the 32nd military district, had incorporated their lands into France.[36]

The mediatized were further divided by their unequal prospects for restoration. Those from Bavaria and Würtemberg were already doomed by the terms of Ried and Fulda, and every subsequent treaty of accession would shatter the hopes of dozens more. Their fortunes would then depend more than ever on the creation of a strong central authority in Germany, one that would uphold their local rights and guarantee them a voice in state government, even if it did not restore their immediate status. Those, however, who came from Berg, Westphalia, the grand duchy of Frankfurt, and the military district had greater expectations. The largest of the annexed territories, like Hanover, Brunswick, and Hesse-Cassel, had particularist traditions of their own, which had persisted despite the most strenuous efforts of the French rulers to introduce centralized administration.[37] Hanover and Brunswick, in addition, had guarantees of restoration in the Anglo-Prussian agreement of Reichenbach. The lesser houses and the Hanseatic cities had no such ironclad assurances, but the flight of their French rulers and the arrival of governors from the central department offered hope.

Badgered by the "swarming envoys and deputies, all soliciting," [38] and with dissonant voices ringing in his ears, Metternich reflected on the coming negotiations. He knew that the bargaining must affect the German question at every level. There was his own almost personal struggle with Stein. There was the party struggle between the sovereign princes and the mediatized. There was the constitutional struggle between the idea of voluntary union among equals and that of organic unity under an empire. To these could be added the power struggle between Austria and Prussia. Yet this was the one thing he hoped to set aside if he could. For in the larger question of the European equilibrium, which was the supreme object of the Frankfurt meeting, he was prepared to make every effort to

[36] d'Arenberg, *Les princes du St-Empire,* 195–196.
[37] Heffter, *Deutsche Selbstverwaltung,* 106.
[38] Metternich to Hudelist, 7 Nov. 1813, in Fournier, *Congress von Chatillon,* 241.

conciliate the Prussians and draw them away from Russia. Such matters as this and the equally portentous resumption of negotiations with Bonaparte he kept in his own hands. The actual signing of German treaties he left to his deputy, Baron Binder, chief of the mobile unit of the chancellery, while Humboldt acted for Hardenberg and Baron Anstett for Alexander.[39] The ministers were always available in the inner rooms, however, when their subordinates, interviewing suppliants in the antechambers, required advice. They had to be, for the arrival of Stein on November 13 and of Stadion a little later virtually guaranteed that there would be discord even within delegations.

If one views Metternich primarily as the archenemy of German nationalism and his policy as directed mainly toward sabotaging German union, then the accession treaties signed at Frankfurt can only be regarded as Austrian defeats. For when the allies met on November 15 to discuss the wording of the treaties, they finally agreed that territorial integrity as well as "sovereignty" and "independence" must be limited, "in conformity with the arrangements which shall be judged necessary in peacetime for preserving the independence of Germany." [40] For the current war, moreover, the acceding princes had to subscribe to elaborate regulations governing the common war effort—in contrast to Bavaria and Würtemberg, which had undertaken merely to contribute a stated number of troops. Considering that one of the princes concerned, the grand duke Carl of Baden, had sent his plenipotentiary to Frankfurt merely to gain recognition of Baden's neutrality,[41] the terms were severe, at least more severe than the Metternich of Ried and Fulda would have been expected to approve.

That Metternich did give his consent could be explained on grounds of duress, for it was not until agreement was reached on these new treaties (November 15) that Prussia and Russia

---

[39] Metternich, *Memoirs*, I, 212f. On Binder, a ubiquitous but little known figure, see Erich Zöllner, "Aus unbekannten Diplomatenbriefen an den Freiherrn Franz Binder von Kriegelstein," in Leo Santifaller (ed.), *Festschrift zur Feier des zweihundertjährigen Bestandes des Haus- Hof-und Staatsarchiv*, Bd. I (Vienna, 1949), 746–766.

[40] Texts in Martens, *Nouveau recueil*, I, 649–650, and *IV*, 96–117.

[41] Wolfgang Windelband, "Badens Austritt aus dem Rheinbund, 1813," *Zeitschrift für Geschichte des Oberrheins*, Bd. xxv, Neue Folge (1910), 115–119.

ratified the two earlier ones (November 16).[42] Yet it was not part of his program to keep Germany weak and, even if it had been, his desire to appease Hardenberg at this juncture was more important still. The case of Baden is again revealing. When the plenipotentiary, Baron Carl von Reitzenstein, arrived at Frankfurt, he found that, next to Nesselrode, Metternich was the least friendly of all the allied ministers. Reitzenstein erroneously assumed that the cause of Metternich's attitude was the Austrian intention of reclaiming the Breisgau, but he could hardly have been mistaken about the reception itself. It was at any rate hostile enough so that the envoy advised his master to come in person to Frankfurt, if possible before Stein arrived on the scene. This Carl did, arriving about November 13, while there was still time to influence the drafting of the treaties. Immediately he appealed to Frederick William and Alexander. This was not easy for the man who was both the husband of Stephanie Beauharnais and the brother-in-law of the tsar, and he was convinced that the latter would regard him as a traitor. His fears were groundless. Alexander, who had earlier kept pace with Metternich in appeasing Bavaria and Würtemberg, was equally anxious to restore his former influence in Baden. Accordingly he pleasantly surprised Carl with the warmth of his greeting, as did Frederick William, who was always courteous to his fellow sovereigns.[43]

The records do not disclose the actual course of debate, and in particular whether Alexander seriously tried to obtain better terms for Baden. The important point, however, is that he, not Metternich, was regarded by the men from Karlsruhe as their champion. Under these circumstances Metternich probably could have obtained the same terms for Baden as for Bavaria—or at least Würtemberg—had he insisted upon them, especially as the negotiations were well within his mandate to deal with the South German courts. That he did not is probably due, first to his convictions about the matter, and second, to the cal-

[42] This point has hitherto been overlooked owing in part at least to the fact that the ratification text given in Martens, *Nouveau recueil*, carries the date of November 4 without specifying that this is the old-style Russian date. The correct date is given in Martens, *Traités par la russie*, VII, 119.

[43] Windelband, "Badens Austritt," *ibid.*, 121–127.

culation that a possible rapprochement with Hardenberg was worth the risk that Baden would gravitate toward St. Petersburg rather than Vienna. Finally, Reitzenstein's explanation may not have been entirely amiss, though wrong about the Breisgau, since Metternich's plans did call for the cession of Baden's northern provinces to Bavaria, especially the Palatinate.

Thus the clause that amounted to a blank check with respect to a future German union was a victory for Metternich as much as for anyone. This issue, however, was only secondary in his policy, and it is doubtful that he himself regarded the clause as either better or worse than the comparable article in Würtemberg's treaty, except that it was less awkwardly composed. He had far greater success in placing in the treaties guarantees of sovereignty and compensations for ceded territory, the two principal safeguards against the reincarnation of an emperor and the restoration of the mediatized domains. Without such assurances the Rheinbund princes either would take their chances with Napoleon, signing no treaties at all, or would sign at the cost of losing the greater part of their territories. In either case most of Germany would sooner or later fall, as Saxony and Westphalia had already fallen, under the rule of Stein's administrative department. As it was, all the princes who signed treaties were assured that their contacts with the department were to be merely through agents with advisory powers, not governors with dictatorial powers. Consequently, apart from the aforementioned guarantees, the important thing about the accession treaties was not what was in them but who signed them. As at Teplitz and Leipzig, so now at Frankfurt, the primary struggle was over territorial spheres of influence rather than the German constitution.

In this respect Metternich's first success came between November 20 and 22, when Baron Binder signed treaties with Baden, Nassau, and Hesse-Darmstadt, thereby completing the alignment of South Germany against Bonaparte and Stein. On the grave issue of the Thuringian states Austrian diplomacy was no less triumphant. All the states but Saxe-Weimar and the four principalities of Reuss gained the coveted guarantees. Saxe-Weimar did not because the duke, Goethe's celebrated patron

Carl August, insisted on unconditional sovereignty, which was refused. To the duke it was a matter of principle—he had long been a friend of the patriots and was even a general in the Russian army. To some of his admirers in Saxony it was a matter of power, since they hoped to place him on the vacant throne and wanted no encumbrances.[44] He never did sign a treaty, but since he kept his freedom, there was no reason for Metternich to complain.

Satisfactory too, because of the claims Russia had once made, was the settlement regarding Frankfurt. If the defiance of the king of Saxony was Hardenberg's greatest stroke of luck, the flight of the Prince Primate was Metternich's, for he needed the grand duchy in order to compensate Bavaria for her cessions to Austria. He could not, of course, snatch the land from under Stein's jurisdiction, but he did obtain the right to appoint the occupation governor, and that assured Austria the preponderance of influence. The governor he chose was Prince Philip of Hesse-Homburg, an Austrian field marshal. To the duchy, moreover, he added the principality of Isenburg, taking advantage of the ill repute its ruler had acquired by organizing a regiment of brigands and deserters for the French service.[45] The prince received no compensation; he was simply dispossessed. Metternich's attachment to the doctrine of legitimacy was no more serious than Hardenberg's to German nationalism. As for the city of Frankfurt, Stein separated it from the rest of the duchy, restoring its charter from imperial times and—*mirabile dictu*—giving it a mayor who had served as municipal prefect in Rheinbund days! [46] In matters of city government Stein was a professional; his usual prejudices did not apply.

What Metternich achieved by these agreements was nothing less than the primacy of Austrian influence not only in the south, where it had been virtually conceded all along, but also in the hotly disputed central tier of states from Saxony to the Rhine. One further success, the restitution of Hesse-Cassel, was an incursion into the north. The event was of utmost impor-

---

[44] Treitschke, *History of Germany*, I, 611; and Huber, *Deutsche Verfassungsgeschichte*, I, 496 and 509–510.

[45] d'Arenberg, *Les princes du St-Empire*, 201.

[46] Cf. Huber, *Deutsche Verfassungsgeschichte*, I, 497–498.

tance because it linked the sovereign states of the center with the newly restored kingdom of Hanover and its dynastic affiliate, the duchy of Brunswick. Together with Frankfurt and Hesse-Darmstadt, the three formed a belt of free states from the Main to the North Sea, a barrier that stood squarely between the stem lands of Prussia and any provinces she might reacquire or newly acquire in the west. Resistance from Hardenberg was therefore to be expected, but Metternich had much to support his case. The elector of Hesse-Cassel had cleaner hands than most; his title dated back only to the Imperial Recess, but it was equal to those of even the highest Rheinbund sovereigns; morally he had the advantage of having chosen exile rather than submission, and he had, as previously noted, contributed money and enthusiasm to the crusade of 1809. Stein himself succumbed easily to such credentials, although it meant contracting his own domain.[47]

Metternich also had the benefit of Hardenberg's sanguine assumptions about the future. On one hand, the annexation of Saxony would lessen Prussia's stake in the west; on the other, leadership of a North German union would allow her indirectly to control the secondary states of the north and west anyway. The assumptions, though erroneous as things turned out, were by no means unwarranted. Metternich had already, as we have seen, given indication of yielding on the Saxon question— although he was not explicit about it, as far as we know, until January, 1814.[48] Hardenberg could scarcely have desired to appear unreasonable about a request seemingly made in the spirit of obtaining a modest *quid pro quo*—Metternich, after all, was not seeking to *annex* Hesse-Cassel. As for the future union, that, as Hardenberg conceived it, seemed adequately covered in the pledges given by all the new allies, to submit to whatever regulations were later deemed necessary to preserve Germany's independence. Be that as it may, the Austrians finally gained the point, and Binder was able to conclude the treaty on December 2, 1813,[49] more than a week after most of the other accession

[47] Treitschke, *History of Germany*, I, 606–607.
[48] See below, Chapter x, p. 281.
[49] Text in Martens, *Nouveau recueil*, I, 251–254.

instruments were signed. From that moment on, for fifty years, Hesse-Cassel (or Electoral Hesse, as the ruler liked to call it even though the title had no meaning in the absence of an empire) was to be a storm center, partly because of the elector's own follies, partly because of the state's location and the nature of its restoration.

Elsewhere in the German North Metternich's diplomacy left the field to Prussia and Russia—sometimes voluntarily, sometimes because there was no help for it. Prussia named the governors in two of the occupation districts that Stein established: Berg, and a zone between the Rhine and Weser composed of miscellaneous fragments left over from Westphalia. In the latter Hardenberg appointed Baron von Vincke, who served concurrently as governor of Prussia's own nearby lands. Though Vincke had to satisfy two masters, the Prussian government and the central department, he knew which came first and proceeded to treat both zones as one.[50] Metternich did not insist on guarantees for the petty states of the North; he could not have enforced them if he had. The three Anhalt duchies were necessarily satellites of Prussia. Lippe-Detmold and Schaumburg-Lippe, two principalities on the middle Weser, and Waldeck on the upper Ruhr were left to the vagaries of the final territorial settlement between Prussia and Hanover. Whatever his principles, Metternich had no more strategic interest in these fragmentary sovereigns than Hardenberg had in the two Hohenzollern dependencies in South Germany. People had not yet begun to talk much about legitimacy.

Still farther north, on the Baltic and North Sea coasts, where British frigates appeared on the horizon and the German question merged with the Danish one, Metternich's diplomacy encountered not the hypothetical actions of Stein's governors but the reality of the Russo-Swedish armies. In the two Mecklenburg duchies he faced a situation not unlike that in Saxe-Weimar, except that it had dragged on longer.[51] Knowing that Stein's August constitutional plan consigned them to Prussia, the two dukes continued to insist on unconditional guarantees,

---

[50] Huber, *Deutsche Verfassungsgeschichte*, I, 506–507.
[51] See above, Chapter VII, p. 195.

and Stein still refused. With Alexander's backing Metternich could doubtless have forced Stein's hand, but in an area where the Russian army held sway the tsar saw no reason to commit himself. It was enough simply to exclude Stein's department and appropriate to himself any gratitude the dukes, his cousins, might feel for their continued independence. The dukes, therefore, never did sign treaties even though they were treated as if they had. With the Russian army streaking across the North German plain to restore another cousin, the duke of Oldenburg, in his estates on the North Sea, Metternich was apprehensive, but there was nothing he could do about it. Still less could he rejoice in the Russian action in Bremen, the great seaport adjoining Oldenburg, where General Baron Carl von Tettenborn marched in and, without consulting Stein, declared the city independent. Metternich may well have relished Stein's embarrassment, so evident in his awkward retroactive approval of the deed,[52] but there was small comfort in discovering that the waning of Austrian influence in the North was not so much Stein's or Hardenberg's gain as it was Alexander's.

To this discomfiture must be added the fact that Metternich had still been unable to change anything in Saxony and Poland, both of which remained firmly in Russian hands. Nor could he delude himself about the regions where he did have his way: his victories may not have been due to active assistance from Alexander, but they had been attained with his permission. Still, he had saved the states that mattered most; he was assured of the good will of most of their rulers; and since military governors were barred from their territories, he knew that the princes would retain control of their military forces.

Within these limits and upon these principles Metternich was just as eager as his allies to mobilize the military resources of the third Germany. The stronger the armies of the German states and the more divisions there were whose rulers looked to Vienna for advice, the weaker relatively were the armies of Austria's rivals. Hence in drafting the military clauses of the accession treaties he and Binder were not the advocates of the Rheinbund states, bent on securing them the best available

---

[52] Huber, *Deutsche Verfassungsgeschichte*, I, 498.

terms, but solicitors, seeking to persuade them to make all possible sacrifices for the common cause—or what everyone kept saying was a common cause.

The main lesson Metternich learned from the protracted, wearisome negotiations was that his clients were little disposed to shower him with gratitude. Most of them had not abandoned the Rheinbund, with its onerous military burdens, merely for the chance to make even more strenuous efforts under another banner. They treated every demand for cooperation as an attack on their sovereignty. Both before the treaties were signed, and long after, they struggled to scale down financial and military quotas; to reject popular militias like the Prussian *Landsturm* or the volunteer legions Stein was organizing in the conquered territories; and to resist all regulations that involved the accommodation of troops and officials from other states or from the central department. The very egoism which Metternich so admired in the middle states, and on which he might have to rely if it came to leading them out of the war, proved also to have its disadvantages and embarrassments. It was his first major encounter with the dilemma it took him a decade to solve: how to persuade the middle states to do voluntarily what he could not force them to do, for fear of driving them into the arms of the other powers.

Metternich had one advantage now that he would never hold again: the fact that Stein, Hardenberg, and Alexander were even more impatient than he to force the German states into the allied war machine. Acting with rare concord, which owed much to the common professional outlook of the military men —Schwarzenberg and Count Joseph Radetzky for Austria, Baron Ludwig von Wolzogen for Russia, and Gneisenau for Prussia—the powers were able to exact a high price in military cooperation in return for the guarantees of sovereignty and territory. The treaties, as previously noted, pledged all the states to participate in a "general military system for all of Germany." Exceptions were Bavaria, Würtemberg, and Hanover, but they too, along with Prussia and Austria, joined the system. All states were assigned financial quotas proportionate to their customary annual budgets, and military quotas more

than double those Napoleon had exacted. The manpower obligation included a contingent of line troops amounting to two
per cent of the population, a *Landwehr* contingent of equal
strength, and a much larger *Landsturm* or home guard.[53] For
purposes of command and operations the contingents were
grouped into corps and attached to the existing allied armies.
Bavaria, Würtemberg, and Hesse-Cassel provided whole corps
of their own. The others combined their forces so as to form
five corps, each of which came from at least one middle state
and a number of small ones.[54]

The arrangements bear witness to an extraordinary victory
of military convenience over political friction. The subordination of the small states to the large, within corps, was no mean
accomplishment in itself; and after the angry recriminations en-
gendered by the quarrel over occupation assignments, the geographical compactness and homogeneity of the corps areas was
remarkable to behold. The only actual political decision was
the assignment of the Saxon corps to the northern army instead
of to the much nearer Silesian army of Blücher, which could all
too easily have become a school for Prussian citizenship. Even
in this instance, however, one could hardly say that military
efficiency had been impaired.

It was far more difficult to reconcile the former Rheinbund
states to the authority of the Central Administrative Council,
which was given broad supervisory powers over recruitment,
supply, munitions production, hospital administration, and
other supporting activities. Many of the powers Stein had sought
in vain at Leipzig he now obtained in the sheaves of protocols
and conventions signed at Frankfurt. Recruiting was placed in
the hands of a general commissioner for German armaments,
and the man Stein chose for the post was the Prussian colonel,
Rühle von Lilienstern, a patriotic publicist who promptly
brought to headquarters a host of nationalist writers. These included some noble spirits like the poet Max von Schenkendorf,

[53] "Convention relative à la défense commune des états de l'Allemagne,"
24 Nov. 1813, in Martens, *Traités par la russie*, VII, 143–147. Slightly different
drafts in Martens, *Nouveau recueil*, I, 624–626, and IV, 101–103.
[54] *ibid.*, I, 613.

but also some like the uncouth rabble rouser, Father Jahn, whom even Stein despised.[55]

Recruiting armies of the line presented no special difficulties: in most cases the existing conscription laws needed only slight amendments to yield the norm of two per cent of population required by the treaties. Elimination of the right of substitution and certain exemptions recognized under the Rheinbund generally sufficed. The contribution, though burdensome, fell far short of the strenuous Prussian effort to three per cent, which neither Stein nor Hardenberg allowed anyone to forget. Organizing a *Landwehr* proved more irksome. This organization, an active reserve for ablebodied men from eighteen to forty, with its strong civilian and middle-class outlook, was not beloved of sovereigns who doted on cabinet wars, the more so as Stein emphatically recommended imitating the renowned Prussian system, the work of the great reformers. But most of all the middle states resented the provisions for a *Landsturm,* which, again following the Prussian practice, obligated all men not otherwise in service to organize for home defense and garrison duty within the state. It was bad enough to arm the population in this way, but far worse was the fact that Lilienstern set up the *Landsturm* on an all-German basis, totally disregarding the state authorities. He marked out districts that cut across state lines, he personally appointed district commanders, and he encouraged the popular election of local defense committees. Another division of the department, the general commissariat, undertook a comparable program, sending its agents into the states to collect food, enforce deliveries from powder mills, establish regional hospital facilities, and devise uniform procedures for military police.[56]

The possibilities for clashes were endless, and in the months that followed many materialized. The states were by no means helpless, for the Leipzig convention safeguarded their institutions. They complained that their military and financial quotas

---

[55] Ritter, *Stein* (1958 ed.), 463–464.
[56] Pertz, *Steins Leben,* I, 721ff; Huber, *Deutsche Verfassungsgeschichte,* I, 501–505.

were too high; they protested both the behavior of "foreign" troops on their soil and the measures taken by allied military police to correct it; and in one notorious case, Bavaria actually refused hospital admittance to non-Bavarian troops. Even the mediatized princes complained. In the regions where the central department ruled directly and could have restored many of their rights, it did nothing. Stein ignored their petitions and scolded them for putting their interest in gaining sovereignty above their desire to contribute taxes, raise troops, and take up arms themselves for the common fight.[57]

The source of most strife was the *Landsturm*, which had ominous revolutionary overtones, the more so as its military effectiveness alone could hardly explain Stein's and Lilienstern's almost fanatical interest in it. When in February, 1814, Stein finally threatened to set aside state governments that did not meet their quotas, it looked indeed as if he was making a last desperate effort to overthrow "the petty despots" and reorganize the third Germany to his taste. In the end he had to back down. Metternich's previous victories had deprived him of sufficient means—and taught him, long before Winston Churchill learned it, that one cannot carry out grand enterprises from a secondary post. In the confusion of war and rapidly moving events Stein could act independently in a wider range than was originally intended for him, but eventually he had to face the ministerial council, to which he was ultimately responsible. Bavaria, Würtemberg, and Hanover he could influence only through conventional diplomatic channels, and when he failed to persuade them to join the *Landsturm* system, it did not seem much worse to make concessions elsewhere. In Baden, Hesse-Darmstadt, and Nassau he finally agreed to withdraw the district commanders and allow the sovereigns to occupy the posts themselves. Thus did his dreams of a monolithic national juggernaut fade away.[58]

Considered strictly from a military point of view, the demise of a national *Landsturm* had slight bearing on the outcome of the war. There is little reason to believe that the kind of mass

---

[57] *ibid.*, I, 498; Ritter, *Stein* (1958 ed.), 464–465; and d'Arenberg, *Les princes du St-Empire*, 209.
[58] Cf. Huber, *Deutsche Verfassungsgeschichte*, I, 505–506.

army Stein envisaged would have performed better than the quasi-professional units which bore the brunt of the fighting. In the north, where volunteer units were encouraged and patriotism fanned, enlistments were not spectacular and the main fighting was done by the regulars. The former military wards of Napoleon performed respectably, though not perhaps heroically. By the end of the war their line armies and *Landwehr* totalled 165,000 and the *Landsturm*, such as it was, about twice that.[59] The crown prince of Würtemberg proved himself one of the ablest allied commanders. Altogether the forces rounded up by the allies at Frankfurt more than balanced the new levy voted at the same time by the French senate.

But Metternich's interest in the German contingents derived not so much from their showing on the battlefield as from their place in the bargaining over Europe, which still proceeded at Frankfurt. Binder and Schwarzenberg had done their work well. How well becomes clearer as we turn to the affairs which Metternich kept in his own hands—Prince Metternich, we should say, for after several weeks he had become accustomed to his new title, and so ought we.

[59] *ibid.*, I, 502.

CHAPTER IX

GERMANY AND EUROPE

Not the least of the advantages of Metternich's German policy was that it served equally well whether the war continued or not. Binder conducted the negotiations on the assumption of war but he did not know with certainty what the circumstances would actually be. Metternich meanwhile devoted himself to the mission of St. Aignan. Reduced to its essentials, what he proposed was a peace conference to be opened as soon as Napoleon had pledged himself ready to negotiate on the basis of the Rhine-Alps-Pyrenees frontier. The only enthusiastic support he found was from Frederick William, who was as pacific as his generals were warlike. Hardenberg was strongly opposed, but could not prevail against his king. To make the offer palatable to Alexander, Metternich continued to represent it as a propaganda device, predicting that Napoleon would never cooperate. It was a surmise he could honestly make since he himself had little hope that "Napoleon will really follow the thing up." [1]

To obtain British consent was more difficult, since the Rhine frontier would leave France in control of the Scheldt estuary, the port of Antwerp, and much of the Channel coast. Here Metternich resorted to a subterfuge as brilliant as it was shady. While keeping the two most rigid British diplomats, Charles Stewart and Lord Cathcart—attached to the Prussian and Russian courts respectively—completely in the dark about the project, he convinced the young Lord Aberdeen, one of his warmest admirers, that the offer was well within the scope allowed by previous instructions from Castlereagh. Aberdeen even let a reference to French maritime rights slip by—a flagrant departure from the British postulate that maritime problems were beyond the realm of discussion. Metternich calculated that by the time Castlereagh learned what had happened, Napoleon

[1] Metternich to Hudelist, Frankfurt, 9 Nov. 1813, in Fournier, *Congress von Chatillon*, 242.

would have replied. If the answer was negative, the offer still had the propaganda value which commended it to the tsar; if affirmative, Castlereagh would hardly dare to boycott a peace conference no matter how outraged he felt about the duplicity, and the blame for that in any case rested on Aberdeen.

But the proposal could hardly pass as a solemn British pledge. Metternich, therefore, had to be equally indirect with Bonaparte, giving him an impression of allied unanimity which did not exist. His solution was to have St. Aignan convey an oral message, a summary of conversations to be held at an imformal meeting which Aberdeen was coached to join as if by accident. The meeting took place on the evening of November 9. Nesselrode also attended and claimed that he spoke for Hardenberg as well. Aberdeen arrived as planned. St. Aignan drafted a précis of the conversation which everyone approved and the next day departed for Paris.[2]

St. Aignan's notes contained, besides the offer of France's natural frontiers and those maritime rights "which France had a right to claim,"[3] a reference to Germany. Germany was to be unconditionally independent, but "France need not for that reason renounce the influence which every large state necessarily exercises on a state of lesser size. . . ."[4] The clause was presumably St. Aignan's, but it was sanctioned by Metternich. It restated the position he had taken at Dresden and Prague, the plan he had covertly insinuated into the Teplitz pact and the accession treaties: the appeal to Napoleon that, although France might not dominate Germany, she might still participate in a system of international guarantees of a neutralized Germany. It was, in short, a bid for French support in the Saxon-Polish question, should "the amicable arrangements" stipulated in the Teplitz pact prove impossible. If the allusion was obscure, it was the most that could be said in that company. But in Paris there was a man who would understand: Caulaincourt,

[2] Aberdeen to Castlereagh, 8 Nov. and 9 Nov. 1813, in Webster, *British Diplomacy*, 107–110; Webster, *Castlereagh*, 170–171; Sorel, *L'Europe*, VIII, 206–211.

[3] Quoted from French original by Webster, *Castlereagh*, 171. Versions given by Kissinger, *World Restored*, 100, and Webster, *British Diplomacy*, 110, slightly different.

[4] German version of text in Wilhelm von Humboldt, *Wilhelm von Humboldts gesammelte Schriften*, ed. by Bruno Gebhardt, XI (1903), 93.

who had heard the proposal at Prague; Caulaincourt, who, along with Talleyrand, favored a peace of moderation; and who, as Metternich had told St. Aignan at Meiningen, knew of a similarly dictated memorandum that could end the war in twenty-four hours.[5]

And so to Caulaincourt, as leader of the peace party in France, Metternich now turned. To communicate across the lines, he had originally planned to issue immediately the manifesto he had been authorized at Meiningen to compose. But when he presented his draft at a conference on November 8, both Aberdeen and Nesselrode objected.[6] Not only was it designed to dramatize the moderation inherent in the allied offer and to turn the eyes of Europe on the St. Aignan mission; it also contained an assurance that *the terms would be no different even if an invasion of France should prove necessary*—a gratuitous addition, the purpose of which could only have been to bind the allies, not to impress Bonaparte.

Pleading that the document had been difficult to write but that he had written it "from the bottom of my heart," Metternich nevertheless withdrew it and agreed to await the outcome of St. Aignan's mission.[7] Hence, instead of a public proclamation at this time, he had to turn privately to Caulaincourt, in a personal note informing him of the mission and vouching for its authenticity.[8] It was his way of conveying to friendly eyes the assurance that Austria, though too closely bound to her allies to offer official terms, was willing and perhaps able to lead her allies to a peace congress if France should display a willingness to negotiate. Metternich could go no further without risking the rupture of the coalition, a risk he could not take unless guaranteed in advance that a chastened Bonaparte meant to end the war on the basis of the Frankfurt proposals. The entire intricate maneuver was reminiscent of his earlier attempts at mediation, in which he had also dissembled to both sides, hoping that the contradictions could be ironed out if they were brought to a congress. The difference was that in the summer

[5] Sorel, *L'Europe*, VIII, 204.
[6] Aberdeen to Castlereagh, 8 Nov. 1813, in Webster, *British Diplomacy*, 108.
[7] Fournier, *Congress von Chatillon*, 24–25.
[8] Sorel, *L'Europe*, VIII, 209–210.

it had been Napoleon who had required delicate handling; now it was Russia and Britain.

Metternich's approach to Caulaincourt, reminiscent of his earlier association with Talleyrand and Fouché, should not occasion surprise, but it is an especially forceful reminder of how limited even yet were the claims of the state on the individual vis-à-vis foreign powers. It was true everywhere, not only among the old imperial nobility serving the Austrian government. Trained, experienced men of affairs—diplomats, administrators, military officers, lawyers—served governments, in the early nineteenth century, in a spirit that can only be compared to that with which able men now serve business corporations. Their loyalty derived from professional pride and a ,sort of gratitude for the opportunity to express themselves and exercise power; it was an elemental institutional loyalty, not a total commitment, nor did it include the enthusiastic element of patriotism. Gentz, for example, thought nothing of seeking fees from other governments when he thought he had done them favors; and Baron Andreas von Merian, at one time the Austrian envoy to Karlsruhe, honorably resigned in 1812 to enter the Russian service, when he realized that Metternich's policies were too tame for him.[9]

High-level government service was particularly appealing to men whose talents or ambitions, both financial and political, soared beyond the opportunities available in some petty seigniory or county, and, after the mammoth dislocations that the aristocracy of France and the Holy Roman Empire had experienced, such employment was often a necessity. Metternich's father, a Westphalian Catholic, had entered the Habsburg service; Stein, a protestant, the Prussian service and, when that became untenable, the Russian. Nesselrode, Schwarzenberg, Colloredo, and Stadion, already mentioned, as well as Stollberg-Wernigerode and Windischgrätz, to be noted presently, were mediatized counts and princes. Among the *Hofräte* of the Austrian government were Count Andreas von Mercy, a French émigré, Franz Rademacher from Coblenz, Baron Kaspar Spiegel from Westphalia, and Baron Kress von Kressenstein, of a pa-

---

[9] Sweet, *Gentz*, 205; and Rössler, *Österreichs Kampf*, I, 205.

trician family in Nürnberg.[10] The duke of Richelieu, a French émigré and later premier, spent the Napoleonic wars as governor of Odessa. Alopeus and Anstett of the Russian foreign service were Germans. One could perhaps add Pozzo di Borgo, Czartoryski, La Harpe, and Capo d'Istria to the list, but their relationship to the tsar was of a special kind: it was not their professional competence, but their ideologies and enthusiasms that interested him most.

These and many others found employment readily, partly because of rulers' compassion for dispossessed nobles, but mainly because their skills were a scarce commodity. Throughout the continent there was a shortage of trained personnel, particularly in Central and Eastern Europe, which lacked a strong middle class. The demand had first arisen in response to the state-building activities of the seventeenth and eighteenth centuries, but it was Napoleon's example which compelled rulers to take serious cognizance of talent and to recruit it where they could find it. They especially prized university training. Many of the Rheinbund princes liberally supported their universities, viewing them as training grounds for their burgeoning bureaucracies. Metternich was a university man. Stein, Stadion, and Hardenberg were all products of Göttingen, renowned in the field of public administration. Metternich, Nesselrode, Hardenberg, Caulaincourt—they all belonged, one might say, to a *Begabtenrepublik,* which existed side by side with the *Gelehrtenrepublik,* a popular subject with the literati of the period.[11]

In short, the states of that day, still emerging from the rule of custom and the vaguely defined restraints of a feudal order, were no more closed or exclusive institutions than were the business corporations which a generation later began to arise in a laissez faire economic order. The great exception, the most nearly monolithic enterprise, was Revolutionary-Napoleonic France, and it is hard to say which worried the other political entrepreneurs more: the horizontal monopoly Napoleon had extended over Europe or the vertical monopoly he had created

[10] Josef Karl Mayr, *Geschichte der österreichischen Staatskanzlei im Zeitalter des Fürsten Metternich* (Vienna, 1935), 17–20.

[11] On the *Gelehrtenrepublik* see Kemiläinen, *Auffassungen über die Sendung des deutschen Volkes, passim.*

at home. Metternich was among the few who discerned the dual nature of the problem, and now that the horizontal monopoly had been broken he believed Austria could live with the other.

He was also prepared to accept a large measure of Bonapartism elsewhere in Europe, in the Rheinbund states and Naples, so long as it was a matter of domestic political structure and did not lead states to sacrifice their ordinary power interests to the claims of ideology. He calculated—and on the whole, correctly—that the former was a far stronger impulse in statecraft than the latter, and on it an equilibrium was possible. Conversely, an equilibrium was not possible if some governments should upset all calculations by crusading for justice, or otherwise seeking alignments based on the similarity of social philosophy. Both the tight controls he insisted upon maintaining at home and the laissez-faire attitude he observed (with rare exceptions) toward the domestic systems of other states arose from his fundamental conception of politics, *das Primat der Aussenpolitik*. The balance of power, he sensed, is not primarily a doctrine but a condition, a condition which exists when the various states, each pursuing its selfish interests, reach mutually recognized points of diminishing returns. In her struggle with France Metternich believed Austria had reached that point. Whether Napoleon thought this was also true of France and whether he believed that his position at home could be dissociated from the wreckage of his continental empire, could only be answered when he and his ministers replied to St. Aignan's message.

St. Aignan had left Frankfurt on November 10. On the 14th he reached Paris, and two days later the foreign minister, Bernard Maret, Duke of Bassano, drafted a reply. On November 24 a new courier presented himself at the military outposts of Frankfurt, under a flag of truce, and delivered the message. Almost everyone had expected that Napoleon would appear to be accommodating, if only to gain time for further military preparations.[12] Great was the surprise, therefore, when Bonaparte, not so much as mentioning the Frankfurt base, offered only to attend a conference at Mannheim without any pre-

---

[12] This was the view of Cathcart among others. Cathcart to Castlereagh, 24 Nov. 1813, in Webster, *British Diplomacy*, 41–42.

liminary commitments save for a pointed reference to *Britain's* willingness to make sacrifices. Metternich was quick to respond. The next day in an official dispatch, which spoke for all the allies, he solemnly insisted that there could be no congress until France had first accepted the Frankfurt base. This he followed up with the proclamation to the French people which a month earlier he had had to postpone. Released on December 1, it publicized the generous peace terms that had just been offered, emphasized Bonaparte's intransigeance, and blamed him for the continuation of the war. One cherished statement, however, Metternich had had to drop from the previous draft—the clause making the terms a standing offer regardless of the coming invasion of France. The new version, a concession to Alexander, simply proclaimed the allies' desire to see France remain "great, strong and prosperous," and vouchsafed "to the *French Empire* an extent of territory such as France never knew under her kings." [13] This was a vague promise, but it publicly committed the allies to a mild peace, one signed with Bonaparte himself.

Again the question arises: was Metternich in earnest or was he, as he claimed later, merely waging psychological warfare, hoping to divide the French nation and stiffen the determination of Frederick William and Francis? The latter view, a favorite with those who think of Metternich as the unscrupulous nemesis of Napoleon, can hardly be squared with the over-all structure of his policy. Yet the former thesis, almost universally held in Germany by Metternich's admirers and detractors alike (the first group stressing the European balance as the purpose, the others adducing timidity, lack of patriotism, or naïveté regarding Napoleon's motives), is not wholly satisfactory either.[14] Even if the devious approach to Napoleon via St. Aignan's oral message and the private letter to Caulaincourt can be explained, as we have done here, as being the most Metternich could exact

[13] Text in Meyer, *Corpus Juris*, I, 204–206. Italics mine.

[14] An important exception is the intermediate view held by Fournier, *Congress von Chatillon*, 20ff., who contends that while Metternich earnestly desired peace, he believed further military successes were necessary to bring Napoleon to reason and accordingly promoted a relatively early resumption of hostilities, accompanied by psychological pyrotechnics. This position is very sound as far as it goes, but in neglecting the anti-Russian aspects of Metternich's maneuvering, it puts the emphasis in the wrong place.

from his allies, the peremptory and literal insistence on the Frankfurt base, after Napoleon had met him halfway, does not sound like the Metternich we have come to know in these pages. Sorel, for one, is quite right in arguing that Napoleon, in receipt of a mere oral and unofficial proposition, was justified in using a noncommittal counterproposal to test the *bona fides* of his enemies.[15] Indeed, the allied manifesto, which proclaimed to the world Bonaparte's guilt for the coming slaughter, seemed to confirm his suspicions.

Neither hypothesis does justice to the complexity of Metternich's calculations. First of all, the two views are not mutually exclusive since the allied maneuver had undeniable propaganda value regardless of the fate of a peace congress. Secondly, both the allied reply of November 25 and the manifesto of December 1, for all their seeming intransigeance, were actually forward steps in the negotiations. The former made official the offer of France's natural frontiers, and the latter publicly committed the tsar to a moderate peace. How else could such an improbable result have been achieved? Alexander, as so often before, was as much the object of Metternich's circuitous methods as Napoleon.[16] Finally—and here is the crux of the matter—the question of peace could not remain unaffected by other developments which occurred while the negotiations were in progress.

During the two-week interval between the departure of St. Aignan and the receipt of Maret's reply Metternich's position improved in three ways. His first success concerned the coming military campaign. Over the vehement objections of the Prussian generals, all of whom except Knesebeck favored a frontal assault across the middle Rhine and a drive direct to Paris, the Austrians won adoption of Schwarzenberg's more cautious strategy, based on a plan presented by General Radetzky. At a council of war held on November 19 it was decided to avoid the great fortified belts between Mainz and Paris and send the main army on a detour across Switzerland, through the Burgundian gate, and on to the plateau of Langres. The plan contained

[15] *L'Europe*, VIII, 214–226.
[16] Lauber, *Metternichs Kampf*, 120. Cf. Gentz to Metternich, 16 Jan. 1814, in Gentz, *Briefe von und an*, III, 228, where Gentz says that "the effect in France" was not the major consideration.

enough sound, if conservative, military reasoning to win the approval of Frederick William and the grudging endorsement of Alexander, who was ready to appease Metternich at all costs so long as the war continued. For Austria the maneuver had the added advantages of striking at the French communications to Italy and possibly opening the way for a juncture with the British forces marching over the Pyrenees. To Metternich, however, it was a device for keeping a tight reign on the progress of the campaign and applying his motto of "negotiating but while negotiating, advancing." If Napoleon should prove adamant on the Rhine there would be a chance to try him again when the main army reached Langres.[17]

Metternich's next success was the provisional settlement of the German question. Radetzky's war plan was adopted on November 19. On the 20th Binder signed the first of the Frankfurt accession treaties and in the next two days concluded most of the others. On the 24th came the adoption of the corps organization plan for the German contingents. That this was the very day on which Maret's note arrived at allied headquarters was purely fortuitous. Nevertheless, had the German negotiations been stalled at the time or had they been developing in Stein's favor rather than Metternich's, Austria's foreign minister must surely have given a more conciliatory reply, perhaps going so far as to announce that whatever his allies might do, he would make the trip to Mannheim. As it was, his victories in Germany caused him to shrink from such a drastic step. Though hoping for peace, he was not yet prepared to break up the alliance. Hence he avoided the two things that would have caused a rupture: full acceptance of Maret's counteroffer and a showdown on the Saxon-Polish question.

The third factor in Metternich's reaction was Austria's relations with Great Britain. As we have seen, he had always valued Britain as a counterweight to Russia—a useful counterweight if France remained strong, an indispensable counterweight if she became weak. Theoretically Austria and Britain were natural allies. The British interest in a continental balance

---

[17] Fournier, *Congress von Chatillon*, 34–35; Ritter, *Stein* (1958 one-volume ed.), 469; Lauber, *Metternichs Kampf*, 120-125; and Sorel, *L'Europe*, VIII, 213.

had been a matter of historic fact for over a century. Territorially there were few conflicts. To an independent Spain and an independent Holland Metternich had no objections in themselves, provided they did not make peace with France impossible. In Italy their interests coincided. Britain's sea power in the Mediterranean and Austria's Alpine military frontier were both in jeopardy so long as France controlled the peninsula. Both powers, moreover, had disquieting memories of the past: the Suvorov expedition in 1799 and the Russian attempt on Malta; they were determined that the removal of French forces should not open Italy to the Russians. Castlereagh, therefore, was fully prepared to grant Austria a position of preponderance in the north,[18] more perhaps than Austria herself wanted to take on. In the south both favored an independent Naples. Although Castlereagh preferred to restore the Bourbons, and his principal agent in Naples, Lord William Bentinck, schemed to introduce an English-style constitution, Aberdeen's instructions from August on permitted acquiescence in Metternich's solution, which was an alliance with the reigning king, Napoleon's brother-in-law Murat.[19] In Germany, too, British and Austrian interests were compatible. Although in the fall of 1813 Castlereagh shared Münster's view that the Reich should be restored, there was certainly no reason for him to insist upon it, especially as Münster's purpose, like Metternich's, was primarily to establish a Central European defense system. Such common interests, once Austria had entered the war, made possible the treaty of alliance and subsidy signed October 3.

But Anglo-Austrian relations remained far from cordial. It was largely a case of lack of confidence and understanding, ultimately traceable to the inherently different outlooks of the insular power and the centrally located continental one. Substantively, their interests were almost identical, but they were not of identical import. Austria was still fighting for her life, still trying to arrange the elementary conditions of her existence. England, on the other hand, already assured of survival by her

---

[18] By a convention signed 27 July 1813 at Prague. Griewank, *Wiener Kongress*, 140.

[19] Castlereagh to Aberdeen, 15 Oct. 1813, in Webster, *British Diplomacy*, 102ff.

sea power, which she was even then asserting against the United States of America, was attending to the more remote supports of her security, groping toward her coming century of world leadership.

For this reason Castlereagh did not share Metternich's alarm at *potential* developments. If Alexander posed a threat to Europe, comparable to the French threat proved by a century of experience, let Metternich produce the evidence for it. What difference did it make if Russia acquired Poland so long as Austria received compensations? Absorbed in the one simple task of overthrowing Bonaparte, Castlereagh tended to interpret Austria's dilatory tactics as a mixture of cowardice and dynastic, Bonapartist sympathies. And as long as Castlereagh's understanding penetrated no deeper than this, he could hardly qualify as an ally whose appearance on the scene would compensate Metternich for the disappearance of Napoleon. Before a stern attitude toward France was even thinkable, let alone advisable, Metternich had to find some means to win Castlereagh to his policy even if he could not teach him the need for it.[20]

The means were forthcoming during the interval in which everyone awaited the results of the St. Aignan mission. It came in the form of a rift between Great Britain and Russia, hitherto bound by their enthusiasm for crushing France. The point at issue was the creation of a grand alliance, which Castlereagh came more and more to cherish both as the means to cement the ramshackle coalition, and as the basis of a postwar system of collective security, "a perpetual defensive Alliance for the maintenance of such a peace." As war aims he endorsed the Reichenbach terms and the cession of Norway to Sweden, adding that Holland should have "an adequate barrier" against France.[21] He made no reference, however, to extra-continental affairs: maritime rights, British colonial conquests, and the war against America. With a certain obtuseness born of being shielded by the Channel from the grossest facts of international life, Castlereagh thought his country entitled to a major voice in continental affairs while refusing others a corresponding voice in non-

[20] Cf. Kissinger, *World Restored*, 88–104.
[21] Castlereagh to Cathcart, 18 Sept. 1813, in Webster, *British Diplomacy*, 25–28.

European matters. On the continent, balance of power; on the high seas, British hegemony. It was the 1805 formula of Pitt, whom Castlereagh acknowledged as his mentor.

Although the project was dispatched from London on September 18, 1813, it did not reach Cathcart until October 20 and, owing to the confusion following the battle of Leipzig, was not presented to the tsar until October 26. Alexander's reply was noncommittal. On November 5 Castlereagh informed Aberdeen of the project but not until the 11th, the day after St. Aignan's departure, was it earnestly discussed again. Thereafter hardly anything was discussed more.[22]

Throughout, Alexander's attitude ranged from defiance to evasiveness. To be sure, the points Castlereagh specified were all to the good as far as they went, but except for the reference to an adequate barrier for Holland, they implied a strong France. Whatever interest the tsar may once have had in defining war aims was gone, now that the Rhine had been reached, a point he made abundantly clear when he told Cathcart that "such a Treaty should be framed according to existing circumstances and not as matters stood two months ago. . . ."[23] Alexander now felt strong enough to play Castlereagh's game in reverse: to assert Russia's right as a world power to a voice in maritime and colonial questions, while remaining silent about his peace program for the continent. This attitude was no mere pose, adopted to point up the one-sidedness of the British proposals. Recalling Czartoryski's maxim of ten years earlier that England was the one abiding enemy of Russia, the tsar was conceivably looking ahead already to compensating a weakened France with the return of lost colonies, and to assisting the other maritime powers—Spain, Portugal, Holland, the United States —to flourish at sea as challengers of Britannia's rule.[24]

With France still strong under Napoleon, Alexander was not ready to embrace her, nor was Metternich yet willing to foresake her for England. Nevertheless the Anglo-Russian dispute, auguring as it did greater clashes in the future, gave him enor-

[22] Cathcart to Castlereagh, 30 Oct. 1813, and Castlereagh to Aberdeen, 5 Nov. 1813, in Webster, *British Diplomacy*, 35–38 and 106–107 respectively.
[23] Cathcart to Castlereagh, 11 Nov. 1813, in Webster, *British Diplomacy*, 37.
[24] Cf. Pirenne, *La sainte-alliance*, I, 37–60.

mous new bargaining power with Castlereagh. He did not recklessly dissipate this power by loudly extolling the alliance project; even though a postwar system of guarantees was his own cherished goal, there was no need of saying so immediately. Instead he joined Alexander in finding all manner of faults with the proposal. In this way he might increase the tsar's trust in him at a critical juncture in the German negotiations, and at the same time hold something in reserve to trade for British support on the German and Polish questions. This new prospect for an entente with England, together with the adoption of Schwarzenberg's campaign plan and the favorable developments in Germany, did not make peace with France less desirable. But the balance of risks had shifted, and for that reason Metternich concluded that he must take his stand on the Frankfurt base, which after all represented only a change of means, not of goal. Ultimately it was because of England that Metternich dared not insist upon the more moderate program so deviously planned in the "sine qua non" of Teplitz.

In France, meanwhile, the friends of appeasement grew stronger. On November 20, even before Maret's message had reached Frankfurt, Caulaincourt became foreign minister. It was he, Metternich's friend, who received the allied reply rejecting the Mannheim conference. It was he, the longtime advocate of a negotiated peace, who now accepted the terms and on December 2 dispatched the official French note to that effect. Metternich was elated. "I hope you will be satisfied with Caulaincourt's answer," he wrote to Baron Hudelist, his deputy in Vienna. "I have every right to be since we can regard it as the direct result of our carefully calculated political and military limits." [25] What Caulaincourt and Metternich had failed to accomplish at Prague now seemed within their grasp.

And yet it was not to be. By December 5, when the note was received in Frankfurt, the allied manifesto of war aims had already been issued. More important, Aberdeen's rash concessions had become known in London, and Castlereagh's fury, aggravated still further by Bonaparte's impudent comments

[25] Metternich to Hudelist, 6 Dec. 1813, in Fournier, *Congress von Chatillon*, 245.

about British sacrifices, knew no bounds. At allied headquarters Cathcart and Stewart had finally learned the contents of St. Aignan's memoir and were likewise vexed with Aberdeen. Not France but England now loomed as the chief opponent of the Frankfurt base, and Alexander was only too happy to stand with Castlereagh on the matter. For Metternich the situation was exceedingly delicate. Even if he had been willing to risk it, he could not have allowed England to go her way while he sided with France, for Caulaincourt's acceptance of the original terms was contingent on British participation. It is, in fact, most likely that Napoleon's sole purpose in permitting Caulaincourt's démarche was to attempt to break up the coalition. In desperation Metternich turned to Alexander, agreeing to support Russia's demand for subsidies and a voice in the distribution of colonial conquests, if he would join in a plea to London to send an emissary with full authority to act. They entrusted both demands to Pozzo di Borgo, who set out on December 6.[26]

Meanwhile answer had to be made to the French foreign minister, and under the circumstances Metternich could only state the truth, namely, that he had received the French note with satisfaction and was then in process of bringing it to the attention of his allies, but that no formal conference could begin until the British plenipotentiary arrived. In the meantime the war must go on.[27] The coolness of the answer was hardly likely to strengthen French confidence in allied intentions. Yet to have promised more than could be delivered might well have alienated Britain and Russia without impressing Napoleon, in whose good intentions Metternich still did not fully believe. Within these limits he kept the negotiations alive. He continued with preparations for a conference and, whatever London might think, took the view that the British envoy was coming to a peace conference, not just to patch up the alliance.[28] As it happened, the plenipotentiary was Castlereagh himself; he was appointed on December 20. That same day Schwarzenberg invaded Switzerland at Basel and began a new phase of the war.

[26] Cf. Webster, *Castlereagh*, 176–177.

[27] Fournier, *Congress von Chatillon*, 34; Sorel, *L'Europe*, VIII, 225.

[28] Metternich to Hudelist, 16 Dec. 1813 and 3 Jan. 1814, in Fournier, *Congress von Chatillon*, 245f and 248 respectively.

The invasion of Switzerland did more than implement the strategy agreed upon for the campaign against France: it brought into the open the primordial antagonism between Metternich and Alexander. It is a matter of some wonder that this antagonism could have been veiled, that a veneer of bonhomie could have been maintained through all the stresses and strains of the German question, only to crack on the peaks of Switzerland, especially as in the process the two adversaries completely reversed their previous positions. For it was Metternich who ordered Schwarzenberg to the attack, choosing a moment when Alexander was away from headquarters, and it was the tsar who tried to halt the advance in order to preserve Swiss neutrality.

It was a political question of the highest order. Since Alexander had not dared as yet to speak out in behalf of a liberal Poland and had been maneuvered by Metternich into abandoning Stein in Germany, Switzerland offered him the first real opportunity to proclaim his sponsorship of the inchoate liberal nationalism which Napoleon had once ridden to victory. For this reason he was determined to protect the existing liberal regime in Switzerland. For this reason he was willing, despite his desire in every other way to swell the ranks of the conquering allied armies, to overlook the continued presence of Swiss regiments in Napoleon's armies and to recognize the regime's professed neutrality. For this reason, too, he retained his old teacher, Frederick Caesar de La Harpe, in his entourage, intending that the veteran Swiss reformer should be the link between Russia and the diet in Zürich, a publicist who would advertise the tsar's benevolent program.

To Metternich a pro-Russian government in Switzerland would be scarcely less menacing than a Russian-controlled Poland. To make matters worse, there was, in contrast to the situation in the German states, no way to outbid Alexander for the favor of the existing government. How could one possibly offer more than a recognition of neutrality to a country which still had troops fighting on the other side? Every pressure was in the opposite direction. The German press described Swiss neutrality in abusive terms. In the pages of the *Rheinische Merkur* Joseph Görres included the Swiss in the German

Volkstum he sought to unify. At allied headquarters, Hans von Gagern, the German representative of the House of Orange, pleaded with Swiss envoys to enter the war as Holland had just done.[29] In the chancelleries plans for Germany began to appear, and even the conservative ones took for granted a Swiss contribution to the common defense system.[30] In Austria itself there was Archduke John's plan for a synthetic state composed of Switzerland, Vorarlberg, and Tyrol; and all those who demanded the restoration of Austrian power on the upper Rhine were in effect proposing that Switzerland be part of the Austrian sphere of influence.

There was only one solution: to overthrow the existing regime and bring to power one that *desired* to become part of the Austrian system, for reasons of political philosophy if not for protection—a conservative regime that would be more likely to ban La Harpe than to welcome him. The means Metternich chose were subversion backed by the invading allied army. When arguing the merits of the detour through Switzerland, he had assured Alexander that the operation could be managed without violating her neutrality. In a sense this was true, because a newly restored conservative government could probably be persuaded to grant free transit to the allied armies or even to greet them as liberators. To bring about a change of governments required all of Metternich's cunning, and nothing contributed more to his already considerable reputation for craft than the intrigue he now carried out in the Swiss cantons. When Alexander learned of this activity he was angrier than ever. Not only did he halt Russia's part in the military preparations but he recklessly conveyed to his friends at Zürich his personal guarantee of Swiss neutrality. It was under such circumstances that Metternich suddenly became the champion of precipitate action and behind the tsar's back ordered Schwarzenberg to cross the frontier and seize the Rhine bridge at Basel.[31]

[29] Hellmuth Rössler, *Zwischen Revolution und Reaktion. Ein Lebensbild des Reichsfreiherrn Hans Christoph von Gagern 1766–1852* (Göttingen and Berlin, 1958), 148.

[30] E.g., views of Stadion and Hardenberg. Griewank, *Wiener Kongress*, 118.

[31] Edgar Bonjour, H. S. Offler, and G. R. Potter, *A Short History of Switzerland* (Oxford, 1952), 240–241; Fournier, *Congress von Chatillon*, 36–42; Ritter, *Stein* (1958 ed.), 469–470; and Metternich *Memoirs*, I, 217–221.

Alexander was stunned. "As one of the allied monarchs I have nothing more to say to you," was his helpless response when Metternich told him the news; "but as a man I declare to you that you have grieved me in a way that you can never repair." [32] To add to the tsar's frustration, the Austrian prestidigitator was able, by ignoring the Swiss troops in the French service and arranging for handfuls of demonstrators here and there to hail the allied armies as liberators, to prevent Alexander from taking any action based on his guarantee. In Switzerland the result was the demise of the centralistic liberal constitution and the restoration of a loose federalism under the conservative leadership of canton Bern. In the coalition the result was an open breach between Metternich and Alexander that ushered in the most trying period of the common war effort. When the tsar added to the words quoted above, "you do not know the peculiar circumstances of my position," Metternich replied: "I know them, and I believe I know them fully." [33] A period of pretense had come to an end. Henceforward Alexander knew that his Austrian adversary was not the timid and indolent dilettante he pretended to be but a rival of high intelligence and, it would seem, with unsuspected resources of energy and decisiveness. He was the Metternich of old, the man who in 1805 had seconded Alexander's highhanded treatment of the king of Prussia.

From then on the struggle with the tsar was in the open on all fronts. In Saxony, Austria employed former Saxon officers under General Alois Langenau to sabotage Prince Repnin's military government and agitate for the restoration of King Frederick August. When the tsar threatened to arrest the agents, Metternich had to back down. He repudiated the plots and ordered Langenau to desist.[34] In Denmark his diplomacy defended King Frederick VI against the demands of Alexander's protégé, Bernadotte. To the latter he offered a compromise: Denmark to cede only the part of Norway north of Trondheim, not all of it. The prince royal of Sweden refused. Heartened by military success in Holstein and an advantageous armistice (December 15), he

---

[32] *ibid.*, I, 222.
[33] *ibid.*, I, 222–223.
[34] Pertz, *Aus Steins Leben*, I, 735.

appealed to the tsar on the basis of long-standing treaty pledges. Alexander supported him and again Metternich retreated, withdrawing the mediation.[35] By the treaty of Kiel (January 14, 1814,) Denmark was compelled to cede all of Norway. To be sure, she received Swedish Pomerania as compensation, but this was due to British intercession, not Austrian.[36] Only in Naples, where Austria's immediate opponent was merely Lord Bentinck, the unmanageable representative of Castlereagh, did Metternich enjoy success comparable to that in Switzerland. Wearying of Bentinck's attempts to establish constitutional government under the Bourbons, he finally ordered his own agent, Count Neipperg (another mediatized prince in the Austrian service), to settle with Murat alone if need be. On January 11 Neipperg did so, concluding a treaty which recognized Murat as king of Naples in return for placing an army of 30,000 at the disposal of the allies. With Austrian troops pouring into the north and an ally in the south who was none the less useful for being a Bonapartist, Italy, for the time being at least, was secure.[37]

On the perimeter of Germany, therefore, Metternich at year's end had victories in Switzerland and Italy to balance against rebuffs in Saxony and Denmark. But these were local issues and, important as they were, they provided scant consolation for his inability to bring about peace on the Rhine. To be sure, as the allied ministers, now assembled at Freiburg, lifted their glasses to the new year, the Frankfurt proposals were still the official allied offer, and Metternich continued to maintain an official air of preparing for a conference on that basis. But Castlereagh was already in the Hague promising the newly installed prince of Orange that he would obtain Belgium for the restored Dutch state,[38] and in Germany there was such tumultuous rejoicing at the crossing of the Rhine that only a miraculous recovery of Napoleon's military fortunes would have made the old offer again acceptable. The invasion of French soil was in itself

[35] Metternich to Hudelist, 3 Jan. 1814, in Fournier, *Congress von Chatillon*, 248–249.
[36] Texts of treaties with Great Britain and with Sweden in Martens, *Nouveau recueil*, I, 666–680.
[37] Webster, *Castlereagh*, 253–260.
[38] *ibid.*, 194–198.

enough to fire the imagination, but when the poet Arndt supplied a slogan to go with it—"the Rhine, Germany's stream but not Germany's boundary"—even the unimaginative were caught by that enthusiasm which Metternich so dreaded. "The world thinks and speaks," observed Gentz, "as Kleist did in the year 1809: 'Strike him dead—humanity's court will ask thee not for reasons.'" [39]

Left-bank conquests on the lower and middle Rhine had always been an unspoken war aim of almost everyone except Metternich, Schwarzenberg, and Frederick William. Now the talk was of Alsace too. Sentimentalists recalled that Alsace had been cruelly torn from the Reich by Louis XIV. Military men, notably Blücher and Gneisenau, coveted the great military base at Strasbourg. "Shall the Rhine again become the boundary of the French Empire?" asked Crown Prince Ludwig of Bavaria, who did not share his father's Francophilism. "No!" he exclaimed to the Austrian envoy in Munich. "I proceed from this principle: the fortresses of the Rhine shall come into German hands, the Vosges and the Ardennes forest shall be the boundary of France." [40] In similar vein Humboldt envisaged a belt of German buffer states controlling the fortifications on both sides of the Rhine from Switzerland to Holland. On Austria's side, meanwhile, Stadion leaped at the chance to add Alsace to the Breisgau and anchor Austria more firmly than ever on the upper Rhine. In this purpose Hardenberg heartily concurred, the better to justify his own claims to Saxony.

These longings would have been alarming enough if they had involved nothing more than a dangerous weakening of France before the westward march of the allied army. But the outlook became immeasurably blacker when Alexander, early in January, began to talk freely about placing his protégé Bernadotte on the French throne. Metternich was now faced with the specter of a Franco-Russian entente. At best such a rapprochement portended the sort of condominium over Ger-

[39] Gentz to Metternich, 16 Jan. 1814, in Gentz, *Briefe von und an*, III, 227. The Kleist quotation is from his poem "Germania an ihre Kinder."

[40] Count Apponyi to Metternich, 19 Dec. 1813, in Anton Chroust (ed.), *Gesandschaftsberichte aus München 1814–1848. Zweite Abteilung: Die Berichte der österreichischen Gesandten*, I, 7–8.

many that Napoleon and Alexander had exercised in the days of the *Reichsdeputationshauptschluss.* At worst it could mean a new Tilsit, this time with Russia giving the orders. Metternich acted with characteristic vigor, informing Schwarzenberg of the new development, ordering him to halt the army on the Langres plateau, and not to budge from there until further notice, all in one dispatch. "It does not enter into our point of view," he explained, "to sacrifice a single man to place Bernadotte on the throne of France." [41]

The same developments imparted new urgency to the problem of the German constitution. Almost everyone, it seemed, who had ever expressed an opinion on the subject, was present at the new headquarters to add his voice to the excitement of "the Freiburg days." Besides Metternich and Hardenberg there were Stadion and Humboldt, and for Russia Prince Razumovsky and Nesselrode. Gentz, who had remained at Prague sulking over his exclusion from the select company at headquarters, at length received Metternich's summons and arrived on December 15.[42] Stein, delayed by administrative duties at Frankfurt, missed most of the talks but finally appeared on the 20th.

In the generally ebullient atmosphere of Freiburg Metternich found little to relieve his own gloom. True, even the most ardent imperialists had to admit that the middle-state accession treaties had all but eliminated a revival of the Reich, at least in its previous form. But the new plans being circulated in a steady effusion of memoranda almost without exception postulated a weak France and made the assumption that Russia would be either benevolent or compliant.

One of the chastened imperialists was Count Stadion. Facing the fact that sovereignty had been promised the middle states, he had reduced his hopes to a confederation consisting of Austria and Prussia and seven or eight middle states, all enlarged by absorption of their smaller neighbors. His primary concern was the defense of the Rhine, for which he considered Stein's plan of joining the fragmented western territories into a union

[41] Metternich to Schwarzenberg, 16 Jan. 1814, in Alfons Klinkowstrom (ed.), *Oesterreichs Theilnahme an den Befreiungskriegen* (Vienna, 1887), 797–798. Cf. Fournier, *Congress von Chatillon*, 43–55.

[42].Gentz, *Briefe von und an,* III, 226, note 2.

separate from Prussia and Austria wholly inadequate. Nor did he have confidence in a league among equals, which Metternich championed at the time; distant Austria, he claimed, could hardly compete with adjacent France in asserting influence on the Rhine. "Does the ministry in Vienna," he asked, "flatter itself that by its importance and prestige alone it can be effective with these petty sovereigns against all the wiles of human frailty and emotion . . . ? These difficult problems are not yet solved, indeed not yet seriously discussed." [43] To Stadion the only solution was a sweeping rearrangement of territory which would enable the two great powers to overwhelm the lesser states and divide the task of supervising Germany.

Accordingly he desired that Prussia receive Cleve, Berg, Mark, Recklinghausen, Münster, and Westphalia, which would give her control of the Rhine from Mainz to the Dutch border, while Austria would acquire the entire right bank from the Breisgau to Strasbourg, together with a strip of southern Würtemberg to provide a connection with the Austrian crown lands. Should it prove necessary to placate Bavaria, she could be given a place on the middle Rhine and be bound with the two great powers in a special pact to coordinate the defense of Germany's western frontier. The other states, surrounded by Austrian and Prussian territory and cut off from their French protector, would then have no choice but to submit to whatever federal instruments were devised in concert between Berlin and Vienna. The particular federative provisions Stadion considered a routine matter and did not elaborate, except to make it clear that he meant— like the good imperial patriot he was—to include adequate safeguards for the mediatized houses.

Since France was the main target, he was anxious to settle the German question quickly in order to deny her a voice in it. Yet he was not blind to the danger from the East. If defense of the Rhine was uppermost in his plans, it was because France was the present enemy and because he, no less than Metternich, feared a Franco-Russian entente. If anything, he was even more obsessed with it, and therefore he concluded that a strong France would only compound the calamity. Rather than gamble that

[43] This and following from Rössler, *Österreichs Kampf*, II, 173–176.

Bonaparte, even if he could be brought to terms and his throne preserved, would be pro-Austrian and would not attempt to entice the middle states into a new Rheinbund, Stadion preferred the certainty of permanently eliminating at least one of the dangers. Then, and only then, could Austria, from her firm base in Germany and allied to Great Britain and Prussia, concentrate her full strength against Russia, whether in the Balkans, in Poland, or in Germany itself.

Stadion's general conception of the Austrian predicament did not differ fundamentally from that of Metternich. Both strove for a system of collective security in Central Europe. Both attached utmost importance to undertakings with Britain and Prussia. Since in the winter of 1813–14 these were Austria's most urgent tasks, it is understandable that in the bargaining Metternich should assign Stadion a role second only to his own. They differed, in short, not so much in their schematic representation of the situation as in their assessments of contingencies. Superficially Stadion appeared the greater realist: in his distrust of Napoleon, in his desire to remove the French threat once and for all, in his plea for coercion against the German middle states, and in his readiness to grant Prussia hegemony in North Germany. The program was simple and direct, partly because Stadion was that kind of man, partly because his subordinate position allowed him certain liberties of speculation not available to the responsible policy maker. His realism, in truth, was that of a Felix Schwarzenberg, a Schlieffen, or a Clemenceau: bold, straightforward, decisive, but by these very qualities inflexible, and involving risks the more dangerous for being unperceived rather than calculated.

Such so-called realism has its moments of success, but it commits the often fatal error of being simpler and more direct than reality itself. "Men of this sort," said Metternich of Stadion some years later, "always incline to extremes; for them there are no transitions, and since these nevertheless do exist, when they come before them, instead of knowing how to wait, they often act at random." [44] Stadion understood the need for a rapprochement with Prussia and was lavish in his offers of aggrandizement, yet

[44] "Autobiographical Memoir," Metternich, *Memoirs*, I, 98.

he stopped short of the one concession necessary for success—Saxony. Regarding the German question as a whole, he perceived that the main problem was how to achieve the acquiescence of the middle states. But when he further argued that coercion must be used and that, if necessary, Austria should threaten a separate peace to bring the tsar to sacrifice his South German relatives, one is at a loss to understand how he still expected to crush France. Stadion's solution of the German problem begged the question. By contrast, Metternich's policy of reconciliation and cooperation with the middle states, though it had its difficulties, was consistent; and it required, as matters stood in December, a minimum of dependence upon the unpredictable decisions of either Napoleon or Alexander. His was the realism of non-commitment, of keeping all roads open as long as possible in the fashion of a Bismarck or a Napoleon. It was not the less realistic for eschewing grand moves on the European chess board; victories are also won by a superior pawn position at the end of the game.

How to win the game—that was, despite their differences, the common purpose of the two Austrians. An entirely different note was sounded by Wilhelm von Humboldt, who in mid-December finally completed, in answer to Stein's August memorandum, his own version of a German constitution.[45] "Germany must be free and strong," he wrote in words that have echoed through generations of German thought, "not merely so that she can defend herself against this or that neighbor or against any enemy whatsoever, but because only a nation externally strong can preserve within itself the spirit from which all internal blessings flow." [46] Germany, Humboldt insisted, was by nature a land of diverse peoples and diverse traditions which were her glory. "It is the destiny of Germany to be a *Staatenverein*," he concluded, not a unitary mass like France or a cluster of totally disconnected entities like Italy. As a result he favored neither a strong central authority nor a further consolidation of territorial units. The restoration of the Reich he

---

[45] "Denkschrift über die deutsche Verfassung," in Gebhardt, *Humboldts Schriften*, XI, 95-112.
[46] *ibid.*, XI, 97.

opposed as infeasible, while the defensive advantages of greater consolidation he considered outweighed by the stultifying effects on Germany's kaleidoscopic culture.

Nevertheless, insofar as his Prussian loyalties permitted, Humboldt's sympathies lay with the restorers. The purpose of his "mutual defense alliance" was to secure not only the "tranquility and independence of Germany," but also "in the individual states a just order founded on law." The latter aim encompassed a few innovations like an embryonic customs union, but mainly it covered the restoration of *Landstände* ("an old German institution," he called them), special regulations protecting the mediatized princes, and, in states too small to provide adequate judicial machinery, the right of subjects to appeal to the high courts of a neighboring state—preferably one of the big four: Austria, Prussia, Bavaria, and Hanover. As these four were also to arbitrate interstate disputes, they would really exercise the functions of the old *Reichskammergericht* and, in lieu of an emperor, constitute a supreme directory. "This entire treatise," Humboldt explained for Stein's benefit, "is only an attempt to show what can still be done even if, as I believe, the restoration of a constitution with a true *Reichs-Oberhaupt* is impossible."

For the rest, Humboldt, like most of his contemporaries, viewed the German question mainly as one of defense. The *Staatenverein* must be permanent, he said; the members must be forbidden to enter treaties contrary to the terms of the covenant; all states must provide military contingents just as in the Rheinbund; and the great powers, particularly Great Britain and Russia, must guarantee the security of the confederation. The key to the system was the supervisory role of Austria and Prussia. They would inspect the army, set quotas and standards, and they alone would determine when hostilities should commence and end. In contrast to Stadion, however, Humboldt believed the two powers could act more effectively if they were separated from France by small buffer states than if they themselves attempted to keep the watch on the Rhine.[47]

Thus Austria and Prussia were to have a dual function: together with Britain and Russia they would determine Germany's

[47] *ibid.*, XI, 102.

place in the European order; in company with Bavaria and Hanover they would regulate Germany's internal order. In both cases, however, the scope of the guarantors' authority was to be confined to specified *ad hoc* situations. There was to be no sovereign chief, no German court, no executive machinery, no over-all legislative organ, not even a congress of diplomats such as Gentz had provided for in his plan of 1808. The reason was not far to seek. To Humboldt the nation was mainly a cultural concept; in politics he was a Prussian statesman. A Reich implied too large a role for the Habsburgs, a congress of diplomats too many voices for the lesser states. The limited condominium he did propose would grant Prussia parity with Austria, regardless of the territorial settlement, and without seriously restricting her freedom of action as a great power. All in all Prussia stood to gain from the system at least as much as she gave—in terms of her European position alone, to say nothing of the opportunities she would have to extend her influence in Germany through her appellate courts and her powers of arbitration, both of which would come into play among the petty states of the north more often than in Austria's sphere.[48]

This observation is certainly no criticism of Humboldt, merely a reminder that his oft-quoted obeisance to the German nation should not be confused with the concrete solution he actually proposed. There was much in his plan which even Metternich could well accept: the primacy of foreign policy and defense; the belief that the Reich was both irretrievable and undesirable; the desire to avoid further consolidation of the lesser states; and above all the necessity for intimate cooperation between Austria and Prussia, not in the sense of separate spheres of influence as favored by Stadion and Hardenberg, but in a joint direction of the whole. Even the privileged status of Bavaria and Hanover was a solution Metternich was willing to try, as we shall see.[49] Only Humboldt's determination to regu-

---

[48] Cf. Friedrich Meinecke, *Weltbürgertum und Nationalstaat. Studien zur Genesis des deutschen Nationalstaates,* 5th ed. (Munich and Berlin, 1919), 192–204; Huber, *Deutsche Verfassungsgeschichte,* 519–526; Ritter, *Stein* (1958 ed.), 483; and Griewank, *Wiener Kongress,* 116, note 58, all of whom exaggerate the unitary effects of the plan and neglect the elements of Prussian *Realpolitik.*

[49] See below, Ch. x, p. 306.

late the internal affairs of the states was alien to the Austrian's outlook. The correspondence of viewpoints is not surprising. Three years as Prussian ambassador at the *Ballhausplatz* had taught Humboldt something of Metternich's plans, and he could hardly disregard them. On the contrary, he had great respect for them.[50]

Nevertheless, he himself was impressed with the gulf between him and the Austrians, as indeed he might be after hearing Gentz's ideas on the subject. Gentz, into whose hands a copy of Humboldt's memorial was thrust almost upon his arrival in Freiburg, directed his criticism at the three-class system of states. At the very least, he argued, Bavaria and Hanover would have to be admitted to a voice in matters of war and peace, and this would leave all the others even more disgruntled. Still worse was the effort, however mild, to regulate internal affairs, for all alike, from the pettiest principality to the great powers themselves, would boggle at this infringement of their sovereignty. To form a league of equals, Gentz declared, was hard enough under any circumstances, but to start with equals, diminish the status of some, and *then* try to form a league would be foolhardy. Only a month earlier he had said of a Habsburg Reich that "in short order the whole thing would degenerate into such a tumult of anarchy, internal feuds and external cabals that no one would know any more who was first and who last." [51] This would be just as true of an Austro-Prussian condominium, which differed from an "empire" only in providing Prussia an equal place at the top. If invidious distinctions were to be made, Gentz favored mediatizing some of the smallest states, preferably through mergers of closely related dynasties, and then forming a system of alliances among the fourteen or so remaining sovereigns on the basis of strict equality. The suggestion was not rigorously consistent, but it proved one thing: Gentz was not a doctrinaire legitimist, merely making excuses to Humboldt. He was a realist, like Metternich carefully gauging the bargaining power of the sovereign princes.[52]

[50] See his report of 31 March 1813, in Gebhardt, *Humboldts Schriften*, XI, 25ff.
[51] Gentz to Metternich, 5 Nov. 1813, in Gentz, *Briefe von und an*, III, 197.
[52] Gebhardt, *Humboldts Schriften*, XI, 95 and 113–116.

In reply Humboldt was quick to observe that further mediatizing would cause more resentment than milder gradations of status, the more so, he added somewhat waggishly, as relatives would quarrel more than anyone else. As to the other points, he amiably conceded that Hanover and Bavaria might be accommodated as Gentz wished. Toward the remaining states, however, he was more disdainful than ever, arguing that their subordination would be slight enough, and would offer little cause for complaint. So far as German unity was concerned, Humboldt was possibly correct, but this was not the main issue. The crux of the matter was the regulation of the rights of the *Stände*. Although this, for all but the very smallest courts, was the only invasion of internal affairs, it was the one thing the sovereigns were bound to resist. It was also the one thing Humboldt insisted upon, and he painted for Gentz a lugubrious picture of the blight on German public life if the mediatized were not aided and the rights of the other *Stände* not secured against the leveling, bureaucratic programs of the despots.[53]

Since the conclusion of the Frankfurt accession treaties in November the matter of restoring a corporate order in the former Rheinbund states had grown daily more important. In guaranteeing sovereignty the treaties had, as we have seen, dashed almost all hopes of restoring a hierarchy of estates under the mild dominion of an emperor. Whatever protection the mediatized could now hope for must come from state constitutions or, to use the ambiguous nomenclature of the period, *landständische Verfassungen*. Recovering with surprising rapidity from their defeats at Frankfurt, the mediatized houses organized for action. A few, mostly from Westphalia, banded together under Prince Bentheim-Steinfurth to ask the Central Administrative Council to restore their former rights. Their efforts were futile because Baron Stein, however sympathetic he was in most respects, had other things in store for them[54] and conferred his patronage on another organization. This, proposed on December 10 by the two princes of Loewenstein and half a dozen others, developed almost immediately into a formal as-

[53] *ibid.*, XI, 113–116.
[54] Huber, *Deutsche Verfassungsgeschichte*, 498.

sociation of mediatized princes under the leadership of Count
Friedrich Christian Solms-Laubach, a close friend and colleague
of Stein. Their goal was not sovereignty but the maximum possible restoration of the old regime, or, barring that, a protective
"legal order" and full compensation for their losses.[55]

Stein reached Freiburg on December 20 and immediately
plunged into the debate on his favorite subject. To Stadion he
presented a lengthy memorandum dated December 25, which
contained his new ideas on the German constitution.[56] For
Humboldt he prepared a critique, written in the margins of the
latter's draft.[57] To both he gave encouragement, though with
somewhat divergent suggestions. In the note to Stadion he proposed vesting executive powers in "an hereditary chief." In his
remarks to the Prussian he placed such powers in the hands of a
four-power directory, an adaptation of Humboldt's committee
of guarantors. To Stadion he was sympathetic with Austrian
territorial demands and made no mention of Saxony. With the
Prussian diplomat, fortunately, he did not have to discuss territory at all, since Humboldt had conveniently omitted this
pivotal issue.

Otherwise Stein addressed the Austrian and the Prussian in
similar language. Since both had glossed over the precise work-
ings of a federal apparatus, he obligingly made them explicit.
In addition to a stronger executive he demanded an "assembly
of representatives meeting periodically," the two central organs
to have competence over customs, posts, coinage, fortresses, and
several police functions of general concern—approximately the
same powers he had earlier proposed. He was even more specific
about the internal order within the states. The state assemblies
or *Landtage* should meet periodically, participating in legislation, appropriations, raising of taxes, and the supervision of
army and bureaucracy. The costs of the princes' courts should
be defrayed from their own private domains, not the public
treasury. Each state constitution, moreover, should contain a
bill of rights guaranteeing freedom of person and property, the

---

[55] d'Arenberg, *Les princes du St-Empire*, 208–209; Ritter, *Stein* (1958 ed.), 486;
and Hoff, *Die Mediatisiertenfrage*, 17–25.
[56] Rössler, *Österreichs Kampf*, II, 172ff.
[57] Text in Stein, *Briefwechsel*, IV, 528–530.

277

right of residence and employment anywhere in Germany, and protection against arbitrary seizure of property. An independent judiciary, trial by jury, and public trials were other liberal measures which Stein advocated. There can be little doubt that, measured against a policy directed solely against absolutism, Stein's program was in the great liberal tradition then in the making.

Nevertheless the spirit was conservative—if indeed the terms liberal and conservative are applicable to the problem. Privilege lurked in the corporative structure of the *Landtage,* and in the status of the mediatized houses it strode brazenly forward. For them Stein demanded exemption from military service, as well as partial exemption from taxes, a privileged position before the law, hereditary seats in the *Landtage* and, with revealing personal sensitivity, full social equality of the imperial knights to the higher nobility, the *Standesherrn.* He did not explicitly include in this list the nobility's ancient manorial rights, or the traditional powers over local governmental functions such as police, schools, churches, charities, and lower courts of law. But in fact the whole scheme would have left the sovereigns so enfeebled that they could hardly have curbed their titled subjects even in these realms.

Under such circumstances could the great reformer have put through the emancipation of the serfs in Prussia? It is a fair question. Many a burdened peasant of western Germany might, had he been familiar with the issues, have judged his prospects better under the enlightened rule of a Carl Frederick in Baden or even under the less distinguished Rheinbund rulers, most of whom had already eliminated personal bondage,[58] than under a regime dominated or paralyzed by the great landlords. On the other hand, it is hardly fair to Stein to suggest, as several of his biographers have done, that since he regarded his great reforms only as a means to victory, he was no longer interested now that Napoleon was almost driven from German soil.[59] The whole

[58] Theodore S. Hamerow, *Restoration, Revolution, Reaction. Economics and Politics in Germany 1815–1871* (Princeton, N.J., 1958), 38–49.

[59] Ritter, *Stein* (1958 ed.), 485; and Max Lehmann, *Freiherr vom Stein,* one-vol. ed. (Leipzig, 1921), 510.

matter is extremely complex and beyond the scope of this study.[60] It is raised here only to show that in backing the much maligned "petty despots" Metternich was far from committing himself *ipso facto* to the cause of reaction.

Metternich's interest of course was not ideological. He only knew that Stein, Humboldt, and Stadion alike were asking that Austria desert her middle-state protégés at a time of extraordinary difficulty. From a strictly Austrian point of view such a course would have eliminated her only leverage for dealing with Prussia, just when Hardenberg was about to declare officially his government's right to Saxony. But even from a joint Austro-Prussian standpoint the assault on the sovereignty of the middle states was unrealistic. The thesis that Austria and Prussia could have imposed almost any terms at this time rested on the premise that France was to be permanently weakened, possibly even deprived of the Vosges. It further presupposed that, with French influence removed, the middle states would be helpless. Both assumptions Metternich dismissed. Whatever the effect on Germany, the European balance required a strong France; but with or without France a Russian protectorate over the middle states was a possibility too real and too ominous to be ignored.

Alexander's hand in fact continued to grow stronger. To overcome Metternich's "spirit of frivolity, conceit, and . . . lack of respect for truth and principle," [61] Stein had no scruples against admitting Russia to the most intimate councils on the destiny of Germany. Anxious to obtain results while France was still excluded, he proposed on December 30 the creation of a German-constitution committee, on which the Russian Prince Razumovsky would sit with Humboldt and Stadion. The tsar refused. Metternich, he explained, would counter by coming to terms with France, and in any case the exclusion of France would be accomplished in the coming peace treaty.[62] These were good

[60] Especially useful on these issues are Wolff, *Die deutsche Publizistik;* Wilhelm Mommesen, *Stein, Ranke, Bismarck. Ein Beitrag zur politischen und sozialen Bewegung des 19. Jahrhunderts* (Munich, 1954), 15–76; Heffter, *Deutsche Selbstverwaltung,* 63–137; and Leonard Krieger, *The German Idea of Freedom* (Boston, 1957), 139–216.
[61] Stein's memorial of 30 Dec. 1813 with tsar's reply in margins, in Stein, *Briefwechsel,* IV, 508–509.
[62] *ibid.*

reasons. An even better one was his reluctance to disillusion Stein just at that moment about Russia's German policy. He wanted to postpone all decisions, whether in Germany or Poland, until the capture of Paris and the overthrow of Bonaparte, in the meantime enjoying the advantages of hunting with the hounds and running with the hares.

So ended the year 1813, the year of liberation. All eyes looked to Paris. Alexander's right to be consulted at every turn was almost unquestioned. Bernadotte's prospects for ascending the French throne had never been better. On all sides voices were raised demanding an immediate settlement of the German problem and the subjugation of the Rheinbund states. Count Münster for Hanover and Hans von Gagern, representing Nassau for William of Orange, though pro-Austrian, still accused Metternich of Francophilism and urged the restoration of the Reich, with all its benefits for the mediatized. The Rheinbund states themselves were of inadequate weight and uncertain loyalty. In Bavaria Montgelas ridiculed the allied war effort and went out of his way to express his affection for France.[63] In Würtemberg, on the other hand, King Frederick was so determined to find favor with the tsar that he denounced Austria's hesitant military policy, and alone among the former wards of Napoleon zealously maintained a strenuous war effort. He fielded a contingent of double his assigned quota for Alexander, just as he had done in 1809 for Napoleon.[64] Elsewhere, too, there was scarcely a court but had its pro-French and pro-Russian factions. One by one all the dangers that Metternich had foreseen were coming to pass. They were crystallizing, moreover, at a time when he had neither come to terms with Napoleon nor reached an understanding with Castlereagh. Even the weather was bad. It was the severest winter that that generation was to see, like the one at Canossa so many centuries before, when Henry IV had had to make his agonizing decision. Metternich, too, knew what he must do. Turning to Hardenberg, he acquiesced in Prussia's annexation of Saxony.

[63] Reports of Count Apponyi, December, 1813, in Chroust, *Berichte der österreichischen Gesandten*, I, 1–12.
[64] Hölzle, *Württemberg im Zeitalter*, 162.

CHAPTER X

RAPPROCHEMENT WITH HARDENBERG

AND CASTLEREAGH

Metternich's démarche on the Saxon question was a sensation, producing exclamations of disbelief in headquarters, and a torrent of rumors which to this day have not been fully clarified. That the offer was made there can be no doubt. "Conference with Metternich," reads a laconic entry from Hardenberg's diary of January 8, 1814. "Metternich dines with me. He accedes to the plan concerning Saxony." [1] It also seems indicated that the whole of Saxony was meant, not just a part of it, for the very next day the chancellor, reporting the interview to his ally Alexander, wrote that Metternich had indeed "conveyed from his chief the assent of his court to the acquisition of Saxony. . . ." [2] What the conditions were, however, we can only guess. One stipulation, the omission of which is hardly imaginable, must have been Prussia's repudiation of the Russian program in Poland, and Hardenberg hinted as much in his report to Alexander. Another possibility was a more favorable attitude toward the middle states in the German constitution question, even though the evidence for this is largely circumstantial.

Hardenberg went to work, in the days immediately following, on a comprehensive program which included many concessions to Austria. Although he professed to believe that Europe had nothing to fear from Alexander personally, he insisted that in the long run "the massive strength which France presents from the one side and Russia from the other imposes on the intermediate powers . . . the [need for the] most intimate union and alliance. . . ." [3] Accordingly he proposed a Central

---

[1] Text in Fournier, *Congress von Chatillon*, 361.

[2] Hardenberg to Alexander, 9 Jan. 1814, in Martens, *Traités par la russie*, VII, 156.

[3] This and following from Hardenberg's "Mémoire donnée à Lord Castlereagh en janvier 1814.' Text in Karl Griewank, "Preussen und die Neuordnung

European defense league which would include Holland and Switzerland, and possibly even Denmark, Sweden, and Turkey, with Britain lending diplomatic support from outside. The German states were to be joined by a *lien fédératif*, and though Hardenberg clung to Humboldt's principle of subordinating smaller states to larger ones to some extent, he also took seriously Gentz's suggestion and granted Bavaria and Hanover full equality to Austria and Prussia by admitting them into the supreme executive organ. Not only would they take their turn in directing the whole under a system of rotation, but they would also retain control of their own foreign policies and military establishments. It was a remarkable retreat from the conception of an Austro-Prussian protectorate, and even though British pressure in behalf of Hanover also figured in it, it must be regarded primarily as a concession to Metternich,[4] a *quid pro quo* tied to the Saxon question.

No less gratifying to Metternich was Hardenberg's attitude toward Poland. He explicitly stated that "in the East the security of Germany will depend essentially on the arrangements agreed to for Poland," and the territory he claimed far exceeded the strip connecting Silesia and East Prussia stipulated in the Kalisch pact and confirmed at Teplitz. Bounded by the Warthe river in the east and a line from the Warthe's main bend through Dobrzyn to Soldau, south of East Prussia, the area Hardenberg sought encompassed the strong points of Czentochowa and Kalisch and the great fortress on the lower Vistula, Thorn. Cracow, the corresponding rampart on the upper Vistula, the chancellor assigned to Austria. Territorially the claims were modest compared to those recommended on January 18 by the Prussian Russophobe, General Knesebeck, but the essence

Deutschlands," *Forschungen zur brandenburgischen und preussischen Geschichte,* LII (1940), 265–267. Cf. Karl Erich Born, "Hardenbergs Pläne und Versuche zur Neuordnung Europas und Deutschlands 1813/1815," *Geschichte in Wissenschaft und Unterricht,* 8. Jahrgang (1957), 554–555. I cannot accept Born's view, based solely on Hardenberg's profession here, that the chancellor trusted the tsar. Closer to the mark on this matter is Hausherr, *Die Stunde Hardenbergs,* 322, although he offers no concrete evidence.

[4] The four-power directory was already present in a memorandum of Staatsrat Hoffmann under the date of 12 Jan., i.e., *before* Castlereagh arrived at headquarters. Griewank, "Neuordnung," *ibid.,* 244, note 3.

of the Polish question was not so much the square miles of territory to be bartered as strong military frontiers. Their acquisition was the goal of Hardenberg and Metternich, their breaching the aim of Alexander. The presentation of the Prussian plan supported Metternich's efforts to force Alexander to divulge his own intentions before France was removed as a factor in the European balance. Within a month the Prussian monarch was scolding his chancellor for toying with "a sort of league" against the tsar.[5]

Actually it was not an anti-Russian front that Hardenberg sought, so much as a position of independence, and he was simply taking full advantage of his bargaining position to attain it. If he was goaded by Alexander to take Saxony and by Metternich to help himself in Poland, he had Castlereagh's encouragement to reach out for territory beyond the Rhine. For on January 18 the British minister had at last arrived at allied headquarters, and had profoundly altered the course of the negotiations. Besides insisting on the transfer of Belgium to Holland, he made no secret of his intention of "bringing forward Prussia" to participate in the barrier against France—"a favourite scheme of Mr. Pitt," as he rightly called it.[6] Accordingly Hardenberg included in his list of claims much territory on both banks of the Rhine. That he demanded nothing south of the Mosel may be viewed as another concession to Austria, inasmuch as Metternich had always believed he could, as a last resort, concede Saxony, provided Prussia did not also dominate the Rhine-Main confluence.

Nevertheless, the claim to left-bank territory was a direct rebuff to Metternich. On the plane of European politics it signaled the repudiation of the Frankfurt base, which was still the official allied offer to France. On the German level it transgressed one of the essential conditions of the concession regarding Saxony. The European implications Hardenberg understood well enough, though in view of the British attitude he had in all likelihood already dismissed the Rhine frontier as obso-

<hr />

[5] *ibid.*, 258; Griewank *Wiener Kongress*, 151–155; Ritter, *Stein* (1958 ed.), 487; and Treitschke, *History of Germany*, I, 626.

[6] Castlereagh to Liverpool, 22 Jan. 1814, in *British Diplomacy*, 135.

lete. The connection with Saxony he probably did not perceive, for it is doubtful that Metternich had made the condition clear. At no time apparently had the Austrian stated explicitly what Prussia might have if peace was made immediately and, alternatively, what would be hers if the war continued. On this subject he was entangled in his own web. He had naturally avoided commitments based on further conquests. Yet he could not undertake candid discussion of anything postulated on allowing France her natural frontiers without betraying the deception he had practiced all along: namely, the pretense that the Frankfurt base was only clever propaganda, not a genuine peace move. Such matters were better reserved to a European peace congress in which France participated.

Meanwhile, Metternich even more than Hardenberg had reason to rejoice at Castlereagh's coming. Indeed, the British minister's appreciation of Austria's predicament exceeded his wildest hopes. Regarding Poland Castlereagh recognized the seriousness of the tsar's silence and agreed "to press an early decision on these arrangements." [7] Alexander's plans for France he learned of in shocked amazement and vowed that Bernadotte would never ascend the throne. Though partial to a restoration of the Bourbons, he met the Austrian halfway, offering to leave the decision about the throne entirely to the French, and in the meantime to deal with Napoleon. This formula, both men agreed, would confine the choice to Bonaparte himself or to the ancient dynasty.[8] "Lord Castlereagh is here," Metternich gleefully reported to Schwarzenberg, "and I am very pleased with him. He has everything: grace, discretion, and moderation." [9]

There remained, however, the difficulty of Castlereagh's stand on Belgium, which was incompatible with the Frankfurt base. To eliminate the contradiction, to be "delivered from the embarrassments of the Frankfurt negotiation," the Englishman proposed that the preliminary offer be omitted altogether and the outline of a general settlement drafted, which would then

[7] ibid., 134.
[8] ibid., 138.
[9] Quoted in Webster, Castlereagh, 203, note 1.

be submitted to France as an ultimatum.[10] From Metternich's point of view the remedy was worse than the ill. It meant not only the abandonment of the Frankfurt base but also the elimination of France from a share in determining the peace settlement beyond her borders. It granted one of Alexander's most coveted objects and forced Metternich to choose at last between France and England. And so he chose, acquiescing in Castlereagh's desires.

It was a momentous decision, and Metternich did not make it lightly. Nor did he, as a more emotional and dramatic statesman might have done, shift to the other extreme and place his hopes exclusively on Castlereagh. For until the French army had actually capitulated, France *was* still a factor regardless of interallied resolutions to the contrary. Metternich, the master of the gradual transition, still held out for France *and* England as the combination to pit against the tsar in shaping the future of Central Europe. Nevertheless, he was hedging his bets increasingly in favor of Great Britain. "Metternich's geographical notions are improved," the British foreign minister reported, "he will *listen at least* to modifications of the Rhine in advance of Dusseldorf (sic)." [11]

But if the Rhineland was to be the focal point of accommodation among Austria, Britain, and Prussia, Metternich could only regard the Saxon offer as obsolete, especially as the despondency and sense of isolation that had driven him to make it had considerably abated. The problem was how to withdraw an offer which had strings attached that he had never bothered to mention. Typically he proceeded by indirection, avoiding a personal confrontation with Hardenberg and placing the matter in the hands of Stadion, a man who scarcely needed instructions when it came to diverting the Prussians from Saxony to the Rhineland. The task was made easier, as it happened, by the magnitude of the Prussian designs. Altogether Hardenberg claimed a population of 13,000,000 against less than 10,000,000 in 1805. When he presented his case on January 20, Stadion was

[10] Cf. Castlereagh to Liverpool, 29 Jan. 1814, in *British Diplomacy*, 143 and 144.
[11] Castlereagh to Liverpool, 22 Jan. 1814, in *British Diplomacy*, 135.

genuinely shocked. "Exorbitant! Scandalous!" he exclaimed, and urged the chancellor to be satisfied with the part of Saxony east of the Elbe or, better yet, to forego the Wettin property entirely and take more territory in the Rhineland instead. Hardenberg refused, repeatedly invoking Metternich's promise of January 8, and pleading that the existence of many competing claims made title to the Rhenish lands uncertain, whereas Saxony could be occupied immediately. He was also influenced by Humboldt's buffer-state doctrine, which counseled against a common frontier with France.[12]

He defended the figure of 13,000,000 on the ground that many of the western territories should not really be counted in the Prussian totals. They consisted of mediatized lands over which Prussia would exercise only a partial dominion [13]—the assumption being that in the future German league a federal statute would guarantee numerous liberties to the mediatized houses. The argument was not so specious as it sounds, particularly in the mind of a bureaucratic centralist like Hardenberg. In league with Stein, Humboldt, and Solms-Laubach he was plotting to undermine the middle-state princes in this same fashion, and so he could not help but fear for Prussia's own internal administration if her compensations included very many such privileged territories. The issue was clear. If Prussia must replace provinces over which her sway had once been complete with an assortment of principalities and counties where the local landlords claimed nominal sovereignty, controlled all local government, and could defy *Kreis* directors appointed in Berlin, then she could not be strictly bound to the population scale of 1805. What Hardenberg forgot was that where he saw mainly internal complications, others would see increments to Prussian power: new recruiting grounds for the army, command of stra-

---

[12] Rössler, *Österreichs Kampf*, II, 188–190. Both Rössler and Lauber, *Metternichs Kampf*, 127, regard Stadion's conversations with Hardenberg as a mere personal protest. It was at least that, but unless all was chaos in the ministry of foreign affairs, we must assume that Stadion spoke for Metternich. Griewank, "Neuordnung," *ibid.*, 250, is closer to the truth, saying Metternich had left Stadion behind to deal with these matters.

[13] Griewank, "Neuordnung," *ibid.*, 245 and 250. Griewank seems to confuse the problem of the mediatized houses with that of sovereign states subordinated to Prussia in a *Kreis* type German constitution.

tegic heights, and influence on neighboring small states. In any case, it was hardly the kind of argument to appeal to an old *Reichsgraf* like Stadion, and so the discussions faded away without an accord, as Metternich had doubtless anticipated. At least Prussia was put on notice that Austria no longer considered herself pledged to deliver Saxony.

But the Saxon gambit had had its advantages. Hardenberg now knew that Austria's opposition was relative, not absolute; henceforward, he could be more independent of Russia, knowing that this most prized territory could, under certain circumstances, be acquired via Vienna as well as via St. Petersburg. And Metternich came away with the knowledge that territorial concessions would yield copious returns in the German constitutional question. Almost as important for Metternich was the effect on Stadion. The leader of the German national party in Austria, and a potential threat to Metternich's internal position, emerged from his interviews considerably chastened. Hardenberg's solicitude for the mediatized nobility, he discovered, stopped at the Prussian border. A common policy for the two German powers was not so simple as it had seemed.

Thus, ironically, it was Metternich's retreat on the Rhineland issue rather than his concession regarding Saxony that won support for his peace program. Both Castlereagh and Hardenberg were now willing to negotiate with Napoleon and to make one more attempt to force a definition of war aims—Castlereagh for the sake of the continental equilibrium, Hardenberg because, having presented his own claims, he needed to know if they were compatible with Alexander's. Castlereagh eased matters by volunteering to specify Britain's colonial demands, while Metternich contributed a memorandum which reminded his allies that they were still pledged to negotiate with Caulaincourt, indeed to do so on the basis of a Rhine-Alps-Pyrenees frontier.[14]

This last reference, in view of what had gone before, could hardly have been more than a bluff directed at the tsar. If so, it had little effect. The only war aim Alexander deigned to dis-

[14] Metternich's *Vortrag* of 27 Jan. 1814, in Fournier, *Congress von Chatillon*, 62–65.

cuss was the award of Alsace to Austria, and this Metternich emphatically refused, fearful that it presaged a Russian demand for Galicia.[15] Beyond that the tsar only reiterated his previous argument that the detailed claims of individual members of the coalition were inseparable from the terms tendered France, and that these in turn depended on the military situation. It was an unabashed affirmation of the right of conquest. When Alexander refused to countenance even a formal four-power meeting to discuss the subject, the Austrian minister once more responded with the threat of a separate peace.[16] And once more the threat had the desired effect, for the bargaining power which Austria had lost by virtue of victory she had at least partially regained in the entente with England. Alexander, finding himself virtually isolated at headquarters, and sure that mounting military success would annul any decisions made, finally consented to formal conferences. "I have been to the brink of a rupture," Metternich reported with bravado, "and I have carried it off." [17]

These conferences took place at the end of January at Langres. Here Metternich continued his bluff, vigorously defending one after another the positions he had already privately abandoned. He demanded a cessation of hostilities while peace was negotiated, took the Frankfurt proposals as a starting point, and extolled the Bonapartist regime in France. The Russian delegates, Nesselrode, Razumovsky, and Pozzo di Borgo, dutifully, though not always with conviction, opposed all peace negotiations, went so far beyond the Frankfurt base as to thrust Alsace at the Austrians, and of course held out for overthrowing Napoleon. The way was clear, as Metternich had no doubt intended, for Castlereagh to interpose "compromise" proposals, and these for the most part were adopted. Thus it was agreed to institute peace negotiations but without relaxing military pressure—precisely the formula Metternich himself had employed ever since the battle of Leipzig. It was further agreed to offer France her "ancient frontiers," a solution into which

[15] Münster to the Prince Regent, 30 Jan. 1814, in Fournier, *Congress von Chatillon.*
[16] Webster, *Castlereagh*, 204; and Sorel, *L'Europe*, VIII, 254–255.
[17] Quoted in *ibid.*, VIII, 254.

Metternich "entered very liberally," as Castlereagh reported it, although Metternich did insist on some token concessions to bring the new peace program into line with the promises contained in the December manifesto: viz. to leave France greater than she had been under her kings. The conference of ministers similarly adopted the British formula of allowing France to settle her own dynastic problem. In return she was to have no voice in the settlement beyond her frontiers, though she was to be informed of allied plans in that regard.[18]

Castlereagh had offered the last proviso with the best of intentions, to give France some idea of the over-all peace settlement, and hoping not only to assuage French feelings but also to force Alexander at last to divulge his plans. This, however, the tsar still refused to do. Consequently when Metternich was assigned to put in writing something that could pass as a concerted allied peace program, he was able to frame only the most general statements.[19] Switzerland and Holland, as he explained it, were to be independent and the latter enlarged. Spain was to be restored to the Bourbons—one of the few instances of literal, legitimist restoration. Italy, "between the possessions of France and Austria," he described as consisting of independent states. Regarding Germany he was still more vague. The territorial settlement he had to ignore completely, whether in Saxony, Poland, or the Rhineland—not to mention the reciprocal gains and losses of the middle states. Such questions were to be settled later, at a conference to be held in Vienna. Only in the question of the German constitution could he record some progress. "Germany," his phrasing ran, was to be "composed of sovereign princes united by a federal bond which will secure and guarantee the independence of Germany." [20]

The clause lacked the literary grace that usually adorned Metternich's prose, but it was not wanting in other subtleties. The term "federal bond," which appeared here for the first time in the official interallied agreements, bespoke a measure of German unity not contained in the Teplitz pact, which had

---

[18] Castlereagh to Liverpool, 29 Jan. 1814, in *British Diplomacy*, 141–144.
[19] Text in Fournier, *Congress von Chatillon*, 306ff.
[20] *ibid.*

mentioned only "the entire and absolute independence" of the intermediate states. At the same time it obviated any remaining possibility of reading into the Frankfurt accession treaties a mandate to restore the Reich—a hope which even so experienced a diplomat as Count Münster had entertained until now. The article was meager enough from the national standpoint, but for the purpose at hand the information it contained was adequate. After all, it was not meant to be a pledge to the German people; it was simply part of an allied concession to France: a glimpse of future arrangements *d'outre le Rhin*. Neither was the clause hostile to Prussia. In it Metternich said nothing about the *equality* of all states, which would have precluded an Austro-Prussian condominium as well as a four-power directory, or about *existing* states, which would have prohibited further mediatizing. As a matter of fact, the expression "federal bond," far from constituting the smashing victory over Hardenberg and the German unity movement that Metternich's foes and apologists alike have claimed for it,[21] was in reality borrowed, as we have seen, from Hardenberg's memorial of January 22. Even Stein was satisfied: Germany would be a political entity, he said, not an "aggregate of despots," when the clause was later inserted into the treaty of Chaumont.[22] Altogether, it was a fair and straightforward statement of what the accession treaties had provided: sovereignty, yes, but modified by Germany's security requirements.

The fact was that now more than ever Metternich wished to avoid commitments. With France eliminated as a factor in the German negotiations, Russia's influence was greater than ever. Henceforth, it was Metternich's policy to postpone a definitive settlement of the German question until France had been readmitted to the deliberations or, better yet, until Russia and France had both been barred. In the coming year he was to discover that he would have to resort to the former in order to accomplish the latter.

[21] E.g., Lauber, *Metternichs Kampf*, 136; Kissinger, *World Restored*, 132; Srbik, *Metternich*, I, 195; and many others. The sole voice to the contrary is Ritter, *Stein*, II, 250, who regards the clause as a triumph of the national constitution idea.

[22] Stein to Solms-Laubach, 7 March 1814, in Stein, *Briefwechsel* IV, 590.

In this policy Metternich stood alone. Castlereagh had come to regard Alexander as an uncooperative and ungrateful ally but not yet as an enemy, let alone the *main* enemy. Snatching at every possible means to cement the coalition, he began to speak of the four great powers as not merely representing themselves but as constituting a sort of directory responsible for all Europe —a philosophy which found mature expression a month later in the treaty of Chaumont. To Hardenberg this was heady wine indeed, a foretaste of the fine Mosels he hoped to enjoy when his western territorial claims were realized. Prussia, which for so many years had had to content herself with marauding in North Germany and Poland, now had a chance to displace France in the highest councils of Europe. This was an honor and an advantage not to be scorned by a state which had witnessed so many changes in Europe—and changes made without her participation. That Hardenberg valued such recognition for its own sake is debatable, but the fact remains that after Langres he constantly endeavored to exclude France from European deliberations, and to perpetuate her isolation by a postwar treaty system which would recognize Prussia as the equal of Russia, Austria, and Britain.[23] Without such recognition was it not possible that the other powers would return to that system of North German neutrality which had often before been attempted—even as Humboldt and Hardenberg himself were plotting to strip the German middle states of their treaty and warmaking powers?

The suggestion that Hardenberg had his inner doubts about Prussia's great-power status may have surprised a European public that thrilled to the exploits of the fanatical Gneisenau and the dashing Blücher, fondly called "Marshal Forward." It is even more at variance with the opinion of historians who have consistently taken the campaigns of the *Befreiungskriege* at face value, seeing in the brilliance of the Silesian army and the dullness of Schwarzenberg's leadership a measure of the relative prowess of the Austrian and Prussian military systems. At headquarters, however, where the political issues were understood, and where military potential was still predicated on the area

---

[23] Cf. Born, "Hardenbergs Pläne," *ibid.*, 557ff.

and population of provinces, the belabored caution and cumbersome maneuvers of the Austrians were not mistaken by everyone for ineptitude, nor was Prussian valor taken for enduring might. The Poles, too, fought gallantly in that generation without, in the end, having much to show for it.

Hardenberg, at any rate, was not deluded, nor was Frederick William, who held an even more modest opinion of Prussia's capabilities. But whereas the king, in his unimaginative way, had no more ambitious solution to offer than to rely docilely on Russia to look after the Hohenzollern patrimony, the chancellor saw in Prussia's status as a great power the surest escape from the eastern colossus whose ruler still refused to say whether he would award Prussia a stout frontier in Poland. If he had a vote in the reorganization of Europe, the Prussian chancellor could defend his own claims; otherwise the tsar must speak for him. It was more than a matter of prestige. The material basis for such rank was the ability to play Russia against Austria, as in the January conversations with Metternich. And this in turn was possible only so long as Austria did not have France to lean on; otherwise Austria was the mediator between east and west and Prussia an ineffectual satellite of Russia, as the spring of 1813 had proved all too well.

Indeed, the point can be demonstrated mathematically, in a way that Metternich and Hardenberg themselves might have calculated it. Let us assign France and Russia a value of 4 each, Austria 3, and Prussia 2. At once it is evident that in a contest between France and Russia, Austria, not Prussia, must hold the balance, for her weight plus that of France would equal 7 as against 6 for the Russo-Prussian total. Prussia's choices would then be to remain isolated, to join the side where she was not needed, or the side where her contribution would not suffice. Now let France be removed from the system, and it is Prussia which makes the difference. A Russo-Prussian combination would equal 6 against Austria's 3, an Austro-Prussian one 5 against Russia's 4. Britain, curiously, did not affect the relationship between Austria and Prussia as much as one might suppose. Only a part of British might was disposable on the continent, and that part Castlereagh, who aimed at reconciling the two central powers, added to both states alike. The British factor therefore only diminished, but did not eliminate, the disadvantage to Austria and the advantage to Prussia of ostracizing France.

In human affairs logical structures are not causative but permissive; they define in a rough way the field within which action occurs—action with all its contingent qualities of courage and cowardice, wisdom and folly, blunders and successes, passion and calculation, imagination and obtuseness. Our model is admittedly crude but, unless we are prepared to banish the intellect entirely from history, it is relevant.[24] The basic fact was that Prussia was weaker than Austria. Hence came Hardenberg's exorbitant territorial claims, his bid for parity with Austria in the German constitutional structure, and even his toleration of the fire-eating generals—for until France was beaten he needed military prestige more than he needed flexibility. Hence too came the paradox that whereas Metternich sought deliverance from Russia through collaboration with France, Hardenberg sought it through the isolation of France.

Our model also serves to explain the *common* interests of Prussia and Austria: the one thing both had to dread was the union of France and Russia, the major cause of the debacle of 1809. Against such a union their combined might would not be likely to prevail, even if augmented by that of the smaller states, coordinated with theirs in a defense league. Indeed, in such a case it was more likely that the flanking powers, not the central powers, would control the third Germany. "Today," observed Gentz, who believed a Bourbon France would be a Russian satellite, "the independence of the German great powers is secured or jeopardized exactly in proportion as the probability of a close union between Russia and France diminishes or increases. For me this . . . principle is now the main and cardinal point throughout the whole gamut of European politics." [25]

It was this specter which arose when Alexander proposed to

---

[24] That Metternich did in fact literally use figures in this way has recently been shown by Guillaume de Bertier de Sauvigny, "Sainte-Alliance et Alliance dans les conceptions de Metternich," *Revue historique*, ccxxiii (1960), 260–261.

[25] Gentz to Metternich, 15 Feb. 1814, in Gentz, *Briefe von und an*, iii, 251.

place Bernadotte on the French throne. Metternich's reaction, as we have seen, was to make the concession of Saxony; Hardenberg's was to present his territorial claims quickly, to strike before a Franco-Russian entente became a reality. Beyond that he resisted the temptation to burn all his bridges. Though insisting on the diplomatic *isolation* of France, he did not demand either her physical *destruction* or the installation of a French government friendly to Russia. In short, the more France was isolated the more sympathetic he became toward a mild peace. Over the enraged protests of Gneisenau, Blücher, Stein, and all others who made the cession of Alsace the test of a good peace, he accepted without a murmur Castlereagh's solutions of the dynastic and boundary questions. Then, hardly two weeks after the Langres conferences, he signed a secret convention with Metternich (February 14, 1814), by which he agreed to support the Langres program to the end, no matter how complete the rout of the French army might be. "Considering the position of a Prussian minister," Gentz remarked again when he heard of the compact, "it took courage to speak so clearly and emphatically against Russia." [26]

At the Langres conferences, therefore, a rapprochement between the two central powers arose as much from Hardenberg's side as from Metternich's. Its basis was not the Austrian concession regarding Saxony—a plausible enough explanation save for the Hardenberg-Stadion conversations—but the common judgment of the chancellor and the foreign minister, both of them champions of a diplomatic *Mitteleuropa*, that Alexander's aspirations in France menaced both their governments, though not in identical ways. The entente was a tentative one—at times, it seemed, resting on nothing more solid than their mutual fondness for champagne and actresses. Saxony, compensations for Bavaria, and the German constitution were nagging irritants. Neither man, moreover, was sure that the other could carry his government with him. Both steered wary, unpopular middle courses, Metternich between the imperial school and the *stockösterreichische* group, Hardenberg between the pa-

[26] Gentz to Metternich, 21 March 1814, in *ibid.*, III, 280; Lauber, *Metternichs Kampf*, 134; and Kissinger, *World Restored*, 124.

triotic aggrandizers and the king, who viewed his relation to the tsar as one of feudal loyalty more than of political convenience. The Austrian minister might be overthrown at any time if he renewed his offer of Saxony, which scandalized imperialists and isolationists alike; while Hardenberg risked dismissal if he demanded too much in Poland or too little on the left bank of the Rhine. These forces of domestic opposition did in the end ruin the collaboration between the two. They managed to get along for the moment, however, and for months to come, with their points of friction oiled from time to time by Castlereagh—but with his difference: that whereas Metternich endeavored to postpone a settlement in Central Europe until French influence had been restored or that of Russia eliminated, Hardenberg had to act while the other powers were still bidding for his services.

The close relations which Metternich established at Langres with Castlereagh and Hardenberg were gratifying accomplishments. The agreements themselves, however, were fragile and provisional, since their efficacy depended upon peace actually being made at Châtillon. As Alexander had foreseen, if peace was not made the armies would advance to Paris, Bonaparte would be overthrown, and even the generalizations about the larger European settlement would be out of date. When the congress opened on February 5 it was a moot question who was now the greater obstacle to peace—Napoleon, who had instructed Caulaincourt to hold out for the natural frontiers offered in the Frankfurt proposals, or Alexander, who had ordered his envoy Razumovsky to stall the proceedings and if necessary bolt the conference. The question was soon answered. On February 9, the day on which Caulaincourt privately accepted the ancient limits of France, provided an armistice was granted immediately, Razumovsky received orders to report to his master for new instructions. On that same day at Troyes, the site of the new headquarters, Alexander grimly informed Metternich that he intended to march to Paris and unseat Napoleon. He also revealed a plan conceived by La Harpe that would conform to the Langres formula about the dynasty and still allow the tsar to determine the future government: the

French would make the choice, but through an assembly of notables elected under the supervision of a Russian governor. La Harpe's preference was a liberal republic with Bernadotte as a first consul.[27] Alexander still made Bernadotte his first choice too, whether as monarch or something else, but if Castlereagh and Metternich wished the Bourbons, then let them, he said in effect, take the duke of Orleans or the duke of Berri. He was grooming both of them for the post anyhow, and was also considering the latter as a husband for the Romanov grand duchess Anne.[28]

Solid military advantages lay behind Alexander's flaunting. While still at Langres he had moved to protect himself from a repetition of Austrian peace threats, wringing from Frederick William a pledge to remain with him "to the last extremity." [29] Shortly thereafter occurred the allied victories at La Rothière and Brienne, which shattered Caulaincourt's composure and shook even Bonaparte. The tsar could now seriously contemplate withdrawing the 61,000 Russian troops from Schwarzenberg's Bohemian army, joining them to Blücher's Silesian army, two-thirds of which was Russian anyway,[30] and leaving the Austrians to their own devices. Were Alexander to try it, and were he to succeed, his hegemony of the continent would be an accomplished fact. Not since Wagram had Austria faced a darker future.

And now it was Napoleon, often enough in the past year Metternich's nemesis, who came to the rescue. Striking at a flank of the Silesian army exposed by a combination of Blücher's haste and Schwarzenberg's caution, he defeated the Prussian in four

---

[27] Franklin D. Scott, "Bernadotte and the Throne of France 1814," *Journal of Modern History*, v (1933), 470–471. Cf. Sorel, *L'Europe*, viii, 254, who, following Metternich's unreliable "Autobiographical Memoir," *Memoirs*, I, 226–229, has Alexander revealing the plan at Langres. It is far more likely that Metternich many years later dated the interview too early than that he would have accepted the Langres formula had he known of the plan then.

[28] Lobanov-Rostovsky, *Russia and Europe*, 297–298; Sorel, *L'Europe*, viii, 262–267; Lauber, *Metternichs Kampf*, 131; and Gentz to Karadja, 11 April 1814, in Friedrich von Gentz, *Dépêches inédites du chevalier de Gentz aux hospodars de Valachie* (Paris, 1876–1877), I, 77.

[29] As reported by Münster to the Prince Regent, 30 Jan. 1814, in Fournier, *Congress von Chatillon*, 58, note 2.

[30] Lobanov-Rostovsky, *Russia and Europe*, 291.

successive enagements from February 10 to 14. The battles, though not catastrophic, were more than the "slight reverses" Castlereagh called them [31] and, magnified by the name of Bonaparte, they created consternation at allied headquarters. Politically they had the effect of adding the weight of France to Metternich's position, the more so as the immediate victims were the Russians and Prussians, not the Austrians, who were concentrated mainly in Schwarzenberg's lumbering Bohemian army. General Wrede, the commander of the far from insignificant Bavarian corps, made bold to hint to Metternich that if Austria withdrew from the war she would find most of the German princes ready to follow her example. Even Alexander momentarily favored an armistice, while Frederick William, though upbraiding Hardenberg for his anti-Russian attitude, did not prevent the chancellor's closing ranks with Metternich. "The losses," said Gentz with some glee, "at least had the advantage that the voice of calm and sensible men was listened to with a little more indulgence." [32]

Firmly and methodically Metternich pressed his advantage, threatening a separate peace, boasting of full support from Bavaria and Würtemberg, urging Castlereagh and Hardenberg to join the exodus, and finally giving the ground necessary to accommodate them. In this way he isolated Alexander diplomatically at the very time it had become clear that Russia was not strong enough to continue the war alone. What a difference if Napoleon had given her two more years to prepare! The Austrian now framed a compromise, in the dual form of a preliminary peace treaty and an interallied convention, and the tsar acceded to it on February 15. Both the military campaign and the peace negotiations were to continue, but regardless of the success of the former or the failure of the latter, allied terms would remain those offered at Châtillon. If Napoleon accepted these conditions he might keep his throne, but if he was repudiated by the French themselves, without any allied inter-

[31] Castlereagh to Metternich, 18 Feb. 1814, in *British Diplomacy* 159.
[32] Gentz to Karadja, 8 March 1814, in *Dépêches inédites*, I, 67; Metternich to Stadion, 8 Feb. 1814, in Fournier, *Congress von Chatillon*, 314–315; Castlereagh to Liverpool, 26 Feb. 1814, in *British Diplomacy*, 160; and Lauber, *Metternichs Kampf*, 134.

ference, only the Bourbons, specifically Louis XVIII unless he voluntarily renounced his claims, might take his place. If the allies captured Paris, Russia might appoint a military governor —in honor of her unique contribution to the victory—but actual administrative powers would be vested in a commission consisting of Russia, Prussia, and Austria. The principle invoked was that all conquered territory was occupied "in the name of all allied powers," the same formula Metternich had exploited at Leipzig in regulating the occupation of Germany.[33] In other agreements, designed to correct one of the difficulties at Châtillon and give Caulaincourt a sharper picture of the European settlement, Castlereagh revived his still unexecuted offer to specify the colonies his government would return to France; Metternich officially renounced the Austrian claim to Belgium; and Hardenberg conceded the British a voice in the disposition of the territory between the Rhine and the Maas "in such manner as to offer security and protection to [Holland] and north Germany." [34] For the rest the provisions were as stated at Langres, with this difference: before they had been *ad hoc;* now they were permanent pledges among the allies themselves. At last it was official: Germany would be composed of sovereign states joined by a federal bond.

There was still no mention of Poland. In this respect as well as in the recognition that the war must continue—to Paris, if necessary—Metternich had failed. But he had gained something more important: the assurance that France would remain a great power, and no one knew better than he that whatever limitations treaties might impose, a great power will eventually obtain "the influence which every large state necessarily exercises on a state of lesser size," as he had put it in the famous session with St. Aignan at Frankfurt. The Austrian minister in effect conceded Alexander his victory march but robbed him of its fruits. "All my toil, troubles, and worries are . . . richly compensated," he triumphantly announced to Hudelist in Vienna,

[33] Article III as given in Oncken, "Die Krisis der letzten Friedensverhandlungen mit Napoleon I," *Historisches Taschenbuch,* 6. Folge, v (1886), 34; Fournier, *Congress von Chatillon,* 133–136.
[34] Text in *British State Papers,* I, 119–120. Cf. Sorel, *L'Europe,* VIII, 280; and Webster, *Castlereagh,* 214–215.

"by the accomplishment of my sleepless nights and overburdened days. This is where we stand: the Emperor Alexander leaves the conduct of military affairs entirely to *us*—the political questions to me. . . ." [35]

This grandiloquent appraisal no doubt made good reading in the salons of Vienna, but it was hardly an example of Metternich's celebrated flair for precision. "I will not strike up the victory song too early," replied Gentz, to whom Hudelist had shown the dispatch, "nor severely rebuke Hudelist for being gloomier than I." [36] And they were right. Had the Austrians really been in charge of military operations, they would have sounded a general retreat, possibly back to the Rhine. As it was, they had to face, first, Napoleon's rebuff of the allied offer of an armistice, and then a threat from Alexander that he would pull his contingent out of the Bohemian army. Threatened with isolation in the face of Bonaparte's light but deadly attacks, they had to give in, limiting their retreat to Langres and granting freedom of action to the Silesian army. The latter concession was especially galling since it allowed the impetuous Blücher to keep himself in continual difficulty, which held the Austrians under constant pressure to rescue him, and brought down on their heads Frederick William's cries of treason when they hesitated to do so. Schwarzenberg and Metternich managed to block the tsar's scheme for merging the two armies, but in all other respects they were swept along with the tide.[37]

Politically there was even less to justify Metternich's self-assured reports. At Châtillon the negotiations proved more sterile than ever. Caulaincourt had ended the first stage of the meeting with a plea for an armistice and the "ancient limits." Now, on February 17, the allied envoys offered both, and the draft of a preliminary peace treaty as well. But the same victories which made Alexander pliable made Napoleon adamant, and Caulaincourt, now stripped of the *carte blanche* Napoleon had earlier granted him, could only beg for time. Finally Stadion consented to March 10 as the date for a definite answer,

[35] To Hudelist, 16 Feb. 1814, in Fournier, *Congress von Chatillon*, 257.

[36] Gentz to Metternich, 25 Feb. 1814, in Gentz, *Briefe von und an*, III, 260.

[37] Lobanov-Rostovsky, *Russia and Europe*, 295–296; and Lauber, *Metternichs Kampf*, 209, note 367.

but neither he nor Metternich nor the well-intentioned Caulaincourt himself really believed there would be one.[38]

At headquarters, which had been drawn back to Chaumont, developments were no better, as Metternich perceived with a shudder one day when he caught a glimpse of Czartoryski strolling with the tsar. Nothing would have cleared the air more than a solution of the Polish problem, but not one that Czartoryski was connected with. For his very person was a reminder of the Grand Design of 1804 and the dreams of the Poles for a territorial restoration of their own "old regime," which had ended in 1772. This vision indeed still illumined Czartoryski's musings, so much so that he maintained an emissary in England, Felix Biernacki, to cultivate the Whigs in Poland's behalf in case Alexander should prove a disappointment—either by obtaining too little for Poland or by subjugating her completely. This latter possibility was the theme of an article written in January for the *Edinburgh Review* by one of Biernacki's converts, Lord Henry Brougham. Brougham flatly accused the tsar of "dividing the spoils" in preference to terminating "slavery and oppression." Alexander could ill afford such publicity if Poland was to be the showcase of his vaunted liberalism and nationalism, and he now reassured Czartoryski that Russia would set a good example by transferring her own Polish provinces to the Polish crown.[39]

What this portended for Austria was not certain. An exchange of Alsace for Galicia seemed excluded by the convention of Troyes, but there was still the possibility of losing Galicia *without* compensation, and it was far from clear which territories figured in the Russo-Polish plan—only Western Galicia, Austria's contribution to the Duchy of Warsaw, or Eastern Galicia, which was still part of the Habsburg realm, as well. The latter possibility was almost too horrible to contemplate. The loss of Eastern Galicia would remove the friendly bulwark of the great Carpathian Wall just as Prussia's acquisition of Saxony would eliminate the *glacis* provided by the *Erzgebirge*. Poland,

[38] Kissinger, *World Restored*, 129–130.
[39] Kukiel, *Czartoryski*, 112–114.

and through her, Russia, would command the passes that debouched into the greater and lesser Hungarian plains, threatening the empire's major cities.

When Alexander had first proposed the exchange of Alsace for Galicia, in January, he probably had had in mind nothing more than the western part—despite rumors to the contrary. At any rate a bargain on that basis would have corresponded to the Teplitz formula, by which Austria was to receive her territorial extent of 1805. But now after his defeat on the French boundary question, and under the pressure of liberal circles to do something for the Poles as a nation better than juggling the boundaries of the Duchy of Warsaw, who could tell how far he would go, especially since he himself refused to say? The plan to hand over Russia's own Polish provinces implied an attempt to re-create old Poland, and the arrival of Czartoryski, the aristocratic patriot, seemed to remove all doubt.[40] Münster charged that if the Austrians procrastinated in France, it was because they desired "to keep their army intact in order to preserve their influence on the affairs of Poland." [41] Metternich inaugurated private negotiations with the French outside the official channels at Châtillon.[42] And Castlereagh, though not as much upset, nevertheless regarded the presence of the Polish prince at headquarters "as calculated to create dissension," [43] and persuaded him to leave.

Münster's remark, though not literally correct, struck close to the heart of the problem. Since Napoleon would not make peace on allied terms and Alexander would not allay fears about Poland, there seemed little else for Austria to do but withdraw unilaterally from the war and shift her troops to Galicia, there to face the new formations that Alexander was assembling in

[40] Münster to the Prince Regent, 23 Feb. 1814, in Fournier, *Congress von Chatillon*, 302. Cf. Oncken, "Die Krisis," *op.cit.*, 33.
[41] Münster to the Prince Regent, 25 Feb. 1814, in Fournier, *Congress von Chatillon*, 303.
[42] Sorel, *L'Europe*, VIII, 289.
[43] Castlereagh to Liverpool, 26 Feb. 1814, in *British Diplomacy*, 160–164. Münster, in his above cited dispatch of 25 Feb. is our witness that Alexander did finally clarify that he meant only Western Galicia; but if so, this only left matters where they had been, and that was serious enough.

Poland—formations which by summer amounted to more than the strength Russia deployed in France. Had Metternich possessed the soul of a bookkeeper, as Stein had once claimed, he would surely have chosen this course, condemning Europe to another round of looting, aimless marching to and fro, and all the barbarism of military campaigns without clear object. That would have been the way of mechanical, uncreative calculation. That, perhaps, was the way Gentz would have taken, a man whose keen intellectual insights were blunted by his pawn-broker character.[44] It was also the way Napoleon expected Austria to take. "Your emperor does not seem to love his daughter," he told Wessenberg some time later when the game was almost up. "If I had married a Russian princess, I would not be where I am now." [45] But Metternich, steeped though he was in a Newtonian view of nature, did not regard human affairs as identical with nature's mechanics. He did not liken the European state system to the solar system with its endless motion, its recurrent actions and reactions. What he envisaged was a system that would finally come to rest, a system within which a balance would exist without permanently mobilized armies and interminably marching troops. Austria's immediate interest may have indicated a separate peace, but long-range stability required more than the fortuitous stalemate of armies: it required intelligent design.

Each day he saw Napoleon parade his scorn for any design but his own, gambling ever more recklessly that the coalition must eventually collapse. Each day Metternich saw the Corsican demonstrate anew that force alone would induce him to make peace or keep it afterward. Castlereagh, on the other hand, time and again had proved his moderation, his sympathy for Austria, his distrust of Russia, his concern for order. Only when Schwarzenberg had offered Napoleon a truce did the British minister heap abuse on Metternich and warn him against the "fatal sacrifice both of moral and political consideration, if . . . the great edifice of peace were suffered to be disfigured in its pro-

[44] Cf. Metternich to Hudelist, 12 March 1814, in Fournier, *Congress von Chatillon*, 264; and Gentz to Metternich, 15 Feb. 1814, in Gentz, *Briefe von und an*, III, 245

[45] Quoted by Sorel, *L'Europe*, VIII, 306.

portions." [46] Despite the rebuke, here was someone Metternich could understand. It had become a choice between two men, and making one of his rare leaps from the realm of calculation to that of assessing personality, he moved most of his remaining bets from Bonaparte to Castlereagh. The decision was solemnized in the treaty of Chaumont.

The treaty,[47] signed on March 9, 1814, pledged each of the four allied powers to maintain in the field an army of 150,000 and to sign no peace until France had accepted the conditions laid down at Troyes. Great Britain, in addition, was to supply subsidies to her three allies totalling £5,000,000 for the rest of the year, paid in prorated monthly installments extending two months (in the case of Russia, four months) beyond the signing of a peace treaty and renewable the following year, "if (which God forbid) the War should so long continue." Thus the immediate importance of the treaty was that it rallied the coalition once and for all behind the peace agreed upon, and ended any hope Napoleon may have had for salvation through a falling-out of his enemies. At the same time an honorable peace was still available to him as the ruler of France if he would accept it. In this way Castlereagh had at last forged iron bands around the coalition; Alexander was spared further prattle from Metternich about a separate peace; and Metternich himself could hope that the declaration of allied solidarity would do what the crossing of the Rhine had not done: bring Bonaparte to his senses.

Precisely because the treaty envisaged peace with the insatiable emperor, it contained articles extending the alliance for a period of twenty years, guaranteeing to the signatories "the protection of their respective States in Europe" against French aggression, and pledging them to assist the power attacked with a body of 60,000 men. Thus the treaty also constituted a mutual assistance pact, aimed for years to come at a France which would be strong within her ancient limits, and might in addition remain Bonapartist. Finally, in three secret articles the treaty confirmed the decisions already made regarding Holland, Italy, Spain, Switzerland, and Germany; invited Spain, Portugal, Hol-

[46] Castlereagh to Metternich, 18 Feb. 1814, in *British Diplomacy*, 159.
[47] Text, public articles only, in *Brit. State Papers*, I, 121–129.

land, and Sweden to accede; and required the signatories to maintain their forces on a war footing for a year after the peace was signed.[48]

In regard to Holland debate was especially lively. Castlereagh endeavored to obtain, for the new state, not only Belgium but also the territory between the Maas and the Rhine as far south as Cologne. Hardenberg resisted, piously acting as if his own claim to the area had no other motive than service to Europe. If Prussia could not be strong on the left bank, he sputtered, she would accept no land there at all. He accepted Castlereagh's counteroffer, however, the vague statement that Holland was to have a "suitable" boundary.[49] The tsar, too, raised objections. At Langres and again at Troyes he had complacently, almost as a matter of routine, consented to the addition of both Belgium and the Maas-Rhine area to Holland,[50] assuming that the ghosts of sea-dogs and freebooters would stir the waters between England and Holland and bring the enlarged maritime state into the Russian sphere. To help matters along he toyed with the idea of a marriage between the young prince William of Orange and his sister Catherine, who had once been betrothed to Ludwig of Bavaria and was now, at twenty-four, the widow of the duke of Oldenburg. Then suddenly, toward the end of February, the British announced the forthcoming marriage of their own princess Charlotte to William. As both were in line to inherit, a dynastic union in the near future and a *personal* union in the next generation were in the offing. "Holland resembles an English colony," wrote the disappointed Catherine on March 18,[51] not knowing that before long Charlotte would change her mind and leave the Oranges to the Romanovs after all. Alexander, who could neither avow his secret hopes nor chance a rupture of the coalition at this point, vented his rage in petty ways, haggling over minutiae and finally demanding that Britain take over the Russian debt in Amsterdam.[52] On this

[48] Secret articles published, oddly enough, only in Martens, *Traités par la russie*, III, 155–165.

[49] Fournier, *Congress von Chatillon*, 180–181.

[50] Anglo-Russian convention in Martens, *Traités par la russie*, XI, 200f.

[51] Catherine to Alexander, 18 March 1814, in Mikhailowitch, *Correspondance de . . . Alexandre avec . . . Catherine*, 174.

[52] Webster, *Castlereagh*, 231 and 297ff.

basis Castlereagh carried his point and thereby completed the postwar organization of Western Europe. Then, by insisting on the right of Spain, Portugal, and Holland to accede to the treaty, he won the assurance that the fleets and home ports of the maritime states would not again be pressed into French service—at least by armed assault.

Castlereagh's great achievement at Chaumont was to hem France in both on land and sea, but his beloved treaty did nothing to protect the allies from each other. In this respect, it fell far short of the original project of alliance, dispatched to the Leipzig headquarters the previous fall.[53] It did not pertain to *all* the territories of the signatories but only to "their respective States in Europe"; and instead of "mutual protection" it provided assistance only "against every attempt which *France*[54] might make." Both limitations were victories for Alexander. The first made it possible, should he succeed in installing a pro-Russian government in Paris, for him to goad France into colonial adventures against Britain with no more than normal risks. It was indeed the loophole through which slipped the later schemes of Russia, France, and Spain to revise the colonial order—the schemes often, if erroneously, attributed to the Holy Alliance.

The second limitation helped Alexander even more. The treaty guaranteed a well-defined peace settlement in Western Europe against French revisionism but formed no similar system of collective security against Russian ambitions. In Central and Eastern Europe the treaty did not even prescribe a settlement, let alone guarantee one. True, for Italy and Germany it reaffirmed the principles previously adopted: Italy to consist of independent states, Germany to be united in a federal bond. But these statements merely cloaked the disagreements that prevailed; they avoided the thorny territorial questions completely, and the statement regarding Germany was, as we have seen, broad enough to accommodate Metternich's and Hardenberg's plans with equal ease. There remained the Reichenbach and Teplitz treaties of the previous year, but, as already noted,

[53] See Ch. IX, p. 260.
[54] Italics mine.

neither was precise enough to be patently inconsistent with Russian ambitions; and in any case it could now be argued that they had both been superseded by the treaty of Chaumont, since the latter contained whole sections, notably the collective-security clauses, which had been copied almost verbatim from the Teplitz pact. And so the treaty of Chaumont resembled the Locarno pact of a century later: it regulated the affairs of Western Europe in detail, but it left the rest of the continent—to say nothing of other continents— unaccounted for. What was needed was an "eastern Chaumont," and that was to be the central purpose of the Congress of Vienna.

For Metternich the lacunae in the treaty were perhaps less distressing than the reasons for them, as he learned when he and Hardenberg made one further effort to add substance to the provisions for Germany. Article XV of the treaty provided that "the powers most exposed to a French invasion" be invited to accede; so far as location was concerned, almost all the German states could qualify. But the two ministers quickly realized that signing the treaty would be *ipso facto* an act of full sovereignty; an invitation to accede, therefore, would be tantamount to formal certification of independence, since the right to make treaties was the primary distinguishing characteristic of a sovereign power.[55] If Metternich still desired for Germany nothing more than an "extended system of alliances among equals," such as he had suggested before Leipzig, here was the place to speak up in behalf of the secondary states. Conversely, it was Hardenberg's cue to insist that none of the German states sign. But instead of engaging in polemics on the German question, the two statesmen stood together, agreeing that the invitation be limited to Bavaria and Hanover, the states whose sovereignty was least equivocally guaranteed in the accession treaties of 1813.

In accepting this solution Metternich for all practical purposes approved Hardenberg's proposal of January: a four-power directory for Germany. The available evidence does not disclose whether he had agreed to this previously; in all probability, however, the directory, like Saxony, was one of the many subjects that stayed fluid until precipitated by some external

[55] Fournier, *Congress von Chatillon*, 180.

event. The event in this case was the treaty of Chaumont, and the ministers of the two central powers were agreed that it would be prejudicial to the future German union if others than Bavaria and Hanover among the secondary states should accede to it. The four-power plan was a genuine compromise between the Prussian preference for an Austro-Prussian condominium and Metternich's notion of a treaty system among equals and, left to themselves, the two men would probably have made it the starting point of their respective German policies.

They reckoned, however, without Würtemberg, lying to the west of Bavaria, which had perhaps a still greater right to be classed among the powers exposed to French invasion. As a royal family, the house of Würtemberg was equal in rank to the Wittelsbachs and Hanoverians—the Hohenzollerns too for that matter. Moreover, the treaty that King Frederick had signed in November, 1813, at Fulda, though in the final analysis slanted, as we have seen, toward commitments to unspecified "future arrangements" in Germany, was most ambiguous and by many held to be no more than a variation of Bavaria's treaty of Ried.

Among those who chose to interpret it this way was Alexander. In December he had instructed his new envoy to Stuttgart, Prince Golovkin, to cultivate good relations with Würtemberg on the basis of a strict observance of the treaty,[56] and in January he had sent his sister Catherine—the lady he hoped to marry to the Prince of Orange—on a special mission to King Frederick to offer him Russian protection. Catherine found the monarch full of bitterness at Austria, dreading what Vienna's and Munich's territorial claims might be, and resentful that Metternich had chosen Bavaria rather than Würtemberg to be "the bastion of Germany." So he leapt all the more eagerly at his nephew's overture. "The king told me to count firmly on his good intentions," the grand duchess reported, "and [said] that the only worry he has in this connection is that of being so far away from Russia and, consequently, from your effective protection, the moment calm is restored in Europe."[57] Cather-

[56] Martens, *Traités par la russie,* VII, 126.
[57] Catherine to Alexander, 16 Jan. 1814, in Mikhailowitch, *Correspondance de . . . Alexandre avec . . . Catherine,* 161–163. Cf. Hölzle, *Württemberg im Zeitalter,* 162–163.

ine, who later married the crown prince of Würtemberg, did not, ironically, altogether admire the king's regime and advised him to be less antagonistic to the Austrian cabinet. The tsar, however, distant or not, was true to his word, and so at Chaumont, when Metternich and Hardenberg acted to limit treaty-making rights to Bavaria and Hanover, it was he who insisted on similar rights for his Swabian relatives.

It is a measure of Metternich's determination to appease Hardenberg that he did not waver in the face of such formidable opposition, for the inclusion of Würtemberg among the privileged German states would have hampered his plans far less than Prussia's. Neither he nor Alexander gave in, and it was once more up to Castlereagh to break the deadlock. His solution was to delete any reference to the German states by name and simply say that besides Spain, Portugal, Holland, and Sweden, others would be invited "as occasion shall require." This was the formula finally adopted, it being understood that Germany, once a union had been formed, would accede as a whole and thus complete the *cordon sanitaire* around France.[58]

The compromise, though it removed one more obstacle from the consummation of the grand alliance, was not one of Castlereagh's more brilliant moves. He himself, unwilling to await the establishment of a German league, was determined to complete the barrier against France immediately, especially as there was every reason to be suspicious of the Francophile sentiments of Count Montgelas, who held on to his office in Munich despite the upsurge of patriotic fervor against him. Within a month the British envoy to Munich, George Rose, privately invited Bavaria to accede. Montgelas, though not unmindful of the advantages of signing, was reluctant to commit Bavaria for twenty years to a system which would deny her access to her old friends in Paris. Their material support might be worth more to Bavaria, even in German affairs, than the inferences to be drawn from her having signed a European treaty. His reply to Rose, therefore, was a haughty reminder that he already had a pleni-

[58] Fournier, *Congress von Chatillon*, 179–180; Webster, *Castlereagh*, 229, note 1; and Martens, *Traités par la russie*, III, 164.

potentiary at allied headquarters for that purpose,[59] and Bavaria never did sign the treaty. Münster, by contrast, was sharply disappointed at the outcome, lamenting the lost opportunity which "would have established in principle the sovereign rights which one of course desires to conserve for us." [60] Furthermore, as he grimly reported to the Prince Regent, the difficulty with Würtemberg was not remedied, only postponed.

In this judgment he was certainly right, not perhaps in the sense that Würtemberg's sovereignty was now more secure or that of Hanover and Bavaria irrevocably lost, but rather in the knowledge that Würtemberg had a spokesman among the great powers just as Bavaria had Austria and Hanover had England. Alexander, who had several times brushed aside Stein's entreaties to appoint a deputy to serve on a German constitution committee, was only too happy to weight German affairs in his favor in this less direct and potentially less embarrassing manner. Not since the preceding August, when he had rushed the generous inducement to Bavaria over Metternich's head, had he so brazenly encroached upon Austria's recognized primacy in South Germany. The trouble was that defending Würtemberg was an affront to Hardenberg too, and the time was coming when the Russian autocrat would learn, as Metternich already knew, that to please both Prussia and the former Rheinbund courts simultaneously was virtually impossible.

But these were halcyon days for the tsar: the French capital was in sight, Austria was barred from a separate peace, and Alexander was little inclined to modesty and caution. One thing is certain: thereafter no German plan was seriously put forward which omitted Würtemberg from a place at the top. As for Metternich, he could console himself, for what it was worth, that his major premise had again been proved: in dealing with the German states any departure from the principles of sovereignty and equality would encounter the resistance of one or both of the flanking powers. It was Alexander, not Metternich,

[59] Count Carl Hruby (Austrian minister in Munich) to Metternich, 9 April 1814, in Chroust, *Berichte der österreichischen Gesandten*, I, 23.

[60] Münster to the Prince Regent, 10 March 1814, in Fournier, *Congress von Chatillon*, 304.

who placed the ceiling on the sacrifices that one could exact from "the thirty-six petty despots."

Under the circumstances Metternich's pleasure at the results of Chaumont could hardly be expected to match Castlereagh's —*my* treaty, the Englishman called it. Against the advice of Gentz Metternich had handed over his trusty weapon, the option of a separate peace, and for what? Little enough in most respects. For him the alliance was an attempt—and a desperate one—to convince Napoleon that Austria meant business, that he, Metternich, was not merely waging a war of nerves, expecting to back down at the last moment, but was seeking a rational European order. Beyond that, the treaty was just one more milestone in his tortuous course which aimed at maximum agreement while there was still a French army in the field; and so far as France alone was concerned, he was successful. Her boundaries were settled in a way to keep the country reasonably strong, and there was still at least a formal hope that Bonaparte could be saved.

These were no mean achievements, and the minister surmised to his ambassador in London, Count Merveldt, that the treaty was "perhaps the most extensive ever concluded." [61] Still, the only points he saw fit to mention in transmitting a copy to Hudelist in Vienna were the moderation of the treaty and the good effects this would have on public opinion [62]—Rheinbund and French opinion, that is, since opinion elsewhere was anything but moderate. And remarkably enough, to Stadion, still negotiating at Châtillon, he did not so much as mention the pact. It is difficult to escape the conclusion that Metternich's main interest in the treaty was that it led straight to Castlereagh's heart. The actual provisions were less important than the British determination to have a hand in affairs on the continent. If for the moment that commitment lay in Western Europe only, the machinery, the precedents, the principles, and the predispositions were at hand to shift British commitments, in time, to Eastern Europe as well. It was, as we have noted, an

---

[61] Quoted in Sorel, *L'Europe*, VIII, 290.
[62] To Hudelist, 12 March 1814, in Fournier, *Congress von Chatillon*, 263–264.

adventure in judging character, one of Metternich's rare departures from diplomatic calculus.

In the war against France the only real question remaining was whether Napoleon or the Bourbons would be the recipients of the moderate peace terms. Now more than ever Metternich strove to save his emperor's son-in-law; he no longer bothered to pretend that his efforts were only psychological stratagems aimed at public opinion. When March 10 arrived, the date set for Napoleon's reply to the base of Troyes, and Caulaincourt did nothing but denounce the allies for withdrawing the Frankfurt base, Metternich not only begged his allies to give France more time, but openly blamed the tsar for the fact that peace had not been signed a month earlier when Alexander's deputy had bolted the conference. "Treason," retorted Frederick William, while the tsar asked point blank if Schwarzenberg had been ordered not to fight. "They are all mad and belong in the lunatic asylum," Metternich wrote to Stadion. "We are treated always as if we wanted to barter away the monarchy . . . as if Austria coveted foreign slavery, in short, as if we were blockheads. I believe, though, that we alone are not crazy." [63]

Mad or not, foolish or not, Metternich carried his point one more time, and on March 13 Caulaincourt was told to have an answer ready in forty-eight hours, else the congress would be terminated. Only when the answer came two days later and proved more arrogant than before, did the Austrian minister decide to end the proceedings at Châtillon—that "wretched comedy," to use Stadion's expression. The final meeting took place on March 18, and Stadion read an allied declaration which detailed Napoleon's responsibility for the rupture. Even then Metternich had not abandoned hope; he brought the congress to an end because he believed "peace nearer without the negotiations than with them." [64] He was also able to exact a price: a promise from Hardenberg to redouble his efforts to obtain concessions from the tsar on the Polish question.[65]

[63] Quoted in Srbik, *Metternich*, I, 175.
[64] Metternich to Schwarzenberg, 16 March 1814, in Klinkowstrom, *Oesterreichs Theilnahme*, 820.
[65] Lauber, *Metternichs Kampf*, 138.

In the end, however, Metternich's persistence was to no avail. On such a forlorn issue he risked becoming the clown in the comedy, and when the city of Bordeaux raised the banner of the Bourbons, he too bowed to the inevitable. By the time Bonaparte made another overture, through Baron Wessenberg, who had been captured en route from his post in London, it was too late: Austria was committed to the Bourbons. To Hudelist, who had dreaded this outcome all along, Metternich gave reassurances. "Have faith," he said, "that we nowhere just tag along, that I remain true to my eternal principle that developments which cannot be prevented must be directed and only weak men hesitate." [66] It was only now, in a certain sense, that Austria's armed mediation had come to an end. For better or worse Metternich's course must henceforth be with Castlereagh and Hardenberg.

[66] Metternich to Hudelist, 23, March 1814, in Fournier, *Congress von Chatillon*, 266.

CHAPTER XI

CONCLUSION:

THE CONTEST ENDED AND BEGUN

Some have seen in the collapse of Napoleon's regime a complete rout for Metternich's policy, others see its supreme victory.[1] It was neither. It was not a rout because Metternich's hopes had not been his expectations, and his diplomacy in the spring of 1814 had brilliantly succeeded in offsetting the worst consequences of Napoleon's last-ditch resistance. On the other hand, Napoleon's downfall was certainly not a victory for Metternich since his two main goals, a strong, independent France and a neutral Germany, were both still in question. Territorially the Troyes agreements, as ratified in the treaty of Chaumont, had solved the problem of a strong France tolerably well, but the internal vitality of the country was another matter, about which there was grave concern. Those closest to the Austrian foreign minister at the time, Hudelist and Gentz, though they spent much of their time running to their chief with petty complaints against each other, were as one in their belief that a Bourbon France would be a weak France, probably in the throes of civil war, and that "the little strength which would still remain to France after these convulsions, far from being set against the designs of Russia, would serve rather to favor them."[2] The fact that Britain was the main advocate of the Bourbon restoration made little difference to Gentz, for he thought of England as the natural ally of Russia, perfectly willing that the colossus of the east should "attain to a truly alarming preponderance over her neighbors."[3]

Metternich was scarcely so vehement on the subject, else he

---

[1] Arguing the former are notably Rössler, *Österreichs Kampf*, II, 202f. and Lauber, *Metternichs Kampf*, 137f. Defenders of the latter thesis include Sorel, *L'Europe*, VIII, *passim*; Rohden, *Klassische Diplomatie*, 104ff; and Josephine Bunch Stearns, *The Role of Metternich in Undermining Napoleon* (Urbana, 1948).

[2] Gentz to Karadja, 11 April 1814, *Dépêches inédites*, I, 72.

[3] *ibid.*, I, 71–72.

would have signed a separate peace long before. He called Gentz "impractical," a typical intellectual,[4] and he knew that the publicist was completely wrong about England. But at the same time he was in an even better position than Gentz to see how fragile the Bourbon movement was. Before March 20 there had hardly been such a movement, outside the British cabinet. The action at Bordeaux signified more the despair for Napoleon's prospects than enthusiasm for the count of Provence. And even after Napoleon had abdicated on April 11 and the count entered Paris as King Louis XVIII on May 4, his reception was cool, so far as Metternich could tell—in vivid contrast to the tumultuous welcome accorded Alexander a few days previously. Although the tsar had almost to the end favored Louis' rivals, the duke of Orleans or the duke of Berri, he stood a good chance of being the principal beneficiary after all, as Gentz had feared.

Metternich, therefore, was compelled a second time—Switzerland was the first—to abandon his principle of non-intervention in the internal affairs of other states. All the allies had very clear notions of the kind of government they desired in France, and these they were unwilling to leave to chance. Alexander hoped to play protector to a liberal regime patterned after the constitution of 1791; Castlereagh wanted a limited monarchy that would not commit suicide at the outset; and Metternich, hoping to preserve Bonapartism even if he could not save Bonaparte, intended as much as possible to keep the economic and social *status quo,* both to preserve stability and to prevent what Gentz called "the counterrevolution." Accordingly, when the Emperor Francis at last deserted his son-in-law and joined Castlereagh in manufacturing a Bourbon movement, the terms that the Austrian envoy, Count Ludwig Bombelles, carried to the Bourbon headquarters included the establishment of a constitutional monarchy, acquiescence in the confiscation of noble estates, a guarantee of the public debt, and the retention of existing office-holders, military and civilian.[5] These provisions, which most reasonable men favored, were soon written into the

---

[4] Metternich to Hudelist, 12 March 1814, in Fournier, *Congress von Chatillon,* 263.
[5] Webster, *Castlereagh,* 243–244.

charter grudgingly accepted by Louis XVIII. But the Bourbon restoration did not prove to be an adequate solution from Metternich's point of view until months later, when Talleyrand placed France in the Anglo-Austrian camp against Russia and Prussia at the Congress of Vienna.

In Germany, meanwhile, the fall of Napoleon aggravated Metternich's difficulties, just as he had feared. In the first place, it removed one of his principal advantages in dealing with the former Rheinbund states, namely his function as mediator, as the one moderate man between the overweening emperors of East and West. Now the intermediate states could play Austria and Russia against each other as they had once played Austria and France. The king of Würtemberg, as we have noted, professing to believe that Austria and Prussia intended to replace Napoleon as overlords of Germany, had already sought and found protection in St. Petersburg; by July, 1814, he was even proposing a "Union Russo-Germanique," an alliance of the German middle states under Russian direction.[6] King Max Joseph of Bavaria, on the other hand, still anxious about Prussian designs in his Franconian lands, took advantage of the situation to extract ever greater concessions from Vienna. In June he was rewarded by a convention in which the towns of Wetzlar, Frankfurt, and Mainz, with a belt of territory connecting these lands to the Rhenish Palatinate, were added to the Bavarian claims Austria had already recognized.[7] If the concessions had not been made, Metternich explained to the disappointed Francis, "Bavaria would have been thrown into a sort of wavering which Russia and Prussia quite naturally would have used to strengthen themselves in all respects which would detract from ours."[8]

If the concessions had reflected nothing but Bavaria's augmented bargaining power, they would have been serious enough, but they signified more. They were in fact rendered

---

[6] Hölzle, *Württemberg im Zeitalter*, 163–164.

[7] Text of convention of 3 June in Comte d' Angeberg, *Le Congrès de Vienne et les traités de 1815*, I (Paris, 1864), 179–181.

[8] Metternich to Emperor Francis, 25 June 1814, in August Fournier, "Londoner Präludien zum Wiener Kongress (Geheime Berichte Metternichs an Kaiser Franz)," *Deutsche Revue*, Jgg. 43, Bd. II, 26–27.

desirable even from Metternich's point of view by the activities of Prussia, which had also derived new bargaining power from the fall of Bonaparte. Hardenberg, anxious to gain his ends while Alexander still needed him and before France could again oppose him, on April 29 set forth all his territorial demands. These included not only Saxony and the western lands previously claimed but, for the first time, Rhenish territory south of the Mosel, a strip fifty kilometers wide on the left bank of the Rhine up to and including the great fortress at Mainz.[9] Stadion, whom Metternich delegated to negotiate with Hardenberg, favored recognition of the new claims, hoping that Hardenberg might in return moderate his demands in Saxony.[10] Metternich, however, sided with the army, which was almost unanimous in the judgment that Mainz was one strong point Austria must at all costs keep from Prussian hands.[11] On May 31 the dispute with Prussia was provisionally settled by arranging for a joint Austro-Prussian garrison in the fortress,[12] but when Metternich on June 3 signed the convention awarding Mainz to Bavaria, he served notice that the problem would be a prime source of dispute at the Congress of Vienna, which was scheduled to open in August.

A third result of Napoleon's fall was an alarming acceleration of the restorative movement, which had been temporarily arrested by the middle-state accession treaties and the lingering vitality of the French empire. In March Baron Stein, anxious to extract the most from the reference to a "federal bond" in the treaty of Chaumont, composed still another outline of a German constitution, the most distinctive features of which were a four-power directory (in reality obsolete by then because of Russia's patronage of Würtemberg) and a federal legislature composed not only of governmental envoys but of deputies from

[9] Born, "Hardenbergs Pläne," *op. cit.*, 555ff.

[10] Rössler, *Österreichs Kampf*, II, 199.

[11] The importance of Mainz was also recognized in Prussia, where the question was discussed on 29 May. "South Germany," read the protocol of a conference attended by Humboldt, Gneisenau, Boyen, and Knesebeck, "would be compelled by this point to join the Prussian system." Pertz-Delbrück, *Das Leben von Gneisenau*, IV, 694ff.

[12] Protocol of four-power conference 31 May 1814 in Martens, *Traités par la russie*, III, 166–168.

the state parliaments. He also redoubled his efforts to use his central administrative department and the *Landsturm* organization to harass the German sovereigns and give aid and comfort to the mediatized houses.[13]

The latter were likewise active, through the association headed by Count Solms-Laubach. At a meeting attended by about fifty of the mediatized princes at Amerbach on February 15 the association appointed Baron H. Gärtner, a privy councillor of the prince of Wied-Neuwied, as envoy to allied headquarters, with instructions to lobby for a restoration of the old regime and full compensation for the hardships of the Napoleonic era.[14] When Gärtner arrived at Chaumont on March 12, he found Metternich totally unsympathetic. At that time the congress of Châtillon was still in session and there was still hope for Bonaparte. Two weeks later, however, when Metternich was casting his lot with the Bourbons, he had to make a corresponding retreat in German affairs. At a ministerial conference held at Bar-sur-Aube on March 23, he faced the almost unanimous opposition of the other ministers, all of whom gave Gärtner a friendly reception, believing that whatever justification there might once have been to appease the middle states was gone now that their protector was gone. On a motion by Count Münster the conference adopted a resolution condemning "arbitrary" measures already taken against the mediatized, and authorizing Count Solms to draft a minimum set of rights to be enjoyed by the *Landstände*. The latter was then to be made the basis for a public declaration by the allies.[15] On May 30, when the Chaumont terms were formally accepted by France in the first treaty of Paris, Metternich—next to Gentz perhaps—would have been the last to view Louis' signature as a signal victory for Austria, save only in the sense that the worst had been averted.

Metternich, who now had to direct his appeasement efforts

---

[13] Stein, *Briefwechsel*, IV, 619ff; Ritter *Stein*, II, 265–268.

[14] D'Arenberg, *Princes du St-Empire*, 208–209.

[15] *ibid.*, 209; Ritter, *Stein*, II, 268; Rössler, *Österreichs Kampf*, II, 200f; and Gebhart, *Humboldts Schriften*, XI, 201. All but the last have the conferences taking place at Dijon on March 23, but as other evidence shows that the allies did not reach there until the 24th, Bar-sur-Aube is probably correct.

toward Hardenberg and Castlereagh, reluctantly acquiesced. Later, to be sure, he rekindled Stein's wrath by obstructing the hoped-for declaration and seeing to it that the treaty of Paris merely repeated the "federal bond" formula adopted at Chaumont. But in the long run, he had no choice but to support Hardenberg in the protracted and grueling struggle at the Congress of Vienna to impose controls on the internal regimes of the unwilling German sovereigns. As a result, the Federal Act of 1815, even if it established a mere confederation instead of a Reich, did contain provision for *landständische Verfassungen* and an aristocratic bill of rights. Thus in Germany, as in France, the victory over Bonaparte and Bonapartism was more complete than Metternich had intended.

Traditionally the moderation of Metternich's policy toward Napoleon has been explained either as a campaign of deception necessary to expose the conqueror's insatiable lust for power and so undermine his support at home and among his allies— or as a campaign of genuine appeasement necessary to preserve a favorable dynastic tie for the Habsburgs, to maintain a useful ally against the pretensions of Prussia and Russia in Saxony and Poland, or simply to prevent the revolution that might fill the vacuum left by Bonaparte's removal. The first explanation has a certain contingent merit in that Metternich's repeated peace proposals did possess propaganda value regardless of how Napoleon reacted to them; but in the whole structure of Metternich's policy this was a minor consideration, a good reason but not the true reason. The second line of argument, therefore, is much the sounder, indeed essentially correct as to the aims of Metternich's policy—though his motives are open to question. Its main deficiency is that it explains Metternich's French policy better than his German policy; for, granted the need to preserve a strong French counterweight to Russia, why did Metternich also strive so hard to preserve the Rheinbund states?

Perhaps the most widely offered explanation—certainly the one longest held—is the contention recently revived by Henry Kissinger, that Metternich was determined "to prevent a unification of Germany on the basis of national self-determination," [16]

[16] Kissinger, *World Restored*, 51.

fearing that the triumph of nationalism anywhere would be a grave danger to the multi-national Austrian Empire. For generations this argument has appealed to German nationalists, particularly of the Prussian school but also to certain *grossdeutsch* or Pan-German groups, who have never forgiven Metternich for putting the egotistical interests of the Austrian state ahead of what they have deemed his sacred obligation to the German people.[17] The outstanding scholarly advocate of this point of view is Hellmuth Rössler, whose voluminous work, *Österreichs Kampf um Deutschlands Befreiung* (Hamburg, 1940), is an indispensable source of information for this period. A comparable indictment has come from liberal writers, both German and non-German, who have seen in Metternich not only the foe of national aspirations but the relentless enemy of parliamentary liberalism, a haughty eighteenth-century nobleman bent on maintaining the privileges of the European aristocracy.

A much more sophisticated account of Metternich's motives emerged in the 1920's from the masterful works of Heinrich Ritter von Srbik, whose views have been accepted even by people who have never read them. Srbik saw that Metternich's situation was a circumscribed one. He pictured the Austrian minister as fighting to wring concessions from the German middle states, only to be frustrated by the strength of Napoleon on the one hand and the military weakness of the allies on the other. Beyond that he held Metternich's policy justified by the necessity of resisting Prussia's unjust encroachments in Germany.

The arguments are undoubtedly sound as far as they go. But Srbik's apologia is largely negative: what Metternich did was justified by military necessity or by the fact that the policies of other states were equally self-seeking. And the results were regrettable. In the end Srbik reproaches Metternich for his lack of national sentiment, the absence of any feeling for *das Volk,* and concludes that his great blunder (not his crime, however)

---

[17] A more puzzling view is that of Lauber, *Metternichs Kampf,* 177–183, who ruins his otherwise perceptive account of Metternich's Central European diplomacy by trying to make it a precursor of Pan-Germanism.

was his refusal to countenance the restoration of the Reich, a policy which he attributes not alone to practical necessity but to Austria's particularism and her "worries about liberalism and the German national idea." [18] Had Metternich earnestly desired it, Srbik contends, he might even have had Russia's help in restoring the Reich.

Thus "the New Metternich" launched in 1925 [19] was not so new after all: at bottom his German policy was still governed by ideological considerations which required him to resist liberalism and nationalism, and by the power-political necessity of blocking Prussia, which, in pursuit of its own power interests, was to some degree in league with the revolutionists. His conservatism was sublimated, to be sure, so that it produced a consistent and enlightened *Weltanschauung* which found expression in a balanced European order; but it still resisted change, it still sought to stifle revolution, and it still expressed the primacy of ideology over foreign policy.

One deficiency in the vast literature which produced this portrait of the *grand seigneur* is the relative neglect of the period before the War of Liberation, and particularly before Metternich became foreign minister in 1809. That is why in the present study we have taken such pains to treat Metternich's problems as he inherited them and not as they appeared to posterity. With what results?

In the first place, one looks in vain for any consistent ideological outlook on the part of the young Metternich, at least so far as foreign policy is concerned. The impassioned concern which produced his early fulminations against the Revolution quickly gave way to a certain cynicism, and to a spirit of compromise evident at the congress of Rastatt. From then until the peace of Pressburg in December, 1805, he seems to have regarded Napoleonic France as amenable to reason, a peace of equilibrium as possible, and the rivalry with Napoleon as a more or less equal contest, carried on within the rules of con-

---

[18] Srbik, *Deutsche Einheit*, I, 204.

[19] I.e., in Srbik, *Metternich*, I and II. For still more sophisticated and laudatory but still basically Srbikean views, see Guillaume de Bertier de Savigny, *Metternich et son temps* (Paris, 1959), and Jacques Droz, *L'Europe centrale. Évolution historique de l'idée de "Mitteleuropa"* (Paris, 1960), 31–51.

ventional statecraft. Indeed, it was with real zest that he tackled his assignment in Berlin and threw himself into the work of out-witting the Corsican. Then, with the treaty of Pressburg and the founding of the Rheinbund, Napoleon went too far, proving that he was insatiable, that he made war against the powers, as Metternich put it, as Robespierre had made it against the cha-teaux. Thereafter it was only a question of time. When Spain offered the opportunity, Metternich threw himself into the preparation of a people's war with more fervor than ever—a war replete with a mass army, national appeals, and incendiary propaganda, a war in which his comrades were men like Stadion, Stein, Kleist, Arndt, and other great figures of the liberation movement.

Obviously 1809 was the turning point in Metternich's career, but in what direction did he turn? Did the young diplomat, dis-illusioned and burdened with the responsibilities of office, sud-denly become reactionary? It was not so simple, and here is the second dividend gained from a closer look at the period before 1809: namely, an insight into the true character of the move-ment Metternich supported in 1809 and repudiated in 1813. For it should be clear by this time that despite the presence of some genuinely revolutionary elements—among the intellectuals, in the ranks of student volunteers, and here and there among Prussian officers and Father Jahn's gymnasts—the over-all direc-tion of the liberation movement was restorative. It is difficult to examine the step-by-step liquidation of the Reich and the strug-gle by the mediatized houses against the centralistic, leveling policies of the Rheinbund period without surmising that if the defeat of Napoleon was ever to generate a reaction, it would come from these victims. And that is exactly what happened, both in 1809 and in 1813–1814, though in 1809 they rallied around Austria whereas later they looked to Russia for de-liverance. The nature of this movement has been obscured by many things—notably by the habit of equating the Reich with German unity, and the rights of the *Stände* with the Rights of Man—actually its models were Magna Carta in England and the Estates-General of old France, not the legislation of the Revolu-tion.

In stressing the restorative rather than the national-liberal character of the movement associated with Stein and Stadion, the present study makes no claim to originality; it merely insists that the issue is crucial for an appraisal of Metternich's German policy. In 1809 Metternich, though never quite typical of the imperial aristocrats, was exactly where one would have expected him to be, fighting side by side with other émigré noblemen in a campaign to return home. Had he heeded only the promptings of family interest, class prejudice, and a genuinely conservative political credo, he would no doubt have stood with Stein and Stadion in 1813 as well—precisely as his father did. Yet he did not rush into the War of Liberation, and he refused in any way to be a party to a restoration in Germany save for the elimination of Napoleon's power east of the Rhine. To reconcile his course with the family interest, he implored Franz Georg to sell Ochsenhausen—a plea which the old *Reichsgraf*, an active lobbyist for the mediatized nobility, rejected.[20]

The real clue to Metternich's thinking is not the Federal Act of 1815, with its concessions in favor of the mediatized nobility, but the project of 1813 by which he hoped to mediate an end to the war. That plan called for the preservation of the Rheinbund as it was, but under international guarantee instead of Napoleon's exclusive protection. It is difficult to see how this implicit endorsement of the Bavarian and Westphalian constitutions, to say nothing of the regimes of King Jerome and Grand Duke Napoleon Louis of Berg, can be construed as a defense of conservatism. Gentz, it is true, concocted a doctrine of legitimacy to demonstrate that the rule of Napoleon and all his wards was sanctioned by law.[21] But this formulation took place after the utility of some such argument had become apparent, and there is no evidence that Metternich took it seriously. On the contrary, where it suited his purposes, as with the prince of Isenburg or the Prince Primate, who had dozens of treaties to prove his right to the Duchy of Frankfurt, Metternich seized Rheinbund territory as readily as did Stein.

[20] Corti, *Metternich und die Frauen*, I, 421.
[21] See Gentz to Metternich, 15 February 1814 in Gentz, *Briefe von und an*, III, 245–251.

This is not to say that Metternich was necessarily an admirer of the reforms of the Rheinbund period—the constitutions, the assaults on serfdom, the drafting of law codes, the egalitarian principles by which the sovereigns hoped to curb their noble subjects—but merely that he set aside his personal feelings in the interests of what he regarded as the only practical object of foreign policy: an enlightened concept of Austria's interests.

On this subject above all we can learn much from the years of Metternich's apprenticeship. As he came of age and entered upon his diplomatic career, the great debate in Vienna concerned the value of the Holy Roman Empire. On the one hand, the Reich was an important area of military recruitment, the source of some revenue and some trading benefits, and of those intangible advantages inherent in the *status quo*. On the other hand, it dangerously extended Austria's defense commitments, involved her in wearisome bickering with the so-called armed estates, prejudiced an accommodation with Prussia, and by the very nature of things compelled her to ally with the weak—the ecclesiastical estates and the lower imperial nobility. On balance the advantages seemed to outweigh the disadvantages, but the margin was very narrow, and the temptation to sacrifice status in the Reich for territorial acquisition near to home was correspondingly great.

In any case a voluntary withdrawal was manifestly impossible. Even if the Reich was of dubious value as an institution, the territory it covered was the key to the continental balance of power, and Austria could not by default allow her rivals to replace her influence there. This was the real issue in the contest with France, and Napoleon recognized it by deciding that he could best perpetuate his control of Germany, not by appropriating the Roman crown to himself, as many urged and many more feared he would do, but by founding a league based on the real centers of power in the Reich, the former armed estates. That solution was tested in 1809, in 1812, and again in 1813, and on the whole it was proved successful.

Austria's other rival in the contest for Germany was Russia. Here again, if one begins only with the defeat of the Grand

Army, the Russian threat appears to consist of local ambitions in Poland and the Balkans and Alexander's more generalized but nebulous schemes to save humanity. From this perspective Russia's interest in Germany appears an indirect one, compounded of a selfish reason for supporting Prussia's claims to Saxony, and a more benevolent though vacillating endorsement of Stein's program. A longer perspective, however, shows that Russia must be counted as one of the powers *directly* interested in Germany, both through dynastic ties with such states as Baden, Würtemberg, Oldenburg, and Mecklenburg, and through a variety of international instruments from the treaty of Teschen to the treaty of Tilsit. Russia's record, from the Austrian point of view, ran the gamut from the arrogant Franco-Russian mediation resulting in the Imperial Recess of 1803 to the enigmatic policy which contributed to Austria's defeat in 1809. In Vienna, during those years, almost any subject of debate could be reduced to the question of whether France or Russia was after all the more dangerous foe.

Metternich spent his formative years in the midst of that debate, from its small beginning at Tsar Paul's withdrawal from the Second Coalition to its culmination in the armistice of Znaim. When, therefore, he considered the opportunities presented by Napoleon's catastrophe in Russia, he did not need intercepted letters and other tangible evidence of Alexander's malevolence; he already had a doctrine about Russia's probable course of action. This doctrine told him that the defeat of Napoleon would lead to a new contest for Germany, a contest, moreover, in which Austria's territorial claims in South Germany and her association with the old Reich would put her at a disadvantage. The Reich was a burden that even Napoleon had been unwilling to assume. Metternich concluded that Austria's cause in the Rheinbund capitals must not be hampered from the outset: therefore she must identify herself as much as possible with the *status quo*. In this connection it is important to remember that the issue of Reich *versus* Bund was not so much a question of German unity as of counterrevolution in the internal order of the Rheinbund states. Among the allies Austria, and Austria alone, so Metternich meant to tell the German sovereigns, could prevent a return to the old regime in the third Germany. This was the true meaning of his renunciation of the Reich.

As for German unity on a federative basis, Metternich's plans varied according to circumstances. His first idea was simply to neutralize the Rheinbund. In that way Napoleon's continental hegemony might be broken and Saxony saved from the fate prepared for her at Kalisch. Neither Napoleon nor the eastern powers were interested. The next plan, necessitated by the Teplitz pact of September, 1813, conceded the dissolution of the Rheinbund but sought to save the member states by generous accession treaties. These in effect recognized the permanence of the acts of mediatization in exchange for pledges to acquiesce in "the arrangements which shall be judged necessary in peacetime for preserving the independence of Germany"—in other words, to cooperate in the formation of a new German defense league. Since Metternich at the time still hoped to end the war at the Rhine, and since the arrangements necessary to preserve the independence of Germany could conceivably still include neutralization under international guarantee, the second plan was essentially a variation on the first.

But Napoleon continued to resist, Alexander's attitude became increasingly dangerous, and Metternich could not dispense with the support of Castlereagh and Hardenberg. To the former he conceded the reduction of France to her "ancient frontiers" and, later, the recall of the Bourbons to the French throne. To Hardenberg he offered territorial aggrandizement, at first in Saxony but later in the Rhineland; and in the German constitutional question he apparently agreed to a four-power directory even at the risk of antagonizing most of the former Rheinbund courts. In the meantime, Alexander likewise shifted course. At first he had seriously compromised himself with the states of the third Germany by endorsing Stein's program, by authorizing the Kutusov declarations, and conniving in the despoliation of the king of Saxony; now he turned, as Metternich had foreseen, to competing with the Austrians in the appeasement of the middle states. He gradually abandoned Stein, he aided in the drafting of the conciliatory accession treaties, and took Würtemberg under his special protection. By the time Napoleon abdicated in France, Alexander's task in Germany was to find a formula that would win maximum support in the third Germany without losing the support of Prussia. And Metternich's problem was how to win Prussia without losing his hard-won gains in the third Germany. The contest with Napoleon had become a contest with Alexander—but that is the subject of another volume.

BIBLIOGRAPHY

I. UNPUBLISHED DOCUMENTS

From the *Haus- Hof- und Staatsarchiv* in Vienna I have consulted the following materials from the *Staatskanzlei* section:

Frankreich, Berichte, 1808–1809, Fascicles 289, 290, 291, 292, and 293.
Frankreich, Varia, 1808–1809, Fascicles 71 and 72.
Vorträge, 1808–1809, Fascicles 267, 268, 269, and 270.
Kriegsakten, 1809, Fascicle 488.

II. PUBLISHED DOCUMENTS

I have included here memoirs, letters, and documents published at the time for official use as well as documents published later for the historical interests of posterity. Also included is a genre very common for the events of this period: the document publication presented in the context of or as an appendix to a narrative essay. It is in this form that most archival material has been published.

Angeberg, Comte d', *Le congrès de Vienne et les traités de 1815*, 4 vols. (Paris, 1864).
[Austria. K. k. Hof- und Staats-Druckerey.] *Hof- und Staats-Schematismus des österreichischen Kaiserthums* (Vienna, 1808).
Carl von Österreich, *Ausgewählte Schriften*, ed. von Malcher, 6 vols. (Vienna, 1893–1894).
Caulaincourt, Armand, "Conversation de M. le Comte de Metternich avec l'empereur Napoléon, telle que que S. M. me l'a raconté," ed. Jean Hanoteau, *Revue d'histoire diplomatique*, XLVII (1933), 424–440.
———, *Mémoires du general de Caulaincourt, duc de Vicence, Grand Écuyer de l'empereur*, ed. Jean Hanoteau, 3 vols. (Paris, 1933).
Chroust, Anton, *Gesandtschaftsberichte aus München 1814–1848. Abteilung II: Die Berichte der österreichischen Gesandten*, 4 vols. (Munich, 1939ff.).
Clausewitz, Carl von, *On War*, translated by C. J. M. Jolles (New York, 1943).
Demelitsch, Fedor von, *Actenstücke zur Geschichte der Coalition vom Jahre 1814*. Vol. XLIX:2 in *Fontes Rerum Austricarum*, Abteilung 2 (Vienna, 1899).
Fournier, August, *Gentz und Cobenzl. Geschichte der österreichischen Diplomatie in den Jahre 1801–1805* (Vienna, 1880).

————, *Der Congress von Chatillon. Die Politik im Kriege von 1814* (Vienna and Prague, 1900).

————, "Londoner Präludien zum Wiener Kongress. (Geheime Berichte Metternichs an Kaiser Franz)," *Deutsche Revue,* Jahrgang 3, Band II, pp. 26ff.

————, "Zur Vorgeschichte des Wiener Kongresses," in August Fournier, *Historische Studien und Skizzen* (Vienna and Leipzig, 1908), 290–327. Also published as "Zur Geschichte der polnischen Frage 1814 und 1815," in *Mitteilungen des Instituts für österreichische Geschichtsforschung,* XX, pp. 444ff.

Gentz, Friedrich von, *Aus dem Nachlasse Friedrichs von Gentz,* 2 vols. (Vienna, 1867–1868).

————, *Briefe von und an Friedrich von Gentz,* ed. Friedrich Carl Wittichen and Ernst Salzer, 3 vols. (Munich and Berlin, 1910–1913).

————, *Dépêches inédites du chevalier de Gentz aux Hospodars de Valachie pour servir à l'histoire de la politique européenne (1813 à 1828),* ed. Graf Anton Prokesch von Osten, 3 vols. (Paris, 1876–1877).

[Great Britain. Foreign Office], *British and Foreign State Papers,* I:1 (London, 1841).

Grunwald, Constantin de, "Le mariage de Napoléon et de Marie-Louise. Documents inédites," *Revue des deux mondes,* Series 8, XXXVIII (15 March 1937), 320–352.

————, "Les débuts diplomatiques de Metternich à Paris (documents inédites)," *Revue de Paris,* Année 43, IV (July–August, 1936), 492–537.

————, "La fin d'une ambassade. Metternich à Paris en 1808–1809. Mémoires inédites," *Revue de Paris,* Année 44, V (September–October, 1937), 481–513, and 819–846.

————, "Metternich et Napoléon," *Revue des deux mondes,* Series 8, XLI (September–October, 1937), 607–639.

Guglia, Eugen, *Friedrich von Gentz: Österreichische Manifeste von 1809 und 1813* (Vienna, n.d.).

Humboldt, Wilhelm von, *Wilhelm von Humboldts gesammelte Schriften,* ed. Bruno Gebhart, 15 vols. (Berlin, 1903–1918).

Klinkowstrom, Alfons, *Oesterreichs Theilnahme an den Befreiungskreigen. Ein Beitrag zur Geschichte der Jahres 1813 bis 1815 nach Aufzeichnungen von Friedrich von Gentz nebst einen Anhang: "Briefwechsel zwischen den Fürsten Schwarzenberg und Metternich"* (Vienna, 1887).

Langsam, Walter C., "Count Stadion and Archduke Charles," *Journal of Central European Affairs,* VI (1946), 147–151.

Lebzeltern, Ludwig Graf von, *Un collaborateur de Metternich:*

Mémoires et papiers de Lebzeltern, published by Emanuel de Lévis-Mirepoix (Paris, 1949).

Londonderry, Robert Stewart, Second Marquess of, *Memoirs and Correspondence of Viscount Castlereagh, second Marquess of Londonderry,* ed. by his brother, Charles William Vane, Third Marquess of Londonderry, 12 vols. (London, 1850–1853).

Martens, Fedor Fedorovitch, *Recueil des traités et conventions conclus par la russie avec les puissances étrangères,* 15 vols. (St. Petersburg, 1874–1909).

Martens, Georges Frédéric de, *Recueil de traités d'alliance, de paix, de trêve, de neutralité, de commerce, de limites, d'échange etc. et plusieurs autres actes servant à la connoissance des relations étrangères des puissances et états de l'Europe depuis 1761 jusqu'à présent,* 8 vols. (Göttingen, 1817–1835).

———, *Nouveau recueil de traités . . .* [Continuation of above], 16 vols. (Göttingen, 1817–1842).

———, *Nouveau suppléments au recueil de traités . . .* [Continuation of above], 3 vols. (Göttingen, 1839–1842).

Metternich-Winneburg, Clemens Lothar Wenzel Fürst von, *Aus Metternich's nachgelassenen Papieren,* ed. by Prince Richard Metternich, 8 vols. (Vienna, 1880–1884). Published in English as *Memoirs of Prince Metternich,* 5 vols. (New York, 1880–1882).

Meyer, Philipp Guido von, *Corpus Juris Confoederationis Germanicae,* 2 vols. 3rd ed. (Frankfurt a/M, 1858–1859).

Mikhailowitch, Grand-Duc Nicolas (ed.), *Correspondance de l'Empereur Alexandre Ier avec sa soeur la Grande-Duchesse Catherine Princesse d'Oldenbourg, puis Reine de Wurtemberg 1805–1818* (St. Petersburg, 1910).

Napoleon I, Emperor of the French, *Correspondance de Napoléon Ier,* published by order of the emperor Napoleon III, 32 vols. (Paris, 1858–1870).

Ompteda, Ludwig von, *Politischer Nachlass des hannoverschen Staats- und Cabinets-Ministers Ludwig von Ompteda aus den Jahren 1804 bis 1813,* ed. by Friedrich von Ompteda, 3 vols. (Jena, 1869).

Oncken, Wilhelm, *Oesterreich und Preussen im Befreiungskriege, Urkundliche Aufschlüsse über die politische Geschichte des Jahres 1813,* 2 vols. (Berlin, 1876–1879).

Pertz, Georg Heinrich, *Aus Stein's Leben,* 2 vols. (Berlin, 1856).

———, *Das Leben des Ministers Freiherrn vom Stein,* 6 vols. (Berlin, 1849–1855).

Puttkamer, Ellinor von (ed.), *Föderative Elemente im deutschen-Staatsrecht seit 1648.* Vol. VII in *Quellensammlung zur Kulturgeschichte* (Göttingen, 1955).

Schmidt, W. A., *Geschichte der deutschen Verfassungsfrage während der Befreiungskriege und des Wiener Congresses 1812 bis 1815*, ed. by Alfred Stern (Stuttgart, 1890).

Stein, Heinrich Friedrich Karl Freiherr von, *Freiherr vom Stein: Briefwechsel, Denkschriften und Aufzeichnungen*, ed. by Erich Botzenhart, 7 vols. (Berlin, 1931–1937).

[U.S.S.R., Ministry of Foreign Affairs], *Vneshniaia politika Rossii XIX i nachala XX veka. Dokumenty rossiiskogo Ministerstva inosctannykh del* [Foreign Policy of Russia in the xixth and the Beginning of the xxth Century. Documents of the Russian Ministry of Foreign Affairs], 1st Series, 2- vols. (Moscow, 1960–   ).

Webster, Charles K., *British Diplomacy 1813–1815. Select Documents Dealing with the Reconstruction of Europe* (London, 1921).

III. BASIC STUDIES

The following are historical monographs, usually of large scope, without which I could not have undertaken the study of Metternich's German policy. Some encompass the subject in its entirety, others limited phases of it, but in all cases they are indispensable.

Beer, Adolf, *Zehn Jahre österreichischer Politik 1801–1810* (Leipzig, 1877).

Bitterauf, Theodor, *Geschichte des Rheinbundes. Bd. I: Die Gründung des Rheinbundes und der Untergang des alten Reiches* (Munich, 1905).

Corti, Egon Cäsar Conte, *Metternich und die Frauen, Bd. I: Von der französischen Revolution bis zum Wiener Kongress (1789–1815)* (Zürich and Vienna, 1948).

Demelitsch, Fedor von, *Metternich und seine auswärtige Politik* (Stuttgart, 1898).

Driault, Edouard, *Napoléon et l'Europe*, 5 vols. (Paris, 1910–1927).

Dunan, Marcel, *Napoléon et l'Allemagne. Le système continental et les débuts du royaume de Bavière 1806–1810* (Paris, 1942).

Greulich, Alfred, *Österreichs Beitritt zur Koalition im Jahre 1813* (Leipzig, 1931).

Hölzle, Erwin, *Württemberg im Zeitalter Napoleons und der deutschen Erhebung* (Stuttgart and Berlin, 1937).

Huber, Ernst Rudolf, *Deutsche Verfassungsgeschichte seit 1789. Bd. I: Reform und Restauration 1789 bis 1830* (Stuttgart, 1957).

Lauber, Emil, *Metternichs Kampf um die europäische Mitte. Struktur seiner Politik von 1809 bis 1815* (Vienna and Leipzig, 1939).

Ritter, Gerhard, *Stein: Eine Politische Biographie*, 2 vols. (Stuttgart and Berlin, 1931; one vol. ed. Stuttgart, 1958).

Rössler, Hellmuth, *Österreichs Kampf um Deutschlands Befreiung. Die deutsche Politik der nationalen Führer Österreichs 1805–1815*, 2 vols. (Hamburg, 1940).

Sorel, Albert, *L'Europe et la révolution française*, 8 vols. (Paris, 1885–1904).

Srbik, Heinrich Ritter von, *Metternich der Staatsmann und der Mensch*, 3 vols. (Munich, 1925–1954).

Vandal, Albert, *Napoléon et Alexandre Ier. L'alliance russe sous le premier empire*, 3 vols. (Paris, 1893).

Webster, Charles K., *The Foreign Policy of Castlereagh 1812–1815* (London, 1931).

Wertheimer, Eduard, *Geschichte Oesterreichs und Hungarns im ersten Jahrzehnt des 19. Jahrhunderts*, 2 vols. (Leipzig, 1890).

IV. SPECIAL STUDIES

These include articles, dissertations, and short books incorporating intensive research either on limited topics or on topics which are only partially concerned with the substance of this study.

Berney, A., "Reichstradition und Nationalstaatsgedanke 1789–1815," *Historische Zeitschrift*, CXL (1929), 57ff.

Bertier de Sauvigny, Guillaume de, "Sainte-Alliance et Alliance dans les conceptions de Metternich," *Revue historique*, CCXXIII (1960), 249–274.

Bonjour, Edgar, *Swiss Neutrality, Its History and Meaning*, tr. by Mary Hottinger (London, 1946).

Born, Karl Erich, "Hardenbergs Pläne und Versuche zur Neuordnung Europas und Deutschlands 1813/1815," *Geschichte in Wissenschaft und Unterricht*, VIII (1957), 550–565.

Buckland, C. S. B., *Metternich and the British Government 1809–1813* (London, 1932).

Chroust, Anton, *Geschichte des Grossherzogtums Würzburg 1806–1814. Die äussere Politik des Grossherzogtums* (Würzburg, 1932).

Deutsch, Harold C., *The Genesis of Napoleonic Imperialism*. Vol. XLI in *Harvard Historical Studies* (Cambridge, Mass., 1938).

Ford, Franklin L., *Strasbourg in Transition 1648–1789* (Cambridge, Mass., 1958).

Fournier, August, "Oesterreichs Kriegsziele im Jahre 1809," *Beiträge zur neueren Geschichte Österreichs* (December, 1908) Heft IV, 216ff.

Gollwitzer, Heinz, *Die Standesherren: die politische und gesellschaftliche Stellung der Mediatisierten 1815–1918, ein Beitrag zur deutschen Sozialgeschichte* (Stuttgart, 1957).

Griewank, Karl, "Preussen und die Neuordnung Deutschlands,"

Forschungen zur brandenburgischen und preussischen Geschichte, LII (1940), 245ff.

———, *Der Wiener Kongress und die Neuordnung Europas 1814/15* (Leipzig, 1942).

Haas, Arthur G., "Kaiser Franz, Metternich, und die Stellung Illyriens," *Mitteilungen des österreichischen Staatsarchivs,* XI (1958), 373–397.

Hamerow, Theodore S., *Restoration, Revolution, Reaction. Economics and Politics in Germany, 1815–1871* (Princeton, N.J., 1958).

Haussherr, Hans, "Hardenberg und der Friede von Basel," *Historische Zeitschrift,* CLXXXIV (1957), 292–335.

Haussherr, Hans, *Die Stunde Hardenbergs* (Hamburg, 1943).

Hölzle, Erwin, "Das Napoleonische Staatensystem in Deutschland," *Historische Zeitschrift,* CXLVIII (1933), 279ff.

Hoff, Johann Friedrich, *Die Mediatisiertenfrage in den Jahren 1813–1815.* Heft XLVI in *Abhandlungen zur mittleren und neueren Geschichte* (Berlin and Leipzig, 1913).

Horstenau, Edmund Glaise von, "Altösterreichs Heer in der deutschen Geschichte," in *Deutsche Heeresgeschichte,* ed. by Karl Linnebach (Hamburg, 1935).

Hubatsch, Walther, "Deutsche Grenzprobleme 1813–1815," *Welt als Geschichte,* XVI (1956), 179–195.

Kann, Robert A., "Metternich: a Reappraisal of his Impact on International Relations," *Journal of Modern History,* XXXII (1960), 333–339.

Kemiläinen, Aira, *Auffassungen über die Sendung des deutschen Volkes um die Wende des 18. und 19. Jahrhunderts* (Helsinki, 1956).

Kipa, Emil, *Austria a sprawa polska w r. 1809* [Austria and the Polish Affair in the Year 1809] (Warsaw, 1952).

Kukiel, M. *Czartoryski and European Unity: 1770–1861* (Princeton, N.J., 1955).

Langsam, Walter Consuelo, *The Napoleonic Wars and German Nationalism in Austria* (New York, 1930).

Luckwaldt, F., *Oesterreich und die Anfänge des Befreiungskrieges 1813.* Vol. x in *Ebelings Historische Studien* (Berlin, 1898).

Markert, Werner, "Metternich und Alexander I. Die Rivalität der Mächte in der europäischen Allianz," in *Schicksalswege deutscher Vergangenheit,* ed. by Walther Hubatsch (Düsseldorf, 1950).

Martens, F. von, "Russland und Preussen während der Restauration," Part I, *Deutsche Revue,* XIII:2 (April–June, 1888), 291–317.

Meyer, Arnold Oskar, "Der Streit um Metternich," *Historische Zeitschrift,* CLVII (1937), 75–84.

Mommsen, Wilhelm, "Zur Bedeutung des Reichsgedankens," *Historische Zeitschrift* CLXXIV (1952), 385–415.

Oncken, Wilhelm, "Die Krisis der letzten Friedensverhandlung mit Napoleon I," *Historisches Taschenbuch*, 6th Folge, v (1886), 1–53.

Robert, André, *L'Idée nationale autrichienne et les guerres de Napoléon; l'aspostat du Baron de Hormayr et le salon de Caroline Pichler* (Paris, 1933).

Rössler, Hellmuth, *Napoleons Griff nach der Kaiserkrone; das Ende des alten Reiches 1806*. Vol. III in *Janus-Bücher: Berichte zur Weltgeschichte* (Munich, 1957).

Rohr, W., "Scharnhorsts Sendung nach Wien Ende 1811 und Metternichs Politik," *Forschungen zur brandenburgischen und preussischen Geschichte*, XLVIII (1930), 76–128.

Schroeder, Paul W., "Metternich Studies Since 1925," *Journal of Modern History*, XXXIII (1961), 237–260.

Schwarz, Hans, *Die Vorgeschichte des Vertrages von Ried*. Heft II in *Münchener historische Abhandlungen*, 1st series (Munich, 1933).

Scott, Franklin D., "Bernadotte and the Throne of France, 1814," *Journal of Modern History*, v (1933), 465–478.

Shanahan, William O., *Prussian Military Reforms 1786–1813* (New York, 1945).

Simon, Walter, "Prince Hardenberg," *Review of Politics*, XVIII (1956), 88–99.

Srbik, Heinrich Ritter von, "Metternichs Plan einer Neuordnung Europas 1814/15," *Mitteilungen des österreichischen Instituts für Geschichtsforschung*, XL (1925), 109–126.

———, *Die Schicksalsstunde des alten Reiches. Österreichs Weg 1804–1806* (Jena, 1937).

Stählin, Karl, "Ideal und Wirklichkeit im letzten Jahrzehnt Alexanders I," *Historiche Zeitschrift*, CXLV (1932), 90–105.

Tiedemann, Helmuth, *Der deutsche Kaisergedanke vor und nach dem Wiener Kongress* (Breslau, 1932).

Viereck, Peter, "New Views on Metternich," *Review of Politics*, XIII (1951), 211–228.

Windelband, Wolfgang, "Badens Austritt aus dem Rheinbund, 1813," *Zeitschrift für die Geschichte des Oberrheins*, Neue Folge, XXV (1910), 102–151.

Wolff, Karl, *Die deutsche Publizistik in der Zeit der Freiheitskämpfe und des Wiener Kongress 1813–1815* (Plauen, 1934).

Zöllner, Erich, "Aus unbekannten Diplomatenbriefen an den Freiherrn Franz Binder von Kriegelstein," *Festschrift zur feier des zweihundertjährigen Bestandes des Haus- Hof- und Staatsarchivs*, I, ed. by Leo Santifaller (Vienna, 1949).

Zwehl, Hans Karl von, *Der Kampf um Bayern 1805. I: Der Abschluss der bayerisch-französischen Allianz,* Heft xiii in *Münchener historische Abhandlungen,* 1st Series (Munich, 1937).

V. GENERAL WORKS

Here are listed all those substantial books which, because they treat the period as a whole or some important phase of it, have provided essential reference material and background.

Arenberg, Prince Jean-Engelbert d', *Les princes du St-Empire à l'époque Napoléonienne* (Louvain, 1951).
Arneth, Alfred Ritter von, *Johann Freiherr von Wessenberg. Ein österreichischer Staatsmann des neunzehnten Jahrhunderts,* 2 vols. (Vienna and Leipzig, 1898).
Bertier de Sauvigny, Guillaume de, *Metternich et son temps* (Paris, 1959).
Bibl, Viktor, *Der Zerfall Österreichs. Bd. I: Kaiser Franz und Sein Erbe* (Vienna, Berlin, Leipzig and Munich, 1922).
Doeberl, Michael, *Entwicklungsgeschichte Bayerns,* 3 vols. (Munich, 1908–1912).
Droz, Jacques, *L'Europe centrale. Évolution historique de l'idée de "Mitteleuropa"* (Paris, 1960).
Du Coudray, Helene, *Metternich* (New Haven, 1936).
Fournier, August, *Napoleon I. Eine Biographie,* 3 vols. (Vienna and Leipzig, 1913).
Fisher, H. A. L., *Studies in Napoleonic Statesmanship, Germany* (London, 1903).
Fugier, André, *La révolution française et l'empire Napoléonien.* Vol. iv of *Histoire des relations internationales,* ed. by Pierre Renouvin (Paris, 1954).
Gebhardt, Bruno, *Wilhelm von Humboldt als Staatsmann,* 2 vols. (Stuttgart, 1899).
Grunwald, Constantin de, *Metternich,* tr. by Dorothy Todd (London, 1953).
Hantsch, Hugo, *Die Geschichte Österreichs,* 2 vols. (Graz-Vienna, 1937 and 1950).
Hartung, Fritz, *Deutsche Verfassungsgeschichte vom 15. Jahrhundert bis zur Gegenwart,* 6th ed. (Stuttgart, 1950).
Heffter, Heinrich, *Die deutsche Selbstverwaltung im 19. Jahrhundert. Geschichte der Ideen und Institutionen* (Stuttgart, 1950).
Kaltenborn, Carl von, *Geschichte der deutschen Bundesverhältnisse und Einheitsbestrebungen von 1806 bis 1856,* 2 vols. (Berlin, 1857).

Kann, Robert A., *A Study in Austrian Intellectual History from Late Baroque to Romanticism* (New York, 1960).

Kissinger, Henry A., *A World Restored. Metternich, Castlereagh and the Problems of Peace 1812–1822* (London, 1957).

Klüber, Johann Ludwig, *Öffentliches Recht des Teutschen Bundes und der Bundesstaaten* (Frankfurt a/M, 1840).

Krieger, Leonard, *The German Idea of Freedom* (Boston, 1957).

Lehmann, Max, *Freiherr vom Stein*, one-vol. ed. (Leipzig, 1921).

Lobanov-Rostovsky, Andrei A., *Russia and Europe 1789–1825* (Durham, N.C., 1947).

Meinecke, Friedrich, *Weltbürgertum und Nationalstaat. Studien zur Genesis des deutschen Nationalstaates*, 5th ed. (Munich and Berlin, 1919).

Mommsen, Wilhelm, *Stein-Ranke-Bismarck. Ein Beitrag zur politischen und sozialen Bewegung des 19. Jahrhunderts* (Munich, 1954).

Pertz, G. H., and Delbrück, Hans, *Das Leben des Feldmarschalls Grafen Neithardt von Gneisenau*, 5 vols. (Berlin, 1864–1880).

Phillips, Walter Alison, *The Confederation of Europe: A Study of the European Alliance 1813–1823 as an Experiment in the International Organization of Peace* (London, 1913).

Pirenne, Jacques-Henri, *La sainte-alliance. Organisation européenne de la paix mondiale*, 2 vols. (Neuchâtel, 1946).

Ritter, Gerhard, *Staatskunst und Kriegshandwerk. Das Problem des "Militärismus" in Deutschland*, 2 vols. (Munich, 1954–1960).

Rohden, Peter Richard, *Die klassische Diplomatie von Kaunitz bis Metternich* (Leipzig, 1939).

Rössler, Hellmuth, *Reichsfreiherr vom Stein*. Vol. II in *Persönlichkeit und Geschichte* (Berlin and Frankfurt, 1957).

———, *Zwischen Revolution und Reaktion. Ein Lebensbild des Reichsfreiherrn Hans Christoph von Gagern 1766–1852* (Göttingen, Berlin, and Frankfurt, 1958).

Schaeder, Hildegard, *Die Dritte Koalition und die Heilige Allianz*. Vol. XVI in *Osteuropäische Forschungen*, Neue Folge, ed. by Otto Hoetzsch (Königsberg and Berlin, 1934).

Schnabel, Franz, *Deutsche Geschichte im neunzehnten Jahrhundert*, 4 vols., 2nd ed. (Freiburg, 1949ff.).

Simon, Walter M., *The Failure of the Prussian Reform Movement 1807–1819* (Ithaca, N.Y., 1955).

Srbik, Heinrich Ritter von, *Deutsche Einheit. Die Idee und Wirklichkeit vom Heiligen Reich bis Königgrätz*, 4 vols. (Munich, 1935–1942).

Stählin, Karl, *Geschichte Russlands von den Anfängen bis zur Gegenwart*, 4 vols. in 5 (Königsberg and Berlin, 1923–1939).

Sweet, Paul R., *Friedrich von Gentz, Defender of the Old Order* (Madison, Wis., 1941).

Treitschke, Heinrich von, *Treitschke's History of Germany in the Nineteenth Century,* tr. Eden and Cedar Paul, 7 vols. (New York, 1915–1919).

Ulmann, Heinrich, *Geschichte der Befreiungskriege,* 2 vols. (Munich and Berlin, 1914–1915).

Valjavec, Fritz, *Die Entstehung der politischen Strömungen in Deutschland 1770–1815* (Munich, 1951).

Waliszewski, K., *La russie il y a cent ans. Le règne d'Alexandre Ier,* 3 vols. (Paris, 1923–1925).

VI. REFERENCE WORKS AND WORKS OF OCCASIONAL VALUE

The following have contributed in some small way without being essential.

Allgemeine deutsche Biographie, published by the historical commission of the Royal Academy of Sciences (Leipzig, 1875–1912).

Bibl, Viktor, *Metternich, der Dämon Österreichs* (Vienna and Leipzig, 1936).

Bonjour, Edgar, Offler, H. S., and Potter, G. R., *A Short History of Switzerland* (Oxford, 1952).

Cecil, Algernon, *Metternich 1773–1859: A Study of His Period and His Personality* (London, 1947).

Cresson, W. P., *The Holy Alliance. The European Background of the Monroe Doctrine* (New York, 1922).

Dictionnaire de biographie française, under the direction of M. Prevost and Roman d'Amat (Paris, 1933ff.).

Gulick, Edward Vose, *Europe's Classical Balance of Power: A Case History of the Theory and Practice of One of the Great Concepts of European Statecraft* (Ithaca, N.Y., 1955).

Mayr, Josef Karl, *Geschichte der österreichischen Staatskanzlei im Zeitalter des Fürsten Metternich* (Vienna, 1935).

Meynert, Hermann, *Geschichte der k. k. österreichischen Armee, ihrer Heranbildung und Organisation so wie ihrer Schicksals, Thaten, und Feldzüge von der frühesten bis auf die jetzige Zeit,* 4 vols. (Vienna, 1852–1854).

Missoffe, Michel, *Metternich 1773–1859* (Paris, 1959).

Nicolson, Harold G., *The Congress of Vienna: A Study in Allied Unity 1812–1822* (New York, 1946).

Rall, Hans, *Kurbayern in der letzten Epoche der alten Reichsverfassung 1745–1801.* Vol. xlv in *Schriftenreihe zur bayerischen Landesgeschichte* (Munich, 1952).

Regele, Oskar, *Der österreichische Hofkriegsrat 1556–1848*. Supplementary Vol. I, Heft I, *Mitteilungen des österreichischen Staatsarchivs* (Vienna, 1949).

Springer, Anton, *Geschichte Österreichs seit dem Wiener Frieden 1809*, 2 vols. (Leipzig, 1863).

Stearns, Josephine Bunch, *The Role of Metternich in Undermining Napoleon*. Vol. XXIX, No. 4 in *Illinois Studies in the Social Sciences* (Urbana, Ill., 1948).

Note: Two valuable studies which appeared too late for inclusion above are:

Falk, Minna R., "Stadion, adversaire de Napoléon (1806–1809)," *Annales historiques de la revolution française*, No. 169 (July–September, 1962), 288–305; and

Haas, Arthur G., *Metternich, Reorganization and Nationality, 1813–1818. A Story of Foresight and Frustration in the Rebuilding of the Austrian Empire*, Vol. XXVIII in *Veröffentlichungen des Instituts für europäische Geschichte, Mainz, Abteilung Universalgeschichte* (Wiesbaden, 1963).

INDEX

Aberdeen, George Hamilton-Gordon, Earl of, 223, 250f, 259, 261f

Alexander I, Tsar of Russia, 27; relations with Napoleon, 38, 96f, 122f; and War of 1809, 66, 73f; at Erfurt congress, 67f; Polish policy of, 129, 161, 324 (see also Poland, Polish question); and Würtemberg, 130f, 325; in War of Liberation, 148–52, 157–60, 179, 191f, 195–97, 220f, 258, 260–62, 265–67, 279f, 288f, 295–97, 300–10; German policy of, 148–52, 156, 159f, 176f, 195–97, 200f, 206n, 208–13, 220f, 230f, 232–34, 239f, 307–10, 315, 324–26; Grand Design of 1804, 150, 300; and Baron Stein, 150f, 158f, 194–97, 324; Austrian policy of, 166f, 179, 184; British policy of, 261; and Switzerland, 264–66; Dutch policy of, 304f; French policy of, 172, 295f; and Baden, 238f

allied manifesto of 1 Dec. 1813, 256f, 289

allied war aims, 287–90

Alopeus, Baron Maximilian von, Russian diplomat, 38f, 42, 130, 254

Alsace, 268, 288, 294; proposal to exchange for Galicia, 300f. See also French boundary question

Altenburg, peace conference of, 93f, 96, 106–16, 121

Amerbach meeting of mediatized princes 15 Feb. 1814, 317

Anglo-Austrian preliminary treaty of alliance 3 Oct. 1813, 207, 259

Anhalt, duchies of, 54, 228–31, 243

Anna Pavlovna of Romanov, Grand Duchess, 122f, 296

Ansbach, 40, 170, 193, 212

Anstett, Baron Johann von, Russian diplomat, 181–84, 254

Anton of Habsburg, Archduke of Austria, Grand Master of the Teutonic Order, 59, 112, 117

Antwerp, 250

Arenberg, Duke of, 128–30, 140, 236f

armed estates, 5, 323. See also Reich

Arndt, Ernst Moritz, 71, 150, 227, 268, 321; author of "Die Leipziger Schlacht," 219

Aspern-Essling, battle of, 83, 85, 88f

Augusta of Wittelsbach, Princess of Bavaria, 62

Aulic Council, 35

Austerlitz, battle of, 41, 57; Kaunitz estate at, 18

Austria

army: recruiting rights in Reich, 18, 51, 323; reforms in, 65f; in War of 1809, 82f, 87, 100f, 321; *Landwehr*, 65f, 103; in treaty of Schönbrunn, 117f, 133; auxiliary corps in 1812, 142, 168; in War of Liberation, 171, 184, 187–89, 211, 231, 291f

foreign relations: with Prussia, 7, 19f, 23, 37–42, 54–56, 101f; with France, 21–26, 35f, 51f, 58–60, 69f, 84–118, 134f, 142f, 147; with Russia, 26f, 39–41, 73–75, 86–88, 102, 134–36; with Rheinbund, 51f, 70ff, 73–81, 130–33; alliance with Russia, 1804–05, 39–41; alliance with France, 1812, 142f, 147; convention with Bavaria, June 1814, 315f; declaration of war on France 1813, 184, 189; influence in North Germany, 244

government: crown lands, 13, 21; state chancellery, 13f; finances, 17, 133, 140, 171; Pragmatic Sanction 1723, 3, 33, 36, 119; Austrian Empire created, 36; refugees in state services, 71f, 253f

Austrian Empire, created by Cobenzl, 36

Austrian Netherlands, 7, 13f. See also Belgium

Austrian school, 55, 167, 212, 294f, 323

Austro-Bavarian convention of 3 June 1814, 315f

Austro-French alliance, 1812, 142f, 147

Austro-Russian alliance, 1804–1805, 39–41

Bacher, Théobald-Jacques, 60, 130

Baden, in Imperial Recess, 32; and Russia, 27, 239, 324; and mediatized houses, 61, 236; and territorial settlement of 1810, 126; and Prussia, 197f; and German occupation, 230; accession treaty with allies, 240

balance of power, see European equilibrium

339

Baldacci, Baron Anton von, 65, 71, 85, 99, 115, 120, 165, 171, 209
Balkans, *see* Eastern question, Turkey, Ottoman Empire
Ballhaus, government building in Vienna, 3, 120, 139, 146, 153, 199f, 206
Barbarossa, Frederick, Holy Roman Emperor, 195
Bar-sur-Aube, ministerial conference of, 317
Bartenstein, convention of, April 1807, 55f, 158, 197
Basel, treaty of, 20, 39, 155, 235; allied Rhine crossing at, 265
bastille, the, 12
Batavian Republic, 38. *See also* Holland, Netherlands
Bautzen, battle of, 172, 177
Bavaria, relations with France, 19, 94f; with Austria, 27, 34f, 39, 131, 170, 207–13, 217; with Russia, 27, 95, 196; with Prussia, 197f; constitution of 1808, 60–62, 322; in peace of 1809, 94f; treaty with Würtemberg, 1810, 126; treaty of Ried, 211–18; military contribution to allies, 245–48; in treaty of Chaumont, 306f
Bayreuth, 85, 88, 94, 126, 170, 212
Beauharnais, Eugene, Viceroy of Italy, 62, 144
Beauharnais, Josephine, *see* Josephine
Beauharnais, Stephanie, Grand Duchess of Baden, 239
Belgium, 14, 267, 284f, 298, 304. *See also* Austrian Netherlands
Bellegarde, Count Friedrich Heinrich, Austrian general, 115
Bentheim-Steinfurth, Prince von, 276f
Bentinck, Lord William, Earl of Portland, 259, 267
Berchtesgaden, 32, 43, 94, 117, 126, 208
Berg, Grand Duchy of, 80, 164, 198, 204, 212, 226, 237, 270. *See also* Bonaparte, Napoleon Louis
Bern, canton of, 266
Bernadotte, Jean Baptiste Jules, Prince Royal of Sweden, 133, 266–68, 284, 294, 296
Berri, Duke Charles Ferdinand of, 296, 314
Biernacki, Felix, Polish agent in England, 300
Binder von Kriegelstein, Baron Franz von, Austrian diplomat, 232, 238–40, 242, 249f, 258

Bismarck, Prince Otto von, 135, 272
Blücher, General Gebhard, 169, 187f, 201, 246, 268, 291, 294, 296, 299
Bohemia, Kingdom of, 3, 33, 87, 132
Bohemian army, 184, 296f, 299
Bombelles, Count Ludwig von, Austrian diplomat, 314
Bonaparte, Jerome, King of Westphalia, 56, 62f, 80, 144, 205, 322
Bonaparte, Joseph, King of Naples, then of Spain, 63
Bonaparte, Louis, King of Holland, 63
Bonaparte, Napoleon, *see* Napoleon I
Bonaparte, Napoleon Louis, Grand Duke of Berg, 205, 322
Bonapartism, 254f, 314, 318
Bordeaux, 312, 314
Bourbons, restoration of, 284, 298, 311, 313–15; in Spain, 289
Boyen, Hermann von, 76, 150
Brandeis, Austrian town, 183
Braunau, Austrian town, 58
Bray, Count François Gabriel, Bavarian diplomat, 95
Breisgau, 8, 32, 43, 209, 239, 268, 270
Bremen, 244. *See also* Hanseatic cities
Brenner Pass, 42, 209
Brienne, battle of, 296f
Brixen, Bishopric of, 32, 42, 209
Brougham, Lord Henry, 300
Brunswick, Duchy of, 198, 237, 242
Brunswick, Duke Charles William of, 12, 54, 72
Bubna, General Count Ferdinand von, 92f, 113f, 153, 175f, 177, 183
Bucharest, peace of, 1812, 139
Bülow, General Baron Friedrich Wilhelm von, 201
buffer states, doctrine of, 286
Buol-Schauenstein, Baron Joseph von, Austrian diplomat, 71
Burgundian gate, 257
Burke, Edmund, 30

Campo Formio, treaty of, 20f, 26
Capo d'Istria, Count John, Russian diplomat, 149, 254
Carinthia, 165
Carl of Habsburg, Archduke of Austria, 39, 54f, 69, 74, 82f, 85–89, 99, 113, 120, 142, 187, 192, 209
Carl August, Duke of Saxe-Weimar, 66f, 241
Carl Frederick, Grand Duke of Baden, 61, 236, 238, 278

Carl Theodore, Elector of Palatinate-Bavaria, 61

Carniola, 117

Castlereagh, Robert Vane Stewart, Viscount, British foreign minister, 200, 250f, 260–63, 280, 283f, 291, 294f, 298, 301, 304–10, 312–14, 318, 325

Cathcart, Lord William, 223, 250, 261, 263

Catherine II, Empress of Russia, 19

Catherine of Romanov, Grand Duchess of Russia, 128, 236, 304, 307

Catherine of Würtemberg, Queen of Westphalia, 63

Catholics, 54

Caulaincourt, Count Armand Augustin de, Duke of Vicence, French ambassador and foreign minister, 68, 96, 114, 179f, 182–84, 188, 204f, 251–56, 262f, 295f, 299, 311

censorship, in Austria, 121f; in the German Confederation, 213

Central Administrative Council, 159, 170, 193–97, 208, 223f, 225, 229f, 234, 237, 240, 244–46, 276

Central European defense system, 259, 281f

Champagny, Jean Baptiste de, Duke of Cadace, French foreign minister, 58, 89, 91f, 96, 103–05

Charles VI, Holy Roman Emperor, 33

Charlotte of England, Princess of Wales, 304

Châtillon, Congress of, 295, 298f, 310f, 317

Chaumont, allied headquarters, 300; treaty of, 290, 303–10, 313, 316, 318

Chernyshev, Count Alexander, Russian Colonel, 111f

Churchill, Sir Winston, 248

Cisalpine Republic, 38. See also Kingdom of Italy

classical diplomacy, 186

Clausewitz, General Carl von, 187

Clemenceau, Georges, 271

Cleves, 19, 26f

Cobenzl, Count Ludwig von, Austrian diplomat and foreign minister, 21f, 26, 28, 33, 35, 38–42; becomes court and state vice-chancellor, 27; Bavarian policy of, 34; resigns, 43

Cobenzl, Philip von, Austrian diplomat, 50

Colloredo, Count Franz von, vice-chancellor for imperial affairs, 33, 37f, 43, 253

Cologne, Archbishopric of, 8, 32

colonial question, 260, 287, 298

committee for a free Germany, 149

Commotau, 213

Comorn, Austrian headquarters in Hungary, 87, 91, 113–15

compensation, principle of, 22

Confederation of the Rhine, see Rheinbund

conspiracies in Germany, 72, 138–41, 149f, 152, 157–60, 165

continental system, 127, 144

Cotta, Johann Friedrich, publisher, 232

counterrevolution, 314, 324

Cracow, 19, 84, 282

Croatia, 117

Crumpipen, Baron Heinrich von, Austrian diplomat, 71

Czartoryski, Prince Adam, 136, 157, 161, 254, 261, 300f

Czentochowa, fortress of, 282

Daiser von Sylbach, Carl von, Austrian official, 28

Dalberg, Carl Theodore von, Archbishop of Mainz, Archchancellor of the Holy Roman Empire, Prince Primate of the Rheinbund, 32, 44–46, 60, 62n, 126, 130, 212, 226, 241. See also Prince Primate

Dalmatia, 21, 42, 58, 103

Danish question, 243. See also Denmark

Danubian Principalities, 56, 84, 99, 134

Danzig, 56, 131

Declaration of Rights, 12

Denmark, 5, 195, 225, 266

Dennewitz, battle of, 201

Dietrichstein, Prince Franz Joseph von, 111

Dohle, Austrian councillor of legation, 131

Dresden, in War of 1809, 85, 88; conference of 1812, 143–46; meeting of Metternich and Napoleon, 1813, 173, 179f, 199; battle of, 201, 210

Driault, Edouard, French historian, 130

East Prussia, 148

Eastern question, 26, 134–36, 324. See also Turkey, Danubian Principalities

ecclesiastical estates, 6, 23, 31, 33, 323. See also Reich, constitution of

Edinburgh Review, 300

Egyptian campaign, 25f
émigrés, at Coblenz, 1792, 13; in Austrian service, 71f, 92, 98, 106, 118, 121, 253f, 322
Enghien, Duke of, 38
Enlightenment, 6, 9
Enns River, 109
Erfurt, 93, 128, 229; congress of, 66–68, 134
Estates-General of France, 321
Esterhazy, Prince Paul, 88
European directory, Castlereagh idea of, 291
European equilibrium, 11, 161, 167, 184, 203, 220f, 227, 237, 255, 259, 261, 279, 287, 302, 320

Fassbender, Mathias von, Austrian official, 71
Federal Act of 1815, see German Confederation
Ferdinand, Archduke, Duke of Modena-Este, uncle of Emperor Francis I, 27, 32, 43, 82f, 102
Ferdinand, Archduke, Grand Duke of Tuscany, Grand Duke of Würzburg, 27, 32, 43, 59, 97f, 113f, 212, 229; and the Rheinbund, 48–50
Ferdinand, Crown Prince of Austria, 143f
feudalism, 254
Fichte, Johann Gottlieb, 150
Finland, 84, 134, 139
Fiume, 93, 117
Floret, Peter Johann von, Austrian diplomat, 161
Fontainebleau, convention of, 10 Oct. 1807, 59
Fouché, Joseph, Duke of Otrante, 68, 253
Fournier, August von, Austrian historian, 256n
Fourth Coalition, 192. See also War of Liberation
France, ancient frontiers of, 288f, 325; assembly of notables, 296; charter of 1814, 314f; constitution of 1791, 314; corps législatif, 122; German policy of, 5, 7, 21ff (see also under Alexander I, Metternich, Clemens, and Napoleon I); natural frontiers of, 202, 257, 284, 295; senate, 129f
Francis of Habsburg, Holy Roman Emperor, Emperor of Austria, abdicates as Holy Roman Emperor, 53; abdica-

tion question in 1809, 97f, 105, 114f; aims in 1813, 209; and Metternich, 180f; and Rastatt congress, 21; and the Reich, 44; and the Rheinbund, 130; and Stadion, 64, 125; and treaty of Lunéville, 26; at Dresden conference 1812, 143–45; coronation of 1792, 9, 12; deserts Napoleon, 314; in Third Coalition, 41f; in War of Liberation, 220, 222, 315; receives Metternich, July 1809, 89; rejects Napoleon's request for armistice extension, 113
Franco-Austrian alliance 1812, 149, 169
Franco-Austrian convention of 30 June, 1813, 180
Franconia, 7, 34f, 125f, 170, 212, 315
Francophilism, in Munich, 210, 268, 308; in Vienna, 55, 135, 152, 280
Franco-Prussian alliance, 1806, 42
Franco-Prussian alliance, 1812, 142, 149
Frankfurt accession treaties, 238–43, 258, 290, 325; military clauses in, 244–46
Frankfurt base, see Frankfurt peace proposals
Frankfurt, city of, 12, 241; as allied headquarters 1813, 222, 234ff
Frankfurt, Grand Duchy of, 226, 234, 237, 241f, 322
Frankfurt peace proposals 1813, 250–52, 255f, 262f, 283–85, 288, 295
Frederick I, King of Würtemberg, 34f, 61, 126, 130f, 172, 233f, 280, 315
Frederick II, King of Prussia, 33
Frederick VI, King of Denmark, 266f
Frederick August III, Elector and King of Saxony, Grand Duke of Warsaw, 54, 132, 144f, 158, 266
Frederick William III, King of Prussia, during War of Third Coalition, 38–42; neutrality in 1809, 66, 102; in War of Liberation, 156f, 180, 188, 239, 258, 292, 311
Freiburg, allied headquarters, 267–69
French boundary question, 167, 202, 223, 250–52, 287–90. See also France, ancient frontiers, and natural frontiers
French imperialism, 184
French Revolution, 12; Metternich and, 320. See also under Metternich, Clemens
Friedland, battle of, 53, 56
frontier of the Rhine, the Alps, and the Pyrenees, see France, natural frontiers

Fulda, Bishopric of, 126
Fulda, treaty of between Würtemberg and Austria, Nov. 1813, 230f, 233f, 237, 238f, 307

Gagern, Hans von, 265, 280
Galicia, 57, 84, 93, 95–97, 100, 120, 132, 137; guaranteed in Franco-Austrian treaty of 1812, 143; in peace negotiation of 1809, 102f, 107, 109–12; partitioned, 117; proposal to exchange for Alsace, 300f
Galitzin, Prince Serge, Russian general, 84, 102, 109–12
Gärtner, Baron H., 317
Gelderland, 19, 26
Gentz, Friedrich von, in War of 1809, 83, 190, 209, 274; in War of Liberation, 253, 268f, 297, 299, 310, 313, 314, 317; on German constitution 1808–09, 74f, 163; on German constitution 1813, 275f; on Russian danger, 75, 293
George III, King of England and Elector of Hanover, 5, 214
George IV, King of England and Hanover, see Prince Regent of England
German Confederation, 227; army of, 213; censorship in, 213; Federal Act of 1815, 75, 318, 322
German conspiracies, 82f, 88, 90, 160, 165, 209f
German constitutional question, 213, 269–80, 287, 289, 294, 298, 306–10, 325; in accession treaties, 240; plan for four-power directory, 276–78, 282, 306f, 307, 316f, 325
German defense system, in Humboldt plan, 273f; question of in 1813, 214f, 325
German law, 10
German liberties, 6
German nationalism, 194, 241, 274, 319; and Metternich, 75–78, 238, 319; in Austria, 71f, 78f, 287, 319, 321
German nobility, see Standesherren, imperial nobility, and mediatized houses
German union, 289
Germany, allied occupation policy, 222–31, 238ff; neutralization of, 231, 251, 313. See also Reich, Rheinbund, the third Germany, German constitutional question, and German conspiracies

Gneisenau, General Count Neithardt von, 65, 76, 150, 188, 218, 227, 245, 268, 291, 294
Goerlitz meeting 13 May 1813, 175
Görres, Joseph, German publicist, 264f
Görtz, 117
Goethe, Johann Wolfgang von, 66, 240
Göttingen, University of, 10, 254
Golovkin, Prince, Russian diplomat, 307
Goltz, Count Carl Heinrich Friedrich, von der, Prussian major, mission to Vienna, Feb. 1809, 72, 101
government service, 254f
Gravenreuth, Baron Carl von, Bavarian diplomat, 48, 52
Grand Army, 148, 152, 188, 323f
Great Britain, courier captured, 165; German policy of, 199f, 210; in Second Coalition, 25f; peace objectives 1813, 207. See also Castlereagh
Greulich, Alfred, German historian, 185n
Grossbeeren, battle of, 201
grossdeutsch movement, 319
Gruner, Justus von, Prussian councillor, 149

Habsburg, House of, 5, 32f, 86, 124, 194f, 197, 201, 210, 214, 274, 318
Hamburg, see Hanseatic cities
Hanau, 126
Hanover, Electorate of, 5, 20, 38, 40f, 72, 127, 195, 198–200, 225f, 242, 306–09. See also Münster, Count Ernst von, and Hardenberg, Count Ernst von
Hanseatic cities, 32, 127f, 177, 188f, 205, 237
Hardenberg, Baron (later Prince) Carl August von, Prussian minister and chancellor, 39, 55f; appeals to Vienna, Jan. 1813, 148; French policy of, 140–42, 294f; German policy of, 148, 154f, 160–63, 171, 175, 178, 197, 200f, 206f, 212, 238, 242f, 268, 281–87, 291–94, 306–08, 316; mediation plan in 1813, 154f; Metternich's appeasement of, 318; personality of, 198f; Polish policy of, 282f; Russian policy of, 199, 292–94. See also Metternich, Clemens, and Prussia
Hardenberg, Count Ernst von, Hanoverian diplomat, 147f; interview with Metternich, 215–17

Harrowby, Lord, British envoy in Berlin, 40n
Haugwitz, Count Christian August von, 39–42, 55
Hausrück District, 94, 117, 126, 208f
Helvetian Republic, 38. *See also* Switzerland
Hesse-Cassel, Landgraviate (later Electorate) of, 20, 23, 32, 54, 72, 237, 241–43, 246
Hesse-Darmstadt, Grand Duchy of, 230f, 240, 242
Hesse-Homburg, Prince Philip of, Austrian field marshal, 241
historical law, 11
Hofburg, imperial residence in Vienna, 35, 80
Hofer, Andreas, 72, 79, 88, 120
Hofkriegsrat, 39, 55, 77
Hohenlinden, battle of, 26
Hohenzollern, House of, 5, 36, 56, 307; principalities of, 126, 243
Holland, 127f, 167f, 207, 259, 261, 289, 303–05
Holstein, Duchy of, 5, 193
Holstein-Gottorp, House of, 128
Holy Roman Emperor, 6, 13f, 86. *See also* Francis of Habsburg
Holy Roman Empire, 3, 162, 218, 253; importance to Austria, 323f. *See also* Reich
Hormayr, Baron Joseph von, Austrian official, 71, 79, 165
Hruby, Count Carl von, Austrian diplomat, 211
Hudelist, Baron Joseph von, Austrian official, 298f, 310, 312f
Humboldt, Wilhelm von, 181–84, 206, 213, 225, 238, 269, 279, 286; on buffer states, 268; German constitution plan of, 272–76
Hungary, 33, 87, 140

Illyrian Provinces, 117, 124f, 137, 141, 143, 152, 165, 168, 180f, 184
imperial free cities, 6, 31f, 236. *See also* Hanseatic cities
imperial knights, *see Reichsritterschaft*
imperial nobility, 3–5, 34f, 227, 323. *See also Standesherren* and mediatized houses
Imperial Recess, 31–34, 37, 57, 71, 80, 151, 195, 208, 242, 269, 324
imperial school, 214, 294f
Inn District, 94f, 103, 117, 126, 141, 208f

Isenburg, Principality of, 212, 235, 322
Isonzo River, 58
Istria, 21, 42, 103
Italy, Kingdom of, 26, 42, 58f, 62, 207, 303

Jahn, Friedrich Ludwig, 150, 227, 247, 321
Jena, battle of, 53f, 96
Johannisberg, Metternich estate, 12
John of Habsburg, Archduke of Austria, 65, 71, 76, 79, 87, 165, 265
Jomini, Baron Henri de, Russian General, 192
Joseph II, Holy Roman Emperor, 7, 14, 71, 119
Josephine, Empress of the French, 88
Josephinism, 14, 197

Kageneck, *see* Metternich, Countess Beatrice von
Kaiser, *see* Francis II and I, and Holy Roman Emperor
Kalisch, treaty of, 156–58, 165f, 171, 177, 199, 282, 325. *See also* under Russia, Baron Hardenberg, and Alexander I
Kaulla, Würtemberg banker, 232
Kaunitz, House of, 28, 121
Kaunitz, Prince Ernst von, 17
Kaunitz, Prince Wenzel Anton von, Austrian chancellor, 17
Kaunitz, Princess Eleanor von, marries Clemens Metternich, 17
Kiel, treaty of between Denmark and Sweden, 267
Kissinger, Henry A., American historian, 318f
Kleist, Heinrich von, poet, 71, 268, 321
Kleist von Nollendorf, Friedrich Heinrich, Prussian general, 201
Knesebeck, Carl Friedrich von dem, Prussian colonel, 160–62, 197, 257, 282f; mission to Comorn 1809, 101; mission to Vienna, Jan. 1813, 154–56
Koch, Christopher William, 10, 12
Königsberg, 141
Königswart, Metternich estate in Bohemia, 3, 17
Kotschubey, Count, Russian diplomat, 224
Kress von Kressenstein, Baron von, Austrian official, 253
Kutusov, Count Michael, 159; Kutusov declaration, 159f, 165f, 169f, 175, 185, 195f, 201, 210f, 228, 325

LaForest, Count Antoine de, French diplomat, 50f

La Harpe, Frederick Caesar, 149f, 254, 264f, 295f

Landeshoheit, 5

Landstände, 79f, 197, 214f, 218, 273, 276–78, 317f, 321. *See also landständische Verfassungen*

landständische Verfassungen, 276–78, 318

Landsturm, 245–49, 317

Landwehr, in Austria, 65f, 103; in War of Liberation, 246f

Langenau, Alois, Saxon-Austrian general, 266

Langres, conferences of, 288–90, 294f, 304; peace program of, 288–90; plateau of, 257f, 269

La Rochefoucauld, Count Alexander de, French diplomat, 50

La Rothière, battle of, 296f

Lauber, Emil, Austrian historian, 319n

Lauenburg, 127f

Lebzeltern, Baron Ludwig von, 160, 162f, 164, 173, 192

legitimacy, doctrine of, 241, 243, 322f

Lehrbach, Count Ludwig von, Austrian envoy, 21f

Leiningen-Westerburg, Count Christian von, 140, 149

Leipzig, battle of, 208, 219f, 222, 224, 232, 261, 288

Leipzig, interallied convention of, 225–27, 246, 298

Leopold II, Holy Roman Emperor, 9, 12

Levant, *see* Eastern question

Leyen, Prince von der, 235

liberalism, 61, 79, 278, 319

Liechtenstein, House of, in Austria, 18, 28

Liechtenstein, Prince Johann, Austrian general, 89, 91, 113, 115–17, 120

Lippe, principalities of, 54, 243

Lobau, island in Danube, 83

Lombard, John William, Prussian councillor, 39

Louis XIV, King of France, 268

Louis XVI, King of France, 144

Louis XVIII, King of France, 298. *See also* Provence, Count of

Louise, Empress of Austria, 143–45

Lowenstein, princes of, 276f

Lower-Rhine-Westphalia, 3

Ludwig, Crown Prince of Bavaria, 94f, 128, 131, 170, 268, 304

Lübeck, *see* Hanseatic cities

Lützen, battle of, 172

Lunéville, peace of, 25f, 31

Lusatia, duchies of, 132

Magna Carta in England, 321

Mainz, University of, 11, 13; fortress of, 26, 270, 316. *See also* Rhine-Main confluence

Malta, 259

Mannheim, projected conference of, 255f, 258, 262

manorial system, 79

Marcolini palace, 143

Marengo, battle of, 26

Maret, Bernard, Duke of Bassano, French foreign minister, 189, 255, 258, 262, 277

Marie Louise of Habsburg, Archduchess of Austria, Empress of the French, 95, 122f, 145

maritime question, 250, 260

Mark, County of, 270

Markov, Count Arcadi, Russian diplomat, 27

masterless lands, 226

Maximilian I Joseph, Prince of Zweibrücken, later King of Bavaria, 4, 12, 34f, 39, 60, 95, 170, 172, 196, 210, 315

Mecklenburg, duchies of, 7, 57, 156, 159, 193, 195f, 200, 243f, 324

mediatized houses, 194, 197f, 218, 234, 240, 248, 273, 276–80, 286f, 316–18, 321–25; at Frankfurt, 1813, 235–37; convention of restitution to, 124f; status in Rheinbund, 47f

Meiningen, 230f, 252

Mercy, Count Andreas von, French émigré, 253

Mergentheim, capital of Teutonic Order, 58, 81, 112, 117

Merian von Falkach, Baron Andreas von, Austrian diplomat, 71, 149, 253

Merveldt, Count Maximilian von, Austrian diplomat, 71, 310

Metternich, Count (later Prince) Clemens Lothar Wenzel von, social standing, 3f; education, 8f; marriage, 4, 17f; assignment in Netherlands, 13; in England, 14; in Rastatt, 21–25; in Saxony, 28–31, 34–37; in Berlin, 37–42, 321; moves to Vienna, 17; residence at Austerlitz, 43; plan for a

Metternich, Clemens (*continued*)
Confederation of the East, 1806, 44f, 51; assignment in Paris, 50f; author of pamphlet on popular militia, 14; and treaty of Pressburg, 58f; and Erfurt Congress, 66f; and War of 1809, 64–70, 75; recalled to Vienna, Dec. 1808, 68f; detention in Paris, 82; prisoner in Vienna, 88f; unofficially replaces Stadion, 90; strategy in peace negotiation, 98–113; at Altenburg conference, 106–16; appointed foreign minister, 118; mediation in 1813, 162–86, 315; plan to neutralize Rheinbund, 164, 168; ultimatum to Napoleon, 183, 190; made prince, 220, 249; Frankfurt peace proposals, 223; entente with Hardenberg, 294ff, 325; and German constitution, 306–10

attitude toward: Bonapartism, 254f; censorshp, 122, 213; conservatism, 164, 185, 278f; insurrections in Germany, 76–78; German nationalism, 79, 238; German unity, 205f, 213f, 217, 233f, 289f, 324f; legitimacy, 241; public opinion, 65, 121; revolution, 14–17, 28; sovereignty, 216–18, 221f

policy toward: Baden, 238–40; Bavaria, 131, 170f, 208–13; Great Britain, 147, 167f, 178, 207, 250f, 258–62, 280, 284f, 302ff, 312; Denmark, 133, 266f; Eastern question, 134–36; France, 75f, 104–15, 121, 137, 153, 165f, 168f, 173, 179–85, 189, 250–53, 255f, 262f, 288f, 290, 302f, 313–15, 318, 320f; Hanover, 213–17; Hesse-Cassel, 241–43; Hesse-Darmstadt, 231; Naples, 133, 164, 255, 259, 267; Poland, 29, 100, 109–13, 136f; Prussia, 29, 101f, 141–43, 148, 155f, 160–62, 171f, 174f, 281–83, 288–90, 294, 306–08, 311; Rheinbund, 51f, 57, 62f, 69, 76–78, 132f, 164, 168; Russia, 29, 68–70, 102f, 138f, 147, 174f, 179–84, 191f, 200, 221, 230–32, 234, 323–26; Saxon-Polish question, 162, 199, 207f, 251, 258, 266, 280–83, 286, 300–02, 311, 318, 325; Saxony, 131f, 169f; Sweden, 133; Switzerland, 264–66; Würtemberg, 231–34, 307f

principles and political philosophy: 14–17, 28–31, 63, 65, 185f, 191, 212, 255, 302, 319–23

relationship with: Alexander I, 38–41, 51, 264–67, 279f, 298f; Archduke Carl, 104f; Cobenzl, 35–40; Emperor Francis, 81, 105, 120, 181, 187f; Frederick William III, 42; Gentz, 30f, 38, 40, 51, 120: Hardenberg, Baron Carl von (*see* policy toward Prussia); Humboldt, 274f; Napoleon, 116–18; Schwarzenberg, 123, 139, 142, 168, 187f, 219f, 257, 264, 269; Stadion, 50, 65, 68f, 78–81, 89ff, 124f, 165, 173–76, 270–72, 285ff; Stein, 194, 213, 224–31, 244, 302, 318; Thugut, 20

Metternich, Count (later Prince) Franz Georg von, 3, 8–10, 21f, 26, 124, 135, 253, 322; minister in the Netherlands, 13ff; moves to Vienna, 17; made prince, 33

Metternich, Count Joseph von, brother of Clemens, 8

Metternich, Count Victor von, son of Clemens, 81n

Metternich, Countess Beatrice von, born Kageneck, mother of Clemens, 8f, 17

Metternich, Countess Eleanor von, born Kaunitz, first wife of Clemens, 22, 25, 123

Metternich, Countess Pauline von, sister of Clemens, 8

Mieg, Geheimrat von, 236

Mitteleuropa idea, 198, 294

Mohr, General von, Austrian officer, 110

Moldavia, *see* Danubian Principalities

Montgelas, Count Maximilian Joseph von, Bavarian minister, 94f, 131, 170f, 196, 210, 214, 234, 280, 308f

Moravia, 87; Moravian Gateway, 19, 57, 84

Moreau, Jean Victor, 192

Münster, Count Ernst von, Hanoverian minister, 147f, 151, 159, 199f, 214–17, 225, 259, 280, 290, 301, 309, 317

Murat, Joachim, Grand Duke of Berg, then King of Naples, 63, 133, 144, 164, 259, 267

Naples, 255, 259. *See also* Murat, Joachim

Napoleon I, Emperor of the French, at Rastatt, 23f; and Second Coalition, 25f; becomes First Consul, 27; and Imperial Recess, 32; German policy of, 35, 45–50, 60–62, 143–45 (*see also* under Rheinbund); made Emperor, 36; relations with Alexander I, 38,

122f; at Erfurt congress, 66–68; and War of 1809, 80ff; in Vienna, 89; Polish policy of, 93, 144f; Bavarian policy, 94f; marriage tie with Habsburgs, 118, 122f; and peace negotiations of 1809, 92–98; Russian campaign, 147f; peace overtures in War of Liberation, 222; place of in treaty of Chaumont, 311; fall of, 313, 316, 326

Napoleonic codes, 62, 221

Narbonne, Count Louis de, French diplomat, 168

Nassau, Duchy of, 227, 230f, 240. *See also* Orange, House of

nationalism, 264; in Austria, 71f, 78f, 167; in Poland, 79, 109–11

natural law, 10

Neipperg, General Count Adam Adalbert von, 267

Nesselrode, Count Carl Robert von, 172, 175, 177f, 222f, 229–31, 239, 253f, 269, 288f

Neumark, armistice agreement of, 182

Nollendorf, battle of, 201

Norway, offered to Sweden, 195, 225, 260

Nugent, Count Laval, Austrian general, 92, 147

Ochsenhausen, Metternich estate in Swabia, 33, 37, 43, 45, 47, 50, 61, 124f, 322

Odonell, Count Joseph von, Austrian finance minister, 66, 69, 133

Oettingen, Prince von, Bavarian diplomat, 211

Oldenburg, Duchy of, 57, 128f, 140, 200, 205, 324

Oldenburg, Duke George of, 128

Oldenburg, Duke Peter of, 128, 236f, 244, 304

Opotschna meeting between Metternich and Alexander, 179

Orange, Prince William of, 267, 280, 304, 307

Orange-Nassau, House of, 23, 265

Orleans, Duke of, 296, 314

Ortenau, 32, 43

Ottoman Empire, 136. *See also* Turkey and Eastern question

Oubril, Count Peter, Russian diplomat, 52

Palatinate, 240

Palffy, House of, 18

Pan-Germanism, 319

Paris, First Treaty of, May 1814, 317f

Passau, 32, 209

Paul I, Tsar of Russia, 25–27, 324

Pfuel, Ernst von, 72

Phull, Colonel Carl Ludwig von, 41

Pitt, William, the younger, 261, 283

Pläswitz, armistice of, 173, 182

Podolia, 84

Poland, first partition of, 7; second partition of, 19; third partition of, 20; in War of 1809, 66; in peace negotiation of 1809, 95f; cause of Franco-Russian war in 1812, 136f; Polish aspirations in 1814, 300

Polish question, 158. *See also* Metternich, Clemens, and Saxon-Polish question

Pomerania, 38, 267

Poniatowski, Prince Joseph, 84, 102–12, 132, 136

Portugal, 261, 303

Potsdam, treaty of, 1805, 40f

Pozzo di Borgo, Count Carl Andreas, 10, 121, 149, 254, 263, 288

Pragmatic Sanction of 1723, 3, 33, 36, 119

Prague, Austro-Saxon treaty of, April 1813, 169, 171f; peace congress of, July 1813, 181–85, 188f, 199, 262; ultimatum to Napoleon, 183. *See also* Metternich, Clemens, French policy of

Pressburg, treaty of, 1805, 41–43, 51, 91, 93, 98, 114f, 209, 320f

Prince Primate, 60, 234, 322. *See also* Dalberg, Carl Theodore von

Prince Regent of Hanover-England, 199. *See also* George IV

Prince Royal of Sweden, *see* Bernadotte

Protestants, 32

Provence, Count of, 314. *See also* Louis XVIII

Prussia, German policy of, 7–23; Knesebeck mission of 1809, 101f; territorial claims, 283, 285–87, 316. *See also* Frederick William III, Hardenberg, and War of Liberation

Prussian army, 291f

Rademacher, Franz, Austrian official, 253

Radetsky, Count Joseph, 245f, 257f

Rainer of Habsburg, Archduke of Austria, 99

Rastatt, congress of, 21–26, 31, 320

Razumovsky, Count Andreas, 10, 269, 279, 288, 295

Rechberg, Count Anton von, Bavarian colonel, 210

Recklinghausen, 270

Reformation, 54

Regensburg, 3f, 31f, 94, 126; battle of 1809, 82

Rehdiger, Prussian official, 224

Reich, constitution of, 3–7, 30–32, 35f; government service in, 6; legal theory of, 11f; Austrian recruiting rights in, 18, 44; dissolution of, 52f, 233; restoration movement, 80f, 166f, 214f, 236f, 316–18, 320–24; Alexander's view of, 195. See also Third Germany and Holy Roman Empire

Reichenbach, Anglo-Prussian-Russian treaty of alliance, 1813, 178, 237; Austro-Prussian-Russian treaty of, 1813, 179–84, 190, 200f, 207, 218, 260, 305

Reichsdeputationshauptschluss, see Imperial Recess

Reichskammergericht, 5, 193, 236, 273

Reichsritterschaft, 4, 6, 22, 34, 172. See also imperial nobility and mediatized houses

Reichstag, 3f, 14, 18f, 33, 194

Reign of Terror, 9

Reitzenstein, Baron Carl von, minister in Baden, 214, 239

Repnin, Prince Nicholai, Russian official, 228, 266

Reuss, Prince Henry of, Austrian general, 211

Reuss, principalities of, 54, 228–31

Rheinbund, in treaty of Pressburg, 43, 45; constitution of, 46–48; status of mediatized houses in, 47f; Act of Confederation, 48, 52, 94, 124, 128, 130, 235; founding of, 48–50, 321; members of, 50, 54, 56f, 128, 234f; reform of, 60–62, 67; and War of 1809, 81, 93–95; and peace of Schönbrunn, 117; territorial settlement in, 125–27; and Dresden conference, 144f; dissolution of, 160, 173, 175f, 178, 190, 203f, 211f, 325; question of French protectorate, 168, 174–80, 183, 185, 189f; international guarantee of, 185; neutralization of, 189, 201, 322; armies of, 190

Rheinische Merkur, German newspaper, 264. See also Görres, Joseph

Rhenish Confederation, see Rheinbund

Rhineland, 3, 7, 17, 283, 325

Rhine-Main confluence, 212, 283

Richelieu, Duke Armand of, 149, 254

Ried, treaty of, 211–18, 228, 232, 237–39, 307

Robespierre, Augustin, 63, 321

Rössler, Hellmuth, German historian, 46n, 319

romanticism, 71f

Rombeck, Countess von, 28

Roschmann, Baron Anton von, 165

Rose, George, British diplomat, 308f

Rosenberg, Prince Franz Seraph, Austrian general, 87

Rühle von Lilienstern, Otto, Prussian officer, 246

Rumiantzev, Count Nicholai Petrovitch, 70, 95

Russia, German policy of, 5, 7, 25–27, 95; invaded by France, 147f; note to Bavaria, Aug. 1813, 196, 208, 210f. See also Alexander I

Russophilism, in Vienna, 135, 139, 152, 189, 280

Russo-Prussian peace program of 16 May 1813, 176, 201f

St. Aignan, Baron Nicholas Auguste Marie de, French diplomat, 223, 230, 250–52, 255–57, 260f, 298

Salm, princes of, 128–30, 140, 236f

Salzburg, Archbishopric of, 32, 43, 94, 103, 109–12, 117, 126, 141, 208f

Savary, General René, 89, 105

Saxe-Teschen, Duke Albert of, 87n

Saxe-Weimar, Duchy of, 240f, 243; constitution of, 61. See also Carl August, Duke of Saxe-Weimar

Saxon Duchies, 54, 228–31. See also Thuringia and Rheinbund, members of

Saxon-Polish question, 179, 199, 207f, 229f, 242, 244, 251. See also under Metternich, Clemens, Alexander I, and Hardenberg, Baron Carl

Saxony, Electorate (later Kingdom) of, 20, 28ff, 168, 193, 198. See also Frederick August III

Scharnhorst, Gerhard David von, 65, 76, 150; mission to Vienna, 1811, 141f

Scheldt River, 250

Schenkendorf, Max von, German poet, 71, 246

Schiller, Friedrich, 122

Schlamperei, in Vienna, 37

Schlieffen, Count Alfred von, 271

Schön, Theodor von, Prussian official, 224

Schönbrunn, Austro-French treaty of in 1809, 117–20; Franco-Prussian treaty of in 1805, 41f; palace of, 86, 88f

Schwarzburg-Rudolstadt, Principality of, 54, 228–31

Schwarzburg-Sonderhausen, Principality of, 54, 228–31

Schwarzenberg, Prince Carl Philip zu, Austrian general and diplomat, mission to St. Petersburg, 1809, 73, 80, 85; ambassador in Paris 1809–1812, 123, 139, 141f; commander of Austrian auxiliary corps 1812, 142; mission to Paris 1813, 168f, 170; and Metternich, 123, 139, 142, 168, 187f, 219f, 257, 264, 269; as allied commander 1813–1814, 184, 187, 192, 201, 209, 219f, 222, 245, 249, 253, 257f, 262–65, 284, 311

Schwarzenberg, Prince Felix zu, Austrian statesman, 271

Second Coalition, 25f, 324

secularization, in Reich, 6, 22f

Senfft, Count von, Saxon minister, 158

Serbia, 135

serfdom, problem of in Germany, 47f, 79, 278

Seven Years' War, 6, 10

Sherlock affair, 82n

Silesia, 138, 141, 145, 154, 172, 282; Metternich's intentions toward, 142, 168; Silesian army, 246, 296, 299

Simon, Johann Friedrich, tutor of Clemens Metternich, 9, 12

Solms-Laubach, Count Friedrich Christian von, 277, 286, 317

Sorel, Albert, French historian, 257

Soult, Marshal Nicholas, 99

South Germany, 197f, 200, 209, 232, 234, 239–41, 248, 324; fortifications razed, 26. *See also* Baden, Bavaria, Würtemberg

Spain, 63, 65, 167f, 207, 259, 261, 303, 321

Spiegel, Baron Kaspar von, Austrian official, 253

Srbik, Heinrich Ritter von, Austrian historian, 17, 319f

Stackelberg, Count Gustav von, Russian diplomat, 147

Stadion, Count Friedrich Lothar, Austrian official, brother of Philip, 71f, 74, 113

Stadion, Count Johann Philip von, Austrian diplomat and foreign minister, appointment to St. Petersburg, 37; made foreign minister, 43f; favors armed mediation 1807, 54; and treaty of Pressburg, 59; and German refugees, 71f; and War of 1809, 64–66, 69, 72–74, 99, 115; and Erfurt congress, 67; dispute with Carl, 83–87; offers resignation, 90, 106; and German conspiracies 1813, 165; mission to allied headquarters 1813, 173–79; German constitutional plan 1813, 269–72; in War of Liberation, 171, 192, 209, 213f, 268, 279, 285f, 287; and Hardenberg, 285f, 316; and Congress of Châtillon, 299, 310f

Standesherren, 3–5, 278. *See also* imperial nobility

Steigentesch, Baron August von, Austrian colonel, 71, 101; mission to Berlin, 83f

Stein, Baron Heinrich Friedrich Carl vom, and War of 1809, 65, 321; and Alexander I, 149–51, 158ff, 194–97, 324; German constitutional plans of, in 1812, 151, 195; in August 1813, 193f, 243; in December 1813, 277f; in March 1814, 316f; and Metternich, 194, 213, 224–31, 244, 302, 318; and Hardenberg, 197f, 286; reforms of in Prussia, 197, 278; on treaty of Ried, 213f; and the German occupation, 223–27, 230ff, 236

Stewart, Sir Charles, British diplomat, 223, 250, 263

Strasbourg, 4, 43, 88, 270; University of, 10f; riots in, 12; Metternich's detention in 1806, 52

Stroganov, Prince Paul, 10

Stutterheim, General Carl von, Austrian soldier, 41f, 71

Suvorov, Prince Alexander, Russian general, 259

Swabia, 7, 34f, 43, 172, 209

Sweden, 195, 225, 304. *See also* Bernadotte

Switzerland, 289, 303, 314; in allied military plans, 257; disputed by Metternich and Alexander, 263–66

Talleyrand, Prince Charles, French foreign minister, 27, 50, 58, 68, 75f, 77, 252f, 315
Tarnopol District, ceded to Russia, 117
Taube, Count von, Würtemberg diplomat, 126
Tauroggen, armistice of, 154, 165
Teplitz, treaties of 9 Sept. 1813, 202–09, 211f, 218, 223, 226, 228, 232, 282, 305, 325
Teschen, treaty of 1779, 7, 208, 324
Tettenborn, Baron Carl Friedrich von, Russian general, 149, 244
Teutonic Knights, Order of, 32, 43, 58f, 81, 117
Theater am der Wien, 122
Third Coalition, 38–42
Third Germany, the, 7, 23, 32, 190, 193, 325f. *See also* Reich, Rheinbund
Thirty-second military district, 127–30, 177, 188, 204f, 223, 226, 237
Thorn, fortress of, 282
Thugut, Baron Franz von, Austrian foreign minister, 17f, 20, 23, 25, 27f, 120
Thun, Count Anton von, Austrian diplomat, 71
Thuringia, 228–31. *See also* Saxon duchies, Reuss, Schwarzburg duchies, Anhalt
Tilsit, alliance between France and Russia, 93–95, 107, 120, 153, 324; treaties between France and Russia and France and Prussia, 56f
Treitschke, Heinrich von, German historian, 193n, 233
Trent, Bishopric of, 32, 42, 209
trialism, 194. *See also* the Third Germany
Trieste, 93, 117
Trier, Archbishopric of, 6, 8, 32
Troyes, allied headquarters, 295; conferences of, 304; interallied convention of, 294, 297, 311, 313
Tugendbund, 141, 152
Turkey, 57, 64, 97, 99, 134; Russian victory over, 140. *See also* Eastern question, Ottoman Empire, and under Metternich
Tyrol, 125, 152, 165, 209f, 265; and the

Imperial Recess, 32; ceded to Bavaria 1805, 42; rising of 1809, 72, 83, 88, 94f, 103

Union Russo-Germanique, proposed by Würtemberg, 315
United States of America, 260f
Upper Austria, Archduchy of, 109–12

Valmy, battle of, 13
Venice, 21, 42
Vienna, captured by Napoleon, 82; Congress of, 178f, 213, 306, 315, 318
Villach, 117
Vincent, Baron Carl von, Austrian general and diplomat, 50, 52f, 66f
Vincke, Baron Friedrich Ludwig Philip von, Prussian administrator, 243
Vittoria, battle of, 181
Vogt, Nicholas, legal theorist, 11f
Volhynia, 84
Vorarlberg, 42, 85f, 209, 265

Wagram, battle of, 87, 89, 96, 296
Waldeck, Principality of, 54, 243
Wallachia, *see* Danubian Principalities
Wallis, Count Joseph, Austrian finance minister, 133, 171
Wallmoden, Count Ludwig Georg von, German soldier, 71, 80, 149, 152
War of Austrian Succession, 6
War of Bavarian Succession, 7
War of 1812, 260
War of Liberation, 187f, 291f, 320; German military organization in, 244–49, 258; military strategy in, 257f
Warsaw, Grand Duchy of, joins Rheinbund, 56; in War of 1809, 98; receives autonomy, 144; dissolution of, 174–77; in Teplitz treaties, 203
Wessenberg, Baron Johann Philip von, Austrian diplomat, 71, 101, 131, 302, 312; mission to Berlin 1809, 73; mission to Munich, 131; mission to London, 1813, 167
Westphalen, General Friedrich von, 72
Westphalia, counts of, 4, 21; *Reichskreis* of, 3, 7f
Westphalia, Kingdom of, 54, 56, 60, 127f, 155, 164, 168, 195, 198, 204, 226, 237, 322. *See also* Bonaparte, Jerome
Westphalia, Peace of, 1648, 5, 23
Wettin, House of, 123, 228, 286. *See also* Saxony

Wied-Neuwied, Prince of, 317

Wieland, Christoph Martin, German poet, 66

Wieliczka, salt mines of, 117, 132

Willam, Crown Prince of Würtemberg, 234, 249

Winneburg-Beilstein, Metternich fief in Rhineland, 3, 13, 17, 29, 51

Winzingerode, Baron Ferdinand von, Russian general, 38, 149

Winzingerode, Count Georg von, Würtemberg minister, 214

Wittelsbach, House of, 42f, 94, 231, 234, 307. *See also* Bavaria and Maximilian I Joseph

Wolkersdorf, Austrian headquarters 1809, 85, 89

Wolzogen, Baron Ludwig von, Prussian and Russian general, 245

Wrede, Count Carl von, Bavarian general, 94f, 211, 233, 297

Würtemberg, Duchy (later Kingdom) of, 23, 270; and Russia, 27, 130f, 315, 324; in Imperial Recess, 32; "good old law" in, 35; acquires Mergentheim, 59; and Rheinbund, 61; in War of 1809, 95; treaty with Bavaria, 1810, 126; and Prussia, 197f; in War of Liberation, 245–48; in treaty of Chaumont, 307–09. *See also* Frederick I

Würtemberg, House of, 231–34. *See also* Frederick I and William, Crown Prince

Würzburg, Grand Duchy of, 226, 229f. *See also* Ferdinand, Archduke

Yorck von Wartenburg, Count Hans David, Prussian general, 154, 165

Zeppelin, Count Ferdinand Ludwig von, Würtemberg minister, 231–33

Znaim, armistice of, 87f, 101, 324; conference of between Napoleon and Liechtenstein, 91